Pastoral MINISTRY

THEOLOGY & PRACTICE

Richard H. Warneck

CONCORDIA PUBLISHING HOUSE · SAINT LOUIS

Published by Concordia Publishing House
3558 S. Jefferson Avenue, St. Louis, MO 63118-3968
1-800-325-3040 · cph.org

Manufactured in the United States of America

Library of Congress Cataloging-in-Publication Data
Names: Warneck, Richard H., author.
Title: Pastoral ministry : theology and practice / Richard H. Warneck.
Description: Saint Louis : Concordia Publishing House, 2018.
Identifiers: LCCN 2017048927 (print) | LCCN 2017052024 (ebook) | ISBN 9780758658630 | ISBN 9780758658593
Subjects: LCSH: Pastoral theology. | Christianity and culture--United States.
Classification: LCC BV4011.3 (ebook) | LCC BV4011.3 .W375 2018 (print) | DDC 253--dc23

LC record available at https://lccn.loc.gov/2017048927

---

4 5 6 7 8 9 10 11 12 13 32 31 30 29 28 27 26 25 24 23

Praise for *Pastoral Ministry: Theology and Practice*

Distilling a lifetime of experience in the congregation and seminary classroom, Rev. Richard Warneck generously shares his insights for pastoral practice in the midst of contemporary challenges. Readers will find his style conversational and his approach biblically conservative. *Pastoral Ministry* stands in the tradition of the older works by C. F. W. Walther and John H. C. Fritz and seeks to bring their legacy into our own time as pastors continue to shepherd God's flock with the saving Gospel.

—Rev. John T. Pless
Assistant Professor of Pastoral Ministry and Missions
Director of Field Education, Concordia Theological Seminary, Fort Wayne, IN
Author of *Martin Luther: Preacher of the Cross*

Through decades of classroom instruction, Rev. Richard Warneck prepared a generation of Lutheran ministers to lead congregations with theological integrity and pastoral sensitivity. Now, in this timely volume, Warneck delivers his treasury of wisdom for the practice of ministry. The scope and depth of this book is impressive. The insights which it provides are thorough, scholarly, practical, and theologically sound. This resource will be a ready guide for maneuvering through the challenges and opportunities of pastoral ministry in a rapidly changing society.

—Rev. Dr. David Peter
Chairman, Department of Practical Theology
Concordia Seminary, St. Louis, MO

Rev. Richard Warneck's experience as a pastor, his decades of teaching pastoral ministry to future shepherds of the Church, and his great love for pastors shine through in this well-written and most useful work. As the title suggests, this book provides doctrinal *and* practical information and guidance, introducing each segment with a real-life vignette. Complementing the pastoral theologies of Walther, Loehe, Fritz, etc., Warneck's book discusses the most important elements of pastoral ministry from a biblical and dominical point of view, taking into account the witness of the Lutheran Confessions and the wisdom of faithful theologians of our day. Especially useful is Warneck's treatment of the twenty-first-century challenges (sexuality, substance abuse, men and women in the church, etc.) with which today's pastors and parishioners must frequently grapple. *Pastoral Ministry: Theology and Practice* is very timely—a must for every pastor's library.

—Rev. Dr. Christian C. Tiews
Pastor, Trinity Lutheran Church, Okmulgee, OK

Pastoral Ministry: Theology and Practice by Professor Richard Warneck is a helpful guide for pastors desiring to be faithful to their callings and God's Word. It speaks with the authority of one well-seasoned in both practice and study of pastoral theology. It is also as personal as it is comprehensive. In a heartfelt and caring way, Rev. Warneck shares with pastors today God's Word and the voices of faithful theologians, all the time being centered in the Church's confession of the saving Gospel of Jesus Christ.

—Rev. Dr. W. Mart Thompson
Associate Professor of Practical Theology
Concordia Seminary, St. Louis, MO

Grounded in Scripture and shaped by decades of experience in the parish and seminary classroom, Dr. Warneck's insight-rich *Pastoral Ministry: Theology and Practice* belongs on every pastor's shelf (though it will more likely stay on his desk through frequent use). This volume merits a place beside Walther's and Fritz's on the short list of outstanding Lutheran pastoral ministry handbooks.

—Rev. Brent McGuire
Senior Pastor, Our Redeemer Lutheran Church, Dallas, TX

Pastoral Ministry: Theology and Practice by Rev. Dr. Richard H. Warneck gives pastors the mature teaching and counsel that result from many years of experience as a faithful parish pastor, an effective seminary professor, and a serious theologian. This substantial volume, clearly laid out and well-written, promises to be of great benefit to pastors ministering in the challenging times of the twenty-first century.

—Rev. Dr. Paul R. Raabe
Professor of Exegetical Theology
Concordia Seminary, St. Louis, MO

Casuistry questions are hard for any pastor to answer. The clear Word of God can be hard to apply in this sin-muddied world. Rev. Warneck's *Pastoral Ministry* offers foundational principles to help guide the pastor. He does not give easy, one-size-fits-all solutions; rather, he prepares the pastor to examine Scripture, to look at the wisdom of the saints who have gone before, and to implement God-pleasing solutions to the problems that arise in the modern church. This book is a welcome update to Walther's and Fritz's pastoral ministry volumes.

—Rev. Lincoln Winter
Pastor, Trinity Lutheran Church, Wheatland, WY

DEDICATION

The Lord, Jesus Christ

IN HONOR

My parents, the late Rev. Walter J.
and Selma Warneck

My wife, Marlene
Sons, Richard and Stephen

CONTENTS

Foreword

Pastoral Ministry: Theology and Practice by Dr. Richard Warneck begins with the letters *INI*, an abbreviation for the words *In Nomine Jesu*—"in the name of Jesus"—for Jesus remains the source, the authority, and the accountability of the pastoral ministry that is His alone. This awesome confidence in Christ, with an undying commitment to His Word, is the foundation and the motivation of the book, which seeks to prepare candidates for such a calling. As Dr. Warneck says, "[*Pastoral Ministry*] states principles that guide and direct active pastoral life and ministry" for a more effective ministry in these challenging times (p. 10). And that *INI* spirit is not just a slogan; it is authentically reflected in the pages that follow and in the life of the author, who is a professor, a pastor, a father, a husband, and an example of that spirit in action in the name of Jesus for others.

Pastoral Ministry is, above all, an exhaustive resource for those in the public ministry who understand that serving Christ and His Church is *dominical* and *apostolic* at its core. Therefore, preparation, commitment, and even a proper sense of calling are vital to the Church's and the pastor's exercise of this public office as Christ's gift. To that end, the issues engaged in the book range from the very call into the ministry to the personal disciplines needed in ministry to the practices associated with the public ministry in service to the Church (i.e., preaching, teaching, counseling, leadership) and even to the pastor's engagement of the community both missionally and civically. A wide range of issues are discussed, each flowing from deep, theological reflection with stated biblical principles that are then applied to the challenges of ministry in today's modern world.

This work is not only a foundational guide for one's training in the public ministry; it is a helpful resource for one's lifelong growth in service to that ministry for the sake of Christ's Church as well. For those "often burdened," "gripped by malaise," or "overwhelmed" in ministry due to the seemingly endless challenges of modern culture, this is a resource that directs us to the comfort and power of the presence of the real-present Jesus Christ and the enduring wisdom of His Word.

This book is also a very practical guide, filled with real how-tos for ministry. The suggestions throughout, and the appendices at the end, offer real solutions to real questions. Whether the issues are congregational (worship styles, leadership challenges, handling criticism, effective teaching and preaching), cultural (sexual libertinism, egalitarianism, rampant individualism), or personal (the pastor's personal disciplines or family life), this book is an invaluable tool for the pastor who seeks to meet the spiritual needs of His people—for their salvation, their life in Christ for others, and their future hope in Jesus eternally.

For example, in dealing with the very modern tension between the view of the pastoral ministry as a calling to "preach and teach" and the modern pressures to be a "leader" as well, the topic is engaged thoroughly from a biblical and practical standpoint. The final summary says it well:

> The pastor's vocation is that of a missionary in the name of Jesus. This is consistent with his Call to exercise the Office of the Holy Ministry. Complementing his calling as missionary is his role as leader of God's people, a multifaceted profile consisting of numerous roles: *bishop*, *priest*, *prophet*, *watchman*, and *servant*. The pastor utilizes these roles in his leadership of the congregation, whose priorities in ministry are *worship*, *witness*, *teaching*, *fellowship-care*, *service*, and *mission* (*growth*). (p. 102, emphasis in original)

But what differentiates this work from all others is the bold assertion of a dominical and apostolic pastoral ministry that expects God to intervene through the Gospel at every juncture of one's ministry. It's this awesome confidence in God, rooted in the Scripture's proclamation of a God who loves completely: all the way to the cross, through the cross, and into the lives of rebellious humanity through words, water, bread and wine, just to say, "I did it all for you." No matter what the challenges today, that real-present Jesus, that God-for-us-in-Christ reality drives, empowers, and guides the public ministry of the Church for God's people. In full view of the work, empowered by the Lord who comes in Word and Sacrament, as Dr. Warneck says so well, " Let the action begin!" With this book as a guide, you'll be well prepared!

Rev. Gregory P. Seltz, PhD

Executive Director, Lutheran Center for Religious Liberty
Speaker Emeritus, *The Lutheran Hour*

Preface

INI

In Nomine Jesu! This book about the pastoral ministry in the Christian Church opens in the name of Jesus. Similar to the professions of medicine and law, the pastoral ministry lays claim to a cumulative fund of knowledge, learning, and experience. The special pedigree of this profession, however, is its origin as a ministry of Jesus. God had given His Word to His people through Moses and the prophets. Later, the Word Incarnate, Jesus Christ, called and sent His apostles with the Gospel of God's love for the world's people. The apostles' ministry continues, exercised by the pastoral office established by Jesus.

The acronym *INI*, in the name of Jesus, signals that subjects, discussions, and conclusions relative to pastoral practice have but one referent, the Lord Jesus Christ. He is the authority for the pastoral ministry. Also, the purpose of the pastoral ministry derives from Him, namely, the eternal salvation of all who hear the Gospel and believe in Him. It is evident, therefore, that the theology and practice of the pastoral ministry is singularly of the Lord, that is, *dominical*.

The Lord interpreted His ministry according to the Scriptures. The implication is clear. The pastoral ministry today, *dominical* indeed, must practice in accord with that same Word of God. Therefore, discussions of pastoral practice in this work are anchored in biblical theology and they cite the Scriptures liberally, but responsibly. The intention is to frame pastoral practice according to the Scriptures, for they are the Word of God and they both set and norm the disciplines of the pastoral ministry.

This book states principles that guide and direct active pastoral life and ministry. The author is a pastor and professor in The Lutheran Church—Missouri Synod, but the work may also serve pastors and churches of many fellowships where the Scriptures are normative. Pressed by the secular culture, the institutional church as we know it may deconstruct. In that event, Christians may find themselves in settings that are both different and varied. Wherever they congregate—perhaps under conditions unforeseen—this book will inform understanding of the pastoral ministry for both pastors and the laity.

Hopefully, this work will serve a wide range of pastors and assist them in honing pastoral judgment. Accomplished pastors at the top of their game may profit. For the initiate to the profession, the book is an introduction. For some pastors, it may provide a fresh view of their profession that is both *dominical* and *apostolic*. We are concerned for the pastor gripped by malaise. He may be weary or burdened with self-doubt, or he may feel pangs of guilt. Has the pastoral ministry become disappointing? Whatever the pastor's condition or situation—challenges, accomplishments, victories, burdens, failures—we intend to assist his ministry and enrich his life in the profession.

This book appears at a time of diverse pastoral practice. This diversity has resulted, sadly, in division. Unresolved radical diversity finally becomes divisive. Tensions over diversity in practice are legion. To name a few, there are serious disagreements in the Church about open versus close(d) Communion practice, worship forms, mission strategies, and the treatment of marriage, divorce, and remarriage. Pastoral practice on many counts is either lax or legalistic. This work takes a position on many subjects, but it will not arbitrate between different factions. Correctives in regard to questionable diversity and polarity rest with ecclesiastical leadership exercised by responsible church officials. Our hope early in the twenty-first century is that this book brings stability to the pastoral ministry and contributes to the unity of the spirit in the Church.

This book about the pastoral ministry was written for pastors, but always with an eye for the laity of the Church, chiefly their comprehension of their pastor's calling. Many lay Christians seek this understanding. Knowledge in any field can be misused, but properly informed about the pastoral office, Christian people will take interest in their pastor's ministry and support his day-to-day work among them. More significant, they will be comfortable with the dialogue that pastors and people must have over the mission and ministry of the congregation. With this in mind, we commend this book to both pastors and the laity.

The Holy Scriptures are the principal source for this work, followed by the Lutheran Confessions and the writings of Martin Luther and C. F. W. Walther. Contributions abound from theologians and pastors to whom this author is indebted. The late Dr. Robert D. Preus rescued me for the pastoral ministry and started me on this journey. Dr. John F. Johnson, former president of Concordia Seminary, was a valued mentor. Many others whom I esteem are referenced in these pages. I thank many physicians and surgeons. Students in pastoral theology classes at Concordia Seminary contributed. The Rev. Scot A. Kinnaman, senior book editor at Concordia Publishing House, was patient and generous with good counsel. Most appreciated is a supportive family—my wife, Marlene, quintessential pastor's wife, and two sons, Richard and Stephen. Rich was a valued adviser, and Steve served with his talent for writing and editing.

This work, begun in the name of Jesus, advanced under Christ and His Word, serving pastors and the people they shepherd, let the action begin. From the first salvo to the last breath, let all be to the glory of God!

Richard H. Warneck, PhD

CHAPTER ONE

Prolegomena

Pastoral Ministry—*Dominical, Apostolic*

Pastoral Ministry: Theology and Practice addresses the principal parts of the pastoral ministry in the Christian Church. The discussion opens with assumptions and observations that are germane to the larger treatment of the profession. Collectively, these are *prolegomena*, or first considerations. They set the stage for discussing the essential tasks and responsibilities of the pastoral office in a time of diverse practice.

Where diversity reigns, pastors and theologians may not share a quest for common pastoral practice, but reaching a consensus that the pastoral office is transcendent in nature and character should be a goal. We believe and teach that the pastoral ministry is foremost, *dominical*. It is of the Lord Jesus Christ! If this is stating the obvious, why do many pastors wing it in the practice of the pastoral ministry? Perhaps together we may seek to secure our common ministry on the moorings of Christ and His Word.

Confessing that the pastoral office is *dominical*, we assert a *metanarrative*. The pastoral ministry is not a human construct; rather, it was instituted by Christ, who sent His apostles to execute this ministry. He gathered them as disciples, made them fishers of men, and sent them into the public ministry of His making and in His name (cf. Luke 9:1–2; 10:1–12). Through His Church, He continues to call and send pastors to fulfill this pastoral office. Who pastors are and what pastors do is of the Lord (John 20:20–23; Matt 28:19–20; John 21:15–19; Acts 1:8; Eph 4:11; cf. Eph 3:8; Luke 5:1–11).

Furthermore, the dominical pastoral ministry is also *apostolic*, that is, it is ordered by the teachings of the Lord's apostles. Jesus announced that the Spirit would take what is His and declare it to His apostles; in other words, all that Jesus has of the Father the Spirit would declare to them (John 16:13–15). Therefore, the apostles' teaching properly orders pastoral ministry because this *apostolic* teaching is also *dominical*. The apostles' ministry was distinctive in this respect. Note how Peter and John explain their encounter with the lame man at the temple gate in Jerusalem: "Let it be known to all of you and to all the people of Israel that by the name of Jesus Christ of Nazareth, whom you crucified, whom God raised from the dead—by Him this man is standing before you well" (Acts 4:10). *Dominical* indeed!

Dominical: of the Lord Jesus Christ.
Apostolic: ordered by the teachings of the Lord's apostles!

In letters to Timothy and Titus, St. Paul stresses that their ministries were *apostolic* and *dominical.* The charge to Timothy, "Preach the word; be ready in season and out of season; reprove, rebuke, and exhort, with complete patience and teaching," is *apostolic*, under the authority of the Lord's apostle, but it is a charge given "in the presence of God and of Christ Jesus who is to judge the living and the dead" (2 Tim 4:1–2), a ministry accountable to the Lord, *dominical*! Pastoral ministry should be ordered in such a way as to be *dominical* and *apostolic.*

The Lord's Word, the Apostles' Word, the Pastor's Word

Jesus affirmed His apostles' preaching and ministry in His name when He declared, "The one who hears you hears Me" (Luke 10:16). And He announced, "But the Helper, the Holy Spirit, whom the Father will send in My name, He will teach you all things and bring to your remembrance all that I have said to you" (John 14:26). He declared the sequence: the Father's Word to the Son to the apostles. Praying to the Father, He said, "For I have given them the words that You gave Me, and they have received them and have come to know in truth that I came from You; and they have believed that You sent Me" (John 17:8; cf. 15:15b). In the apostles' preaching and teaching, their words are the Lord's words, certainly *dominical* (Acts 1:8; cf. Acts 10:36–43; cf. Titus 1:3).

Clearly, when the pastoral ministry—preaching and teaching—proclaims the *apostolic* Word, this ministry is of Christ and His Word, *dominical.* Our Lord spoke the words of God and gave those words to His apostles, and they to pastors, beginning with servants like Timothy, Titus, and others (John 3:34–35; 1 Tim 1:1–2; 2 Tim 1:13; Titus 1:3; cf. 1 Cor 11:23ff.). Therefore, it is legitimate to say that the pastoral ministry is *apostolic*, and to believe that when the pastor proclaims and teaches the prophetic and apostolic Word, Christ our Lord is speaking the Word of God to His people (cf. Luke 5:1).

Holy Scripture

The pastor proclaims the Word that is *dominical* and *apostolic* when he publicly expounds the Holy Scriptures. The indispensable link—the pastoral ministry and the Scriptures—is by *apostolic* design. St. Paul's exhortation to Timothy is compelling: "Preach the word" (2 Tim 4:2). This exhortation follows his directive to Timothy to continue in what he had learned since childhood from the sacred writings which instruct about the Gospel and salvation through faith in Jesus Christ. Paul directed Timothy to the Scriptures because they had been given *theopneustos*, by inspiration of God (2 Tim 3:14–16; cf. 2 Pet 1:20–21).

Moreover, a pastoral theology frames pastoral ministry in the manner that our Lord interpreted His ministry: according to the Scriptures. The Old Testament—Moses and the prophets and the Psalms—and the New Testament, the *apostolic* Word, is the Word from the Father that our Lord committed to His apostles through the Holy Spirit during His ministry and following His ascension (Luke 24:27, 32, 44–49; 1 Cor 15:1–4; John 14:24b, 16–17, 25–26; cf. John 15:15b, 20; 1 Thess 2:13). For the sake of the Gospel revealed and disclosed through the *prophetic* and *apostolic* writings, the work of the pastoral ministry adheres closely to the Scriptures, the final authority in teaching and practice (Rom 16:25–27). The Lutheran Confessions are mentor in this regard, for they constantly appeal to the Scriptures, the divine Word.[1]

A pastor arrives at certainty that the Scriptures hold God's foundational principles for pastoral ministry not by his own ruminating but only by the *testimonium Spiritus Sancti internum*, the internal testimony of the Holy Spirit. This testimony of the Spirit comes by means of the Scriptures owned by the Spirit. Consider this assessment:

> This *testimonium Spiritus Sancti internum* by which the Spirit moves and enlightens our hearts to believe the Scriptures and promises of God is never something immediate but always *per*

1 See the preface to the Book of Concord 3, 4, 7, 20, 22; preface to the Augsburg Confession 8 and 11, in *The Book of Concord: The Confessions of the Evangelical Lutheran Church*. Ed. Robert Kolb and Timothy J. Wengert. Minneapolis, MN: Augsburg Fortress, 2000. (Hereafter, Kolb-Wengert) The authority of the Holy Scriptures, the inspired and inerrant Word of God, is treated by a vast bibliography of works. We mention the following: A. L. Graebner, *Outlines of Doctrinal Theology* (St. Louis: Concordia Publishing House, n.d.). Francis Pieper, *Christian Dogmatics*, vol. 1 (St. Louis: Concordia Publishing House, 1950). M. Reu, "Luther and the Scriptures," *The Springfielder* 24, no. 2 (August 1960), reprint of the work originally published by the Wartburg Press, Columbus, OH, 1944. *The Gospel and Scripture: The Interrelationship of the Material and Formal Principles in Lutheran Theology; A Report of the Commission on Theology and Church Relations* (St. Louis: The Lutheran Church—Missouri Synod, November 1972). *The Inspiration of Scripture: A Report of the Commission on Theology and Church Relations* (St. Louis: The Lutheran Church—Missouri Synod, March 1975). Robert D. Preus, *The Inspiration of Scripture: A Study of the Theology of the 17th Century Lutheran Dogmaticians* (Mankato, MN: Lutheran Synod Book Company, 1955). Robert D. Preus, *The Theology of Post-Reformation Lutheranism: A Study of Theological Prolegomena*, vol. 1 (St. Louis: Concordia Publishing House, 1970); see chapter 3, "The Doctrine of Scripture," 254–403. For right comprehension of the Bible, see Carl Ferdinand Wilhelm Walther, *Law and Gospel: How to Read and Apply the Bible*, ed. Charles P. Schaum, trans. Christian C. Tiews (St. Louis: Concordia Publishing House, 2010).

verbum. It is, like faith, the work of the Spirit in the believer's heart; and it is also the work of the Scripture itself.[2]

Revelation

Divine disclosure or revelation is generic to the pastoral ministry. For the Gospel preached according to the Scriptures—the forgiveness of sins and peace with God for all through Jesus Christ, His death and resurrection—is a divine mystery that the apostle Paul relates as God's revelation or disclosure. He was especially taken by God's disclosure of the Gospel for the Gentiles (Col 1:27; Rom 16:25–26; Eph 3:3–6).

Principle: A pastor's energy abounds in proportion to his sense that God intervenes through the Gospel at every juncture of his ministry.

Furthermore, divine revelation is also intervention (as in Acts 22:6–11). A pastor senses the intervening action of the Spirit as persons initially respond to the Gospel in faith and confession. Witness the narrative in Acts 10. The Spirit came to hearers at Caesarea upon Peter's preaching the Gospel (Acts 10:44–48); but this occurred in the context of dual intervention: (1) Peter's commission to travel to Caesarea; (2) Cornelius's commission to receive the apostle (Acts 10:1–33). The incident at Caesarea was revelatory. It was divine intervention.

Revelation in terms of the intervening action of the Spirit encourages any faithful and sensitive pastor. Conscious of revelation—disclosure and intervention—the pastor moves with confidence and perhaps even with bounce in his step, a light heart, and a sense of joy and wonder permeating his life and work.

Interpretation

Correct interpretation of the biblical text is essential when engaging Holy Scripture as the *norm* for the practice of the pastoral ministry. As interpreter, the pastor is busy with the *res*, the subject matter of the Bible. God's saving action moving throughout the Old and New Testaments, bringing fallen mankind back to Him by grace, that by faith in Jesus Christ we might be saved, is the *res*, the chief focus of the pastor as interpreter. Reading the Scripture as Gospel is the pastor's calling.[3]

---

2 Robert D. Preus, *Post-Reformation Lutheranism*, vol. 1, 302. See Preus's discussion of the divine origin and authority of Scripture as a work of the Holy Spirit, distinguished from rational criteria for certainty about these factors, 302–303.

3 Martin H. Franzmann, "Seven Theses on Reformation Hermeneutics," *Concordia Theological Monthly* 40, no. 4 (April 1969): 235, 245.

Seeking and finding the *res*, the pastor works with the *verba*, the words of Holy Scripture. We emphasize that the Scripture as writing or text is an objective entity. So the interpreter as exegete pays close attention to the language of the text—vocabulary, usage of words and terms, grammar, syntax, and context—in his effort to comprehend the text and what it states. Historical background augments close exegetical examination, as does the principle "Scripture interprets Scripture." Fanciful as it may sound, this latter principle implies that it is not the interpreter, but the subject—the external Word of the Scriptures—that leads to the meaning of a text studied from the Scriptures.[4] As the pastor works with the Scriptures, he is confident, God does not lie. His Word speaks truth (Titus 1:2; Isa 45:19b).

Today, biblical hermeneutics has moved beyond the traditional discipline. A shift has occurred that is somewhat parallel to the moves in the culture from modernism to postmodernism. Lately, the interpreter himself plays a larger role in the interpretation method.[5] In some models, the postmodern hermeneutic moves away from and beyond the objectivity of the Scripture text, interjects the interpreter's profile in terms of his orientation and subjective perceptions, arriving at a meaning of the text that is framed to meet anthropological needs of a contemporary audience.[6]

There is a relationship—the interpreter to the text—in the interpretation of the Scriptures. This human factor is undeniable. The new hermeneutic goes so far to assert that there is no neutral hearing, that all hearers or readers of a text are conditioned by their situated circumstances (including biases) that affect their reception of meaning from a text. Yet precisely how much preconditioning affects the interpreter's search for meaning remains ambiguous.

Thus, a caution is appropriate for the confessional pastor-interpreter. When a pastor seeks the counsel of God's Word for shaping his judgment, decisions, or actions, his subjective view of a Scripture text shall not override

4 Still useful is the model for exegetical work provided by Dr. Martin Scharlemann, graduate professor of exegetical theology at Concordia Seminary, titled "Fifteen Steps from Scripture Text to a Central Thought." This exhibit served seminary students developing and composing sermons. See Appendix 1. Other exhibits of traditional hermeneutics are Martin H. Franzmann, "Essays in Hermeneutics," *Concordia Theological Monthly* 19 (August to October 1948): 595–605, 641–652, 738–746. Franzmann treats the circles of language, history, and Scripture in biblical interpretation. An earlier exhibit is *Theological Hermeneutics* (St. Louis: Concordia Publishing House, 1924), a translation of the publication *Theologische Hermeneutik* (St. Louis: Concordia Publishing House, 1912).

5 The focus on the interpreter in biblical interpretation is treated by Jeffrey J. Kloha, "Theological Hermeneutics after Meaning," *Lutheran Theological Journal* 46, no. 1 (May 2012): 4–16. See the response to Kloha's essay by Werner R. A. Klän, "Response to 'Theological Hermeneutics after Meaning,'" *Lutheran Theological Journal* 46, no. 1 (May 2012): 17–25. Cf. James W. Voelz, *What Does This Mean?: Principles of Biblical Interpretation in the Post-Modern World* (St. Louis: Concordia Publishing House, 1997).

6 For close tracking of this shift in contemporary biblical hermeneutics, see Armin Wenz, "Biblical Hermeneutics in a Postmodern World; Sacramental Hermeneutics versus Spiritualistic Constructivism," *Logia* 22, no. 3 (Holy Trinity 2013): 15–24.

the objective character and authority of the Scriptures. Barring this restraint, the content and meaning of the Scripture message may be considered variable, according to particular circumstances of time and situation with respect to the interpreter, and also according to his preunderstandings.[7] In a worst-case scenario, the interpretation is the interpreter's construct that arises principally from his reader-response to the text. The objective text and the probable intention of the author are dispensable. Unavoidable, then, is relativity, resulting in the advocacy of *new meaning* that essentially accommodates the text to current situations in pastoral practice.[8]

Again, biblical interpretation is crucial for the Christian pastor. How does our discipline, pastoral theology, arrive at meaning of the biblical text for the enterprise of pastoral ministry? Can we or should we go farther than the Lutheran confessors, who were satisfied that the plain words of Scripture hold the Spirit's intended meaning? Stating the meaning of the Lord's Supper, for example, they cited the clear words of the Scripture text. Those words suffice. They are there, and, most of the time, solid exegetical work discloses their meaning.[9]

Doctrine and Practice

Principle: The pastoral ministry, *dominical* and *apostolic*, possesses authority and legitimacy in doctrine and practice as shown by the initial pastoral theology, the Pastoral Epistles of the New Testament.

Doctrine and practice in the pastoral ministry exercise a complementary relationship.[10] The apostle Paul commits his apostolic teaching to Timothy and Titus, the *words* about Jesus Christ and salvation won by Him (Titus 1:1–4; 2:11–15; cf. 1 Tim 2:3–7; 4:16). This Gospel—*doctrine*—leads to *practice* of the Christian life. So Paul exclaims: "Great indeed, we confess, is the mystery of godliness: He was manifested in the flesh, vindicated by the Spirit, seen by angels, proclaimed among the nations, believed on in the world, taken up in glory" (1 Tim 3:16). The term "godliness" here refers to Paul's previous discussion about behavior within the household of God; the instructions about these matters, *doctrine*, he forwards to Timothy in case he is delayed or prevented from instructing in person (1 Tim 3:14–15).

7 Ibid., 21.

8 This caution serves the practicing pastor because some current models of hermeneutics advance the notion that the text of Holy Scripture in any discussion is merely one factor among many, that the meaning of divine revelation may also be, at least in part, nonconceptual, the inner workings of new consciousness as the psyche interacts with the stimuli of the present time and age. See the discussion by Roman Catholic theologian Gregory Baum in *The Infallibility Debate: Gregory Baum and Others*, ed. John J. Kirvan (New York: Paulist Press, 1971), 25–27.

9 Preface to the Book of Concord, Kolb-Wengert, 18.

10 How doctrine determines and affects the practice of the pastoral ministry, but equally significant, how practice may change and ultimately determine doctrine, are themes explored by Pastor Klemet I. Preus, *The Fire and the Staff: Lutheran Theology in Practice* (St. Louis: Concordia Publishing House, 2004).

Conversely, the Pastoral Epistles mark irreligion or ungodliness, that is, negative practice that results from false teaching, doctrine. For example, corrupt persons on the Isle of Crete who professed to know God but denied Him by their works, their practice, had given themselves to Jewish myths and commands of men who reject the truth (Titus 1:14–16). Error or false doctrine fosters ungodly behavior, that is, false *practice.* Paul calls out lawlessness in practice that is contrary to sound doctrine (1 Tim 1:8–11). Also note his avoidance exhortations. They press for avoiding false doctrine in order to preserve godliness in living, *practice.* Teaching or doctrine bereft of truth (1 Tim 6:5) ruins hearers (2 Tim 2:14–15), upsets whole families (Titus 1:11), threatens those in the faith, and even wrecks faith itself (2 Tim 2:18b).

Paul mentored Timothy and Titus in a manner that shows the complementary relationship between *doctrine* and *practice* in their conduct of the pastoral ministry. His mentoring sparks many discussions in the chapters ahead where doctrine and practice are essential factors that warrant close attention and careful distinctions in pastoral practice today.

Postmodern Pastoral Theology

Doctrine and *practice* come together with interpretation in the discipline of pastoral theology. Lutheran pastoral theology is known for its hefty assertion of doctrine, which is pivotal for confessional pastoral ministry. Lutheran pastors are bound by the Lutheran Confessions, which expound and *interpret* the Scriptures for both doctrine and practice as this passage from the Epitome of the Formula of Concord shows:

> We believe, teach, and confess that the only rule and guiding principle according to which all teachings and teachers are to be evaluated and judged are the prophetic and apostolic writings of the Old and New Testaments alone, as it is written, "Your word is a lamp to my feet and a light to may path" (Ps. 119[:105]), and Saint Paul: "If . . . an angel from heaven should proclaim to you something contrary, . . . let that one be accursed!" (Gal. 1[:8]).[11]

Sound *doctrine* that serves as the norm for practice is essential for Lutheran pastoral ministry. In other traditions, this paradigm is termed theory to practice, but postmodern models of pastoral theology differ significantly. For example, in his work *A Fundamental Practical Theology*, the late Prof. Don Browning of Chicago University took deliberate steps to distinguish his understanding of pastoral theology from other models that appear to operate in

11 Kolb-Wengert, 486.

a traditional mode, essentially *theory* to practice.[12] He asserts that theology can be practical only when we bring practical concerns to it from the beginning and employ practical reason. The interaction of church and culture plays an important role. Where practice is active and poignant, critical questions arise for the Church. As a community of interpreters, the Church receives those questions and addresses them to inherited normative sources, that is, texts—Scripture, creeds, confessions, doctrinal statements, and such. Thus begins a conversation—questions arising from religious and secular practices put to normative texts within the community of faith. The results from this dialogue are significant. What evolves are reconstructed religious meanings and practices, also new or revised understanding of how the texts serve theology as practice in the present context or situation. New understandings about the meaning and the thrust of *norms* for the current practice of the ministry may emerge. Browning recognizes that such a process is *de facto* deconstruction of former traditional meanings and uses of texts.[13]

Browning's paradigm of practical theology is a three-part movement—beginning with *practice*, moving back to *reflection* on norms or texts, and then moving forward again to *practice*. The process is distinctively hermeneutical or interpretive, and it assumes deconstruction of the theory to practice model of traditional practical theology.[14] Browning's model raises critical questions for confessional theology and practice, and these questions are about the status, authority, and use of texts (Scripture, Confessions, etc.) as norms for the practice of pastoral ministry. Shall these norms undergo revisionist handling? Are the norms pliable? If so, what authority do they carry for practice? Can they retain their preservative and protective purposes—their apologetic functions—if they are constantly vulnerable to revision? And what of hermeneutical principles within the norms themselves, which exclude reconfiguration or reconstruction? Finally, how does church and ministry arrive at practice that is

---

12 Somewhat surprising is Browning's confrontation with the Swiss theologian Karl Barth, who, in Browning's estimate, was an epistemological realist who saw theology as the systematic interpretation of God's self-disclosure to the Christian Church. In Barth's view, theology is practical only by applying God's revelation as directly and purely as possible to the concrete situations of life. The theologian moves from revelation to the human, from *theory to practice*, and from revealed knowledge to application. Browning took exception to Barth's strong accent on revelation. He believed that Barth left little room for the interpreting community to verify things morally, experientially, or cognitively. In Barth's theology for practice of the ministry, Browning saw no role for human understanding, action, or practice in the construal of God's self-disclosure. Don S. Browning, *A Fundamental Practical Theology: Descriptive and Strategic Proposals* (Minneapolis: Fortress Press, 1991), 5, 7.

13 Ibid., 6.

14 Browning engages George Gadamer's work *Truth and Method*, which integrates understanding, interpretation, and application. He uses Gadamer's fusion of the horizon of meaning—practical questions and fore-meanings—brought to classic texts and the horizon of meaning that texts themselves project. See *A Fundamental Practical Theology*, 41. Also see a sampling of questions Browning puts to central texts and monuments of Christian faith. Ibid., 48–49.

integral to the divine norms themselves when meaning conveyed by the norms is subject to reconfiguration as a result of interaction with the current situation, context, or experience of the community of faith?

Browning's work was the capstone of former paradigms that differed from pastoral theology, a discipline of applied Bible and biblical principles. The influence of representative models was broad in the twentieth century. Seward Hiltner (1909–1984) championed "shepherding" as the organizing principle for pastoral theology, a discipline consisting of three major components: healing, sustaining, and girding. These pastoral actions are executed, not as applied theology—Bible or Christian doctrine—applied one way directly to acts and functions. Important as Bible and Confessions are—the currencies of faith, Hiltner's respectful term—he suggested that the use of such norms is a process that moves the other way so that a creative study and consideration of events from some significant perspective makes creative contributions to theological understanding.[15] Embracing such contributions, Hiltner emphasized that faith is relevant and faithful only when it dialogues carefully and in a discriminating manner with the culture. Addressing questions of theology, he saw significant potential available in the personality sciences.[16] Distancing the discipline of pastoral theology away from a rigid theology-applied-to-practice model, Hiltner followed his mentor, Anton Boisen (1876–1965), father of the case study method and clinical pastoral education. Like William James, Boisen was concerned more with the function of theological belief than with the substance of belief and confession. He placed a premium on learning theology empirically from the kind of experiences that students and clinicians observed in patients with serious pathologies.[17]

Practical theology, distanced from divine revelation, is the order for numerous postmodern paradigms. J. Poling and D. Miller describe practical theology as a critical and constructive reflection within a community of faith that involves correlation of the Christian story and other perspectives, leading to guidelines and skills for the formation of persons and communities.[18] While Poling and Miller describe practical theology as a process of *reflection*, the British practical theologian Martyn Percy prefers to use the term *refraction*

15 Thus the editors of *The Blackwell Reader in Pastoral and Practical Theology* observed Hiltner's contention that pastoral theology, more than the application in practice of theories derived from academic study of theological ideas, is a venue where theological ideas and contemporary experiences meet in such a way that both are exchanged. *The Blackwell Reader in Pastoral and Practical Theology*, ed. James Woodward and Stephen Pattison (Malden, MA: Blackwell Publishers, 2000), 25.

16 Seward Hiltner, *Preface to Pastoral Theology* (Nashville: Abingdon Press, 1958), 22.

17 John Patton, "Introduction to Modern Pastoral Theology in the United States," in *The Blackwell Reader in Pastoral and Practical Theology*, 51.

18 See Martyn Percy, *Engaging with Contemporary Culture: Christianity, Theology and the Concrete Church* (Burlington, VT: Ashgate Publishing, 2005), 9.

to describe the discipline. Refraction, says Percy, engages the whole range of behaviorist sciences to configure pastoral practice. Practical theology, then, is a process of refraction similar to the dispersal of light into its constituent bands of color as it passes through a glass prism. Percy asserts that practical theology is host to numerous disciplines interacting and coloring one another with richer and deeper hues. Considering theology, church, and contemporary culture, Percy describes a refractive process when an *issue* passes through each of the prisms—sociology, theology, anthropology, cultural studies—and possibly others, too, and that each of these then sees how its own truth is affected by such refraction.[19] The handling of issues—pastoral care, ethical, spiritual, and so forth—through prisms may be configured and processed as shown in this exhibit:

This overview of revisionist models of practical theology poses the question of use for biblical and confessional pastoral theology. How do these models contribute? Certainly, they remind pastors that ministry to people attends to their situation and context. Then practicing pastors are alerted to their subjective biases and attitudes, which may be idiosyncratic and indefensible. These negative traits can accumulate as "theory-laden" factors, to use Browning's term. Orthodox practice consistent with the Scriptures can be legalistic in tone, insensitive or loveless. Pastoral practice that is orthodox for its own sake is problematic. Although such practice may continue to plead confessional character, it may no longer be *dominical.* Sometimes, the rush to get things *right* may outpace the timing of the Holy Spirit. Some pastors who are hasty to enforce orthodox practice assign to patience the pejorative label *laxity.*

This assessment includes a significant caveat. Postmodern practical theology appears to show a better way, but the humanistic orientation of these postmodern models is disquieting for biblical and confessional practitioners. These models have deep roots in psychology and sociology, also ethnography (descriptive anthropology) and ethnology (the science of human family—races, their origins, proliferation, relations, and peculiarities). But theology—God speaking, revealing, and directing through the medium of divine revelation—is rare in these postmodern models. We state this caveat with regret.

19 Ibid., 11.

Biblical and Confessional Pastoral Theology

Contrasted to Hiltner, Browning, and others, the biblical and confessional paradigm of pastoral theology is *theory* to *practice* in genre, though not as inflexible as this category infers. In the late nineteenth century, James M. Hoppin, professor at Yale University, advanced the notion that pastoral theology is both a science and an art. By the term *science*, Hoppin meant that pastoral theology embraces the underlying principles of pastoral work. By the term *art*, he meant the external and somewhat flexible and even subjective use of those principles toward a certain goal or end. Hoppin's work, *Pastoral Theology*, is theory to practice, but certainly not rigid.[20] Nor is the work of G. H. Gerberding, *The Lutheran Pastor*, first published in 1902, inflexible or insensitive. C. F. W. Walther's exhaustive *Pastorale* is quite sensitive to the spiritual needs of people. When properly driven by the Gospel, the traditional theory to practice paradigm still serves well. It has not been upstaged by recent postmodern models of pastoral theology.

Drawing from C. F. W. Walther's *American-Lutheran Pastoral Theology* as a base, John H. C. Fritz defines our discipline in this manner: "*Pastoral Theology* is theology, or the doctrine of the knowledge of God and of divine things, *applied* by the *pastor*, the spiritual shepherd, to the *spiritual* needs of his flock."[21] Expanding his definition, Fritz emphasizes that pastoral theology is *theology* that has its source in the Word of God, stating that the Word reveals the eternal truths and the divine unchangeable principles that the pastor applies to the spiritual needs of God's people. Fritz urges pastors to recall such passages as Psalm 119:105; 1 Peter 1:25; Galatians 1:6–9; John 8:31–32. He adds that all principles for pastoral practice are anchored in the Word of God's revelation, which came by the instruments of His chosen prophets and apostles. The prophets spoke as the Word of the Lord came to them; the apostles spoke and wrote not what men teach but that which the Holy Spirit teaches (1 Thess 2:13; 1 Cor 2:4–13; cf. Acts 26:22–23).

We have shown that the pastoral ministry is *dominical*, of our Lord Jesus Christ. He affirmed the testimony of the Scriptures to His own ministry as the

---

20 Hoppin offers this precise definition: "Pastoral theology is chiefly concerned in carrying into life and practice those fundamental truths which are taught in the Scriptures and in any true and comprehensive system of theological education." James M. Hoppin, *Pastoral Theology*, 7th ed. (New York: Funk & Wagnalls, 1884), 4.

21 John H. C. Fritz, *Pastoral Theology: A Handbook of Scriptural Principles Written Especially for Pastors of the Lutheran Church* (St. Louis: Concordia Publishing House, 1932), 1. See the English translations of Walther's work. C. F. W. Walther, *American-Lutheran Pastoral Theology*, ed. David W. Loy, trans. Christian C. Tiews (St. Louis: Concordia Publishing House, 2017), and C. F. W. Walther, *Walther's Pastorale: American-Lutheran Pastoral Theology*, trans. and abridged by John M. Drickamer (New Haven, MO: Lutheran News, 1995). (Hereafter, Walther, *American-Lutheran Pastoral Theology*).

world's redeemer and to His atoning death and resurrection (Luke 18:31–34; 24:44–47; cf. 1 Cor 15:1–4). Even precursors to that redeeming work—preaching and signs and wonders—were His works according to the Scriptures (Luke 4:16–19; Isa 61:1–2; Matt 11:4–6). Therefore, we assert that the pastoral ministry, *dominical* with respect to *doctrine* and *practice*, functions according to the Scriptures. Further, the discipline, *pastoral theology*, provides principles from Holy Scripture for the practice of this ministry. For reason of their divine source, Fritz emphasizes, they are divine unchangeable principles.

The Spiritual Needs of God's People

God's people share many needs with the rest of humanity—personal, social, economic, and so forth, but pastoral theology assists pastors to meet the *spiritual* needs of His people. As a spiritual shepherd, the pastor applies theology to three important spiritual needs. The first is soteriological, that is, that many be saved (1 Cor 10:33). Nothing in this regard is to be taken for granted (cf. Acts 16:30; Mark 9:24). The Pastoral Epistles convey a sense of urgency when they show that the primary goal of theology directed by the pastor to a Christian congregation through such things as preaching, teaching, and pastoral care is to bring sinners to repentance, and then to faith in Jesus Christ. Consider how the saving work of Christ saturates the letters 1 and 2 Timothy and Titus. One passage is "The saying is trustworthy and deserving of full acceptance, that Christ Jesus came into the world to save sinners" (1 Tim 1:15).[22] In his first days of ministry to a congregation, a pastor poses key questions: How many persons will be led to Christ? How many will be strengthened in their faith in Christ during my ministry here?

A second *spiritual* need addressed by pastoral theology is the drive to live the faith-life, that is, the life of a Christian, a disciple of Jesus. Sanctification is a pressing need for one who is justified before God by His grace alone in Christ Jesus (Rom 6:20–22). The pastor speaks to this need. When the Gospel is preached, exhortation to good works accompanies the *Good News*. It is the way of the apostle Paul's ministry. For example, in Romans 12, the appeal by the "mercies of God," is promptly followed by the exhortation that Christians present their bodies to God as living sacrifices that are "holy and acceptable to God" (Rom 12:1–2). Their minds renewed, these Christians prove or show the will of God. The remainder of the chapter is a list of specific exhortations for those who live by the Spirit and in every situation overcome evil with good (Rom 12:21; cf. Titus 3:1–2).

22 The theme of salvation is dominant throughout the Pastoral Epistles (1 Tim 1:15–17; 2:3–5, 7; 4:10, 16; 2 Tim 2:10; 3:15; 4:8; Titus 1:1–3; 2:11–14, 15; 3:7).

By the Holy Spirit's work of regeneration through Baptism, Christians apply themselves to good actions (Titus 3:3–7; 3:8, 14).[23] A pastor sincerely desires for his people the royalty of a sanctified life (1 Thess 5:23–24; cf. 1 John 2:1, 5–6). A pastor accents Christian love (John 17:26), and love is essential goodness (cf. John 13:34–35; 1 John 3:4–18). In sermons, teaching lessons, and one-on-one conversations, he leads Christians to godly living. The close of the age is at hand. In 2 Peter 3:11, the apostle Peter presses, "Since all these things are thus to be dissolved, what sort of people ought you to be in lives of holiness and godliness[?]" John challenged Christians to sanctified living. In that vision of the bride of the Lamb, he saw her beauteous apparel, the righteous deeds of the saints (Rev 19:7–8).

A third *spiritual* need is *eschatological,* the need for Christians to know they have a part in the coming of the Lord on the Last Day. The culture in early twenty-first-century America narrowly focuses on the present, the preoccupation with self and enrichment for the moment. By contrast, Titus 3 draws the baptized Christian to Christ's appearing for our salvation. Since the incarnation, the present age is a time "waiting for our blessed hope, the appearing of the glory of our great God and Savior Jesus Christ" (Titus 2:11–14). This is not an escape from vocation—calling, responsibility, duty—but a perspective. This is the Christian worldview. The pastor applying theology alerts his congregation to the Lord who speaks, "Surely I am coming soon" (Rev 22:20). Until that day, the pastor attends to the spiritual needs of the people.

The Law and the Gospel—Adiaphora

Pastoral ministry falls under the scrutiny and correction of the Law, which judges practice to be right or wrong. Some aspects of practice, however, fall within the province of activity that is not specifically covered by either God's command or prohibition. These aspects are in the category titled *adiaphora,* a term originally assigned by the Lutheran Confessions to church rites that are neither commanded nor forbidden in the Word of God (FC SD X 5, 8, 9). Whether a practice is directly under scrutiny of the Law or is indifferent with respect to that scrutiny, it must honor the Gospel. Pastor Klemet Preus observed, "The minute a practice is introduced that communicates to the church something contrary to the Gospel, then that practice is no longer indifferent. It is no longer an adiaphoron."[24] Preus prefaced his remark, saying, "If the doc-

23 In the Pauline correspondence, couplets that combine Gospel and exhortation to sanctified living are common (Gal 4:4–7; 5:13–15, 16–26; Eph 2:1–10; 4:17–24; Phil 1:27–30; 2:5–11; 4:8–9; Col 3:1–4; 3:5–11, 12–25; 4:1–6).

24 Klemet I. Preus, *The Fire and the Staff,* 117.

trine of the Gospel is at stake, then a church's practice has significance."[25] Not all issues of pastoral practice, however, are black and white. Therefore, keen pastoral discernment is essential in regard to *adiaphora*.

Casuistry

When exercising discernment, the pastor may quickly find himself embroiled in *casuistry*, matters that call for a decision of conscience when determining if an action or practice is in accord with the Word of God. Usually, casuistry involves deciding whether a practice is right or wrong. That decision can be as puzzling as it is difficult.

Not all situations in the pastoral ministry are casuistry, but some pastors seem to thrive on it. They reduce pastoral practice to configurations where questions and doubt hover closely, calling for pastoral judgment, decision, or action. Arriving at right answers distinguished from wrong responses frequently lacks clarity. Confusion may result. Furthermore, it is impossible to anticipate or foresee all situations that call for, but elude, firm and absolute answers. All of this is true.

Any fruitful discussion of cases of casuistry begins with the clear understanding of principles of pastoral practice that even remotely apply to a particular doubtful situation. Lest participants in the discussion talk past one another, they should be on the same page with respect to biblical hermeneutics, that is, how the Scriptures are understood and interpreted. When discernment is elusive, frequently it comes down to stating, "This much we can say." With clear principles of pastoral practice in hand, the outcome is likely to be sanctified good judgment supported by the Holy Spirit.

Conclusion

The temptation in addressing prolegomena is to discuss the entire work in advance. Conscious of this temptation, we may have omitted topics pertinent to the purpose of setting out first considerations. At this point, however, basic positions with regard to pastoral ministry normed by the Holy Scriptures have been stated. The hope is that the reader will now give fair consideration to the larger contents of the work.

---

25 Ibid., 109. Consider the diversity of church practices, *adiaphora* defended by some or condemned by others, in the light of confession of the Gospel. See Charles P. Arand, "Not All Adiaphora Are Created Equal," *Concordia Journal* 30, no. 3 (July 2004): 156–164.

CHAPTER TWO

The Call to the Office of the Holy Ministry

Introduction

We pass Christian churches in cities, on town squares, and along country roads. A sign or marquee marks not only property and buildings, but also a fellowship of Christians who assemble in this place. The people of this fellowship gather in the name of the triune God. That name they each own in their Holy Baptism, and that name came with baptismal gifts—the forgiveness of sins and peace with God won by Christ on the cross and affirmed by His rising from the grave.

Christ Himself has given His Church the Office of the Holy Ministry. Christian congregations are charged by the Lord with the duty and privilege of calling suitably qualified men to carry out the Lord's Office of Ministry among them. This is the Lord's arrangement, His doing! Transcending what occurs behind the scenes in church life—joy, sorrow, conflict, peace—is the Office of the Holy Ministry. The pastor is called by the Lord Jesus Christ through the local congregation to carry out the Lord's ministry for their sake and on their behalf.

Divine Initiative Establishing the Ministry and the Call to This Ministry

The Lord's Ministry and the Church's Public Ministry

The matrix for the Church's ministry and the call to exercise the same is our Lord's public ministry, visible as that scene outside the house of disreputable Zacchaeus when Jesus announced, "Today salvation has come to this house. . . . For the Son of Man came to seek and to save the lost" (Luke 19:9–10; cf. Mark 1:14–15). The Lord brought into His public ministry the twelve apostles whom He called, trained, and sent, even as He was sent by the Father (Luke 9:1–2; Matt 10:1–5a; cf. John 7:18; 16:12–15; 17:25–26; 20:21). After the apostles, others served in the Lord's ministry, an arrangement that prevails until He comes at the close of the age (Matt 28:20; Rev 22:7, 13; 2 Tim 1:13–14; 2:1–2; Titus 1:5ff; cf. Acts 20:28; 2 Cor 8:16–19; Phil 2:19–24, 25–30).

Framework for the Church's Ministry

Principle: The Church's public ministry in every age may and shall claim identity with the Lord's own public ministry because it is framed by His ministry and exercised according to His institution and by His command.

By His command and promise, the Lord prescribed these components of the Church's ministry: preach the Gospel, teach the Word of God, administer Baptism and the Lord's Supper, declare Absolution to the penitent and withhold the same from the impenitent.[26] The Church's ministry is *dominical.* Therefore, through her pastors, the congregation is sure and certain that it is the Lord Himself who preaches, teaches, baptizes, hosts His Supper, and absolves and retains sins (Luke 10:16; Titus 3:4–7; 1 Cor 11:23–25; 2 Cor 2:10; John 20:23; Matt 18:18; cf. Acts 20:28). The Lutheran Confessions capture the essence of Christ's public ministry committed to the Church in these words from the Augsburg Confession, Articles IV and V:

> Furthermore . . . we receive forgiveness of sin and become righteous before God out of grace for Christ's sake through faith when we believe that Christ has suffered for us and that for his sake our sin is forgiven and righteousness and eternal life are given to us. . . . To obtain such faith God instituted the office of preaching, giving the gospel and the sacraments. Through these, as through means, he gives the Holy Spirit who produces faith, where and when he wills, in those who hear the gospel.[27]

---

26 Shall healing the sick, casting out demons (exorcism), and raising the dead—components of the Lord's public ministry—be named among essentials of the Church's public ministry (cf. Matt 10:1, 8)? Doubtless, these ministries of Jesus (Matt 8:16–17) demonstrated that the kingdom of God had come (Luke 10:9). Whether they are parts of an enduring public ministry beyond that of the apostles is debated. Again, the Lord prescribed: preaching the Gospel of repentance and forgiveness of sins, Holy Baptism, the Lord's Supper, and Absolution (Matt 28:19–20; Luke 24:46–47; John 20:22–23; Acts 1:8; 1 Cor 11:23–25). Certainly, the ecstatic gifts may accompany the Word-and-Sacrament ministry. But test the spirits (1 John 4:1)! St. Paul's exhortations in the Pastoral Epistles and elsewhere do not include mandates to exercise the ecstatic gifts named above. Theologians of two seminary departments of Systematic Theology state: "And the service to which ministers of the Word are called today does not necessarily involve raising the dead or healing the sick, as it did for the Twelve and the Seventy-Two in the Gospels. But the point is that Christ gave the same office that the Father had given Him." See "The Office of the Holy Ministry: Departments of Systematic Theology," *Concordia Journal* 33, no. 3 (July 2007): 244. Also see "The Office of the Holy Ministry," *Concordia Theological Quarterly* 70, no. 2 (April 2006): 113–121. Dr. Joel P. Okamoto authored a paper that became the basis for discussion reported in these articles that led to consensus reached by the two faculties on the subject, the Office of the Ministry.

27 AC IV 1, 2; V 1–2.

The Call to the Church's Public Ministry

The Lord Jesus Christ has given every Christian congregation the right, privilege, and responsibility to call and ordain pastors. The Treatise from the Book of Concord asserts:

> Therefore, where the true church is, there must also be the right of choosing and ordaining ministers. . . . Pertinent here are the words of Christ that assert that the keys were given to the church, not just to particular persons: "For where two or three are gathered in my name . . ." [Matt. 18:20] Finally this is also confirmed by Peter's declaration [1 Peter 2:9]: "You are a . . . royal priesthood." These words apply to the true church, which, since it alone possesses the priesthood, certainly has the right of choosing and ordaining ministers.[28]

The teaching is clear. The whole Church possesses the Keys, which does not license freelancing individualistic public ministry but serves as the Church's right to choose, call, and ordain ministers.[29] The Lutheran Confessions are concerned that these ministers (pastors)—chosen, called, ordained—represent Christ and do His work publicly. This is seen from repeated citations of these words of Jesus addressed to His apostles: "The one who hears you hears Me" (Luke 10:16; AC XXVIII 22; Ap VII/VIII 28, 47; cf. Ap XII 40; XXVIII 18–19a).[30]

The Ministry as *Office*

The Term *Office*

The term *office* in the phrase "Office of the Ministry" is the word *Amt* in German, and so in Article V of the Augsburg Confession there is a very specific office in view, the *Predigtamt* or the "preaching office," which assumes there are actual preachers preaching. It is not merely a vague set of functions with no actual concrete office and office holder. The Lord's Office of the Ministry has these qualities:

- *Responsibility*: The pastor is called to preach God's Word and administer the Sacraments *publice*, publicly for the benefit of all (1 Tim 4:13). He absolves the penitent and withholds Absolution from

---

28 Treatise on the Power and Primacy of the Pope 67, 68, 69. Cf. par. 23, 24. Kolb-Wengert, 330ff.

29 This articulate stating of the matter is by the Systematic Departments of two seminaries, Concordia Seminary, St. Louis, Missouri, and Concordia Theological Seminary, Fort Wayne, Indiana. "The Office of the Holy Ministry: Departments of Systematic Theology," *Concordia Journal* 33, no. 3 (July 2007): 252–253. *Concordia Theological Quarterly* 70, no. 2 (April 2006): 113ff.

30 "The Office of the Holy Ministry: Departments of Systematic Theology," *Concordia Journal* 33, no. 3 (July 2007): 245.

impenitent persons (John 20:23). He sees to it that public worship is conducted in proper order (1 Cor 14:40). He cares for the faith and life of each person in the congregation, guarding souls so that they are not drawn away from Christ and His Word (Acts 20:28–30). What is commanded of the Lord for His people becomes the pastor's responsibility (cf. 1 Cor 14:37; 1 Tim 4:6).

- *Duty (Action)*: The responsibilities above involve active work (1 Tim 3:1), that is, preparation and then effective execution—preaching, teaching, and conduct of the church's sacramental ministry, Holy Baptism and the Lord's Supper. The pastor's duty is to instruct the congregation about these sacraments and their use (cf. 1 Cor 11:17–34). In teaching, the pastor instructs from the Scriptures about the Gospel and its articles, the entire counsel of God (Acts 20:20–21; cf. 2 Tim 3:15–17). The pastor's duty is to mark doctrine contrary to the Scriptures, to counsel proponents of false teaching to correct their error. If they do not heed his counsel, the pastor urges the congregation to avoid such teaching and teachers (Titus 2:1; 1:9; Rom 16:17).
- *Accountability*: The pastor is accountable both to the Lord and to the body of believers. He is accountable for faithful exercise of the Church's public ministry, the Lord's ministry. He is also liable for censure if he is unfaithful in carrying out the duties of this public ministry responsibly. He is accountable to the Lord (Acts 20:28; 2 Tim 2:15; Heb 13:17) and to the Church (Acts 11:4ff.; 15:2ff.; 1 Tim 4:13–16).

The apostle Paul gave order to the ministry in the early churches. For instance, he cited the ministry's components and engaged Timothy and Titus to exercise them. His commission to both of these pastors accords with the paradigm above. There is responsibility to care for the spiritual welfare of churches at Ephesus and the Isle of Crete (1 Tim 1:3; 4:6; 2 Tim 1:8; 2:14; Titus 1:5; 3:8, 14). Second, there is duty to teach, exhort, and so on (1 Tim 1:3; 4:11; 6:2b–3; 2 Tim 1:13–14; 2:1–2; 3:14–17; 4:2, 5; Titus 1:13; 2:1, 15; 3:1–2). Third, Paul presses accountability to them as apostles for conduct of the public ministry, which ultimately is accountability to the Lord of the Church (1 Tim 1:18; 2:3–7; 5:21; 6:13–16; 2 Tim 3:14; 4:1–2, 9; Titus 2:11–13).

The three parts—responsibility, duty, and accountability—compose a framework wherein pastors exercise the Office of the Holy Ministry. In the stead of and by the command of his Lord Jesus Christ, the pastor exercises oversight of doctrine and life in the congregation.[31]

31 For helpful discussions of the Office of the Ministry and its functions, see Kurt Marquart, *The Church*

The Office as Continuum

The founding of new congregations challenged St. Paul. But he was forward looking. He realized that care of many churches had to be entrusted to others (2 Cor 11:28). He charged Timothy to discover able teachers (2 Tim 2:1–2). Also, he commissioned Titus to ordain elders (πρεβυτέρους) at Crete. These elders served as bishops (επίσκοποι). They exercised oversight and care (Titus 1:5).[32] What is apparent is not a succession of bishops for generations following, but the continuum, the office, to which many in various times and places were appointed or called to exercise the Church's public ministry. In the first century, the Office of the Ministry of the Word, once exercised by the apostle Paul, then by his immediate assistants, for example, Timothy, Titus, Epaphroditus, and others, was filled later by the calling and ministry of the bishop or elder.

The Divine Call to the Office

Consistent with His institution of the Office of the Ministry, our Lord is giving *gifts*, pastors, to fill the office in every generation. Recall the sequence. The Father sends the Son, and He sends apostles to exercise the public ministry (John 17:18; cf. John 20:21b; Matt 10:40). The apostles, in turn, prepare for appointment of bishops or elders to this office (cf. Acts 14:23). Thus, a pastor *given* by the Lord can be certain that both the office and his Call are divine.[33] Congregations should also be certain of these things. Observe that it is not protocol if a congregation refuses to have a pastor. This action rejects the giving Lord who places pastors with His people so that His Word and Sacraments may be administered properly among them. Further, a divinely called pastor will apply himself tirelessly in the Lord's public ministry as one who is responsible, dutiful, and accountable.[34]

---

and Her Fellowship, Ministry, and Governance (Confessional Lutheran Dogmatics, vol. 9), (Fort Wayne: Luther Academy, 1990); John F. Johnson, "The Office of the Pastoral Ministry: Scriptural and Confessional Considerations," in *Church and Ministry: The Collected Papers of The 150th Anniversary Theological Convocation of The Lutheran Church—Missouri Synod*, ed. Jerald C. Joerz and Paul T. McCain (St. Louis: Concordia Publishing House, 1998), 77–99. For helpful discussions of the Office of the Ministry and its functions, see David R. Maxwell, "The Function of the Pastoral Office in the Lutheran Confessions," and Scott R. Murray, "Function and Office: Seventeenth-Century Lutheran Dogmaticians and the Ministry," in *Pastoral Theology in the Light of the Lutheran Confessions*, ed. Jason Gehrke and Jennifer H. Maxfield (St. Louis: Luther Academy, 2012), 28–43, 44–64.

32 While the terms *prebyteros* and *episcopus* may not be synonyms in the Pastoral Epistles, each connotes the oversight and care exercised by the *shepherd*, the pastor who is charged to "feed the church of God" over whom the Holy Spirit has made him a bishop or overseer or guardian (Acts 20:28 KJV). See Titus 1:5, 7 where elders (*presbyteroi*) are referenced as bishops (*episcopoi*). For a discussion of these terms and their relationship to each other, see H. G. Brueggemann, "The Public Ministry in the Apostolic Age," *Concordia Theological Monthly* 22, no. 2 (February 1951): 91.

33 The term *Call* is capitalized in order to indicate its essential property with regard to the divine Office of the Ministry.

34 We may speak of the divinity of the Call to the Office of the Ministry. Consider this summary statement: "For reason that the Call or appointment to the pastoral office in a congregation of Christians

Mutual Understanding of the Call —Pastor and People

Understanding Is Essential for All

> **Principle:** Mutual understanding of the office and the Call by congregations and pastors keeps expectations within the boundaries of the Lord's stipulations consonant with His institution of the public ministry.

Calling a pastor is complex. This is due in part to elevated expectations of a pastor by members of the congregation. The higher the expectations are, the more difficult is procurement of a pastor.[35] Add the diversity of preferences, as diverse as the membership itself, and calling a pastor becomes a herculean effort. Should it be this way? Possibly deeper understanding of the Office of the Ministry and the Call to that ministry may temper the frustration generated by anticipation of a new pastor.

The Matter of Expectations

The Lord's Expectations

During the process of calling a pastor, the congregation should distinguish between what the Lord requires of a pastor and what the people find desirable in a pastor from a human perspective. Mark the distinction between *iure divino*, by divine right or command, and *iure humano*, by human preference or arrangement. Clearly, the Lord expects that a pastor perform the duties of the pastoral office, attending faithfully to those components cited above: preaching the Gospel, teaching the Word of God, administering the Sacraments, absolving penitent sinners, and exercising oversight and care of the spiritual welfare of all in the congregation. This prime expectation is *iure divino*.[36]

---

is by the Holy Spirit (Acts 20:28; 13:2–4), and because the Lord of the Church gives men to the public ministry of Word and Sacrament (Eph 4:11; 1 Cor 12:28–29), and when the apostle Paul attests to his own appointment by the Lord to the public ministry of preaching the Gospel to the Gentiles (Eph 3:7–8; Col 1:24–26), and when he attributes his public ministry to the will of God and through Jesus Christ (Rom 1:1; Gal 1:1; Eph 1:1; et al.), and further, when the apostle openly accounts for his ministry as a work for which he is proud before God (Rom 15:15–18), and because the apostle sees the continuation of this same public ministry of Word and Sacrament effected by the appointment of elders or bishops or pastors (Acts 14:23; Titus 1:5; 2 Tim 2:2) who were confirmed by the laying on of hands (1 Tim 4:14; 2 Tim 1:6; cf. 1 Tim 5:22a), therefore we believe that when a man trained and qualified for the pastoral office is duly examined, elected, called, and ordained into said office upon prayerful deliberations of the Church (Acts 1:14), such a Call is indeed a divine Call and should be accorded highest respect by both congregations and pastors as something that is of God (Col 1:1, 24–25; 1 Thess 5:12–13; Heb 13:7, 17)."

35 Working through the myriad expectations of pastors, some congregations spend one or two years calling a pastor.

36 There are boundaries that contain the authority and power of pastors. Sometimes the clergy acquire power *iure humano* in many areas beyond that given *iure divino*. The Lutheran Confessions discuss the

Expectations from a Human Perspective

Can a pastor be all that the Lord expects plus all that the people demand? From their perspective, the new pastor shall be young, but mature; aggressive, yet likable and winsome. He must possess leadership skills—have vision, infuse enthusiasm, foster cooperation, inspire teams. These expectations are for openers. They are definitely *iure humano*. Even if they are not inimical to expectations *iure divino*, human expectations sometimes overshadow those set by the Lord for His pastors. Surely, balance is needed in this matter.

Avoiding Perfectionism

In searching for a pastor, a plethora of expectations smack of perfectionism. Avoid this pitfall. A congregation's desire to have the perfect pastor, or a pastor's desire to serve the perfect congregation, is harmful and unrealistic. Further, a pastor's fierce perfectionist self-expectations may subtly translate into heavy-handed, law-governed ministry. Christians are at the same time both saints and sinners (Rom 7:15–20). And pastors are men who possess weaknesses as well as strengths, having no reason to boast, except in the Gospel (1 Cor 9:18, 23; cf. 1 Cor 2:1–5). The Lord does not send perfect pastors, nor does He commission pastors to perfect congregations. Yet grace abounds for all (Rom 5:12, 15). Let all pray for a faithful pastor, and then heed the words "Make love your aim" (1 Cor 14:1a RSV). The supremacy of love overrides idiosyncratic expectations.

Reasonable Expectations

Desirable qualities in a pastor are fashioned in each generation. Perceptions of productivity and effectiveness in pastoral ministry will influence the selection of a pastor. These perceptions should not dominate, but neither can they be ignored. Expectations come naturally, but let them be reasonable. The New Testament brings together many desirable traits that divide into two general areas—the pastor's calling as a professional, and his posture as a person.[37] This composite of traits will assist congregations to assess candidates for the pastoral office.

The New Testament transcends common assessment of pastors. Here, we are spared the petty and subjective wants often expressed by some persons when the congregation seeks a pastor. Note that a pastor may be evaluated in

---

power of bishops according to the Gospel. They identify two areas of authority: the power of order, namely, the ministry of Word and Sacraments, and the power of jurisdiction, namely, the authority to excommunicate those who are guilty of public offenses or to absolve them if they are repentant and seek Absolution (Ap XXVIII 13).

37 First Timothy 3:1–7 is pivotal. For complementary traits, see Appendix 2, "Thirteen Reminders for the Exemplary Pastor."

light of the New Testament treatment of spiritual gifts, also the variety of gifts and working and services, all of which the Spirit gives openly for "the common good" (1 Cor 12:4–11; cf. Rom 12:3–8). In addition, the Pastoral Epistles prescribe responsibility and duty.

- *Preaching*: Proclaiming the Word of God in the medium of preaching is a primary responsibility (2 Tim 4:2a; 1 Tim 4:13).
- *Teaching*: Teaching that befits sound doctrine is essential (2 Tim 4:2b–3a; 3:16–17; Titus 2:1; 1 Tim 4:13). The discipline includes such factors as the aptitude for teaching (διδακτικός), the ability to communicate well a proper understanding of the articles of the Christian faith (2 Tim 2:2), that is, the sound words of the Lord Jesus Christ (1 Tim 6:3). The pastor sets forth the Gospel and its articles as vital and important for Christians (e.g., Holy Baptism, Titus 3:5–7). The pastor has the capacity to nurture Christians in the disciplines of the God-fearing life (Titus 2:11–12; 3:1, 8, 14; cf. 2 Cor 7:1) and to correct false teaching, admonishing in a spirit of patience and love (Titus 1:9, 13; 2 Tim 2:24–26).
- *Pastoral Care*: When preaching and teaching, a pastor also watches for souls and protects them against spiritual enemies (2 Tim 4:14–15; Titus 1:9; cf. 1 Tim 1:5–7; 4:1–5). The pastor as watchman has courage to protect against the snare of the evil one (2 Tim 2:26; 2 Cor 11:1–3). He is assertive against heresies and heretical practices swarming in these last days (2 Tim 3:1, 8–9). He counters by feeding the flock in the capacity of a responsible overseer (cf. Acts 20:28; 1 Pet 5:1–3; John 21:17).
- *Leadership*: He cares for the church as a leader (επιμελέομαι) akin to a husband and father who rules (προίστημι, 1 Tim 3:5). The terms *bishop*, *presbyter*, and *pastor* all imply leadership and rulership (cf. ηγούμενοι, Heb 13:7, 17).
- *Competence*: In all of the disciplines above, the pastor shows progress (1 Tim 4:15–16) and presents himself before the Lord "as one . . . who has no need to be ashamed, rightly handling the word of truth" (2 Tim 2:15).
- *Character*: In all matters, the pastor exhibits upstanding and exemplary behavior. It is a matter of character befitting a man of God (1 Tim 3:1–7; 4:12; 2 Tim 4:5; Titus 1:5–8; cf. 1 Pet 5:2–3; Phil 3:17).[38]

38 For additional characterization of the Christian pastor, see chapter 4 of this work: "The Pastor and Relationships—Family and Others." On New Testament terms for pastoral leadership referenced above, see H. G. Brueggemann, "The Public Ministry in the Apostolic Age," *Concordia Theological Monthly* 22, no. 2 (February 1951): 103.

Certainty Brought by the Call

Strength for the Pastor

Certainty and comfort for both pastor and congregation accrue from the divine Call. A pastor works confidently and cheerfully, serving his congregation as the Lord's man, His "sent one," even as Christ was sent by the Father (John 17:18; 20:20–21). St. Paul's life and ministry bolsters confidence. He opens his letters with a salutation from one chosen by God who came preaching by the will of God (Gal 1:1; Rom 1:1, 2; Col 1:1; 1 Tim 1:1). Paul was confident that God used him to proclaim the Gospel in person and by his letters (Gal 1:15–16; 1 Cor 2:2–5; cf. 2 Cor 2:4; 4:5–12). This same confidence animates the Christian pastor. He does not come to pastoral ministry as a contestant who wins over other applicants. He does not advertise his candidacy. Nor does he advance his qualifications. He may not be waiting for a Call. Simply stated, the Holy Spirit was with God's people, directing their search for a pastor; and, answering their prayers, the Call was sent to this pastor. He is certain that he is the Lord's man chosen to serve these people. This certainty is vital. Walther comments,

> Therefore one should not consider the call a minor matter. It is not enough, even if one already has the pure and unalloyed Word of God and upright doctrine; rather one must also be certain of the call that it is correct. . . . So this is our comfort that we are in the preaching office, that we indeed have a holy and heavenly office, have been called to it in a correct and orderly way, of which we can also boast against the gates of hell.[39]

Assurance for the Congregation

Assurance brought by the Lord's Call extends to the congregation. Certainty and confidence are their joy. They are Christians, baptized into Christ. He has not left them. He is with them always to bestow His gifts (Matt 28:20), and they receive what the Lord gives, a devout and faithful pastor, even as Christ through them as instruments bestows His gifts.[40] The Call brings congregations together as no other dynamic can.[41] They share a unique and blessed privilege

39 Walther, *American-Lutheran Pastoral Theology*, 17.

40 Luther emphasizes that where the Church is, there must be Sacraments, Christ Himself, and His Holy Spirit. He reflects, "Should we now be a holy Christian church and have the most necessary things, such as God's Word, Christ, Spirit, faith, prayer, Baptism, the Sacrament, keys, the [pastoral] office, etc., and should not have also this the most minor things, namely the authority and right to call some persons to the office, to administer to us the Word, Baptism, the Sacrament, forgiveness [Absolution] (which are already there), and to serve in those things?" (Martin Luther, "Writing on Corner Masses and the Consecration of Priests," 1533. *Luther's Works*, St. Louis edition. ed. Georg Walch 19, 1565, cited in Walther, *American-Lutheran Pastoral Theology*, 22).

41 Issuing a Call to a pastor is the action of the congregation. The congregation's action in this regard is

to call a pastor, and when the pastor accepts the Call, most Christians are content that they can name one among them their pastor.[42] Are there persons in a congregation who are less than elated over their pastor? Are there antagonists determined to oppose the pastor? True, but too much attention is accorded the *sour faces*. The congregation at large has a pastor, and they look to him for God's Word and for the care that he gives to them—their faith, their souls—and they love and respect him for it. This is a blessing of the Call.

Robbing joy throughout the larger Lutheran Church is the enduring conflict over authority to exercise the Office of the Ministry, stemming from a nineteenth-century difference between C. F. W. Walther and Wilhelm Loehe.[43] Professor Hermann Sasse cut to the quick. He addresses this difference and conflict convincingly when he comments on the Lord's call and commission of the apostles, with notes about the action of the New Testament congregation laying hands on already-credentialed apostles (Acts 13). Prof. Sasse states,

> How does the congregation at Antioch (Acts 13) happen to send Paul and Barnabas out on mission work? They had already been sent by the Lord long before. What could the laying on of hands by the congregation give Paul in addition to that which he already had through a commission directly given by the exalted Lord Himself? Nevertheless, commissioning and laying on of hands are consciously repeated here. The pastoral office and the congregation belong inseparably together. Church history confirms this. There is a living congregation only where there is a living pastoral office, exercising the full authority of its commission. And there is a living pastoral office only where there is a living congregation. . . . The pastoral office and the congregation are like reciprocal

a polity matter, but not to the exclusion of other means of extending the Call; for example, appointment by the magisterium of the Roman Church, the episcopal-synodical government of the Anglicans and the Eastern Orthodox, the election of pastors by presbyters, the arrangement of the Presbyterians and other Calvinist bodies. There is no need to be defensive regarding church polity and governance, for the Lord of the Church did not institute nor designate one or another form. Yet we affirm the Lutheran practice, the congregation electing and calling a pastor, a practice that has early precedent when the congregation at Antioch sent forth Paul and Barnabas after fasting and praying and laying on of hands (Acts 13:1–3). Note: These apostles had received their credentials, yet St. Luke reports and accents the congregation's action at Antioch as the Spirit sent Paul and Barnabas. Finally, the constants, the preaching of the Word, the administration of the Sacraments, and Holy Absolution are paramount whatever the polity. They are of the Lord!

42 Walther cites Luther, who states that it is useful and necessary for the people to distinguish among preachers and say of their own called pastor, "This is our preacher whom God has given us." See Walther, *American-Lutheran Pastoral Theology*, 19–20.

43 The literature abounds addressing the differences between Walther and Loehe on the subject of the Office of the Holy Ministry. Recommended is the doctoral dissertation by Erich H. Heintzen, "Wilhelm Loehe and the Missouri Synod, 1841–1853" (PhD diss., University of Illinois, 1964). Heintzen places the subject within the larger context of the friendship and interaction between Walther and Loehe. Other sources are numerous articles appearing in *The Springfielder* 35, no. 3 (December 1971) and *LOGIA* 17, no. 3 (Holy Trinity 2008).

> conduits; the life of the one is the life of the other. The congregation stands or falls with the pastoral office and vice versa. This argument is sufficient to demonstrate that the 19th century alternative, pastoral office or congregation, was falsely posed.[44]

This sober counsel given in Christian love by Prof. Sasse should put at ease—if not to rest—the intense debate over authority for the Church's public ministry, as to whether it resides foremost with the pastoral office or with the congregation.[45]

Extending the Call

Developing the Call

A congregation begins seeking a pastor by developing the Call. This involves two factors: identifying candidates and assessing the congregation's ministry. The membership may suggest names of pastoral candidates. Ecclesiastical supervisors may supply candidate names and, in some instances, counsel a congregation through the Call procedure. Often, they provide assessment tools to help a congregation identify needs in their location and circumstances.

Principle: Congregations exercise their privilege under Christ to call a pastor. They follow proper procedure, conscious of preparation by prayer, faithful deliberation over many factors, and all things done as the apostle Paul exhorts, "decently and in order" (1 Cor 14:40).

Some congregations easily prepare to extend a Call, while others take time as they work through sensitive issues before calling a pastor. An interim pastor may assist some congregations in this process. Once again, the categories appear: what is required *iure divino*—public ministry, worship, preaching, teaching, administration of the Sacraments and Absolution—and what is desired in pastoral candidates *iure humano*—exciting leadership, effective outreach and mission, efficient management, cultivation of a positive spirit in the congregation, among others. Sensible congregations will understand that factors *iure divino* are essential and factors *iure humano* may be desired, though not always available.

The calling of a pastor should engage the larger congregation and the pro-

44 Hermann Sasse, "Walther and Loehe: On the Church," trans. John Sippola and John Drickamer, *The Springfielder* 35, no. 3 (December 1971): 180.

45 Desired is a calming of tension surrounding this debate across a spectrum of pastoral and congregational paradigms, among them *sacerdotalists*, who elevate the pastoral office and designate the pastor's role as priest; the *megachurch pastorate*, where the pastor, a skilled and powerful leader, assists the community of faith to achieve ministry goals; the *therapeutic construct*, which assists individuals toward self-adjustment and fosters strong relationships; and the *church planting mission*, focused on forming and building congregations.

cedure should be clear to all. Prayer for the Spirit's guidance and direction is essential. Corporate worship services and devotions in homes and in small groups are venues for the congregation to petition the Lord for a pastor. Prayer, waiting, and anticipation are clearly consonant with the *sending* action of the Lord (Luke 10:1ff.; Rom 10:14–15; cf. Acts 13:1–4). When the Call process unfolds at this high spiritual level, the congregation will be edified and strengthened through the experience of seeking a new pastor.

Validity and Legitimacy Issues regarding the Call

Validity Issues

Two factors apply to the Call, validity and legitimacy.[46] The issues raised by these factors are useful. A Call is valid when it is extended by those who have the right and authority from God to do so. Normally, the congregation extends a valid Call, though by mutual arrangement, a placement body of the Synod or larger church may serve as the instrument for calling graduates of theological seminaries to pastoral ministry. Previous discussions in this chapter touched on validity issues. The other factor, legitimacy, pertains to how the Call is sent, that is to say, without imposing conditions; also, how the Call is received—for example, without questionable influence through tampering, maneuvering, and the like to satisfy subjective interests other than the cause of the Gospel ministry.

The validity of the Call may be adversely affected. For instance, a takeover by headstrong congregation leaders or imposition of directions from area or district officials may dominate and effectively prevent the congregation's free choice of a pastoral candidate. Luther counseled against such moves. Leave human machinations and sophistication, he said, and turn to the humble people—workers and farmers, even stable boys—who love and hold God's Word. They serve best as electors in developing and extending the Call for a pastor. Affirming the adequacy of lay Christians in these matters, Luther presses repeatedly, "two or three are gathered in My name" (Matt 18:20). In larger congregations, the informed and active participation of two or three hundred Christians in the calling process should be respected.

A Call from a heterodox congregation is valid in so far as the people extending the Call are Christians. In this regard, Lutheran congregations demonstrate orthodox teaching and practice somewhat along the lines set forth by John H. C. Fritz, altered slightly here:[47]

46 These factors expounded by the Lutheran fathers compose a paradigm that has fallen out of use. Whatever the reasons, the issues treated under each topic, *validity* and *legitimacy*, merit attention when a congregation desires to follow appropriate calling procedure. See John H. C. Fritz, *Pastoral Theology*, 34ff.

47 John H. C. Fritz, *Pastoral Theology*, 42. Note, regarding confession, congregations and pastors of The Lutheran Church—Missouri Synod subscribe to all the confessional writings contained in the Book of Concord (1580).

- The congregation desires to be served as an orthodox Evangelical Lutheran congregation.
- The congregation, therefore, accepts the Scriptures of the Old and the New Testaments as the verbally inspired Word of God.
- The congregation publicly acknowledges the symbolical writings of the Lutheran Church, especially the Augsburg Confession and Luther's Small and Large Catechisms, to be a correct exhibition of the true doctrine as it is revealed in the Scriptures, and requires its pastor(s) and teachers and auxiliary personnel to perform their official duties in accordance with the Bible and the Lutheran Confessions.
- The congregation conforms to ceremonies that are consistent with the orthodox teaching and practice of the Lutheran Church normed by the Lutheran Confessions.
- The congregation engages and employs books and literature of all kinds, both hard copy and electronic, that teach the true doctrine for nurture, training, and edification.
- The congregation insists that all who approach the Lord's Table shall be known to the pastor who counsels them appropriately prior to receiving the Sacrament.
- The congregation's disciplines and larger life submit to the Word of God, which has free course to norm all that is said and done.

A Call from an orthodox congregation with these characteristics exhibits validity, and it is legitimate. It is a Call that a confessional Lutheran pastor may consider with good conscience.

Principle: The Call to the Holy Ministry is normally permanent, though not in an absolute sense, for the Lord of the Church, as He wills, may elect to remove a pastor and send him to another ministry. Short of this, the Call is not served by term limits imposed through contractual or other arrangements that effectively render the Call conditional and may be engaged to terminate the Call or unduly remove a pastor from the Office of the Holy Ministry.

The permanent tenure of the Call—not the pastor—is a transcendent factor, one that proves difficult in an age when human expectations of pastors press hard and human involvement is both powerful and assertive. Impatient or restless congregations may determine that their pastor is not productive in ways they expect. They may react and force a pastor to leave. Some congregations frame the tenure of the Call with incremental time blocks, as if to assert that their Call to this pastor is renewable at junctures of his stay. For example, six months into his ministry to a congregation of powerful people—corporate executives, doctors, lawyers, and independently wealthy persons and families—several prominent members approached the pastor and remarked: "We think that you can stay at this church five years, maybe seven."

These sentiments may be solidified into a contract that will limit the Call's tenure. Such action violates the validity of the Call. This was the view held by C. F. W. Walther and John H. C. Fritz, who rejected what they termed "the temporary Call." Principally, they argued that such a tentative Call would hamper the pastor and prevent him from fulfilling his ministry. The issue is poignant when the pastor must address the Word of God to negative circumstances. When that Word must admonish or correct, let us say, influential persons in the congregation, how shall a pastor boldly bring that Word when the tenure of his Call is on the line, and his tenure as well, meaning livelihood and the care of his family? In this circumstance, the transcendent character of the Call fades, and the pastor becomes what the fathers stated, a mere hireling. How does this accord with honor and respect due the pastor who exercises a divinely instituted office by virtue of a divine Call, which he received and accepted[48] (Heb 13:7, 17; 1 Thess 5:12–13; cf. Luke 10:16; 1 Tim 5:17–18; 1 Cor 16:15–16, 18)?

It may appear inconsistent, but the operative principle here does permit contractual arrangements when the Call is to a special ministry requiring specialized gifts and abilities. When the Church issues a Call to service in a special ministry, such as a mission or teaching at seminaries, proficiencies for the special vocation may not be discerned until the candidate accepts the Call and commences with the ministry. The candidate's gifts and abilities must meet the requirements for this ministry. If the candidate is unable to fulfill the special ministry, the contract may be revoked and the Call terminated.

An impatient and restless congregation may illegitimately press this rubric. They ask, "Why is it not permissible to place the initial year of a pastor's ministry on a contractual basis in order to assure that he is proficient to meet the requirements of the Call?" The question is misdirected, and it screens hidden concerns or biases other than determining a pastor's proficiency. The proficiency of pastors for ministry in normal circumstances is well known versus proficiency of candidates that cannot be predetermined with regard to the acute needs of special ministries cited above. Contracts do not serve the Call to normal parish ministry. Indeed, they may incite an independent spirit whereby a congregation quickly becomes dissatisfied with the new pastor. The people claim that he is not a good fit, and they build a case against him. Such initiatives

48 Removal of a pastor from office is treated at the end of this chapter. The rubrics for such formal action by a congregation shall be structured in such a manner that removal is consonant with God's removing action.

are out of order, and ecclesiastical supervisors should not favor any irregular action that offends the *validity* principle related to the Call.[49]

We recognize that mismatches—congregation and pastors—do occur. Do such occurrences call for radical action? We can only view every Call to the pastoral ministry as the Spirit's opportunity. Can the Spirit use a mismatch that is so frustrating from the human viewpoint? Certainly, these unfortunate occurrences should be prevented. Seminaries must recommend candidates with great care. Not every student at a theological seminary is a candidate for the Office of the Holy Ministry. Further, ecclesiastical supervisors involved in the Call process carefully scrutinize both congregations and candidates. Finally, pastors, "Know yourself!" Know your gifts, your capacities, and your level of maturity in the profession. May all pray for the Spirit's guidance and wisdom from above, and keep faith that the Lord continues to send pastors to His Church.

Legitimacy Issues

A pastor may be too assertive when seeking a Call. At the time of the Reformation, Luther pegged individuals going after Calls. He labeled them "sneaks." He stated, "Yes, they can certainly get behind people, sneak in, and wash long enough that they are afterwards chosen and called. One can soon talk people into doing it. But they are thieves, murderers, and wolves (John 10:1)."[50]

Principle: A pastor may legitimately present himself—his gifts, abilities, and experience—and request a Call or opportunity to transition to a special ministry, but his reasons for these initiatives should be well founded. Also he remembers that the Call seeks the pastor, not *vice versa*.

Luther's severity with charlatans, the brazen call getters, should not burden the conscience of a sincere pastor who wishes to move to another ministry, or needs to relocate because he has fulfilled the ministry where he is serving, or is convinced that he is inadequate as the pastor of his present congregation. He is not a charlatan (Deut 13:1–4; Jer 23:21). Are there initiatives available to the pastor who legitimately wants to receive a Call?

Yes, there are three such initiatives. First, Walther advises the pastor who has been faithful and now sees his ministry fulfilled (Col 4:17) to wait patiently and prayerfully. In modern language, "Cool it!" Walther engages Luther's counsel, "If you are learned and understand God's Word well, if you also believe that

49 This judgment may not satisfy those who are convinced that the contract is the only reasonable arrangement that assures a congregation that their pastoral ministry will be productive. Recognize, however, that the divine Call to any ministry accompanied with a contract is something of an anomaly. It is not easily explained or understood in the light of the theology of the Call.

50 Martin Luther, *Sämmtliche Schriften*, 3, ed. Johann Georg Walch (St. Louis: Concordia Publishing House, 1892), 1077, cited by Walther, *American-Lutheran Pastoral Theology*, 24.

you want to present it to others uprightly and beneficially, wait! If God wants it, He will surely find you."[51]

Is there more a pastor may do when he desires to change ministries? Yes, and this leads to the second initiative. The pastor may turn to his present ministry with renewed vigor and enthusiasm. He may be saying, "I am tired, weary, spent. I am a better man, but the people do not appreciate me. I and this congregation are like a bad marriage. I just cannot work here." The antidote to such bitter feelings is to steady the course. A pastor must not give up. He reconsiders how he may be more effective. "How can I improve?" If he is certain that he has fulfilled this ministry, as St. Paul counseled both Archippus and Timothy (Col 4:17; 2 Tim 4:1–5), perhaps he may regroup and open his eyes to see horizons he has not yet explored.

Remember, pastor, that you are the Lord's man. The Lord has placed you here. Examine your preaching, teaching, pastoral care, and your involvement in the congregation's mission to the community. What are the current challenges in this ministry? What more can you do to meet those challenges? Are there persons in the congregation who need a different approach in your care for them? How may you change work and recreation routines in order to bring freshness to your daily ministry? Certainly, it is fair to consider what different pastor's gifts are needed here. Are they really different from your gifts? Or can you exercise your gifts more effectively? Address these questions to your heart, and in prayer present all to the Lord of the Church.

Beyond waiting and reassessment of one's ministry, a third initiative is available. A pastor may consult with his ecclesiastical supervisor, district president or bishop. When meeting with this official who oversees distribution of the Church's professional servants, the pastor should be well prepared. The pastor is sparing with complaints when he relates the circumstances and his desire to relocate. He reviews his ministry. He brings something to the table. He shows faithfulness, productiveness, and how the congregation he serves is stronger because God has blessed his ministry. He is frank about his failings, his inadequacies, and his feeling that the present challenges exceed his gifts or level of maturity as a pastor. He can be equally frank to suggest that his gifts may be used more effectively in serving another congregation. A pastor who reflects seriously about himself and the ministry will receive an empathic hearing from his ecclesiastical supervisor.

The tenure of a pastor is related to the Call. It is not *legitimate* either to overstay or to leave too soon. We understand that the apostle Paul's ministry

51 Martin Luther, *Sämmtliche Schriften*, 11, ed. Johann Georg Walch (St. Louis: Concordia Publishing House, 1892), 2549, 2555, cited by Walther, *American-Lutheran Pastoral Theology*, 24.

Principle: Transcending tenure is constancy. Where a pastor serves, he is constant and consistent in the energetic use of his *gifts*—preaching, teaching, administering the Sacraments, and fulfilling related responsibilities such as pastoral care and leading. He is faithful.

was largely itinerant, but his stay with numerous congregations—long or brief—yields a principle governing the tenure of a pastor.[52]

A pastor may flee, and in fleeing, he may be understaying.[53] Did the apostle Paul encourage Timothy to remain at his post when he counseled the young pastor to be constant, to attend to public reading of Scripture, also to preaching and teaching (1 Tim 4:13)? The inference is plausible in view of Paul's proposed visit to Ephesus. Furthermore, devoting himself to the pastoral disciplines with constancy, Timothy would demonstrate to all his progress (1 Tim 4:14–15). Such a demonstration takes time. It takes staying with a ministry.

Nevertheless, constancy to the point of overstaying does not serve. Stubbornly digging in, staying on, clinging to comfort when a ministry has come to a close, is not *legitimate* relative to the Call.[54] Consider that once fulfilled, our Lord's public ministry closed (John 19:30). St. Paul exclaimed, "I have finished the race" (2 Tim 4:6–7; cf. Acts 20:25). The end of a ministry, like the beginning and all the years between, is best "the manifestation of the Spirit for the common good" (1 Cor 12:7). There comes a time to leave a ministry for another Call, or after full years to retire from active service.[55] By contrast, if a pastor vows that he shall remain in the pastorate of a congregation until his death, he has taken the reins from the Lord. He has renounced the flexible nature of pastoral vocation, that is, ambassadors going where and when the Lord sends His spokesmen (2 Cor 5:20). At length, wisdom suggests that we move on, confident in the Lord's promise in Matthew 28:20, "Behold, I am with you always[!]"

Legitimacy is a factor relative to the Call on numerous counts. In addition

52 With Barnabas, Paul remained at Antioch for an entire year, meeting with the church and teaching a large company of people (Acts 11:25–26; cf. Acts 14:28). Pressed by the Lord, Paul remained at Corinth a year and six months (Acts 18:11). From Corinth, he sailed to Ephesus, stopped briefly, and went on to Caesarea. From there, he departed and went place to place through the region of Galatia and Phrygia, "strengthening all the disciples" (Acts 18:23).

53 What is a reasonable time to remain as pastor of a congregation? Hardly may a pastor fulfill a ministry to any congregation short of three years. This is an opinion. Understaying can disappoint congregations.

54 In an era when vacant pastorates are few, overstaying is probably par for the course. But when vacancies exist in reasonable numbers, pastors who have fulfilled their ministries should have opportunities to receive a Call elsewhere. The unspoken practice of not recommending pastors who have been faithful and whose ministries have come to a close is unconscionable. They should be given an opportunity to accept a new challenge in the pastoral ministry.

55 A beloved pastor of many years serving a vibrant congregation was uneasy about his advancing age. At a district pastor's conference, he rose to speak. He requested, if any of his brother pastors observed him slipping unawares, would they please approach and tap him on the shoulder. What a gracious gesture! The author remembers this moment. He was a seminary student, a vicar attending that pastor's conference in the California-Nevada District of the LCMS, Fall 1958.

to the aforementioned is the unfavorable practice of using the Call as leverage to secure certain privileges. While issuing a Call to a pastor, a congregation may attach riders, so to speak, that limit speaking the Word of God to weaknesses or even heretical practices tolerated within the congregation. The subtle message attached to the Call is "Pastor, don't go there." These restrictions are not legitimate. Nor shall a congregation use the Call to fix or guarantee worship practices. For example, a congregation demands that the pastor accepting their Call lead only one particular liturgical service. Conversely, a pastor may demand that he will accept a Call only when a congregation promises to accept the change and innovation that he will bring to their worship practices. These demands are not legitimate.

Lutheran confessors of the sixteenth century never faced the *worship wars* of our time, the conflicts between advocates of traditional worship form and others who freelance and depart from established form. But the Lutheran Confessions serve as a mediating authority today. First, they allow for flexibility in worship forms; second, they recommend retention of ancient rites and traditional ceremonies. Favoring flexibility, AC VII 3 asserts, for the true unity of the Church it is not necessary that ceremonies instituted by men should be observed uniformly in all places (cf. AC XXVI 41–45; Ap VII and VIII 32b, 40, 45). The right to change, reduce, or increase ceremonies in an orderly way to serve present circumstances is an authority granted to the Christian Church (FC SD X 9). In this passage from the Formula, however, observe the restraints on freelancing in adoption and use of variations in form, and note the caveats stated in FC SD X 5, 7, and 8. Customary rites, remember, foster harmony in the church (Ap XV 51–52). Furthermore, ceremonies of any kind that negatively affect doctrine are unacceptable. By this principle, worship forms expressive of decision theology, prosperity theology, dispensational theology, millennialism, universalism, et al., are disapproved, as are forms that give the impression that Lutheranism does not differ from the Roman Catholic Church (FC SD X 5).

Principle: Pastors and congregations collaborate with respect to the Lord's worship (*Gottesdienst*) celebrated on the Lord's Day. Neither party—pastor or congregation—shall press the Call extended or accepted as leverage to fix and guarantee a particular liturgical form or order or ceremony.

Second, freedom to adopt worship forms is tempered by advocacy for retention of ancient rites and traditional ceremonies. The Lutheran Confessors retained many ceremonies and traditions that preserve order in the church (AC XXVI 40). They caution that the use of worship forms of one kind or another does not acquire merit before God. They emphasize, however, that the observance of ancient universal rites and ceremonies maintains peace and tranquility essential for the unity of the Church, and these rites and ceremonies compose a discipline that serves to educate and instruct the people and the inexperienced (Ap VII and VIII 33). Through such usage, the people learn the Bible, are touched by the Word, and are prompted to pray (Ap XXIV 3). Today, some pastors abandon these rites and ceremonies in the interest of communicating to the now generation. The Lutheran Confessors would consider this unfortunate and foolish (cf. Ap XV 20b, 21a).

Legitimacy related to the Call includes another subject, the pastor's salary. Abuse occurs when congregations reference the Call as ground to underpay a pastor. "The pastor has a divine Call. We are off the hook. He is God's servant, and God will take care of his needs." Or the pastor may react. "This congregation does not pay me well. I shall slack off a bit. They will get what they pay for." Again, the Call is abused.

Principle: A pastor trusts his congregation to provide for his professional needs and to support him and his family because the Lord expects such provision in behalf of His servants who fulfill the Call to the Ministry.

Assume that a pastor serves full time. Is there biblical basis for remunerating this pastor? The distinguished missionary and missiologist Roland Allen asserted that the New Testament urges remuneration for itinerant prophets and evangelists and not for settled clergy. But the case Allen makes is not easily closed.[56] He dismisses the notion that Galatians 6:6 and 1 Timothy 5:18 suggest support for settled clergy. He maintains that these passages do not refer to fixed salaries, which he says were an abomination in the eyes of early Christians. However, when Paul and Barnabas were furloughed from pursuit of their craft, they awaited support from the Christians at Corinth, and Paul also appears to elicit proper support for workers who are married and thus settled (1 Cor 9:5–7). We believe that the New Testament advocates monetary support of those who are called to preach the Gospel.

The matter of clergy remuneration divides in this manner:

1. What the congregation owes the pastor
2. What the pastor owes the congregation

Addressing congregations, recall that the Lord sent the seventy disciples preaching the Word of God with the expectation that those who heard the Word would provide for their daily need. Jesus' expectation reiterated the long-standing principle that the laborer deserves his wages (Luke 10:7). Field hands

56 Roland Allen, *Missionary Methods: St. Paul's or Ours?* (Grand Rapids: Wm. B. Eerdmans, 1962), 50n1, 51.

who mow and gather the harvest are rewarded. Laborers for the Gospel deserve no less. Even farm animals harnessed to tread out the grain are deserving (Deut 25:4; 1 Tim 5:17–18). Furthermore, this principle was clearly understood in the Old Testament. Saul and his servant did not seek a word from Samuel the prophet except they shared with him part of a shekel of silver (1 Sam 9:5–14).

Remuneration of servants of the Gospel is a sensitive subject, but Paul's discussion matches sensitivity with skillful instruction. He hesitates to press the subject, lest the focus on material things "put an obstacle in the way of the gospel of Christ" (1 Cor 9:12b). He is so reserved that he would rather endure stinginess than be feisty by building a case for support. The Gospel is free of charge. That is its nature, and no demands on his part shall abridge that liberty. For Paul, preaching the Gospel was reward enough (1 Cor 9:17–18), but if the Corinthians fulfilled their part as a congregation receiving the Gospel, they owed Paul and Barnabas support even as those who served the temple in the old order received their food from the temple (1 Cor 9:13–14; cf. 9:4–7). The implication is clear. Christian congregations owe their pastor a living wage with accompanying benefits.

What does the pastor owe the congregation? The pastor is called to labor, to work, to perform a multifaceted task. He handles the Word of truth in all aspects of that task (2 Tim 2:15; 4:2, 5). He has no attitude problem over the demands of his calling. He desires the ministry because it is "a good work" (1 Tim 3:1 KJV). With a sense of abandon, he pours himself into his work as one who has made himself a slave to all (cf. 1 Cor 9:19). He does not complain, "If only this congregation paid more, I would do this and that!" The pastor, instead, does both *this* and *that* and *then some* because he works in the spirit of our Lord's counsel to the Twelve, "You received without paying; give without pay" (Matt 10:8b). With this saying, Jesus released His apostles to become absorbed in their mission.

The pastor does not love money (1 Tim 3:3b; Titus 1:7b). His stock is not in material things (cf. Num 18:24–32; Josh 13:33). He graciously receives honorariums for pastoral services that require intensive work, such as weddings and funerals, but he does not solicit for honorariums or perquisites. Nor does he pursue money on the side, for example, engaging in investment schemes, purchasing and managing properties, partnering in business ventures—all distractions from his calling. The pastor is content. He can take less, if need be, and he can endure hardship for the sake of the Gospel (Phil 4:11–13). He wants little more than the satisfaction of sharing the blessings of the Gospel. His fare is not personal gain but personal giving and fulfillment of his ministry (1 Cor 9:15, 19, 23). He trusts in the care God promises to His own (Ps 55:22; 1 Pet

5:7). Finally, when the subject of his remuneration is up for discussion, the faithful pastor communicates to the congregation in no uncertain terms, "I seek not what is yours but you" (2 Cor 12:14).

What the congregation owes the pastor and what the pastor owes the congregation transcends the hard corporate paradigms engaged to determine a pastor's salary and overall compensation. Congregation leaders and district or diocesan officials may wish to indulge the parish pastor in numerous assessments that seek to match results with work and performance. These initiatives may be well intentioned to encourage the pastor's productivity, but let all who engage corporate tools take heed from the Scriptures in the foregoing discussion.

An energetic hard-working pastor need not back away from evaluation.[57] He is prepared to give account to those who are in proper position to hear his report. He is not defensive in the face of the hard inquiries administered to pastors today. He answers candidly. He brings forward strengths in his ministry that may have been overlooked, and he owns up to weaknesses, remaining open to fair-minded commentary by those evaluating him. In exchange, he maintains the right to counter with his own questions. He inquires in the spirit of Christian love and respect for the Call. Hopefully, he shall receive candid and fair replies from those making the evaluation. If these discussions are spirited and brisk, they shall not polarize parties but bring them together as fellows in Christ. Let Christian love prevail.

Handling the Call

Receiving a Call

After receiving a Call to another ministry, the pastor informs numerous parties—a tier beginning with district or diocesan presidents or bishops, then local clergy supervisors, then leaders of the congregation he presently serves, and finally the congregation members. He promptly acknowledges receipt of the Call in a formal letter to the sending congregation. Note that he informs

---

57 Pastors are tacitly evaluated by many Christians. This is a fact of life in the pastoral ministry. Then, congregation or ecclesiastical leaders may administer formal evaluations. Unfortunately, these instruments of assessment may be *result* driven to extremes because they fail to consider a pastor's calling in a larger picture. A pastor is entitled to know in advance what the standards and measurements are. He should be permitted to respond and to request adjustments to the instrumentation. Furthermore, no evaluation instrument covers a pastor's overall ministry. Congregation leaders and church officials should candidly recognize that the pastor's *world* involves much more complexity than their instruments of evaluation comprehend. The approach is not how a congregation critiques its pastor and ministry, but how the laity and church officials may help this pastor to be more effective, how all parties may best honor the Call and its serious implications.

district or diocesan officials where the Call originated. These officials want to know where Calls are and how pastors are deliberating and making decisions. It is improper for a pastor to hide receipt of a Call, because it is the Church's public ministry and the Church in its varied venues should be informed.[58]

Deliberating on a Call

Sound information and fervent prayer are essential to deliberation over a Call. Why not petition the Lord as King Solomon did (1 Kgs 3:3–14)? The Spirit is not stingy with wisdom and guidance. Pastor, go for it! But check ego needs.[59] The Call presents a major decision affecting the work and mission of our Lord. Therefore, in addition to prayer, reliable information is paramount.[60] The official source of information resides with the Call documents and attending papers, but these resources may prompt key questions. What are the needs of the calling congregation? What are the stated special needs? What pastoral gifts and abilities are needed? Do the Call documents provide information about the congregation, the community, and the circumstances relative to care and support for the pastor and his family? Seeking answers to these and other questions, the pastor may consult responsible persons. District presidents or diocesan bishops are primary providers of reliable information.

The calling congregation may choose to cover the pastor's expenses and invite him to visit. The pastor will have the opportunity to meet with staff and lay leaders. The visit will include an on-site viewing of the facilities. Several hours should be reserved for the pastor and his wife to be in the community and inquire about schools, medical services, and such. A visit will not tell all, but it will yield much valuable information.

In the course of such a visit, the pastor may be invited for a formal interview. He is gracious and he cooperates. He answers questions about his theology and confession. He does not brush off serious inquiries in a cava-

58 An insecure pastor may elect to keep receipt of a Call private. This action offends good order. Then, it is possible that a pastor has received a second Call when he is preoccupied with deliberation on the first Call. District or diocesan officials will advise in such an unusual event. A basic principle prevails: attend to *one* call at a time.

59 Called to be senior minister of a large congregation, a pastor let personal interests interfere. The second pastor—seven years an associate—was passed over and was most uncomfortable. The senior-pastor-elect, however, was determined that such tensions would not *rob* him of this Call. He forged ahead and accepted the Call. It did not work out. The two pastors and the congregation suffered from this unfortunate headstrong action. *Kyrie eleison!*

60 Pious pastors of a former generation received Calls by surface mail, unannounced. A pastor would retrieve the Call documents and set the open documents on his desk. Piety suggested that further inquiry would be tampering with the Call, even interfering with the Holy Spirit's guidance. The pastor pored over the Call documents and finally made a decision. Respectful of his devotion, we ask, can the Holy Spirit work with light as well as darkness? Sound information about a Call sheds light and leads to a good and reasonable decision that the Spirit blesses.

lier manner, asserting gruffly, "I am a member of the clergy of The Lutheran Church—Missouri Synod!" This response is insufficient. Better is to frame answers in terms of what he as a pastor believes, teaches, and confesses. A pastor may hesitate when asked hypothetical questions like "If you accept the Call and become our pastor, what will you do in order to advance the evangelism ministry of this congregation?" He is not sufficiently informed to elaborate in detail. He expresses his positive approach to mission and evangelism. Let it go at that.

A formal interview works both ways. The pastor may direct his questions to lay leaders and congregation members. How will he and his family fare in the new environs? While the pastor may seek clarification about salary and benefits, he does not negotiate. This is not a bargaining session. It is advisable to reserve these questions for a smaller circle of congregation leaders, or even the vacancy pastor or local clergy counselor. An open meeting may not be the venue for inquiry about the Call's stated remuneration.

After visiting with the calling congregation, the pastor returns home. Should he disclose details of the Call to his present congregation? Perhaps he may inform about the Call in general, but he is not obligated to share details. Unfortunately, open meetings over the pastor's Call frequently descend to the lowest denominator, dollars and cents. "What's wrong, Pastor, aren't we paying you enough? Are you unhappy here? And what are *they* offering you?" The trap is set. The pastor takes the bait when he hints that the congregation may make a counteroffer in order to keep him. Now the session hits rock bottom. To prevent this scene, the pastor may confide in a handful of trusted lay leaders who will offer sound reflection about his Call, also about the needs of their parish that he presently serves.

There are sensitive and conscientious pastors who waive all of the above because they feel a deep compulsion to accept any Call that is received. They make no inquiry, concluding that God sends the Call as a mandate to accept it without question. Otherwise, they reason, God would not have sent the Call. How shall we respond? Perhaps sensitive pastors should consider that the Lord's instrumentation for sending and placing His shepherds here and there is quite varied. The pastor receiving a Call is one of many players in the Call process. Furthermore, the purpose of the Call may be such that the Lord uses it as a teaching instrument to assist both pastors and congregations in serious reflection upon their ministries. Finally, there is no Scripture teaching that compels acceptance of a Call. There is work for the Lord in many places and times. And He has many who can serve.

Arriving at a Call Decision

When approaching a Call decision, the pastor considers many details. Sort them. Begin by making two lists, one "professional" and the other "personal/family." Organize the data relative to each congregation.

Professional		Personal/Family	
St. Paul	Zion	St. Paul	Zion
1.	1.	1.	1.
2.	2.	2.	2.

When the pastor highlights substantive issues related to public ministry of the calling congregation and the one he presently serves, he is prepared to make a decision. When all is said and done, three considerations will lead to a God-pleasing decision.

1. What are the present and future challenges and needs presented by the calling congregation and its ministry? How may I serve?
2. What are the present and future challenges and needs apparent in the congregation I serve at present? How may I continue to serve here?
3. At what level of maturity have I arrived in terms of gifts, abilities, and skills for pastoral ministry; and which congregation ministry excites eagerness to serve?

Add to these considerations an important factor, the pastor's family. Can the family deal with the realities that affect them—quality of life, education and schools, provision for special needs and so forth? Recognize that the prospect of moving can be traumatic for the family.

Ultimately, the pastor must render a decision that is timely—two or three weeks. If the pastor senses that he is pegged to accept the Call and fulfill its ministry—that this is something he should do—then he better do just that, accept the Call (cf. Jer 1:7). If, however, he is gripped by uncertainty, it is best to remain where he is serving. That is the counsel of numerous advisers. Short of paralyzing uncertainty, what are the pastor's inclinations? What does he want to do? Where is the Lord leading? He should not shrink from a challenge. Nor should he overreach, that is, take on challenges clearly beyond his maturity or ability. Finally, he says either "I think that I will be excited taking on this new ministry" or "I am fine where I am, just fine."

Accepting/Declining a Call

If the pastor decides to decline the Call, he returns the Call document to the originating congregation with an accompanying letter. He expresses how he was honored to receive the Call, but he senses that the Lord has led him to remain with his present congregation. He assures them that he is praying the Lord will soon send them a pastor. He does not comment on the Call and surely he gives no counsel, correction, or censure.[61] Now he follows protocol and communicates his declination to the same parties he had notified when he received the Call.

When accepting a Call, the pastor communicates his decision similarly to the proper parties. He may announce the decision to his present congregation after worship services. Then good order suggests that he receive from the congregation a formal statement of peaceful release. This action frees the pastor to wind down his present ministry, and it permits the congregation to prepare for calling a new pastor. By common arrangement, the pastor's last day on the payroll is followed immediately by his first day on the payroll of the congregation he is slated to serve in the near future.

As he concludes his ministry, the pastor attends to stability on all fronts before he departs. He delegates pastoral care of the sick and terminally ill to a caring pastor. For those he has cared for with pastoral counseling, he arranges continued care with a competent counselor. He instructs those who will serve in his absence, and he is careful not to leave a trail—paper or electronic.

Then the pastor leaves! He has brought God's Word in his last sermon, and he has assured the people of his fondness for them, his love, and his prayers. They are now his former congregation. Certainly, he may return to conduct official acts for member families—weddings, funerals, possibly Baptisms. He should accept these invitations only when they are issued by the present vacancy pastor or the new pastor in residence. As the former pastor, he defers to their leadership in these public services. He does not linger as a shadow, nor does he solicit opportunities to return home to be with his people.[62] He is supportive of his successor! It bears repeating. The pastor wraps things up. He pays bills, closes accounts, and registers his change of address. He leaves!

---

61 A pastor of a large and powerful urban congregation received a Call from a small congregation in a modest community. Hastily, he declined the Call, attaching severe censure. "How dare you call a man of my stature!"—*Kyrie eleison!* We learn from this abominable pastoral behavior "Never treat the Call shabbily! Always treat the Call with respect!"

62 Indiscretions abound. Some pastors do not readily bond with their new congregation because they carry a torch for the former congregation. The Call transcends sentimentality. Leave and let the people go. They should look for a new pastor. Consider this story. A pastor retired from a long ministry to a beloved congregation. He and his wife purchased a home bordering the far reaches of the church parking lot. Each morning at breakfast, they peered out the kitchen window, noting the arrival of the new pastor for his workday. How sad!

Post-Call Decision Reflection

Deliberating on a Call and making a final decision is stressful for the pastor and his family. Who knows all the post-Call anxieties that accompany that end decision? Simplistic as it sounds, this is a time to move on. A pastor and his family may allow a week to regroup and get beyond the pain that comes with hashing over many issues and revisiting a decision that has been made: "Was it right?" "Should we have gone?" "Should we have stayed?" Again, the pastor and family are entitled to a time of grief over these matters, but not to a point of exhaustion. In these anxious times, reflect, "But the Lord stood by me and strengthened me, so that through me the message might be fully proclaimed and all the Gentiles might hear it" (2 Tim 4:17). The Lord stands by us. Now we turn to our present ministry and proclaim His Word fully.

The Pastor's Call Related to the Call of Other Servants

The Call places the Christian pastor in the Church's Office of the Holy Ministry, in which others, too, are appointed or called to specific ministries. Assistant and Associate Pastors serve with the Senior Pastor and under his supervision attend to the essentials of the public office—preaching the Word and administering the Sacraments. After all, they are ordained pastors. In addition to duties of the office *iure divino*, assisting pastors may receive assignments *iure humano*, which the pastor and the congregation arrange for the strengthening of the congregation's ministry.

Other persons hold public offices in the Church's ministry—Christian teachers, directors of Christian education, deacons and deaconesses, to name several. Some of these offices fulfill a part of the one public ministry of the Word. For example, Christian teachers instruct children in the Scriptures. In this role, they assist the Office of the Word exercised by the pastor. Walther urged that these and other helping offices be regarded as ecclesiastical and sacred.[63] Recent practice in the LCMS establishes persons in these offices by

63 C. F. W. Walther, *Church and Ministry*, trans. J. T. Mueller (St. Louis: Concordia Publishing House, 1987), 290. The status of the Lutheran teacher in the congregation with regard to the pastor has been controversial in the LCMS through the twentieth century. When discussions focus on offices with regard to the one Office of the Holy Ministry and Walther's careful argument setting forth distinctions between that one office and the *helping offices* that function as part of the Church's public ministry of the Word, equanimity shall prevail. Regrettably, some misguided persons have pitted not only offices but also personnel against one another. Reportedly, in Wisconsin, a pastor scolded a teacher serving as church organist and reported his "insubordination" to the district president when the teacher politely requested hymn selections earlier than moments prior to the worship service. *Kyrie eleison!* The notion of *helping offices* originates in C. F. W. Walther, *The Church & The Office of the Ministry*, trans. J. T. Mueller, ed. Matthew C. Harrison (St. Louis: Concordia Publishing House, 2012), 284. A. C. Stellhorn addressed the status of teachers in an unpublished essay, "The Lutheran Teacher's Position in the Ministry of the Congregation," 1949. For additional discussion of offices related to the one office and one Call to that office, see Robert David Preus, *The Doctrine of the Call in the Confessions and Lutheran Orthodoxy* (St. Louis: Luther Academy, 1991), 20–25; also see *The Ministry: Offices, Procedures, and Nomenclature: A Report of the Commission on Theology and Church Relations* (St. Louis: The Lutheran Church—Missouri Synod, September 1981).

appointment or call, not to be confused with the one Call to the one public *ministerium evangelii docendi* (AC V).

Ordination to the Pastoral Office

What Is Ordination?

Entry into the pastoral office occurs in the church's Rite of Ordination and nowhere else. Three parties come together in the conduct of this rite. The Lord is present. The candidate-pastor hears and receives the Lord's command to preach the Word, baptize, host His Table, and absolve, all bringing His gift of the forgiveness of sins. Also present are the Lord's people who have the privilege to ordain a pastor whom they have elected and called. The candidate-pastor arrives with resolve to faithfully commit to the office. The congregation is prepared to publicly say of him, "This man is now our pastor."[64]

Ordination Clarified

In a vital sense, the Rite of Ordination is closure to the exercise of a privilege granted to the Church. God's people elect or choose a pastor. They call him. They ordain him. Their privilege and right is to have a pastor, meaning—to elect, to call, to ordain.[65] With the gifts of Word and Sacraments, the Lord gives another gift, a pastor to execute the public office (1 Pet 2:9; Matt 28:16–20; 1 Cor 11:23–26; John 20:23; Matt 16:19; 18:18; cf. Eph 3:7–10; 4:11–14; 2 Tim 2:1–2; Titus 1:5). About the Lord's making of a minister fit for this office, Dr. Norman Nagel observed, "Election, call, and ordination do the job."[66]

Against formidable odds, the sixteenth-century Lutheran reformers determined to possess and use the privilege of ordaining pastors (SA III X 3; Tr 66, 67, 69–71, 72). First, they maintained that ordination attests to the Church's public

---

64 In the Rite of Ordination, Lutheran pastors make an oath that they accept the *doctrinal content* of the Lutheran Confessions, the symbolical books, because (*quia*) they are the true exposition of the Holy Scriptures, understanding that the Church shall always receive, examine, and test their public ministry—doctrine and practice—by this standard (cf. FC SD Rule and Norm, 10ff.). For clarification of this unconditional confessional subscription, see Robert D. Preus, "Confessional Subscription," in *Evangelical Directions for the Lutheran Church*, ed. Erich Kiehl and Waldo Werning (Chicago, IL: Lutheran Congress, 1970), 43–52; also C. F. W. Walther, "Why Should Our Pastors, Teachers and Professors Subscribe Unconditionally to the Symbolical Writings of Our Church," trans. and condensed by Alex. Wm. C. Guebert, *Concordia Theological Monthly* 18, no. 4 (April 1947): 242–253.

65 Elect, call, ordain! Surfacing in seminaries, mid-twentieth century, was the desire by some candidates to be certified for the public ministry and then ordained, but without a Call to a ministry, a *locus*, a local place or setting, specifically a local congregation. This was a practice of general ordination. The Lutheran Confessions, however, attach ordination not to the public ministry at large but to the election and call by the Church, that is, the Call extended to a candidate for the specific *task* of the pastoral ministry in a particular place, serving a particular congregation in the present time and context. In fact, ordination was nothing more than confirmation of this election and Call. See Treatise on the Power and Primacy of the Pope, 69b–70, 72; Ap XIII 9b, 12; SA III X 2–3.

66 Norman E. Nagel, "Ordination Is Not Other Than . . ." *Concordia Journal* 28, no. 4 (October 2002): 433.

ministry, the office instituted by none other than our Lord. Luther emphasized, "The public ministry of the word, I say, by which the mysteries of God are dispensed, is to be established (*institui debet*) by holy ordination."[67] With the Call and ordination comes the office, in other words, the task conferred, a *diakonia*, a ministry carried out publicly, for the Church. Second, the Rite of Ordination is administered only upon the action of the Call and acceptance of that Call by a qualified candidate. Third, ordination affirms the designation of this called candidate as the pastor of this congregation. Such attestation, *comprobatio*, is absolute. In the Rite of Ordination, the Church says, "This is the candidate the Lord sent, the one we called, and now he is our pastor." How firm is this attestation accompanied by the gesture in the rite, the laying on of hands![68]

Ordination—Authority

Ordination conveys authority to the candidate. About the nature and scope of this authority, E. W. Janetzki clarifies,

> Neither call nor ordination confer a status, an indelible character, worthiness or some quality that enables the one so called or ordained to fulfill the office. Neither call nor ordination, make the one called or ordained "a repository of sacral or numinous power."[69]

The power conferred by Call and ordination is none other than *exousia*, authority in terms of mandate and gifts the Lord gives: the Holy Gospel, which is to be preached, and the Holy Sacraments, which are to be rightly administered (cf. AC XXVIII 8–9). This authority derives not from the Office as such,

67 *Luthers Werke: Kritische Gesamtausgabe* (Weimar: Hermann Böhlau, 1883–1993), 12.191:16, 173:2; LW 40:37, 11, cited by Norman E. Nagel, "Ordination Is Not Other Than . . ." 433.

68 The rubric in the Rite of Ordination, the laying on of hands, is doubtless a reference to this gesture administered to Timothy, distinguished from *placing* of the hands for blessings and healings, and probably modeled on the Jewish rite for the ordination of rabbis which found its inspiration in Joshua's ordination, described in Numbers 27:18–23 and Deuteronomy 34:9, at which Moses "laid his hands" ("leaned" or "pressed" would be more accurate) on his prospective successor. The Hebrew word is סמך (Num 27:23). Was it the elders who laid hands on Timothy (1 Tim 4:14), or was it the apostle Paul only who laid hands on Timothy (2 Tim 1:6)? Is the latter action by a party of one reiterated when Timothy is instructed not to be hasty in laying on of hands (1 Tim 5:22)? Our view is that Paul's role at Timothy's ordination must in any case have been the preponderant one; that of the elders must have been one of simple cooperation and assistance. See J. N. D. Kelly, *A Commentary on the Pastoral Epistles: I Timothy, II Timothy, Titus* (New York: Harper & Row, 1963), 105–108. And what is the relationship, if any, between the gift received by Timothy "by prophetic utterance" and the laying on of hands? Note the explanation by Dr. Armin Moellering, who reflects that Timothy's designation by prophets in the congregation may have preceded "any deputizing service" with the laying on of hands. "If this understanding is correct," says Dr. Moellering, "then the laying on of hands did not so much confer the gift as certify its presence and reality" (H. Armin Moellering, *Concordia Commentary: 1 Timothy, 2 Timothy, Titus* [St. Louis: Concordia Publishing House, 1970], 95–96).

69 Elvin W. Janetzki, "Appointment to the Public Ministry, with Particular Reference to the Call and Ordination," *Lutheran Theological Journal* 6 (August 1972): 49. Janetzki references this point to Martin J. Heinecken, "What Does Ordination Confer?" *Lutheran Quarterly* 18 (May 1966): 132.

nor from or through instrumentality of the clerics in the laying on of hands. It is from Jesus Christ, the Lord of the Church.[70]

Ordination—Transcendence

In the Rite of Ordination, the Lord places the candidate into His Office of the Holy Ministry, Word and Sacrament. This is affirmed by Dr. John W. Kleinig, who views ordination as the *ritual call* complementary to the *regular call* (*rite vocatus*, AC XIV). Informed by Luther's view of Call and ordination, Kleinig comments,

> Luther, in fact, equates the call with true consecration and ordination to the office of the ministry (LW 38, 211). For him the rite of ordination was therefore an important part of the call to be pastor. It enacted the call. Hence CA XIV *rite vocatus*, means both regularly called and ritually called. In fact, Luther defines ordination as calling to and entrusting with the office of the ministry (LW 38, 197).[71]

The significance that Luther attached to Call and ordination elevates the office above the limited perceptions—here is a job in the church, you are the person, and this is our mutual agreement or contract. Call and ordination transcend the mundane categories of a legal document, contract, or work agreement. The transcendence becomes apparent when ordination is properly viewed as a liturgical action, which acknowledges and confesses the triune God. Dr. Kleinig captured the essence, the action of the Holy Trinity. He writes,

> We Lutherans have historically understood ordination as a liturgical act by which the Triune God calls, empowers, and commissions the ordinand as a minister of the gospel (Heubach). John 20:21–23 is a key text in this teaching. It shows that all three persons of the Trinity are involved in this act of ordination. The Father sends the Son who in turn sends out the disciples to forgive and retain sin. The Son breathes on the disciples and empowers them to do the work of the Father by the gift of the Holy Spirit. The disciples, and all ministers of the gospel after them, are therefore commissioned by the Triune God.[72]

---

70 Ibid.

71 John W. Kleinig, "The Office of Ministry and Ordination" (paper presented at the NSW Pastors Conference, Lutheran Church of Australia, December 22, 2005), 8.

72 Ibid.

Ordination—Safeguard

Election, Call, ordination—settling a candidate-pastor in the Office and trusting him to the *task* of the public ministry—is an action that protects the congregation in two aspects. First, the practice of ordination or installation protects against subjective takeover and manhandling of the office by spurious aspirants who may lay claim to authority to preach and to teach on the basis of a professed inner call.[73] Second, this practice of election, Call, and ordination protects a congregation from invasive pressure that would override the people's free choice of a pastor. This unwelcome pressure may come from persons within or without the congregation.

Arranging for the Rite of Ordination

The day of ordination when a candidate enters the Holy Ministry ought to live in his memory. Subsequent days of installation at future congregations will add to the joy. The worship service hosting the Rite of Ordination should be planned by the candidate and the calling congregation in consultation with church officials. Normally, good order suggests that the rite be conducted in the presence of the calling congregation, though officials will work with requests to be ordained elsewhere.

The rites of ordination and installation are similar, except for assessment of the candidate by proper examination referenced only in the Rite of Ordination. It is omitted in the Rite of Installation conducted for the seasoned pastor. Of course, substantive in both Lutheran rites is the candidate's public confession and his pledge to preach, teach, and administer the overall pastoral ministry in accordance with the doctrine of the Evangelical Lutheran Church, that is, according to the Scriptures and the Lutheran Confessions. Other exhortations—to set an example of a godly life, to minister to the sick and the dying, and so forth—are salutary.

A candidate prepares himself for ordination and may be caught up in the moment! Heinrich Rengstorf has framed choice words and phrases that enhance meditation on the significance of ordination. Paraphrased, his words read,

73 Elvin Janetzki reports that later Luther used the concepts of Call and ordination synonymously, for the Reformer was concerned about individuals who may assume for themselves what belongs to all, and appoint themselves to the public office. Claimants to an *inner call* should present those *promptings* together with gifts, abilities, and qualifications to the Church. As the Church gives prayerful consideration to such an appeal, the Spirit shall lead, either to call the aspiring candidate or to reject his aspirations (Acts 1:15–26; 6:1–6). This is why district or diocesan officials serve as valuable resources. They provide information about *aspirants* that should be used by congregations. In the absence of credible information, the congregation is well advised to consider other candidates. See Elvin W. Janetzki, "Appointment to the Public Ministry, with Particular Reference to the Call and Ordination," 49. For a discussion of the *inner call* and its implications, see David J. Peter, "A Lutheran Perspective on the Inward Call to the Ministry," *Concordia Journal* 12, no. 4 (July 1986): 121–129.

> Ordination is an hour when consciousness of the office, certainty of the office, rejoicing in the office, and commitment to the office come together. [Ordination] is an hour when the candidate consciously comes to a decision for the way of the apostles, an hour in which absolute clarity is achieved between the Lord of the office and the bearer of the office, also in the direction as to what the bearer of the office may expect from His Lord. [It is . . .] an hour of decision for the office of Christ, for which he is brought to a decision through the will of Christ.[74]

Removal of a Pastor from the Office

Legitimate Cause

The sad antithesis to election, Call, and ordination is the action of removing a pastor from the Office of the Holy Ministry. Let there be cause for this radical action! Removal for negligible reasons—we are tired of him, he doesn't do what we want, we don't like him, and such—is unconscionable (cf. 2 Cor 10:10–12, 18b; 11:5–6; 12:11b). The principle that governs the action of removing a pastor from office is clear.

> **Principle:** The Lord of the Church, working through the congregation mediately, called and placed the pastor where he serves, and only God shall remove a pastor by criteria in accord with His Word.

Can authorities removing a pastor account for their initiative as an action of God? Short of this serious criterion, they abuse the pastor and offend against the Call. This is not healthy. Historically, the Lord handed fierce reprisals to many who persecuted His servants (Amos 7:10–17; Jer 28:10–17; cf. Exod 17:4; 2 Kgs 5:19–27). Furthermore, a pastor deposed by a congregation or church official without cause creates a delicate dilemma for their future ministry. Johann Gerhard observed, "Neither should anyone allow himself to be put in the place of another who has been removed from his position without due process of law (*sine legitimo judicii*)."[75]

Criteria for Terminating a Pastor's Call and Removing Him from Office:

1. Persistent teaching of false doctrine.

---

74 Karl Heinrich Rengstorf, *Apostolate and Ministry: The New Testament Doctrine of the Office of the Ministry*, trans. Paul D. Pahl (St. Louis: Concordia Publishing House, 1969), 109–110.

75 Johann Gerhard, cited by Robert David Preus, *The Doctrine of the Call in the Confessions and Lutheran Orthodoxy* (Luther Academy, Monograph #1–April 1991), 40.

Concerned parties have confronted a pastor about his errorist teaching versus the Scriptures and the Lutheran Confessions. Still, he persists in teaching error. He pleads that he is entitled to hold such views and press them on the congregation. He has been counseled by fellow pastors, theologians, and church officials. He persists. The people are confused. They cannot accept his teaching, but he is a winsome person and they are drawn to him. False doctrine creeps into every avenue of his ministry. He is a false prophet (Titus 1:9; 2:1; 1 Tim 6:3–4; Matt 7:15; Gal 1:6–9; 2 Thess 2:15; 1 John 4:1; cf. Acts 20:27; 1 Tim 4:16; 2 Tim 2:18; 2 Thess 3:14–15; Rom 16:17–18; Titus 3:10–11)!

2. Leading an ungodly life that dishonors Christ, who is our "righteousness and sanctification and redemption" (1 Cor 1:30).

By his ungodly conduct and unseemly behavior, the pastor betrays the Gospel he is sworn to preach and uphold. The erring ungodly life is contrary to the high and noble standard of Christian living prescribed for one who holds the office of bishop, pastor (1 Tim 3:2–4; Titus 2:7–8). The immoral pastor is not a good example to the flock in word and action (1 Tim 4:12). Nor is he respected by the public outside of the Church (1 Tim 3:7). He is no longer fit. He cannot fulfill his ministry. The compelling trait "above reproach" no longer applies to him (Titus 1:7a; cf. 2 Tim 2:19).

3. Persistent unfaithfulness in the performance of the duties of a pastor.

Understandably, a pastor may be afflicted with problems that affect his performance, and most congregations and church officials will remain patient as he seeks good counsel and works through these issues. There are instances of gross and willful negligence on the part of a pastor. He may be noncaring, flippant, disinterested, merely functioning, going through the motions. His heart is not in the work. Love for the people is absent. They hesitate to approach their pastor. It comes to a point that they do not regard him as a pastor. His negligence and defensive behavior create a wall between him and the people. The unfaithful pastor does not work. He is unprepared across the board. Preaching and teaching are insipid, leadership is nil, pastoral care is heartless or neglected altogether. He may refuse to minister to the sick. He does not do the work of an evangelist. He is not interested to counsel the troubled or admonish the erring. He approaches official acts as if these pastoral occasions are a bothersome distraction. The people to be served in the conduct of Baptisms, weddings, funerals or memorial services are impressed that the pastor is just not interested. There are times when he does not show up for appointments or meetings, and the people wonder what to expect on Sunday mornings. He is unfaithful (Acts 20:28, 31; 1 Thess 2:8–9, 17–20; 3:9–10; 2 Thess 2:16–17; 1 Cor 4:2; 1 Tim 3:1;

4:13, 15; 5:20; 2 Tim 2:15, 24–25; 4:5; Jas 5:14–15, 19–20; cf. 1 Thess 2:11–12; 2 Cor 7:2–4; 1 Cor 10:33; 1 Cor 13:1–3; 16:14; Matt 9:35–36; Mark 6:13; 10:43–45; John 21:15–17)!

4. Obvious incapability to meet the responsibilities and execute the duties of the pastoral ministry.

Long-standing dependencies—alcohol, drugs, and such—may render a pastor incapable of the office even after extensive therapy. He persists and wants to remain in the pastoral ministry, but he is disabled. Recognize that disabilities—physical, mental, or spiritual—may render a pastor incapable. Then, in some circumstances, the public ministry and many related duties for edifying and strengthening the congregation may have outgrown the gifts and abilities of a pastor, rendering him no longer competent to serve the pastorate where he was called years ago. He cannot cope, and continuing is a struggle. Still, authorities should not act hastily. Before reaching a point when demands of the ministry severely outweigh competencies, a pastor will assess the situation. Perhaps he may request and accept assistance that would bring strength to his pastoral ministry. Or he may seek another ministry and consider another Call. His God-given gifts may best serve the Lord and His Church elsewhere (cf. Col 4:17; Eph 4:11–12; 1 Cor 12:7; 1 Tim 4:15b; 2 Tim 4:5).

These lengthy descriptions of causes suggest that removing a pastor from office is not an everyday occurrence. God forbid! So the intention is to deter any impetuous action or kangaroo court proceedings that race toward hasty and final expulsion of a pastor. Causes shall not be invented and brought forward beyond those mentioned above, though C. F. W. Walther reportedly advanced two additional causes for removal of a pastor.[76] The first is a pastor's fierce authoritarian demeanor that oppresses a congregation, makes the people uncomfortable, and damages fruitful pastor-people relationships.[77] However, deposing a pastor who has an authoritarian spirit, but is otherwise faithful and effective, may be questioned. Walther's second added cause is more serious. A pastor may impose on others his overly sensitive conscience about many areas in the realm of *adiaphora* (matters indifferent, neither commanded nor forbidden). Thus he may unduly bind the consciences of Christian people. Their choices in areas of adiaphora he holds accountable to his *approval* or *disapproval*. His piety may be commendable, but his *standards* may not have support

76 *Theology and Practice of "the Divine Call": A Report of the Commission on Theology and Church Relations* (St. Louis: The Lutheran Church—Missouri Synod, February 2003), 43.

77 In a rural town, late nineteenth century, one morning a lady and her small child reportedly were walking on the sidewalk of Main Street. Seeing *Herr Pastor* approaching in the distance, the mother and child hurriedly crossed the street and continued on the opposite sidewalk for *fear* of encountering *his honor*.

from the Scriptures. Strictly enforced, his unfounded scruples encroach on the freedom that the people have in the Gospel. They live under tyranny. This pastor has exhausted useful service to God's people.

Executing Removal of a Pastor

Initiatives to remove a pastor from office reside with congregation leaders and/or the board of elders. Persons who are blatantly hostile to the pastor should recuse themselves from these proceedings. This is pastoral work of the highest order. Let all proceed in a spirit of charity (1 Cor 13). When a pastor has persisted in teaching false doctrine or leads an openly scandalous life, it may be necessary to dismiss him with dispatch (cf. 1 Tim 5:19–20). Parties to this action should act on facts, and permit the facts to speak for themselves. Note: A denominational judiciary may consider removing a pastor from the collegium of clergy.

The Church exercises care to minister to the fallen pastor. Opportunity should be available to hear his confession, with the Absolution readily at hand. Repentance, then restoration by the Gospel of the forgiveness of sins in Jesus' name, is a ministry the deposing congregation or other church entity owes the erring pastor. It is doubtful, however, that a pastor who has fallen, though repentant and absolved of his sin, may continue at his post or commence serving elsewhere as a Christian pastor. This is a matter that church officials will address.

When a congregation dismisses a pastor for the reason of inability to fulfill the pastoral ministry in their midst, charity dictates that the pastor's gifts and abilities be conserved, leaving open the possibility that he may minister elsewhere in the Church at large. Instead of putting him out on the street, first consider that this pastor may be called or appointed to an auxiliary ministry—possibly even within the congregation he has been serving—assistant pastor or minister of pastoral care, for example. Or efforts to redirect him to another ministry should be supported. A congregation may be patient and not press for his immediate resignation. They may wait for the pastor to receive a Call elsewhere. They need not *defrock* the man, which injures his reputation and prevents him from receiving a Call to another ministry. Destroy a man's ministry by hasty, forced termination? Or proceed charitably and assist the pastor to find an alternative ministry where his gifts may be used? A congregation that deals patiently with their pastor chooses the right course (cf. 1 Thess 5:12–13, 25).

Retirement from the Office of the Ministry

Retirement—A Modern Phenomenon

A pastor retiring is a modern phenomenon. For centuries, the tenure of pastors was related to the permanency of their Call; and the Call is permanent, that is, God places and keeps a pastor at his post until God decides otherwise and intervenes either by moving him to another ministry or by taking him in death. No party shall interrupt this order. Yet neither the pastor nor others shall press the Call beyond the pastor's ability to fulfill the pastoral ministry. A pastor may outlive his capacity for the ministry. When this occurs, it is time to retire. "For everything there is a season, and a time for every matter under heaven" (Eccl 3:1).

The Call is permanent, but men are frail. They are not permanent. Observe, however, that prophets and apostles did not retire. Does this observation preclude retirement on the part of pastors today? Moses served to the end, until Yahweh retired him (Deut 34:4–5). Elijah wanted to retire. He retreated into isolation, perhaps gripped by depression, but his ministry as prophet was not ended. Yahweh called for him (1 Kgs 19:8–18). Many apostles were martyred. St. John's tenure extended to an advanced age, but these examples are not prescriptive, and they should not be engaged to set the length or brevity of a pastor's years of service. Neither should societal pressure, government stipulation, or ecclesiastical policy determine a pastor's retirement. *Mandatory retirement* is not in the best tradition of the Lutheran Church. The Call is permanent, and the pastor serves as long as he possesses the capacity to fulfill his ministry.[78]

Principle: Barring removal from the pastoral office by death, a pastor shall continue to serve until his capacity—energy, vitality, alertness, sound judgment, wisdom—wanes, and he is no longer able to meet the demands of the Call and fulfill the pastoral ministry. Then, advisedly, he announces that he is retiring from the active pastorate.

Issues Surrounding Retirement

Caveats should be considered. For example, a pastor is aging and the congregation he serves is growing larger and more complex. There is a pressing need for leadership. Soon the pastor's age and capacity become important factors. Perhaps "It is time, brother." Long pastorates are vulnerable in the face of

78 Fritz reflects that a pastor, a man chosen by God for the pastoral ministry, should not forsake that calling without good reason, but should instead continue to serve a congregation, even if it be a small charge with fewer pastoral responsibilities. He reasons that the harvest is great and laborers are needed (Matt 9:37–38; cf. 1 Cor 9:16, 17, 22b; Luke 9:62; 2 Tim 4:6–7). John H. C. Fritz, *Pastoral Theology*, 56.

the congregation's unspoken desires that the pastor retire. Sensing restlessness among the people over his tenure, a mature and wise pastor will not become defensive. When a pastor senses that (1) he has been at this congregation a long time, and (2) that he is advanced in years, it may be time to consider retirement.[79]

Facing the decision either to retire or to continue in a ministry calls for the collective wisdom of the pastor, the congregation, and supervisory officials, but the decision should be left for the pastor. He should make a careful and wise decision. When the pastor retires, cutting ties will be difficult. Postretirement adjustment may be a mixed bag. Ease, relaxation, and new freedom may be combined with frustration and a lack of focus. A sense of fulfillment may be missed. The Lord's Word supporting Joshua in his youth did not fail in his later years. The same assurance awaits the retiring pastor and his wife. "Be strong and courageous . . . for the LORD your God is with you wherever you go" (Josh 1:9).

---

79 For an example of a wise pastor in later years, see footnote 55, page 42.

CHAPTER THREE

The Pastor as Theologian —Study and Devotion

Introduction

The Christian pastor is a theologian. His only capital is divine theology, what God has revealed in Holy Scripture for salvation and the Christian life that awaits the coming of our Lord Jesus Christ (John 20:31; 1 Thess 5:23b; 2 Tim 3:15–17; Acts 20:27). Not all theologians are pastors by calling, but pastors cannot be anything other than theologians in residence for their congregations.

What is a pastor/theologian? Fritz explains that the pastor, trained and equipped by the Holy Spirit, possesses the *habitus practicus theosdotos*. Loosely translated, the pastor is gifted by the Holy Spirit (*theosdotos*) with the (*habitus*) aptitude or disposition of the soul that makes him sufficient for the performance (*practicus*) of pastoral duties. Again, the term *habitus* refers to that sufficiency given by the Holy Spirit (*theosdotos*), who directs and guides the pastor in the practice (*practicus*) of the pastoral ministry (cf. 2 Cor 2:16b–17; 3:5–6).[80]

The calling of the Christian pastor is both theological and practical. Reflecting on theology and practice, David Hollaz stated:

> Theology is eminently practical wisdom teaching all things from the revealed Word of God that are necessary, with respect to knowl-

80 John H. C. Fritz, *Pastoral Theology*, 2. The term *habitus* implies an abundance of gifts supplied by the Holy Spirit (*theosdotos*), but mediately, that is, through the means of the Holy Scriptures that supplies and nurtures such sufficiency (cf. 2 Tim 3:16–17). The heart of the pastor, his sensitive care for God's people, his sixth sense, so to speak, his listening—attention to God and to people—his being in control, his right Word of God at the right time, are nuances of this *habitus*, acquired not by his own acumen but by the Holy Spirit for this purpose, the practice of the pastoral ministry (*practicus*) in many parts such as preaching (2 Tim 4:2), teaching (Matt 28:20; 2 Tim 1:11; 2:2; Titus 1:9), pastoral care (2 Thess 2:16–17; Phil 1:27), worship and the public reading and exposition of Scripture (1 Tim 4:13), leading (1 Thess 5:12; 1 Tim 5:17; Heb 13:7), and setting the example of Christian living to the flock (Titus 2:7–8; 1 Pet 5:3).

> edge, for true faith in Christ; with respect to deed, for sanctification of life; and for the attainment of eternal life by sinful man.[81]

This is theology. This is practice. The implication is clear. The pastor who engages in the study of theology according to the Scriptures, who brings God's Word to bear upon the human condition with need for salvation and sanctification—he is a pastor and theologian.

Theologian in Residence

The pastor-theologian shepherds souls. He communicates all that the Scriptures disclose and teach concerning God and man (Acts 20:20, 27). Not every interaction with the people is "theological," but when shepherding God's people, a theological response satisfies in many instances. Furthermore, the people look to their pastor for interpretation and application of the Scriptures. He is their theologian in residence. Celebrity types—nationally known evangelists, megachurch leaders, television personalities—may catch their attention temporarily, but the people of the local congregation consult their pastor. They trust him to provide truthful answers and theological judgments on the basis of the Scriptures.

Theologian for the Church Today

The people bring to their pastor-theologian long-standing questions and concerns about subjects requiring theological reflection:

- ☐ Infant Baptism
- ☐ Prosperity Theology
- ☐ "Left Behind" Rapture Eschatology
- ☐ Hedonism
- ☐ Open Communion Practice
- ☐ Charismatic Movement
- ☐ Women in Church and Ministry
- ☐ Ecclesiology, Mission, Church Growth
- ☐ The Papacy—Antichrist?
- ☐ Civil Religion
- ☐ Unionism and Syncretism
- ☐ Church and State
- ☐ Crosses, Burdens
- ☐ Theodicy
- ☐ Pluralism
- ☐ Christians and Consumerism

Other questions and concerns arise from interaction with the culture, trends of the day, and other current issues that press for theological assessment and response:

81 David Hollaz, *Examen theoloogicum acromticum*, 4th ed., ed. John Henry Hollaz (Stockholm 1725). Cap. I., Quaestio 18, 14, cited by Henry J. Eggold, "Theology as *Habitus Practicus Theosdotos*: A Lutheran Emphasis," *Concordia Theological Monthly* 33, no. 10 (October 1962): 596.

☐ The Place of Religion in Today's Culture
☐ Roe v. Wade—Abortion on Demand
☐ Obergefell v. Hodges—Same-Sex Marriage
☐ Normalization of Homosexuality
☐ Transgender Transformation
☐ Euthanasia and Assisted Suicide
☐ Marijuana and Proliferation of Drugs
☐ Biogenetic Issues
☐ Sweeping Ethical Relativity and Immorality
☐ Civil Disobedience vs. Violent Protest
☐ Ecological Matters

Issues arise, often unexpectedly. A pastor's response may require fresh research and study. To rely solely on one's seminary education may be inadequate. Therefore, a priority in current seminary education is to help students to become self-educating pastors who will pursue fresh theological inquiry that equips them to meet challenges in their ministries arising from changes in the culture and the public perception of religion.[82] A wise pastor regularly adds to his fund of knowledge. Neither the world nor the church remains static. Meeting the *issues* that surface constantly in church and world, the pastor acquires appropriate theological capital.

As a theologian, the pastor engages in study and learning, a discipline implied by the apostle Paul's counsel to Timothy, "Until I come, devote yourself to the public reading of Scripture, to exhortation, to teaching" (1 Tim 4:13; cf. 2 Tim 4:2, 5b). He urged Timothy to reach for proficiency, saying, "Do your best to present yourself to God as one approved, a worker who has no need to be ashamed, rightly handling the word of truth" (2 Tim 2:15). Theological proficiency is assumed in this mandate for Titus, "But as for you, teach what accords with sound doctrine" (Titus 2:1). In the way of Timothy and Titus, a pastor studies the Scriptures and supplements his studies with the findings of other scholars and theologians.

Theologian in the Making

The pastor as theologian—is he *being* or *becoming*? Most mentors of seminary students project continuing formation of the pastor-theologian that will last an entire career. For this journey, Martin Luther's classic dictum serves well: *Oratio, meditatio, tentatio faciunt theologum* ("Prayer, study, affliction make the

82 This priority was advanced intensely by H. Richard Niebuhr et al., *The Advancement of Theological Education* (New York: Harper, 1957), 219, cited by Connolloy C. Gamble, *The Continuing Theological Education of the American Minister* (Richmond, VA: Union Theological Seminary, 1960), 12.

theologian"). These three rules, as Luther cites them, originate with Psalm 119; and Luther states that they are expounded throughout the entire psalm.[83]

Oratio (prayer). Our Lord's ministry was set within a life of prayer (Luke 6:12; 11:1a). How exemplary is the Lord, His ministry and devotion! Therefore, Fritz comments,

> Since the sufficiency of the minister of the Gospel is not of himself, but of God alone, he should not fail diligently to call upon God to enlighten the eyes of his understanding, Eph. 1, 18, and to open his heart to the understanding of the Scriptures, Acts 16, 14, and pray Him to give him wisdom from above, so that he may apply God's Word in accordance with God's will, without partiality and without hypocrisy, Jas. 3, 17.[84]

Fritz relates how Luther distinguished *prayer* in the making of a theologian from prayer exercised by the pastor for his congregation or in his personal and family life. The pastor prays! He brings the needs of the people before God. He implores the Lord for himself and for his family. Prayer in the making of a theologian differs in this respect. Here, the pastor prays as he approaches the Scriptures, preparing to search and study the Word of God. "Let us know; let us press on to know the LORD" (Hos 6:3). A pastor's mind and heart are occupied with the text of the Bible. Luther counsels the pastor-theologian, "But enter into thy closet and kneel down and implore God with all humility and earnestness that by His dear Son He would grant you His Holy Ghost, who will enlighten you, guide you, and give you understanding."[85]

Meditatio (study). Luther distinguishes between casual reading and rumination versus direct focus externally on the oral speech and lettered words of the Scriptures. He advises reading and rereading the Scripture text. What does the Holy Spirit teach in the lettered words of the Book, which is not the word of man, but the Word of the Spirit?[86] When a pastor studies Holy Scripture, he attends to the vocabulary of the text, also the grammar and syntax. How do the words and phrases and sentences come together? What is the thought progression in the text? How does the context contribute to understanding the text? We are speaking about close and careful exegesis, and this is what Luther presses with this second rule, *meditation*. Discovering what the Holy Spirit teaches

---

83 Pieper, *Christian Dogmatics*, vol. 1, 186. Dr. Pieper cites Luther's *three rules* under the heading "The Attainment of Theological Aptitude." Luther's *rules* are also cited and discussed by John H. C. Fritz, *Pastoral Theology*, 2ff. Also see Luther's *rules* framed by Abraham Calov as requisites for becoming a theologian, set forth by Robert D. Preus, *Post-Reformation Lutheranism*, 219–222.

84 John H. C. Fritz, *Pastoral Theology*, 3.

85 Luther, cited by Pieper, *Christian Dogmatics*, vol. 1, 187.

86 Ibid., 188.

in the letters of the Scripture text is called *doing* theology. This was Luther's view. With diligent focus on the Word of God, the pastor becomes the theologian the Holy Spirit will make him.

Tentatio (affliction, struggle). Studying the Scriptures in search of the meaning of the text, a pastor will experience what Luther himself experienced, *tentatio*, affliction or struggle. The text's meaning does not always make its appearance front and center stage. Frequently, the meaning lingers in the wings, and remains hidden, causing frustration. The pastor wrestles with the text, but Luther assures him that by engagement of the Scriptures, he shall at length experience how right, how true, how sweet, how lovely, how mighty, how consoling God's Word is, wisdom above all wisdom.[87] Luther observes the struggles of King David. Many conflicts erupted around David that countered and contradicted the consoling Word of God (Ps 119). Therefore, Luther advised pastors to study the Scriptures in earnest and expect the onslaught of Satan. Such buffeting and anxiety within and without, however, contributes to the making of a proficient theologian.

How does a pastor handle gnawing *tentatio*, the affliction that accompanies serious study of the Scriptures? Satan takes every advantage to question, attack, mislead, and create damning doubt (Matt 16:21–23; cf. 1 Cor 13:9, 12a; 1 Pet 5:8). For example, how do theologians resolve the apparent tension between God's universal grace and perceptions of particular election (2 Cor 5:19; 1 Tim 2:3–4; John 3:16; Rom 8:29–30; Eph 1:4–6)? How does the last judgment, holding all accountable for what they did in their bodies, whether good or bad, coincide with salvation by grace alone (Eph 2:8–9; cf. Matt 16:27; 25:31–45; Rom 2:6–10; 1 Cor 3:8; 2 Cor 5:10; Rev 22:12; FC SD XI)? How may we exhort Christians to live by the Lord's commandments when emphatically, *lex semper accusat*, the Law always accuses (FC SD VI)? How could Ezra command the men of Israel to abandon marriages to non-Israelite women in light of the prohibition against divorce (Ezra 10; cf. Mal 2:15–16)? Can we reconcile the prophetic promise that both the Lord's men and women shall prophesy in the last days with the practice of not ordaining women to the pastoral office (Acts 2:18; cf. Joel 2:28–32)?

Questions, questions. There is a time to entertain *tentatio*, and a time to put it aside. A pastor-theologian has unanswered questions, but he does not dwell on them. Nor does he put them on the people. He brings no questions or doubts, but the abiding promises of God that bolster faith and offer assurance (cf. 2 Cor 1:19–20). Certain passages of the Bible elude our grasp, either because God has not told us everything or because our capacities are limited.

---

87 Ibid., 189.

Still, there is more certainty available in the Bible than uncertainty. Therefore, we follow Luther's counsel and return to the Scriptures for the light and understanding the Spirit gives.

The Pastor-Theologian as Student

For the serious student of theology, many resources are available. Books, journals, online exhibits, course offerings, forums, conferences are legion. A pastor-theologian has to find his own way, and his study of the Bible is crucial. Here are a few methods of Bible study:

Outlining Sections of the Bible

While unpalatable to some, outlining a book of the Bible as it unfolds from the pen of the holy writer holds fascination for others. The process follows the track set forth by editions of the English Bible, that is, chapter, verses, phrases, and words. Outlining leads the student to major content and themes. Care must be exercised, however, not to impose on the material an arrangement that is foreign to the text itself.

Topical Approach

This method is a search of the Scriptures for teaching about a subject. Examples abound: prophecies of our Lord's death and resurrection; Jesus' conflict with first-century Judaism; St. Paul's contest with Judaizers in the churches of Galatia; the place of men and women in early apostolic congregations; the *basileia tou Theou* (Kingdom of God) in the Gospels, in Acts, in the Pauline letters; the Holy Spirit at work in the Acts of the Apostles, and so forth.

Biblical Theology

Engaging biblical theology is similar to the topical approach. The student poses a proposition or idea in order to discover how the Scriptures address the matter. Some examples are the suffering of Job, paradigm for pastoral care; the bodily resurrection of the Lord, pivotal for Christian faith; the coming of Christ at the close of the age, stimulus to Christian living; the relationship of mission to ecclesiology in the New Testament Church, model for the Church in the twenty-first century, and so on.

Centrifugal Method

Focused study on one book of the Bible will thrust the student outward to the larger corpus of Holy Scripture. Possibly a lifelong pursuit, singular study of John's Gospel, for example, or one of the synoptic Gospels as well as the Book of Acts and the epistles of the New Testament will spark investigation and study outside of the selected book, reaching into the larger field of the entire Scriptures. Careful study of the biblical text catapults the student into the Scriptures at large.

Commentaries

Though not the strongest Bible study method and taboo in seminaries, busy pastors may profitably pursue reliable exegetical commentaries on individual books of the Bible. The recent Concordia Commentary series, for example, brings scholarly acumen to the task of interpretation. These commentaries enable the pastor to follow exposition of the biblical text in the original language verse by verse with attention to grammar, syntax, and context—all leading to the meaning of the text. Interaction with the work of a biblical scholar and commentator is a beneficial exchange.

> **Principle:** Among his intellectual pursuits, a pastor-theologian always pursues some study of Holy Scripture. He may vary study methods, combine them, or attempt new approaches. Always, he is in the Word.

Supplementary Study Opportunities

The Lutheran Confessions

The Lutheran Confessions contained in the Book of Concord (1580) are requisite for the Lutheran pastor. The challenging question is, How do the Lutheran confessors address current subjects in the twenty-first century? Some examples are justification by grace through faith in Christ versus numerous paradigms with work righteousness at the core; conflicts over worship forms and practices; the Church's public ministry—office or function; the sacraments as the Lord instituted them versus revisionist perceptions; the mission of the Church advanced by the Confessions; Lutheran identity, does it matter?

Additional Study Options

An ever-widening circle embraces numerous study disciplines. One is continued study of the biblical languages, Hebrew and Greek. Some pastors pursue extensive reading of Luther's works. Select reading of the Church Fathers is profitable. Dr. Robert Preus counseled future pastors to read C. F. W. Walther's *The Proper Distinction Between the Law and the Gospel* at least once a year. We commend the discipline followed by the late Dr. D. James Kennedy, who read one page from the Greek New Testament daily through his ministry. A pastor also studies when he prepares sermons and for teaching ministry—

Bible classes, confirmation classes, instruction of Sunday School and Bible class teachers, and such. Some busy pastors make exegetical study in preparation for sermons their primary study program. Beyond the confines of his study or office, the pastor may enroll in courses at a local university. He may study with a group of pastors. Theological journals supplement—but should not replace—a pastor's own tailored study. Much on the Internet—blogs, Facebook, Twitter, email, and e-posts—may become distractions with little value for the pastor.

A pastor studies best those subjects that are of interest to him. He is free. Let him choose. In this regard, guilt should not carry the day. The *oughta* impulse dismantles study. When pastoral duties compound and intensify, the study program slows. It is all right. A pastor has study materials accessible. He returns to them when time is generous—twenty minutes, a half hour, an hour. About study, a pastor should simply relax and enjoy!

The Devotional Life of the Christian Pastor

Examples of Devotional Discipline

It was 6:30 a.m. at Lambert International Airport in St. Louis. Passengers were waiting to board a flight. Among them was the author and Dr. Martin Scharlemann, graduate professor of New Testament at Concordia Seminary. He was en route to a midmorning meeting in Chicago. We boarded the aircraft. The plane had taken off and was leveling on course when Dr. Scharlemann interrupted our conversation. He reached in his satchel for a breviary and said, "Excuse me, I did not have opportunity for this earlier." He read quietly and paused frequently. He was about his morning devotion, in the Word and at prayer.

Principle: A pastor's ministry seldom rises above his day-to-day communion with God, that is, his use of the Holy Scriptures, followed by turning to the Lord in prayer.[88]

Beginning the day with Scripture and prayer is a sacred indulgence that needs little discussion, much less defense.[89] Prof. George R. Kraus puts it this way: "Devotional life is aimed at our attitudes, our faith, our ministry, our daily performance as God's prophets to His people. . . . The purpose of a pastor's devotional life is to make him fit for servanthood and faithfulness."[90] For exam-

88 This principle is attributed to both Dr. Martin Scharlemann and Prof. George Kraus.

89 Basic sources for the pastor's devotion are the Holy Scriptures, hymnal, and prayer book. Helpful are these devotional works published by Concordia Publishing House: *Treasury of Daily Prayer* (2008); George R. Kraus's *The Pastor at Prayer*, rev. ed. (2014); and *Reading the Psalms with Luther* (2007). Also useful are John Doberstein's *Minister's Prayer Book* and John Baillie's *A Diary of Private Prayer*. The classic devotional work *The Daily Office*, by Herbert Lindemann, served the spiritual life of a generation of pastors. A two-volume work, *Daily Prayer*, by Robert Sauer provided devotions based on the lectionary.

90 George R. Kraus, "The Lutheran Pastor's Devotional Life," *Concordia Journal* 6, no. 1 (January 1980): 22.

ple, the Rev. Dr. Billy Graham related his morning devotion practice to a large conference of pastors. Arising at 7:00 a.m., Dr. Graham read one or two psalms, a chapter from the Book of Proverbs, a selection from one of the four Gospels, and closed by reading a chapter from a separate book of the Scriptures. Dr. Graham began each day with twenty minutes of Scripture and prayer.

Alternate Devotion Procedures

There are alternate times and patterns of devotional life for the pastor. When he prepares sermons or material for classes, he may pause devotionally. Is it possible to pause during study of the Word and pray as the Spirit prompts praying? Of course these sacred pauses are possible. The pastor prepares to feed the flock. Shall he not partake of the same riches of God's Word? Listen to the Spirit. Pray in the Spirit. Pursuing any study of the Scriptures, the pastor pauses, reflects, and prays.

Pastor, keep your Bible open as you go through the day. This is a cue from Psalm 119:105, "Your word is a lamp to my feet and a light to my path." The Scriptures prepare our way. If travel is part of an afternoon of calls, keep the Bible open on the car passenger seat. Pull into a parking area for a devotional stop. Turn to the Scriptures for a few moments, you and your Lord together. Some pastors benefit from listening to recordings of the Bible. Or place the Scriptures where they are close at hand within the home. This was the tactic developed by Dr. Martin Franzmann, professor of New Testament at Concordia Seminary. In his home, Prof. Franzmann placed a copy of the Greek New Testament in every room. He could reach for the New Testament and read, filling random moments with the Scriptures.

To these alternate means of devotional life, we mention a discipline, the pastor's retreat. Once every three weeks, the pastor retreats from the regular schedule for a half-day or longer. He goes away alone. This is time to commune with the Lord, reflect on many matters, assisted by his repertoire—the Scriptures, prayer book, a hymnal, the catechism, and perhaps other books or articles too. Of Jesus, the Gospels report, "And after He had dismissed the crowds, He went up on the mountain by Himself to pray. When evening came, He was there alone" (Matt 14:23; Mark 6:46; cf. Luke 5:16). Our Lord retreated to commune with the Father, setting an example for His pastors.

A pastor may drive to a state park or other resort area. While walking in the park, he opens his eyes to God's creation—the blue sky, the tiny flowers, the moss on the tree bark or surface of a rock. He walks along the riverbank or lakeshore. Or he just rests on a park bench. He may interject some exercise. He has sneakers and a basketball in the car trunk. Close by is an outdoor basketball court. Why not toss a few and make those baskets? In a little while, the pastor takes from his car a book or journal to read, and his iPad or notebook. He locates the restaurant at the lodge. Through the meal, he pauses and imbibes with the mind. He thinks and he prays. He shares many thoughts with his Lord. Should ideas break in abruptly, they are welcome. Those thoughts and reflections may be his best friends at another time. He jots them down. Pastor, it is all right to spend a few dollars and a little time on such an outing, just you and your Lord together. It may be the retreat that helps you to be the pastor, the husband, and the parent God would make of you.

CHAPTER FOUR

The Pastor and Relationships —Family and Others

The Person of the Pastor

Baptism, Newness of Life, and the Office of the Ministry

The Christian pastor is a person of good character who edifies others: family, congregation, and the larger community. Baptized into Christ Jesus—His death and resurrection—the old self crucified, sins forgiven, the pastor *en Christo* lives for God (Rom 6:5–11). A new person by Baptism into Christ, the sinful flesh and appetites under control, the pastor is free to shepherd Christ's people (Rom 6:3–4, 12–14, 18; cf. Rom 12:1–2; Eph 2:10; Gal 5:1). Within his circle of relationships, the people receive him as the *new* man he is in Christ Jesus.

The life of the new man baptized into Christ is the only life compatible with the Office of the Holy Ministry.[91] The pastor's life and conduct complement the office. The Rite of Ordination, therefore, requires that a pastor publicly affirm his new life in Christ through Baptism. Recall the question put to the candidate, "Will you adorn the Office of the Holy Ministry with a holy life?" This question reflects the harmony between the public ministry as a noble work and the sanctified life of one who aspires to this high calling (1 Tim 3:1–7; Titus 1:7–9). If unbelievers deny God by their actions (Titus 1:16), then pastors who shepherd believers make a good confession by their actions before God and His people. Day-to-day the pastor presents himself—speech, conduct, behavior—in a manner consistent with the apostolic admonition:

91 Naming Christians at Corinth, "the temple of the living God," and citing promises God made (2 Cor 6:16b–18), the apostle Paul exhorts, "Let us cleanse ourselves from every defilement of body and spirit, bringing holiness to completion in the fear of God" (2 Cor 7:1; cf. 1 Thess 4:7–8). The point is obvious. The Church, holy and washed in Baptism, cleansed by Christ (1 Cor 6:11; Eph 5:26) is well served by a pastor who lives by that same Baptism, washing, cleansing. It is a high calling indeed!

> Whatever is true, whatever is honorable, whatever is just, whatever is pure, whatever is lovely, whatever is commendable, if there is any excellence, if there is anything worthy of praise, think about these things. What you have learned and received and heard and seen in me—practice these things, and the God of peace will be with you. (Phil 4:8–9)

Good character, the new life in Baptism, suggests a vital principle for the pastor and his relationships.

Integrity of Person and Office

Principle: Life within the Office of the Holy Ministry is open and transparent; for the pastor is one baptized into Christ, and to the Church and world he shows forth in speech and behavior the Christlike life, setting for all the example of a good man, a man εν χριστώ, *en Christo.*

The Life Set Apart for the Gospel

Where the pastor is, there is the Gospel, affirmed and confessed by his conduct. No less than the apostles "set apart for the gospel of God," (cf. Rom 1:1; 2 Cor 1:1; Gal 1:1), the Christian pastor engages in the Gospel ministry as one who is a fellow worker with God (1 Cor 3:9; 2 Cor 6:1). Thus the pastor lives and works separated from this evil age, yet he is thrown headlong into the world as an ambassador for Jesus Christ (2 Cor 5:20). He comes with the Gospel, and everything about him communicates the Gospel. Literally, he personifies charity, courtesy, helpfulness, hospitality, and purity because the Gospel is the heartbeat of his life (1 Tim 1:5; cf. Matt 5:14–16; Rom 5:12, 17).

The apostolic example set by St. Paul and his partners is instructive. For the sake of the Gospel, they commended themselves "in every way" in the face of rigorous tests put to them—afflictions, hardships, calamities that put life and reputation on the line (2 Cor 6:4–10). In extreme situations when a man could understandably be ruffled or come apart; when he might be expected to lose control or sink into despair and give up on God; when he might have exploded in rage, resorting to violence; when he could have given himself over to alcohol and turned into an unruly combatant, the apostle Paul stood his ground and by the grace of God retained his composure. No one could discredit his ministry because during the low times he persistently gave no reason or cause for any to think less of the Gospel itself. Always the servant of Jesus, he survived with impeccable character, his life integral with the Gospel he preached. In this manner, the apostle Paul personified this cardinal principle governing the pastor's conduct relative to the Office of the Ministry.

The Asset of a Good Conscience

Principle: "We put no obstacle in anyone's way, so that no fault may be found with our ministry" / "giving no offence in any thing, that the ministry be not blamed" (2 Cor 6:3 ESV and KJV).

What the apostle Paul had going for him was a good conscience that freed him for ministry (cf. 2 Cor 6:11; Heb 13:18; 1 Pet 3:21). By contrast, the burdened conscience impedes freedom for pastoral ministry. The burden is heavy, and its weight is sin. The pastor knows how sin is laced through crippling malaise that is somewhat of his own making—overwork, stifling routine, debilitating work habits, chronic inefficiency. Sometimes a pastor is vulnerable because he has been at a post too many years, a situation he is helpless to resolve. Moreover, unacceptable attitudes and behavior are readily noticed by persons who are eager to criticize. R. V. G. Tasker cites Denney, who comments, "There are people who will be glad of an excuse not to listen to the gospel, or not to take it seriously, and that they will look for such an excuse in the conduct of its ministers."[92]

Though caught in these straits, a pastor has not reached a point of no return. He is a man ἐν χριστῷ, *en Christo*, that is, the pastor is a man of the Gospel. As such, he gives heed to the Gospel pointing to the cross where Christ bears our sins away (1 Pet 2:24). To the cross, then *from* the cross, he makes corrections. Good counsel advises, "The Gospel that forgives us is the Gospel that equips." The grace of God in Christ delivers and frees the pastor to minister (Rom 12:1).[93] By this power of the Gospel, the Holy Spirit turns a burdened conscience into a *good* conscience. The pastor resumes his ministry with joy.

Homosexuality and the Clergy

The pastoral office and the pastor's life is a diverse subject. For instance, whether a homosexual may serve as a Christian pastor is a matter at once *dominical*. The Lord who places men in His Office of the Ministry is He who created all things, also the sexes, male and female (John 1:3, 9–10; Col 1:16; Gen 2:21–25; Matt 19:4). Because homosexual orientation is distinct from God's intent in creation, and homosexual behavior is severely judged by God, the question lingers: should a man whose sexual orientation is distinct from the Lord's creation serve that same Lord in His Office of the Ministry[94] (Lev 18:22, 24; Rom 1:24–27; 1 Cor 6:9–10; 1 Tim 1:9–10)?

---

92 R. V. G. Tasker, *The Second Epistle of Paul to the Corinthians: An Introduction and Commentary* (Grand Rapids: Wm. B. Eerdmans, 1968), 92.

93 "Commitments of the Shepherd: Principles of Conduct for Ordained Ministers of the Gospel." A statement adopted by the Council of Presidents (The Lutheran Church—Missouri Synod, September 1990), 3.

94 This judgment is rendered by The Lutheran Church—Missouri Synod, expressed in the document "Guidelines for Ecclesiastical Supervisors of The Lutheran Church—Missouri Synod in Addressing Instances of Homosexuality in the Lives of Professional Church Workers." The document is a policy statement

In regard to the pastoral office, homosexual orientation is problematic, if for no other reason than the difficulty of teaching and counseling about sexuality, male and female, integral with the Scriptures. Understandably, a homosexual pastor may be conflicted over this teaching. Also, assurance that the gay pastor gives, that he will conduct himself above reproach as the apostle Paul requires, is not always convincing (1 Tim 3:2; Titus 1:7). The issue lingers whether a homosexual can be a candidate for the Office of the Holy Ministry.

In Conduct, Examples to the Flock

The *Typos* Principle

In speech, conduct, temperament, inclinations, et al., the pastor is an example to the Christian congregation and to the community. His moral life speaks volumes (1 Pet 5:3b; 1 Tim 3:7). The Lord exhorts, "Let your light so shine before others" (Matt 5:16). He presses for moral behavior consistent with life in the kingdom of God. Pointedly, St. Paul counsels Titus, "Show yourself in all respects to be a model of good works" (Titus 2:7a). The Greek term for *model* or *example* is τύπος, *typos.*[95] Not boasting, yet firmly assertive, the apostle Paul commends the example, *typos*, of his own right conduct for imitation by Timothy and Christians at large (2 Tim 3:10–11a; 1 Cor 11:1; Phil 3:17). Again, to Timothy he wrote, "Let no one despise you for your youth, but set the believers an example [*typos*] in speech, in conduct, in love, in faith, in purity" (1 Tim 4:12). The implication is clear: a pastor should conduct himself in a right manner so no one may have reason to disregard him (Titus 2:15b). From a stance of sterling Christian character, a pastor quietly and unobtrusively communicates to his congregation, "What you have learned and received and heard and seen in me—practice these things" (Phil 4:9). He is an example to the flock.

The High Ground Morally

Living an exemplary life, the pastor is a moral person. Ethicists writing about the pastor's conduct state, "Morality is intentional. A minister is a moral person because that minister intends to be moral and seeks to safeguard that morality throughout ministry."[96] Intentional morality shows up in conduct that is visible and transparent. The apostle Paul asserted that people must see

adopted by the Council of Presidents, The Lutheran Church—Missouri Synod, February 28, 1991.

95 The usage is varied. *Typos* was the mark of a blow, a print (John 20:25), the figures or images of the gods (Acts 7:43), also the form of teaching, that is, the teaching that embodies the sum and substance of religion and represents it to the mind (Rom 6:17); the term also designates the contents and form of a letter (Acts 23:25). In reference to the moral life, *typos* signifies an example or pattern, most often to imitate or follow (cf 1 Tim 4:12; Phil 3:17; 2 Thess 3:9).

96 Joe E. Trull and James E. Carter, *Ministerial Ethics: Being a Good Minister in a Not-So-Good World* (Nashville: Broadman & Holman, 1993), 88.

the pastor's life as irreproachable, ἀνεπίλημπτον (1 Tim 3:2a), and blameless, ἀνέγκλητος (Titus 1:6a; cf. 1 Tim 3:10). No pastor is perfect, but his external conduct must be morally defensible. No one can accuse him of wrongdoing. There is nothing in his conduct that draws accusation. Luther commented that before God no one is above reproach, but before men the pastor is to be so, that he may not be a fornicator, an adulterer, a greedy man, a foul-mouthed person, a drunkard, a gambler, a slanderer.[97] Luther adds, "He should not have public guilt which causes people to stumble . . . that a detractor will find something to cavil at; that is, he should be the kind of person who cannot be accused openly and publicly."[98]

The apostle Paul explains conduct that is unassailable or irreproachable when he lists numerous character traits of one who aspires to be a Christian pastor (1 Tim 3:2–7; Titus 1:6–9).[99] If the pastor is married, Paul teaches that he shall be a *one woman's man*, devoted to one woman, his wife. If he becomes a widower and remarries, he attends to his second wife. Furthermore, Paul teaches, the pastor is vigilant, alert, of sound mind, in control of self and emotions, a person given to good behavior, possessing a measure of sound judgment, tact, and grace. He is hospitable. Translated, the pastor is available to the people! Then, he is διδακτικός, a competent teacher and communicator (1 Tim 3:2; 2 Tim 2:24). He knows the teaching of the Scriptures, and he communicates the Word effectively.

In his personal life, the pastor does not use alcohol as a crutch. If he imbibes, he does so moderately. Even tempered, he does not lash out. He never raises his hand to strike a person. He has no chip on the shoulder. He is not contentious. He avoids conflict. He seeks to be at peace with all persons (cf. Rom 12:18). He is patient, meaning, "The Lord's servant must not be quarrelsome but kindly to every one . . . forbearing, correcting his opponents with gentleness" (2 Tim 2:24–25 RSV). He rises above frustrations over money, more money, and the things money buys. At home, he oversees family life, nurturing children in the graces of Christian living. Finally, the practice of these virtues commends the pastor as a leader of the Church, one who is spiritually mature rather than a novice or a newcomer to the faith (1 Tim 3:6).

Cultivating the Moral Life

Supplementing the high standard of moral living, the pastor examines specific aspects of his life in the profession. For instance, he pushes back on

97 Martin Luther, *Lectures on 1 Timothy* (LW 28:284).

98 Martin Luther, *Lectures on Titus* (LW 29:17–18).

99 The classic exposition of these passages is that by August C. Hardt, "The Pastor after the Heart of God," *Concordia Theological Monthly* 23, no. 11 (November 1952): 797–814.

distractions. We speak candidly. Has a man's ministry subtly become an avocation versus pursuit of the American dream? Is the ministry a springboard from which a pastor leaps in search of leisure? And what of Isaiah's indictment of watchmen who love their ease and their sleep, shepherds who lack understanding as they turn to their own way, each to his own gain, who fill themselves with strong drink, and seek happy times in the tomorrows ahead (Isa 56:9–12)? Do we hear St. John's censure of the flesh and the lust of the flesh, that is to say, gleeful accommodation of the appetites of the flesh, enticed by the world around us—the world that passes away with the lust of it (1 John 2:15–17; cf. 1 Pet 4:1–6; Rom 8:6–8, 12–14; 13:14)?

The lifestyle that pastors cultivate by choice matters because it contributes either positively or negatively to their fitness for the pastoral ministry. Our Lord related that a wise man built his house set on a rock for a foundation (Matt 7:24–27; Luke 6:47–49). He was teaching His audience to listen and to act on His words in the making of a life in the kingdom of God. No question, a pastor's life is anchored in Baptism on the solid foundation of Christ. What of the house that rises from this rock? How are we building that house?

It is sad when the life that a pastor cultivates is taking him down, when conduct descends to our way with alcohol or drugs, leading to crippling dependency; our way with sexual fantasy and indulgence and pornography, which beckons and lures us into its dungeons; our way with material things that reaches for more senseless toys; our way with recreation that is more intense than healthy repast; our way with temperament that lets loose with anger and meanness of spirit. Thus, the moral life, the only life appropriate for the pastor, eludes us. We know what is happening when our behavior behind the scenes adds up to building a life uncharacteristic of the base, the rock, even Christ, in whom we have both life and pastoral ministry. Discovering that the vices of the world have a grip on us, we take the conventional road. We go for therapy. Perhaps we may reflect and, cold turkey, simply shout a resounding "*No*" to the ruinous temptations and indulgences that damage us and our ministries (Prov 14:16). Is it time, further, to intentionally store up God's Word in our hearts that we might not sin against Him (Ps 119:11)?

Moral Failure

The fallout from a pastor's moral failure is precarious. Prof. David Vallesky observes that trust is disturbed as confidence in the pastor is either diminished or destroyed; or offense rears an ugly head when failed pastoral conduct either is cause for blaming or ridiculing the office; or the pastor's failure leads others to take sin lightly, or diminishes the strength of conscience.[100]

100 David J. Vallesky, "The Pastor Must Be 'Above Reproach,'" *Wisconsin Lutheran Quarterly* 96, no. 3

The apostle Paul's articulate catalog of moral virtues is the same list that serves as the basis for assessing moral failure (cf. 1 Tim 3:1–7; Titus 1:7–9). In the instance of public misbehavior and sin, the pastor's tenure is at stake. Presumably, he no longer exhibits that essential example. The principle that emerges here raises key questions.

When a pastor's behavior jeopardizes his ministry, the church inquires, how flagrant is the discrepancy? How public is the sin? Consider that in a public setting, the pastor has used a poor choice of words. An unguarded moment, or an ill-advised action witnessed by a small group, may be addressed by the pastor's apology and then put to rest. The consequences are more serious for egregious missteps. The pastor may seek private Confession and Absolution. Following forgiveness administered in the name of Jesus, he may appear before the congregation and publicly seek their forgiveness. Although the sin is removed, possibly the *skandalon* remains. Residual disappointment, also shattered confidence and trust, are ugly realities that raise questions. Can this pastor recover in this congregation? Can he maintain his standing as *unassailable* or *irreproachable* and remain as the called pastor? Should he seek a Call elsewhere? The indiscretion may entirely dismantle his candidacy for any pastorate or public role in the church's administration. In this event, he must resign and seek another profession.

Principle: In instances of moral failure, acknowledgment of the same, followed with repentance addressed by Holy Absolution, can a fallen pastor as a Christian recover the state of blamelessness and return to the public ministry? Can he again be viewed as *irreproachable* in conduct and reputation so that he is received well by both congregation and the larger community (cf. 1 Tim 3:7; Titus 1:6)?

On the other hand, when an errant pastor is forgiven and restored, his continuance in the pastoral ministry may be considered. The question is not "Did this pastor at one time fail to meet the qualifications of being above reproach?" No, the question must be put in the present tense. Is this pastor *now* conducting his life in a manner decidedly *unassailable* and *irreproachable*? Is his present conduct and behavior a positive example to the flock (1 Pet 5:3)? Even if he cannot shed the residual effect of the *skandalon* in the parish where his failure occurred, possibly he may begin anew and serve another congregation. In their presence, he wins and maintains confidence as he pursues a credible moral life and attends faithfully to the pastoral ministry. Furthermore, these same rubrics apply to men preparing for the Holy Ministry. A student enrolls in a seminary to study for the pastoral office. He arrives with moral baggage unbecoming the

(Summer 1999): 200.

office for which he prepares. He repents, and he is absolved of the sin. Thus, upon graduation, he may be placed into the public ministry with a Call because his conduct and behavior in the present time are above and beyond reproach or accusation.[101]

A Pastor Who Divorces or Is Divorced

The appearance of moral impropriety cannot be overlooked. Clergy divorce, therefore, calls for serious reflection. In Ephesians 5, the marital relationship is said to be a great mystery (vv. 31–32a), and in the same breath the apostle reflects, "And I am saying that it refers to Christ and the church" (v. 32b). In this passage about the marital union, the *mysterion* depicts the innermost relationship of husband and wife, that is, the divine order that is marriage mirrors the transcendent relationship, Christ as head and then servant of His Bride, the Church. Then how shall divorced pastors properly reflect this *mysterion* in their lives and conduct when either they parted or have been parted from their spouse? Dr. Martin Scharlemann commented,

> Here is a New Testament term [mystery] which depicts the matter of two becoming one as a pointer to the redemptive intent God has for the world. That is to say, the marriage bond is an exhibit and a constant reminder, on the level of the obvious and visible, of God's agenda at work in history; namely, to bring the totality of all things under the headship of Jesus Christ (Eph. 1:10). Now, if the shepherds of God's flock are to serve as *typoi* (models) in this whole enterprise, according to 1 Pet. 5:3, then the pastoral office is to be the one place where this "mystery" is to be evident in a particularly noticeable fashion.[102]

Clearly, divorce is not an option for the married pastor. It does not square with conduct expected of a Christian pastor. Though divorce is here, within the culture and the Church, Dr. Scharlemann reminds pastors, there is a sanctity about the Church, especially with respect to the pastoral office, that demands of us that we not conform to this world but that we "be transformed by the renewal of [the] mind" (Rom 12:2). For we all must live and abide by our ordination vows, that we as pastors shall conform our faith and all of our life to the Word

---

101 Ibid., 203–204. Prof. David Vallesky notes that the case for close attention to the present condition is supported by the present tense of the Greek verbs δει and *εστιν* in 1 Timothy 3:2 and Titus 1:7 respectfully. Also see Titus 1:6.

102 Martin H. Scharlemann, "The Pastoral Office and Divorce, Remarriage, Moral Deviation," *Concordia Journal* 6, no. 4 (July 1980): 146. The witness that a pastor's marriage gives is paramount in the document "Guidelines for Dealing with Marital Crisis Involving Separation and Divorce of The Lutheran Church—Missouri Synod Clergy," a Policy Statement Adopted by the Council of Presidents (The Lutheran Church—Missouri Synod, April 29, 1987).

of God. Any sort of compromise, accommodation, concession, and judgments driven by standards decidedly relative in their formulation must be excluded.[103]

The pastor and his wife going through divorce proceedings are vulnerable to misunderstanding. The *skandalon* is ever present. Herein is the liability of giving offense—perceptions that a pastor's divorce is a green light for others to resolve marital problems by ending their marriage. The pastor's breaking marriage may signal license to abandon the challenge of keeping marriage and home together. The *skandalon* is multifaceted. For instance, a pastor is left by his spouse for no reason that may be attributed to him or his conduct. He is simply *done in* by his wife divorcing him. Still, the congregation is likely to be confused, preoccupied with divergent perceptions of their pastor's divorce.

Again, crucial questions stalk incessantly: Can a divorced pastor recover and retain the status of one who is above reproach, who cannot be assailed, who is beyond accusation of wrongdoing? Can he retain the trust and confidence of God's people? Can he be an example to the flock? Can he effectively counsel others with marital difficulties? Answers to these questions do not come easily. Suspicion that the pastor is culpable, that he failed as a husband and/or father, will test confidence and trust in him. One Christian lady opined over her pastor's impending divorce, "You just have to like him, but really he is a scoundrel." This opinion, though expressed with charity, reveals the tenuous standing of a divorced pastor in the congregation.

A divorced pastor may elect to remarry. What steps does he take? First, has he come to terms with his conduct in the former marriage? Did he counsel with a brother pastor and/or his district president or diocesan bishop? Did he submit to close scrutiny, accompanied by repentance and Absolution? Second, has the divorced pastor attended to support for his former wife and their children? Third, has the pastor demonstrated personal growth and maturity? Is he emotionally and spiritually a strong candidate for marriage? Fourth, has the pastor taken initiatives to retain the trust and confidence of the congregation as their shepherd? He should candidly face the situation if, in fact, the congregation does not accept his remarriage. In this event, he should seriously consider resigning from the pastoral ministry of this congregation.

A Pastor's Credible Life and Ministry

Good character, also love and care, constancy and endurance, passion and zeal lend credibility to the pastor's ministry. For Jesus, love is something you do. While teaching in the synagogue, our Lord saw a poor woman afflicted with a spirit of infirmity. She was bent over and could not straighten. In loving care,

103 Martin H. Scharlemann, "The Pastoral Office and Divorce, Remarriage, Moral Deviation," 148.

Jesus called to her, "Woman, you are freed from your disability" (Luke 13:12). In the footsteps of Jesus, the apostle Paul preached the Gospel at Corinth. "And why? Because I do not love you? God knows that I do!" (2 Cor 11:11; cf. 2 Cor 11:7–10; Phil 4:1; 1 Tim 1:5). Paul's care for the churches was marked by enduring zeal to reach even Rome and the ends of the earth so that the entire Gentile world would hear of Jesus Christ (2 Cor 11:28; Rom 15:15–24). Looking out to the congregation from the pulpit, the pastor sees a people to love, senses the need for care, and presses to be fervent in his credible ministry, *dominical* and *apostolic*. The English divine J. H. Jowett was awakened predawn by the sound of iron clogs worn by men coming down the road to the Yorkshire mills, where work began at six o'clock. "The sound of the clogs," he said, "fetched me out of bed and took me to my work."[104] Passionate for ministry to people, the pastor arises in the morning and stays at his post with constant love, care, and zeal. This he does "heartily," serving the Lord (Col 3:23–24; cf. 1 Thess 3:9–10).

The Pastor in the Way of the Professional Person

For all the goofy caricatures of the clergy, in most venues the Christian pastor is regarded as a professional person. He is credible and respected. His demeanor and outward appearance have much to do with retaining respect. These factors either enhance or diminish his standing in the view of others. The apostle Paul counsels, "Put no obstacle" in the way of honor and respect for the Office of the Ministry (2 Cor 6:3). It comes down to particulars. Pastors who are aware of their high calling attend to such matters as grooming and attire so that in all things they commend the pastoral office.[105]

Principle: The Gospel is ever at stake, also the office, which, by the Lord's arrangement, delivers the blessings of the Gospel. In his person and attire, the pastor is intentional that grooming and wardrobe best present him as one called to represent and deliver the Gospel and its blessings to all with whom he interacts in the course of his public ministry.

Consequently, a pastor gets up for his ministry. For starters, he showers and meets the day clean-shaven. He has attended to his fingernails. They are clean and trimmed. His hairstyle befits his facial features. Hair and hirsute growth—either

104 J. H. Jowett, *The Preacher: His Life and Work* (New York: George H. Doran, 1912), 116.

105 Though style may be informal, consider, for instance, sales personnel. They represent their product as they present themselves to the public. A store showing fine furniture does not send the stock boy on the floor to meet customers seeking a living room set. Walk through the cosmetic section of an urban department store. The women selling those products are at their best. Their own tasteful grooming recommends the products. Is the pastor in his person and appearance the best recommendation for the Gospel of Jesus Christ? Luther comments: "A bishop ought not to go about like a vagabond or a mercenary soldier but ought to appear with dignity as befits him. He should not be seen with torn shoes, mountainous mane, ragged shirts, and torn sleeves, but he should wear respectable clothes. That is what κόσμιος means" (LW 28:284–285). For an extended list of traits pertaining to the pastor—person and profession—see Appendix 2, "Thirteen Reminders for the Exemplary Pastor."

beard or mustache—are a matter of personal choice, but they should never make a statement. The only statement the pastor makes is the Gospel! Still acceptable is the clean shirt with tie, accompanied by a coat, either suit or sport coat. Ties may be dispensable in favor of the open collar or clerical collar. The pastor wears pressed trousers and his shoes are shined.

The Pastor's Relationships

The Pastor and His Wife

A Healthy Marriage

The closest person to the pastor is his wife. Their marriage is crucial for the pastor's ministry. Congregations are edified by their pastor's strong marriage—a husband and wife deeply in love and tirelessly devoted to each other. Such a marriage is like the rampart of a castle. It bespeaks strength and solidarity.

Responsibility for the Pastor's Strong Marriage

The pastor's marriage is strong to the degree that he is a good husband. He is responsible for the life that he and his wife share. He dare not rationalize to himself that the pastoral ministry is so demanding that responsibility for marriage and home must shift to his wife. The pastor does not abdicate. But the old debate persists—ministry or marriage—which is the pastor's first obligation? That debate poses a false dichotomy. The pastor fulfills *both* callings.

A pastor's wife is married to her husband, not to his ministry; but she accedes to demands of the ministry on his time and energy when she is assured day-to-day that she is number one in his life. Sadly, many pastors' wives are merely second in the priorities pursued by their pastor-husbands. Worse, some misguided pastors attempt to convince their wives that *second* is okay. "The Lord's work, you know, must come first." This false dichotomy nettles the wife. Either she capitulates to her husband's overinvolvement in the congregation and ministry, or she gathers up her emotional things and seeks a career of her own. She escapes. And she is missed.

The pastor is in charge of his marriage. He takes matters in hand. He knows the cues for sealing love and affirmation. Returning from the evening agenda at church, he finds her waiting, but not to hear the rehash of controversy and conflict over many issues. She is waiting for him. He left the *mess* as he headed for home. Let the Lord take care of things. Now he is with her and for her. The two share a hot chocolate. They talk. The evening is late. They retreat. She knows and believes that she has her man, her husband, and his love. She is none other than *first* in the life of this man. She is happy.

> **Principle:** A pastor shall not be so occupied or busy or overextended that his wife is left to seek and discover emotional support in other venues. Always, the pastor affirms and reaffirms all that she means to him as the *first* lady and person in his life.

Between special moments for the two of them, the pastor's wife receives from her husband a kind word spoken sincerely, a compliment given freely, an errand completed, a house repair fixed, and their children tended. He takes time for her. His affirming love is tangible. Sometimes it is an unexpected bouquet of flowers or a small gift that shows thoughtfulness. He has been gone. He is with many people. Other women move in and out of his professional life, but his remembering, his demonstrable attention to his wife with words and actions and little gifts and favors, affirms her as the lady who is so special in his life. Going off to church and ministry, he turns in the doorway, "I love you!" She knows that he is true to her.

The Pastor's Wife and the Congregation

As a devout Christian woman, the pastor's wife is a blessing to the congregation. Her service to her Savior and His people begins with her family and home, even if she has a career. Each pastor and his wife communicate and share with respect to domestic matters. She focuses on the cleanliness and neatness of the house, the diet and nutrition of the family, and the personal appearance of family members. Together, a pastor and his wife attend to their home and family in a manner that is supportive of his day-to-day ministry.

Beyond the home, many pastors' wives want to be active in their congregations, but they may be unsure to what extent to be active. A guiding principle is helpful.

> **Principle:** The pastor's wife relates to the women of the congregation and their ministries. Then, as a devoted lay Christian, she participates in at least one ministry as she is able. Involvement may vary—Sunday School teacher, choir or handbell choir, evangelism ministry, or such.

The pastor's wife avoids the two extremes—overinvolvement and blanket inactivity. Overinvolvement may lead to a perception of *too much* for the congregation. They may resent the *second pastor* image. If the pastor's wife is underinvolved, aloof, distant, she may be suspect, especially if she is not present for worship services with the congregation. The latter may signal deeper issues. Her best option is to strike a balance and sensibly assume the role of an active Christian.

The Single Pastor

The majority of Lutheran pastors are married. For pastors who are unmarried, it is important that they maintain self-confidence. Each single pastor is a family of one, but a family no less. Living alone, the pastor monitors diet, maintains an up-to-date wardrobe, and keeps a domicile where he can be both comfortable and productive. Cleanliness and good order are supportive. Outside his home, the single pastor monitors relationships. Congregation members may be solicitous and draw him into socializing. He may date women in the congregation, but advisedly and perhaps humorously, too, he dates one woman at a time. With women, he is discreet. He and his special woman friend are careful not to give occasion for offense, especially when they are on church or school premises or at their respective residences. Save expressions of affection for private moments together. What better setting for a Christian pastor to find a companion than in the Christian community where both are situated? Most congregations will rejoice over their relationship. The single pastor, however, should not rush into marriage. He and his companion should seek the Lord's wisdom.

The Pastor and His Children

Regard for Children as God's Gifts

The blessing of children is a quiet witness to our *childless and happy* culture. If they are gifted with children, the pastor and his wife rejoice. "Behold, children are a heritage from the LORD" (Ps 127:3; cf. Gen 4:1; Ps 128:3–4; 1 Sam 1:20). Children in a pastor's home will mature as adjusted Christians if the pastor keeps the apostolic word "He must manage his own household well" (1 Tim 3:4). The paradigm for the pastor's leadership at home is the Law and the Gospel. The difference is huge—whether parents command honor and respect or whether love and care wins the children's hearts.

Parental love both admonishes and restores children, the former by reprimand, the latter by forgiveness and acceptance. Leniency to the point of permissiveness was Eli's sin and mistake (cf. 1 Sam 3:13), but parents may also err on the side of severity (cf. Eph 6:4; Col 3:21). There must be boundaries for children, but let not the foolish need to impress the congregation with the perfect pastor's family fuel senseless severity with children. Boys and girls should obey their parents (Col 3:20), but from the other side, parents to children, let the Gospel prevail. The result will be children who reflect well on their father's calling as pastor. It shall not be otherwise (Lev 21:9).

Nurture of Children in the Pastor's Home

The nurture of children in the pastor's home is twofold. Informally, children pick up much from conversations of parents about church and ministry, theology and mission, and such. What is said, and how it is said, can either edify or harm. Formally, the παιδέια prescribed by the apostle Paul, "the discipline and instruction of the Lord," may take many forms (Eph 6:4). Reading Bible stories, teaching from the catechism, and using prayer books nurtures children from age 2 through adolescence. There is no substitute for the family gathered before the open Bible for reading, discussion, teaching, and prayer.

The Pastor's Children and the Congregation

The pastor's children are normal boys and girls. Unfortunately, some misguided persons in the congregation may expect more of them than is reasonable. Now and then, a child will venture into capers unbecoming the image of the *pastor's kid*. Perhaps he or she seeks attention. Yes, the pastor and his wife may be embarrassed when a little mischief is reported and exaggerated by catty persons in the congregation. If they join in the reprimand and browbeating, they risk alienating their child, who may internalize unfair expectations and later harbor resentment against the Church. Let children be who they are, boys and girls living and having fun. The pastor and his wife should loosen up and accept their children's childhood.

Taking Children into the Ministry

Do the pastor's children have a place in their father's ministry? They burst into his office shouting, "What are you doing today, Dad?" Seize the opportunity! Young Samuel ministered to the Lord in the presence of Eli the priest (1 Sam 2:11). A similar opportunity awaits the pastor's children. He can explain his study of the Scriptures, preparing sermons, and such. Routinely, he returns to the church—signing letters, arranging materials for worship services or classes, sorting out minor administrative tasks for the secretary, and so forth. The children accompany him. They lend a hand with minor tasks—straightening books and papers, touching up displays, and other useful acts. Children will do these tasks just to be with their father. Older children may accompany him on some hospital visits and calls at member homes. Such activities with their father help the children to bond with him and to comprehend his ministry. They are less likely to resent the pressing demands of that ministry. They will understand.

The Pastor's Relationships with the Congregation

Respect for One and All

The pastor's relationships extend beyond his family to the congregation. They are the baptized ones, Christ's people; and the pastor makes no distinctions—socioeconomic, education, class, race, status, culture. Whether they reside in a house trailer or a mansion, the pastor is comfortable with the people. And he makes them comfortable. He dines with members at the country club, and he will pause to chat with his member the trash hauler, who makes a stop on Main Street. The pastor respects all his people whatever their calling or status (cf. Eph 6:1–9; Col 3:18–4:1; Jas 2:1–7). At public gatherings, he speaks to many persons; but he seeks the disabled person, or the person who is socially isolated, the wallflower. He is a friend to all the people, and all look to him, their pastor.

Men of the Congregation

St. Paul remarked about pastoral relationships when he advised Timothy, "Do not rebuke an older man but encourage him as you would a father, younger men as brothers, older women as mothers, younger women as sisters, in all purity" (1 Tim 5:1–2). This counsel is fail-safe. Older men may nettle a young pastor, but he eases away and considers them "Pop" or "Dad." They may be testy, even feisty, yet the pastor humors them by treating them gently and showing his respect. He treats younger men as brothers, peers. He values them as partners.

Women in the Congregation

Equally valuable are younger women whom the pastor treats as "sisters, in all purity" (1 Tim 5:2). This means that any subtle sexually indiscreet advance in conversation or body language is reprehensible. Discipline your eyes, pastor. The leering look is unconscionable! Show interest and care with genuine respect for young women as persons. At the right time, point them to *mothers* in the faith whose reverent lives edify and strengthen the young (Titus 2:3). Honor the exemplary older women as you honor your own mother.

The Pastor's Relationships with Women

It may happen in the ministry that the pastor is with women much of the day. In fact, the pastor may be with women other than his wife—secretaries, staff, volunteers, counselees—more hours than is healthy. All parties may be vulnerable. Proactive measures to prevent unwarranted bonding are essential. Regarding the pastor and women, follow an important principle to the letter: respect the *space* of each individual, and maintain appropriate *distance* in every setting and situation. Further refined, this principle for relationships with women is nonnegotiable.

Principle: Intimacy takes many forms. Unchecked closeness may lead to illicit bonding. Keeping relationships professional by guaranteeing *space* and maintaining *distance* will assist all parties in a ministry situation to be discreet and to fulfill their respective callings to the Lord's mission.

The importance of *space* and *distance* both owned and respected by all parties cannot be overemphasized. The pastor and a woman have separate domains. Let there be his and her *space.* Let there be *distance*—physical and emotional!

A young married woman admires her pastor. She is a Christian, and she requests time weekly in his office when the two may study the Bible together. Soon it is apparent that she is missing much in her marriage, and she welcomes a close and developing relationship with her pastor. Does he see the pitfall? In other venues, a pastor will not spend private time with women—for example, lunch hours, breaks in schedule at local coffee shops, travel, brief trips in town. Office conversations attend to business only. Unless the matter is acutely personal and private, the pastor leaves the door ajar when meeting women in his office. When a pastor is attracted to a woman, or discovers that she is attracted to him, the cardinal principle of *discretion* dictates changes in circumstances that will deter bonding and maintain both *space* and *distance.* It is noteworthy that when working with women, the pastor's best protection against indiscretion is his own happy and healthy marriage.

The Pastor and Brother Pastors

Cultivating the Brotherhood

Pastoral relationships extend to brother pastors. Unfortunately, these relationships are often weak. Distrust among pastors is common. A fractured collegium of pastors is a scandal of first order in the Church. Pastors of the same confession often will not take Communion together. Websites and blogs become the arena for pastors to bludgeon their fellows. It was our Lord who chided His disciples over their aspirations to greatness (Mark 9:33–37), and that was taken to heart by the apostle Paul, who counseled, "If possible, so far as it depends on you, live peaceably with all" (Rom 12:18). These rubrics are offered for pastors and their brothers:

1. Recognize and celebrate commonalities in faith and confession.
2. Discern a brother's struggles, and offer empathic listening.
3. Respect a brother's ministry, and counsel patiently regarding false doctrine or practice.
4. Engage the graces of civility and courtesy when addressing a fellow pastor.
5. Address issues, not persons or personality traits.
6. Avoid cornering, labeling, or stereotyping.
7. In unresolved disagreement, move on.
8. Keep informed about controversy from reliable sources.
9. Avoid fixating on controversy.
10. Stay wary of submovements and groups.

For all pastors caught up in conflict, daily reading and rereading of Romans 6 and 12 for one month may bring some relief and restore the will to be charitable with one another.

Admonishing Pastors

A pastor sins, and his indiscretion goes public. Then brother pastors rally and minister to him, according to Matthew 18:15–18, so that repentance may be met with the Absolution. The sin may be false teaching or leading an ungodly life; and Galatians 6:1 directs admonishment as care in other instances: severity to a point that a pastor is destroying a congregation, loveless response to expressed need, faulty work habits that draw criticism, abrasive speech or rude behavior, blatant insensitivity, a complex verging on paranoia, seeking conflict, neglect of duty, and the like.

When a pastor exhibits negative conduct, caring brother pastors counsel him—in private. Care does not begin with a tribunal of sorts. One brother pastor initially counsels the erring one; next, a group of pastors meet with him; finally, jurisdictional church officials—that is, district presidents or diocesan bishops—admonish in the face of nonrepentance. Delay in these matters and overextending the process is unconscionable. Lengthy proceedings only invite stonewalling.

Furthermore, useless dallying also invites interference. Ecclesiastical tabloids may take advantage of delay and create their own prosecution, jury, and judgment against the erring pastor. Truly, they must give account. Did they counsel with the erring pastor one-on-one prior to exposing his indiscretion publicly? Did they inquire with those who have been caring for the erring pastor and follow their guidance before going public with the matter? Did they allow for the patient but timely care afforded the erring one by brother pastors as outlined above? Short of responsible answers to these questions, interference in care for a pastor is improper.[106]

The Pastor and Conflict

Critics and Criticism

Public accusations against a pastor will only encourage critics in his own congregation. Observe how persons and families who initially befriended the pastor become his most severe critics years later. It happens. Misguided congregants seek to control the pastor. They are like little dogs snapping at the ankles. Always something is wrong, and who is to blame? The pastor is the culprit, of course.

While indeed, it is a hard reality that a pastor's misconduct brings on criticism, and he must deal with this factor, the constant and faithful pastor is also vulnerable, and he is wise to listen to and evaluate criticism. If there is any truth to the critique, he adjusts and corrects. He removes causes for unfavorable comments about himself or his ministry. The point is, a pastor confronts all criticism, constructive and nonconstructive. He learns, adjusts, and grows, but he shall not become a doormat for critics to walk over. To passively take criticism like a beating, lying down, is to lose. To overreact and fight is to lose. To learn from criticism is the winning strategy.

Handling Criticism

A pastor's worth is not measured by the criticism he receives. Still, we have no mandate to put down every unfair and unjust criticism (cf. Rom 12:9, 17, 19). We do have the opportunity to handle criticism in a constructive manner. A number of positive responses are available:

1. Consider both the nature of criticism and its source.

---

106 When a pastor's public error must be censored in order to protect the community of faith (cf. 1 Tim 5:20), responsible officials handle the matter. However, they shall not be upstaged by clawing journalists. Certainly, observe how the prophets excoriated errant priests in Jerusalem (Zeph 3:4; cf. Ezek 22:26). St. Paul publicly rebuked Peter, who flirted with Judaizing (Gal 2:11–16; cf. 1 Tim 5:19–20). Our Lord confronted the money changers in the temple and on many occasions countered the Pharisees and the scribes, the chief priests, and the Sadducees in public (cf. John 2:13–22). Church officials have a major task to counsel erring pastors with dispatch.

2. Dialogue with the critic. "Friend, I hear that you have some concerns."

3. Listen. Seek clarification. "Do I understand you correctly? Did I say that? Is that what you heard?"

4. Show the critic respect and frame a nonthreatening platform for conversation; then state your position. "This is where I am on the issue. This is where I stand. This is my thinking. This is what I believe can be done. I think that we should proceed in this manner. What do you think?"

5. Diffuse emotion. "Friend, I can see why you would say that. I see where you are coming from. I understand your strong feelings."

6. In the course of the conversation, be alert to points of agreement. "Friend, it is well that we discovered a point on which we both agree. This is a start."

7. Show genuine empathy, assuring the person, "Well, I am certainly going to take this matter seriously. I shall think about what you have said and I will give it attention. Can we talk again soon?"

8. Remain teachable. At the right time in the conversation, comment, "I have learned much from our dialogue. I thank you for insights shared today. You have given me much to think about."

9. If the conversation turns ugly and the critic lashes out, call a halt to the person's reaction. Set boundaries. Be firm. Draw a line. "We may have an animated and spirited discussion, but neither you nor I shall resort to verbal abuse."

10. Close the dialogue on a note of Christian love and pastoral concern. "Shall we talk again? Yes. Before we part today, can we pray about this matter and pray for each other?"

Admonishing Antagonists

A more formidable challenge to the pastor is the antagonist. Critics look for something wrong in the pastor's ministry. Usually, however, they still acknowledge that he is their pastor. Antagonists intentionally destroy the pastor and his ministry. We cannot be in denial about antagonists. The reality is, they infect congregations. The drubbing they inflict on the pastor is draining and debilitating. Pastors internalize the oppression, and their ministry suffers.

At a forum for pastors of large churches across numerous denominations, a young but capable pastor from a southern city related that less than two weeks into his ministry to a prestigious congregation, he was invited to lunch by a prominent member of the church who was a powerful CEO of a national corporation. In the course of the conversation at lunch, this member announced, "Pastor, I did not want you to accept the Call to our church, and I want you to know that I am determined to marshal all the resources available to force you out of the pastorate of this church as soon as possible." Observe, long before the pastor's ministry was up and running, this man intended to attack the pastor. He was an antagonist. Such antagonists are members of Christian congregations. They worship and commune at the Lord's Table while pursuing their designs against the pastor. Some analysts call them sociopaths.[107] Their actions are evil.

The pastor in an antagonist's cross hairs may seek help. There is no help. He faces this trouble alone. Church officials do not want to be involved. Good persons in the congregation who normally support the pastor are intimidated by the ferocity of the antagonist. What shall a pastor do? Although he cannot avoid conflict with antagonists, the pastor will not engage in their vitriol. He seeks peace. "Strive for peace with everyone," the apostle Paul counsels (Heb 12:14a).

But the pastor must act, and admonishment is the starting point in his difficult ministry to vicious persons. The antagonist is sinning. He abuses the pastor when he should honor him as a shepherd in the Lord (1 Thess 5:12–13; 1 Tim 5:17; Heb 13:17, especially 17b). The antagonist shows hatred for the pastor, and he dishonors the pastoral office. These are blatant sins (Matt 5:22; 1 John 3:15; cf. 2 Tim 4:14–15). The antagonist's tirades offend against the Fifth Commandment by hurting and harming the pastor and his family. The antagonist's untrue statements break the Eighth Commandment.

When ministering to the antagonist, the pastor takes the initiative and brings the sin forward. He arranges to meet with the person in his office. The pastor may include church elders or spiritual persons who are prepared to support the admonishment the pastor gives. The meeting begins with prayer, followed by frank confrontation of the sin of abusing the pastor. In addition, the pastor addresses the antagonist's actions that fracture the bond of Chris-

107 Two authorities on the subject of antagonists pitted against the Christian pastor are Lloyd G. Rediger and Kenneth C. Haugk. See Kenneth C. Haugk, *Antagonists in the Church: How to Identify and Deal with Destructive Conflict* (Minneapolis: Augsburg Publishing House, 1988). Also see Lloyd G. Rediger, *Clergy Killers: Guidance for Pastors and Congregations under Attack* (Louisville, KY: Westminster John Knox Press, 1997). Preceding Rediger's book are two articles he authored, addressing this phenomenon: "Clergy Killers," *The Clergy Journal* (August 1993): 7–10 and "Beyond the Clergy Killer Phenomenon," *The Clergy Journal* (August 1995): 19–24.

tian love holding the congregation together under one Lord, who loved us and gave Himself for us[108] (Gal 2:20; 3:26–28; 1 John 4:7–9; Eph 4:32; 5:1–2; 1 Cor 13:4–6; 14:1a; 16:14). The pastor directs words to the antagonist. "The proper care for you, friend—and that is what this meeting is about—is the Church's discipline, which begins with seeing the sin for what it is and proceeding to call for repentance in order that forgiveness may be given (Matt 18:15–18; Gal 6:1–2; Luke 17:3). It is the Lord's way."

Frank confrontation with the sin and the sinner likely will be met by the antagonist with indifference or anger that plays out in ranting and raving. The judging Word he will not hear. The Gospel Word, therefore, is thwarted; and forgone at this point is the forgiveness so needed by the antagonist. The pastor contains his emotions, holds in check displeasure, hurt, and anger in the spirit of the apostle Paul's exhortation "Bless those who persecute you; bless and do not curse them" (Rom 12:14; cf. 1 Cor 4:12b). The pastor does not chide, scold, threaten, strive, or argue. Pointedly, he holds before the antagonist the duty to honor and respect pastors, yes, his pastor (Heb 13:7; 1 Thess 5:12–13; 1 Tim 5:17). The pastor cautions, "This you are not doing. Your lack of respect, your abuse of the pastor, are actions well known to the congregation. Now, the best course for you is to repent of your sins, receive forgiveness in Jesus' name, and then turn away from the sin; yes, cease and desist from words and actions designed to hurt and destroy."

If the situation turns explosive, the pastor eases and waits for the moment to meet the angry resistance with a word of judgment, which can be final, that is to say, the last word this pastor shall have with this antagonist (Titus 3:10–11; cf. 2 Tim 4:14–15). This is tragic, but the intransigence comes to this final admonition. The pastor speaks, "These words of admonishment and grace I have offered. You refuse them. Now, lest you continue in your ways and place yourself in the unenviable position of individuals who dared to abuse the Lord's men in earlier times, I urge you to note the punishment that came to Gehazi, who dared to lie to the prophet Elisha (2 Kgs 5:20–27). The leprosy that was Naaman's disease befell this wicked servant, Gehazi. Note also that open and public defiance of the Lord's servant Moses cost the houses of Korah, Dathan, and Abiram great loss of life and goods (Num 16:1–35). Please recall that the priest of Bethel, Amaziah, rejected Amos the prophet at great peril (Amos 7:10–11). The prophet responded with a fierce message from the Lord: the wife of Amaziah would become a harlot, his sons would fall by the sword, and Amaziah himself would die in an unclean land (Amos 7:17). Note also that the false

108 The pastor must have concrete evidence of the antagonist's evil designs, corroborated by people in the congregation.

prophet Hananiah publicly defied the prophet Jeremiah, an action of rebellion against the Lord (Jer 28:10–11, 16). Do you remember what happened? In the seventh month of the same year, 'the prophet Hananiah died' (Jer 28:17b). Add to these accounts the fate of Ananias and Sapphira, who lied to the apostles and to the Holy Spirit, and to the Church at Jerusalem (Acts 5:1–11). Friend, think about God's dealing with abuse of His servants."

The pastor puts before the antagonist signs, vivid and sobering accounts of God's vindication of His abused prophets and apostles. If this counsel from the Scriptures meets rejection, if pastoral care in this matter is met with more hostile and belligerent resistance, the pastor has no other option than to administer the *minor ban*, refusing to give the Lord's Supper to this antagonist. He issues this ban upon consultation with the church elders. The ban continues until the antagonist shows that he is repentant. In the event of an explosive reaction to this disciplinary step, the pastor shall report the antagonist's threats to the congregation's leaders, the elders, and possibly to the civil authorities.

Surviving Confrontation with Antagonists

How shall a pastor survive the onslaught of the antagonist? He seeks the high ground. He follows in the steps of the ancient prophets. This means that he stands up and walks away. The pastor does this symbolically and in real motion. When the antagonist rejects the Law and Gospel ministry of care, the pastor goes his way. This response has sound support. Confronting the violent action of Hananiah against him, "Jeremiah the prophet went his way" (Jer 28:11b). The matter was entirely in the hands of Yahweh. Let it be! Yahweh's action affirmed the word of His prophet Jeremiah. Similarly, the rebuffed pastor goes his way, confident that the Lord stands by him and his family.

The pastor steadies the course. He turns to serious public ministry, no longer distracted by the onslaught. He attends more faithfully to preaching and teaching and caring for the congregation. He carries on, and he assures his family that the Lord cares for them, as He has stood by His servants in every age and generation (Dan 6:6–28; Matt 10:16–23; 2 Tim 4:17–18; 2 Cor 11:23–33; 12:9–10, 19). The pastor prays for the antagonist, but he commits all into the Lord's hands. The Lord will attend to the matter.

Satan is powerful. His henchman, the antagonist, instead of repenting and respecting the pastor and his office, may redouble his efforts to abuse and destroy the pastor. The resources and initiatives to deter the antagonist's damage and destruction are lacking. The evil rages on. Then, the pastor who has stood and gone his way shall go yet farther. He seeks a Call, and he ***leaves***! The pastor's departure is properly a testimony against antagonists and their hostility to the

Word-driven pastoral care that he has attempted to administer (Matt 10:14; Luke 9:5; 10:10–11; Acts 13:51). Furthermore, to remain in this pastorate and struggle with the temptation to duke it out with a person who determines to remain hostile is poor stewardship of a pastor's education, training, and experience, as well as life itself. The pastor's gifts and abilities are too valuable to suffer continued abuse that diminishes and stultifies. The better course, the wise and honorable course, is to leave and take up another ministry. Surely the Lord of the Church shall provide.

CHAPTER FIVE

The Pastor—Missionary and Leader

The Missional Pastor, the Missional Congregation

The Missional Pastor

The Missional Pastor Seeks Prospects for the Christian Faith

The pastor of a start-up Lutheran mission in a new Twin Cities suburb was alert to young families moving to the area. U-Haul trucks and larger vans arrived daily. Before the newcomers could unload their belongings, the pastor was there, extending a warm welcome. He invited them to visit the mission. He witnessed to the purpose of his flock, namely, to believe and to help others toward faith in Christ Jesus and life in Him, the best living in the suburbs of Minneapolis/St. Paul, Minnesota. His name was Paul James Pfotenhauer, and he was an outstanding *missional* pastor.

Mission and the Office of the Holy Ministry

Many pastors would not track vans and trailers to welcome newcomers. Foolish excuses about evangelism prevail, such as "I'm too busy. It is not my calling. Let the laity evangelize. Besides, the Church has the Gospel. If outsiders want it, they can come and get it." These excuses fall apart in the light of the apostle Paul's word to pastors, "Do the work of an evangelist" (2 Tim 4:5). And the next phrase, "fulfill your ministry," suggests that the Office of the Ministry is indeed *missional*. The first occupants of the office under Jesus were apostles, missionaries (Matt 10:1–11; cf. Luke 5:1–11; 10:1–12). They were the *sent* ones, fishers of men. All who follow in their train are in part the Father's answer to Jesus' petition "Pray earnestly to the Lord of the harvest to send out laborers into His harvest" (Matt 9:38: Luke 10:2).

Principle: Pastors are missionaries who search for the lost with the Gospel of Jesus Christ while they fulfill their ministry to the saved.

Reversing Hesitance in Mission Work

The Office of the Ministry is *missional* as surely as it is *dominical* and *apostolic*. The disciplines of the office—preaching the Gospel, baptizing, teaching—are inherently *missional*. Early, the office and mission were perceived distinct and separate, a cleavage that still affects ecclesiastical thinking today. It is telling, however, that the Spirit countered this misperception mightily. The Pentecost event was exploding mission (Acts 2). Before Peter could be too comfortable in Jerusalem, the Holy Spirit sent him to Caesarea, where Cornelius and his friends implored him to tell them all that the Lord had commanded (Acts 10:33).

As the apostles were engaged in mission (Acts 8:14), pastors today should resist any inclination to retreat from mission work or ignore people in their community who have not heard the Gospel of Jesus Christ.[109] Instead, pastors leave their comfort zone and take action when the Spirit opens doors to individuals and families waiting for a Christian to ask, invite, and then tell them about Jesus Christ. Pastors are prepared to say to the unchurched, "Friend, do you know what you have been waiting for? Do you know the quest of your heart after peace with God? Jesus answers that quest. Let me tell you more about Him."

The Missional Congregation

Many congregations conveniently leave mission work to the pastor. "This is why we pay him," they say. How does a pastor reverse this attitude and help Christians to become a *missional* congregation? He begins by looking down an open road. When they assign mission to him, he goes for it. The pastor's initiative to preach and to teach the Gospel to unchurched persons will not go unnoticed. So he employs his prime tool for mission, the pastor's class, which hosts newcomers to instruction in the doctrines of the Christian faith—creation to eschatology and all the doctrines between. The class meets on the church premises or in rented quarters of a community library, for instance—any setting that is cordial and nonthreatening. This class leads inquirers into the Holy Scriptures, which are able to make them wise unto salvation through faith in Jesus Christ[110] (2 Tim 3:14–17). Expectantly, the Word of the Lord grows, and

109 Retiring from active parish ministry, a pastor and his wife relocated in a suburb of a major city. They settled in their home, but did not relate to neighbors on a first-name basis. Familiarity was generally avoided in the neighborhood. Across the street and down a half-block, a mother and daughter resided and kept to themselves. The mother died, and the daughter was in ill health. The pastor and his wife learned of her condition only second hand. Two years later, the daughter died. To this day, the pastor regrets that he did not take the initiative to visit this person, befriend her, and share the Gospel—a mission opportunity missed. *Kyrie eleison!*

110 Dr. Guido Merkens exhausted the mission possibilities of the pastor's adult class at Concordia Lutheran Church, San Antonio, Texas. His class was so renowned that as a young pastor, Merkens returned

conversions occur in these classes. Luther stated that the property of Christ grows and increases.[111] When candidates for Baptism or confirmation emerge from the pastor's class openly rejoicing, some *old* Christians will take notice. They will assist the pastor in gathering unchurched persons for future classes.

Mission as Teaching

The pastor's class is a prime example of mission by teaching (Matt 28:20). The Lord's commission to teach followed His own ministry: "And He went about among the villages teaching" (Mark 6:6b; cf. Mark 2:13; 4:1). After Pentecost, the Early Church was staunch in the teaching of the apostles. Converts received the apostolic teaching as the teaching of the Lord (cf. Acts 2:42). In *Missionary Methods: St. Paul's or Ours?*, Roland Allen observes that the apostle Paul's missionary work was strategically focused within great urban centers of the first-century world, and he conducted classes in synagogues or in the homes of recent converts.[112] The apostolic model shows that teaching is a priority in the congregation's mission. The pastor's class, a teaching ministry, is a vital arm of that mission.

The Missional Pastor as Leader

The Debate over Pastoral Leadership

The pastor is *missional.* Is there biblical support for his role as a leader? Does he have a call to *lead*? Many congregations expect dynamic leadership from their pastor. District or diocesan officials often assert the same expectation. Among pastors, however, the debate over pastoral leadership divides along two distinct lines. Put in radical terms, one pastor states, "I don't have to lead. I won't lead." Another pastor opposes and states, "I lead, and this is who I am, this is what I do."

Numerous pastors would settle if the push for them to be *leaders* had not surfaced in recent decades. For them, initiatives to lead are distractions from vital Word-and-Sacrament ministry. In their view, there is nothing in either the office or the divine Call that mandates *leadership*. They are convinced that

to his *alma mater*, Concordia Seminary, in the early 1960s and presented to an alumni gathering of two hundred-plus pastors his design and development of the pastor's class as a prime mission ministry of his growing congregation.

111 Martin Luther, *Lectures on Titus* (LW 29:23).

112 Roland Allen, *Missionary Methods: St. Paul's or Ours?* (Grand Rapids: Wm. B. Eerdmans; fifth printing, 1969), 16–17, 23. Allen is forceful in his assertion that St. Paul did not gather congregations. He planted churches, and he did not leave a church until it was fully equipped with orders of ministry, sacraments, and tradition. See *Missionary Methods: St. Paul's or Ours?*, 5. We observe that Paul's sustained time with churches he planted was given to teaching and teaching and teaching (Acts 14:3; 15:35; 16:12b; 17:2, 14; 18:3–4, 7, 11, 18; 19:8, 10; 28:23)!

this new role, *leader*, with accompanying expectations, was dragged into the Church from the corporate world. They want none of it, and they maintain that faithfulness is the Lord's mandate, nothing more.

Pastors in the opposing camp aspire to be dynamic leaders. They seek conferences, workshops, and institutes that help them acquire leadership skills because they may feel deficient in these skills. Many say that their theological education did not train them to be leaders, even though some seminaries have introduced courses in pastoral leadership. Moreover, these pastors find nothing in the Scriptures contrary to their aspirations to be effective leaders of their congregations' ministries. For these pastors, leadership is an absolute; they cannot be faithful in the Gospel ministry except as leaders.

The Pastor as Leader

Pastoral Leadership—A Priority

We cannot settle this debate. Cautiously, we take a position. There is no question, Word-and-Sacrament ministry is the core of the pastoral task, but this public ministry also involves the mission of the Church. For this priority, pastoral leadership is a must. There is truth in the assessment that pastoral leadership is crucial for productive congregational life and ministry. What the Church is (identity), what the Church is about (mission), how the Church functions (ministry) are matters of pastoral leadership. Either a Christian congregation is proactive—moving forward with mission and ministry—or reactive, with energies spent on conserving and preserving. There is a difference, and that difference simply may be pastoral leadership.

Clearing Misunderstanding about Pastoral Leadership

Pastoral leadership seeks support from biblical theology, but leaders find few specific teachings about leadership in the Bible. If chapter and verse are in short supply, consider the powerful narratives about leadership—Moses leading the people, the Judges, Samuel, and kings David and Solomon—all stories about leaders. The Gospels portray Jesus Christ as a leader. The apostles also exhibited leadership.

These sentiments will be challenged by pastors who are convinced that the Office of the Ministry, *iure divino*, by divine law, does not in any way accommodate the role of *leader*. They consider leadership only *iure humano*, by human law. Theologians who covet the ministerial use of reason, however, should observe that there is legitimate use of instrumentality—human assets—in the cause of the Gospel. It is not trivial that Jesus engaged the disciples to distribute the loaves and fishes to feed the multitudes and later gather up the leftovers (Matt 14:15–21; Mark 6:35–44; Luke 9:12–17; John 6:5–14).

Confusion reigns over leadership when a congregation calls a new pastor. Shall their Call include a mandate that the pastor be a dynamic leader? Here, the distinction we have used consistently must prevail. The Call, *iure divino*, that is, according to the Scriptures and described by the Lutheran Confessions, is a Call to preach and teach the Gospel in its purity according to the Scriptures, administer the Sacraments as Christ instituted them, and give Absolution (AC V). Still, a congregation may supplement the Call, stating needs that require *iure humano*, pastoral passion and skill to lead the congregation in its mission and ministries. Every ordained pastor is fit and able to execute the pastoral office. Can every pastor lead? Some manage well, but management and leadership require a separate set of skills.[113]

Management is large in the pastor's work with the congregation. Administering various ministries and attending to multiple details is important. Leadership, however, relates people to the big picture with an end in view. It attends to motivation and involvement of people in ministry. Leadership is buoyant, enlisting ordinary people to accomplish extraordinary things. Leadership brings out the potential of others, develops their talents, and helps them to transcend difficulties. With optimism for the future, leadership believes in the capacity of others, strengthens their wills, and supplies the means to achieve.[114] These skills are useful to the pastor as leader.

Biblical Leadership Roles

The pastor as leader is conscious of biblical roles composing pastoral leadership, and he practices them. It may prove futile to construct correspondence between corporate leadership skills and biblical roles, though some observe qualities of the modern leader in the notion of *ruling*[115] (1 Tim 5:17). More

113 James Anderson distinguishes in this manner. In the congregation, management pertains to a broad range of functions, such as planning, organizing, and administering. Leadership more narrowly involves human factors of influencing others to achieve desired ends. James D. Anderson, *To Come Alive: New Proposal for Revitalizing the Church* (New York: Harper & Row, 1973), 45.

114 James M. Kouzes and Barry Z. Posner, *The Leadership Challenge*, 3rd ed. (San Francisco: Jossey-Bass, 2004), 398.

115 Reading 1 Timothy 5:17, the verb in the phrase "Let the elders who rule" is a participle of προίστημι, a verb whose usage in the New Testament principally reflects the meaning "to manage and to guide," in the sense of caring for, possibly suggesting pastoral care (cf. 1 Thess 5:12–13; Heb 13:17). Somewhat parallel to this usage is the notion of administering by leadership the company of the faithful. The notion of *ruling* as guiding, thus leading, is not out of the question. With reference to the bishop or pastor, we read, "For if someone does not know how to manage (*προιστηναι*) his own household, how will he care (*επιμελήσεται*) for God's church?" (1 Tim 3:5). Here, then, "to rule," concludes Bo Reicke, is the same as "to take care of" (cf. Rom 12:8, "the one who leads [gives aid], with zeal"). Also see the exhortation to deacons in 1 Timothy 3:12, where the deacon as head of his household is not given to exercise of power, but to oversight as care for his family. But A. Harnack argues that the term is a reference to real office bearers. Consult *Theological*

often than not, the biblical roles combine leadership with aspects of pastoral care. Consider five roles that are prominent in the Scriptures, roles that place *pastor* and *leader* in a complementary and interactive relationship.

The role of ***bishop***—the ἐπίσκοπος, the overseer—connotes leadership as well as care for Christians and their spiritual life. This term and its synonym, πρεσβύτερος, elder, signify responsibility for others with authority given by the Holy Spirit (Acts 20:28). Specifically, the bishop was designated to oversee the doctrine and life of the Christian fellowship. Proper oversight of teaching is implied in Titus 1:9; 1 Timothy 4:11; 6:3; cf. 2 Timothy 4:3–4. Also, the apostle Paul asserts oversight of the Christian life in 1 Thessalonians 4:1–7, 9–12. Discover the bishop as leader in the authority and actions of the apostles and elders in Jerusalem who took charge, made decisions, exercised spiritual judgment, and commissioned qualified persons for mission and ministry (Acts 15:2, 6, 13, 19, 22–23; 16:4; 21:18–19). Similarly, bishops as leaders oversaw the ministries of other first-century congregations (Acts 14:23; 1 Tim 5:17; Titus 1:5–9).

The ***shepherd***, ποιμήν—provider, protector, and caretaker—is as ancient as Joshua's calling (Num 27:16–23). Clearly, the shepherd is indispensable for the sheep (Num 27:17b; cf. Jer 23:4; Matt 9:36; John 10:11, 14, 27–29). A shepherd leads. He knows where the flock should go. And a pastor directs his flock by the Word that he interprets, proclaims, and teaches. By this same Word, he exhorts the flock to be Christ's people. Leadership is said to be an affair of the heart. More, it is an affair of the shepherd's entire life (John 10:15b). The pastor dedicates his life to the spiritual welfare of the flock. The people are in his thinking, and each person with his or her spiritual need is in his prayers.

The ***priest***, כֹּהֵן, from the cognate verb כּוּן, to stand, signifies another leadership role. As priest, the pastor leads when he assembles the congregation for worship in the name of the Holy Trinity. He positions the congregation to stand and serve in the presence of God. Ahead, in front of pastor and people, stands Jesus Christ as priest. Specifically, by His atoning sacrifice on the cross for sin before God and supplying to us God's grace, mercy, and the forgiveness of sins, Jesus secures our place before God (Heb 9:11–28; 10:11–18). Therefore, within the holy place, the sanctuary—church, chancel, altar—the pastor causes the people to stand before God in order to receive from Him all that He gives in the Word and the Sacraments. The pastor draws them forward, and they yield to God praise and thanksgiving expressed by their very lives in these moments of public worship. In the presence of God, the pastor serves as priest awaiting God's blessing upon the people (Num 6:22–27; cf. Zech 3:6–7; Ezek 44:14). He

Dictionary of the New Testament vol. 6, ed. Gerhard Friedrich, ed. and trans. Geoffrey W. Bromiley (Grand Rapids: Wm. B. Eerdmans, 1968), 701.

instills in the people reverence, a proper sense of the holy when they are in this place where God proclaims His Word and gives His holy gifts (cf. Ezek 44:23).

Moreover, the church lives by nurture from the Word of God (Ps 119:103; Matt 7:24; 11:28; John 5:24; 8:31–32). The pastor's role as ***prophet***, נָבִיא, is that of a leader who exercises this ministry of nurture in preaching and teaching. The Word of the Lord came to the prophet (Jer 1:4; cf. Jer 1:7, 9b, 11a). And the prophet declares as did Amos, "Thus says the LORD" (Amos 7:17). The ancient prophet was gifted with *seeing* or *apprehending* that which is not normally accessible.[116] He was a seer, who saw and then spoke what God revealed, a Word that was not always smooth and pleasing (Isa 30:10). The Word of God engages the pastor and equips him to be a κηρυξ, a herald, a preacher (1 Tim 2:7; 2 Tim 1:11; cf. Acts 20:25ff.; 28:30–31). He brings a Word of judgment that causes pain and anguish over sin and guilt, but he also brings a Word that seals to the people the grace, mercy, and peace of God in Christ Jesus. Always, it is the Word that the Spirit teaches (1 Cor 2:13).

Closely related to prophet is the role of ***watchman***, צֹפֶה or שֹׁמֵר. The ancient watchman was a sentry, normally poised atop the city wall. He watched over fields, lands, vineyards. He was the security guard who notified the king's armored guard if an enemy encroached by night (2 Sam 18:24–25; Jer 51:12). Congregations seek a pastor who is a leader, a visionary, a motivator, an energizer. Just as important, the pastor is a keeper, commissioned to shout warning and secure the safety of God's people (Isa 21:6; Jer 6:17; Ezek 3:17; cf. Isa 62:6). Pastors are alert to attacks from a secular culture without and from crippling attitudes within—apathy, lethargy, traditionalism. These thwart the Church's life and mission. The pastor as leader watches against negative forces for the people.

A leader of Christ's people, the pastor is a ***servant***, עֶבֶד, δοῦλος, διάκονος. He works to lead the Church fulfilling its mission under Christ. Humbled by his calling to serve "ourselves as your servants for Jesus' sake" (2 Cor 4:5), the pastor brings the Word and steps out of the way so that Christ may lead His Church. As a servant, the pastor is expendable (1 Cor 9:22–23). The Lord's mission is the priority, followed by satisfaction and contentment, blessings that accompany the pastor's calling as a servant of Christ.

---

116 Leadership, according to some experts, begins with belief in oneself. It is said that a leader listens within because leadership has everything to do with what we think of ourselves. But leadership in the Church has everything to do with listening to the Word of the Lord as it has come to us *via* His revelation to us. The role of the *prophet* is apprehending that Word and delivering it to the people as it applies to their mission and ministry. Leadership in this sense is revelatory as it is dominical. It is God-given and Spirit-shaped.

Conclusion

The pastor's vocation is that of a missionary in the name of Jesus. This is consistent with his Call to exercise the Office of the Holy Ministry. Complementing his calling as missionary is his role as leader of God's people, a multifaceted profile consisting of numerous roles: *bishop*, *priest*, *prophet*, *watchman*, and *servant*. The pastor utilizes these roles in his leadership of the congregation, whose priorities in ministry are *worship*, *witness*, *teaching*, *fellowship-care*, *service*, and *mission (growth)*.[117]

The pastoral ministry engages the people in these vital New Testament ministries by instruction, counsel, and direction from the Word of God. For example, the Lutheran colony in Perry County, Missouri, in 1839 was at sea with regard to its identity and purpose. The group floundered after Pastor Martin Stephan was separated from the colony. Stepping up were C. F. W. Walther and other pastors, who led the group back to confidence that they were Christ's Church with purpose and mission. How did Walther lead? He came forward with the clear teachings of the Scriptures about church and ministry. If we are indeed serious about the Church's mission—*worship, witness, teaching, fellowship-care, service,* and *mission (growth)*—we shall lead principally by the Scriptures.

117 These priorities are described in Appendix 3, "Priorities for New Testament Congregations."

CHAPTER SIX

The Pastor as Preacher

Introduction

The people in Judea flocked to hear the preacher, John, preparing hearts and pointing to the Messiah (Matt 3:5). People still come to hear from the Word of God delivered by their pastor. They listen, and they want to hear Jesus (Luke 10:16a). When calling a pastor, congregations prioritize their wants and needs:

1. Preaching
2. Preaching
3. Preaching

God owns the same priorities. He pressed Amos, "Go, prophesy to My people Israel" (Amos 7:15). Jesus' first act of ministry was that He came proclaiming the Gospel of God (Mark 1:14). He exhorts pastors, "And proclaim as you go" (Matt 10:7). The Lord was intentional with His preaching, and He seeks pastors who will go and preach intentionally, who are not lethargic or nonchalant, who prepare well for preaching, men for whom the greatest woe must be to not speak the Good News of Jesus Christ and declare the whole counsel of God (1 Cor 9:16; Acts 20:27).

The Textual Sermon

As you go, preach the Gospel of Jesus Christ according to the Scriptures. Yes, preach the Gospel of the crucified and risen Lord (1 Cor 2:1–5; 15:1–4). Preachers proclaim the Gospel as they have heard God speaking to them, and the speaking of the Spirit is by the text of the Holy Scriptures (2 Pet 1:20–21; cf. 1 Pet 1:10–12). To preach the one and only Gospel, the Scripture text is foundational. There is time and opportunity for topical preaching, which can be biblical and Gospel centered. Still, there is strength in the sermon that arises from a text of Scripture and conveys the Gospel according to the uniqueness of that text.

Devotion to the Task of Preaching

In this age, multiple pastoral tasks demand attention, and the work of preaching receives less of the pastor's energy. Pastors attest tongue in cheek that their sermon preparation receives at best five or six hours a week. How may pastors recover preaching as their principal task? Have we vision for preaching? Are we devoted to preaching the Word of God with the expectation that our best efforts serve the Spirit, who works in the hearts and lives of people? Do our sermons ring true with sober honesty about the ravages of sin? Is there clarity about the forgiveness of sin through Christ, of reconciling sinners to God (2 Cor 5:19–20)? Is our preaching a fit tool for the Holy Spirit to strengthen the congregation in their confession of faith in Jesus Christ? Does our preaching show from Holy Scripture how God declares His grace in a variety of ways? Does the congregation's knowledge of the Bible and comprehension of God's Word increase over the years of our pulpit ministry? We observe that preaching, which serves Christians over the long term, commands prime investment of the pastor's time and life.

To paraphrase Dietrich Bonhoeffer, we are speaking about the cost of discipleship as a preacher of the Gospel. Expectantly, the cost for such total effort is incalculable! Not a quickly packaged bundle of random theological thoughts scraped together on Saturday night, the sermon that the pastor takes to the pulpit to deliver is the Word studied, pondered, and absorbed the days and nights from his rising on Monday morning toward next Sunday, with all of his thoughts and emotions pointed to the preaching moment.[118] Finally, a pastor abandons multitasking. He directs time and energy to the work of preaching, much like Joseph Parker, the London divine who resolved, "This one thing I do!" Does a pastor dare to make such a determination? Shall he organize life and work in order to commit major resources to preaching?[119] Dr. Lloyd Ogilvie practiced total dedication to the preaching task. Monday and Tuesday, or Tuesday and Wednesday, then Saturday, he worked on the sermon for Sunday and nothing else. He explained that preparation for Sunday takes three full days of the week. Either you take them as full days, half-days, whatever, but we do not get by with fewer than three days.[120]

---

118 John Killinger, *The Centrality of Preaching in the Total Task of the Ministry* (Waco, TX: Word Books, 1969), 29.

119 Attributed to Harry Emerson Fosdick, formerly of Riverside Church in New York, is this formula: one hour of study and preparation for every minute of preaching from the pulpit. Reportedly, Prime Minister Winston Churchill employed the same formula, spending one hour of preparation for every minute of his radio broadcasts to the people of Britain during World War II.

120 Lloyd Ogilvie. Remarks made in a presentation at a preaching conference hosted by the Methodist Diocese of Southern Illinois at St. Matthew Methodist Church, Belleville, Illinois.

Ogilvie is frank to remind that devotion to thorough preparation for preaching is absolute in its demands. Nothing else dare interfere. Taking the risk to pursue such singular devotion to preparation, a pastor will discover that things fall into place. Homiletician John Killinger observed that pastors who give themselves with devotion to this one task of preaching are generally successful in multiple areas of their ministries, and those who do not focus prime energies on preaching tend to be frustrated and discouraged and fearful that the house is falling in on them.[121] In the thicket and tangle of so many claims upon pastors, in the midst of the confusion, the best thing a pastor can do is to make preaching the center of his life and work. The primacy and priority of preaching will introduce order into the chaos of a man's ministry.[122]

Preaching with Conviction

Well-prepared preaching rings true and vibrant for the preacher himself. Conversely, nothing dismantles preaching like a sermon served as cold leftovers. St. Paul believed what he preached, and he proclaimed in the manner of his believing (cf. Acts 20:24). Though the sermon text is clear, the doctrine orthodox, the preparation meticulous, the delivery articulate, if a preacher lacks conviction, all is for naught. John H. C. Fritz cited M. Reu, who observed that prior to delivering the Word of God to the congregation, that Word must have been received by the preacher in faith and have become wedded to his personality, producing in him a new life.[123] Reu comments, "Nevertheless it is true that the Word of God unfolds its inherent power in a very different manner when it is united with a living personality whom it has gripped in his inmost heart and from whose lips it pours as living testimony."[124] Internalizing the Word during sermon preparation is like J. S. Bach, who knew his Bible in his head and in his heart. "The genius given to him," according to one observer, "was to lift the biblical words off the printed page to be carried by music into the heads and hearts of those who listen to his words."[125]

Preaching benefits from fire in the belly, so to speak. That fire comes by the Spirit through the Word. Conviction and excitement happen through the entire process of preparing sermons: the study of the text, exegesis, focus on the purpose of the sermon, attending to outlining and arranging, followed by writing, rewriting, and fine-tuning. The preacher pauses frequently to pray for un-

---

121 John Killinger, *The Centrality of Preaching in the Total Task of the Ministry*, 28.

122 Ibid.

123 John H. C. Fritz, *Pastoral Theology* (St. Louis, MO: Concordia Publishing House, 1932), 82.

124 Ibid.

125 Advertisement posted for Bach at the Sem, Chapel of St. Timothy and St. Titus. Concordia Seminary, St. Louis, Missouri. January 2016.

derstanding of the Scripture text and for wisdom in arranging and composing a message. Literally, he prays up and out of the Word, and the Holy Spirit binds that Word to the preacher's heart for vigorous proclamation. Then he preaches the Gospel of Christ with power and conviction (cf. Rom 10:17). Lloyd Ogilvie reflects on preparation of the preacher for preaching: "Nothing can happen through us that does not happen in us!"

Text Selection and Attention to Content

That persistent and agonizing question "What shall I preach next Sunday?" is answered in the Lutheran tradition by the lectionary—Old Testament lesson, Epistle selection, and a reading from one of the four Gospels. This resource is ample, but the lectionary does not preclude free texts for sermons. So choose free texts that parallel the content of the lectionary lessons. Then branch out and engage free texts that speak to the preacher and hold the prospect of edifying the congregation. Discipline in free-text selection will prevent settling on texts that are not suited for the design and development of a sermon.[126] There are no spurious passages of Scripture, but we do not comprehend some passages. The pastor should not preach on any text that is unclear to him. Even some lectionary texts may escape his understanding. Then other texts will serve.

Preaching from the Scriptures encompasses doctrine, the teaching of the Christian faith. According to Dr. Martin Scharlemann, one of the fifteen steps in the study of a text leading to a central thought or theme for the sermon is to study the doctrines related to the text.[127] In the Lutheran tradition, preaching through a year will include every revealed doctrine of the Word of God, a sweeping program that comprises the whole counsel of God for salvation. Doctrines surface within texts from the lectionary. Free texts supplement. An occasional sermon series also serves well.

The content of the sermon includes preaching the Law and the Gospel (Jer 1:9–10). The Law exposes and condemns sin (Rom 7:7, 13). The Gospel shows Christ taking away sin in His own body at the cross (1 Pet 2:24; Col 2:13–14). Both teachings are present in the sermon, and the preacher proclaims them either from the text itself or from biblical texts and theology outside the preaching text. The Scriptures as a whole divide into content that is the Law and the Gospel. Therefore, biblical preaching, whatever the form or structure, declares the Law and proclaims the Gospel.[128]

---

126 For helpful criteria in selecting Scripture texts for preaching, see John A. Broadus, *On the Preparation and Delivery of Sermons*, Rev. Jesse Burton Weatherspoon (New York: Harper & Brothers, 1944), 18–23.

127 Appendix 1, "Fifteen Steps from Scripture Text to Central Thought."

128 The mandate to pursue the art of distinguishing between the Law and the Gospel in order to preach well is accented by C. F. W. Walther: "What is he [the preacher] to bring about by his preaching? Remember

Preaching to Controversial Issues

The Church in the world is a reality, and the gap between Christianity and American culture widens. Tensions between Christian and secular worldviews give rise to sensitive issues, many controversial. Shall preaching in the Church address these issues? Some pastors adopt a hands-off approach. They argue that New Testament preaching does not bring the public square into the Church. In their view, the pastor's calling is to nurture the flock of God, nothing else.

Conversely, other pastors recognize that Christians are inseparable from a culture where faith in God is waning. They cannot escape. Therefore, the Church's message should respond to belief systems and life practices that are contrary to the faith. Preaching in this manner supports Christians struggling in a secular culture.[129] How does a Christian live and confess in a time such as this? Hearing a sermon that intended to prepare a Christian for dying, a parishioner remarked after the worship service, "Pastor, I know how to die. What I really need is help to live."

Principle: Preaching that assists Christians to respond in the face of cultural developments contrary to the will of God is not an every Sunday venture, lest the Gospel be overshadowed by attention to the world. However, the Church's preaching ministry should provide a basis for Christian reflection and decision with regard to the secular program exhibited in government, the media, academia, the social network, and so forth.

A pastor may address issues such as abortion, same-sex marriage, church and state matters, and policies that threaten religious liberty. Venues other than the pulpit serve well—groups, classes, assemblies. When a sermon offers counsel, it clarifies issues. This is the approach: this is the issue, and this is what the Word of God teaches. Giving guidance about how to address officials and stating the Christian stance on issues is in order, but pastors shall not instruct congregations how to vote, nor direct votes to particular candidates (cf. AC XXVIII 12–17). They may encourage voting by Christian conscience.

---

that the preacher is supposed to shock secure souls who are asleep in sin. Next, his job is to lead those who have been shocked to faith. Next, he gives believers assurance of their state of grace and salvation. Next, he leads those who have become sure of their salvation to a life of sanctification. And last, he is to confirm those who are sanctified and to keep them in their holy and blessed state to the end. What a task!" C. F. W. Walther, *Law & Gospel: How to Read and Apply the Bible*, trans. Christian C. Tiews (St. Louis: Concordia Publishing House, 2010), 272.

129 Note that the prophets were not hesitant to publicly expose the excesses of wicked kings or rulers in Israel, Judah, and the nations (1 Kgs 18:17–18, 21; Isa 1:4–9; 3:13–17; 5:18–23; 13–23). How vivid are the oracles against Jerusalem and the nations (Jer 21:10; 22:11, 15, 17; 26:1–10, 11b; Isa 23–24; Amos 1:2–8; Mal 2:10–12)! In the New Testament, the apostle Paul cautioned readers in the churches he founded against the world in the grip of the princes and principalities of darkness (Gal 5:19–21; Eph 4:22–24; 6:10–13; 2 Thess 1:5–10).

Preaching as Communication

In preaching, which factor has priority? Is it the content, form, structure, and development of the sermon? Or is it the preacher as self and person? Certainly, both factors are paramount. Former Lutheran Hour speaker Dr. Dale A. Meyer emphasized the latter when he observed, "Preaching . . . is about us as much as it is about ministry." He qualified his statement carefully when he stated that preaching is not self-promotion. He went on to say, "However, preaching is about us, about you and about me in an individual way, because in preaching much of our private faith, our own encounter with Law and Gospel, becomes public."[130] The late Rev. Alton F. Wedel, former pastor of Mount Olive Lutheran Church in Minneapolis, Minnesota, advanced a similar point when he said, "There are three ingredients in vital preaching: well-practiced skills in biblical theology, intimate acquaintance with the facts of life, and a rich imagination that is able to connect the two."[131] More than steps toward getting the sermon, vital as they are, preaching as communication interacts with people. This initiative may involve an amount of introspection. A busy pastor considers his own personal disarray enough to focus on the human condition and deliver the Word of God that edifies the people.

Variety in Preaching

Variety in preaching promotes listening by the congregation. Varied accents in the Church Year, special days in the congregation's life, and specific needs within the fellowship are opportunities for healthy variety in preaching. By contrast, a rigid or lockstep regimen subdues interest in sermons. It is common practice, however, for Lutheran pastors to preach Sunday to Sunday using a single series of lectionary texts.[132] Are there portions of the Bible inadvertently overlooked in the lectionary series? We retain interest in preaching by occasionally selecting a variety of preaching texts from the Bible at large. Topical messages grounded in biblical theology also give variety. The nonfestival half of the Church Year is suited for varied preaching.

130 Dale A Meyer, "A Letter to Pastors of The Lutheran Church—Missouri Synod in Advent," sent from Lutheran Hour Ministries, St. Louis, Missouri, December 1995.

131 Alton F. Wedel, "Vital Preaching," *Entrée*, Campus Ministry Communications—National Lutheran Campus Ministry (December 1984): 4.

132 After years of using lectionary texts provided by the Inter-Lutheran Commission on Worship, a pastor may revisit older series of texts for the Church Year listed in works such as Paul W. Nesper, *Biblical Texts* (Columbus, OH: Wartburg Press, 1955) or *Sermon Texts*, ed. Ernst H. Wendland (Milwaukee: Northwestern Publishing House, 1984). A change in series provides variation.

Varied Preaching of the Law

Variety serves the essence of Lutheran preaching, the Law and the Gospel. It makes proclamation of these two doctrines fresh and vital.

We discover varied ways to preach the Law in the Pentateuch, the Prophets, the Psalms, and the other poetic books of the Old Testament. Begin with the account of the exodus. In scene after scene on the journey from the Red Sea to the Promised Land, Moses struggled with the people's disconnect from Yahweh. Later, the prophets' searing declaration of the Law against the escapades of the kings of Judah and Israel proved that Yahweh had zero tolerance for deviation from the worship of the true God. The Psalms expose devious actions, vile words, hypocrisy, injustice, and blatant rejection of Yahweh. The Proverbs mark wrongdoing that permeates everyday life. Discover variation in expression of the Law in snippets of biography: Samuel leaving Saul; Nathan in the face of David; the sad apostasy of Solomon; the pollution of Israel's worship by Jeroboam; Elijah confronting Ahab and Jezebel; Amos prophesying against Israel; Jeremiah spurning fickle Zedekiah.

The New Testament yields variety for proclaiming the Law. In the four Gospels, Jesus confronted self-serving notions of the kingdom of God as He exposed pride in the Pharisees, heretical teaching by the Sadducees, the smug, know-it-all attitude of the Scribes (cf. Matt 23). See how He calls to account those who are in denial about time, yes, the end time: "Likewise, just as it was in the days of Lot—they were eating and drinking, buying and selling, planting and building, but on the day when Lot went out from Sodom, fire and sulfur rained from heaven and destroyed them all" (Luke 17:28–29). Do these words apply to Christians captive in a culture surfeited with all the *good* things but missing the one thing needful (cf. Luke 10:38–42)? To the Lord's preaching the Law, add the apostle Paul's direct challenge to Judaizers, who advocated righteousness by the Law, making circumcision obligatory for any who call themselves Christian (Gal 2:14–16; 5:1–6). Paul's indictment of disregard for natural law and the Commandments provides variation for preaching the Law (Rom 1:24–32; 2:1–5; 1 Tim 1:8–11; et al.). Though a mere sampling, these references show how the Scriptures vary both proclamation and application of the Law.

At some point, sermons should declare that much neglected doctrine, the ορyή θεου, the wrath of God, revealed from heaven (Rom 1:18). Harsh as this subject is, people may not comprehend the seriousness of sin and sinfulness until God's wrath and judgment are real. Some preachers avoid this subject. They reason that they preach to baptized Christians and God's wrath is irrelevant for the forgiven ones. Or they fear coming off like ranting tent preachers of yesteryear who called down fire and brimstone. In any case, neglecting to take

God's wrath seriously, the Law may amount to nothing more than arousing mild sensitivity to a little naughtiness.

Furthermore, God's fierce anger against sin is continuous, unabated as long as the sinner is unrepentant and the sin is not forgiven (cf. Rom 2:5). Preachers should not conceal this reality. Commenting on Romans 1:18, "For the wrath of God is revealed from heaven," R. V. G. Tasker puts it succinctly:

> Paul is in effect here laying down the essential foundation for the doctrine of grace by a general statement of God's *permanent* attitude to sin; for it is only when men are fully conscious of this attitude that they are inclined to, or indeed are able to accept the good-news of the revelation of God's righteousness revealed in the saving death of Christ. To realize that we are under God's wrath and in disgrace is the essential preliminary to the experience of His love and His grace.[133]

Tasker construes the present tense, ἀποκαλύπτεται, in this passage as a *frequent present*, meaning that God's wrath is continually revealed and covers the whole field of human experience as delineated in the Old Testament. The wrath of God is ongoing and permanent, and there is no relief or refuge except at the foot of the cross of Christ. How well do preachers communicate this *bad news* so that people become frantic to hear and rehear the *Good News*, that for the sake of Christ we are delivered from wrath and reconciled to God in eternal peace (Rom 5:9, 20–21; 1 Thess 1:10; 5:9–10)?

Varied Preaching of the Gospel

The Scriptures provide variety for Gospel preaching. Preaching the Gospel is proclaiming that Gospel *pro nobis*, for us. Walther expresses this truth when he states,

> **Principle:** Proclaiming the Law and the Gospel always begins with the preaching text and its unique expression of these two doctrines complemented by nuances drawn from the Scriptures at large.

> Pastors want to awaken their people and warn them against self-deception. However, that cannot be their ultimate aim. Their ultimate aim must be to lead their listeners to the assurance that they have forgiveness of sins with God, the hope of the future blessed life, and confidence to meet death cheerfully. Anyone who does not make these things his ultimate aim is not an evangelical, [that is, a Gospel-oriented,] pastor.[134]

133 R V. G. Tasker, *The Biblical Doctrine of the Wrath of God* (London: Tyndale Press, 1951), 10.

134 Walther, *Law & Gospel: How to Read and Apply the Bible*, 343.

Preaching the Gospel connects the listener with God's salvation; and Christ-centered preaching is notably soteriological.[135] It was no coincidence that early apostolic proclamation was preaching Jesus Christ, both His person and work (Acts 5:42; 11:20; 13:23, 26–39; cf. Acts 19:13b). The principle here is the key to variety in Gospel preaching.

Principle: Preaching lets the Gospel have its way with the listener on its own terms, which are the person and work of Jesus Christ for the salvation of sinners.

Consider the I AM sayings of Jesus cited in the Gospel of John—I AM the Good Shepherd! I AM the bread of life! I AM the door! I AM the way, the truth, and the life!—sayings that convey the Gospel in terms of the Lord's person. Further, the parables of our Lord were Gospel preaching. His miracles—healing the sick and raising the dead—point forward to His resurrection. These signs were precursors to His rising from the grave and His victory over sin and death.

Moreover, references to the Lord's saving work demonstrate variety in preaching the Gospel. For instance, note how His active obedience—fulfillment of the Law and sufficient righteousness—brings Gospel comfort to persons who agonize over what they have not done and cannot do because of sin (cf. Rom 10:4). Again, variety shows in numerous subtopics to the Lord's passive obedience. Christ was "made sin for us" (2 Cor 5:21), being made a "curse for us" (Gal 3:13). "The LORD has laid on Him the iniquity of us all[!]" (Isa 53:6, 11). He saved us from suffering punishment for our iniquity (Rom 8:1; cf. 1 John 4:14–17). Dying on the cross, Jesus was the propitiation for us—the ιλασμόσ for our sins and for the world's sins (1 John 2:2). He was put forward as the ιλαστήριον, the "propitiation by His blood" for our sins (Rom 3:24–26; cf. Heb 9:11–15, 24–28). When He "bore our sins in His body on the tree" of the cross (1 Pet 2:24), His propitiatory sacrifice turned away God's wrath from us (Rom 5:1, 9; 8:1; cf. Heb 9:28). He has earned for us the forgiveness of sins. All entries against us in God's book are canceled and void for the sake of Christ (2 Cor 5:19). We have fellowship with God, and death cannot touch it. Christ has defeated the one who had the power of death, even Satan (Heb 2:14–15). These blessings are concomitant with justification by grace through faith in Christ (Rom 5:1; Eph 2:8–10, 14–16). In summary, note ten ways to preach the atoning work of Christ: as a curse for us, the sin-bearer, accomplishing rescue, peacemaker making peace with God, winning forgiveness and justification, as

135 Preaching the person and work of Christ for forgiveness of sins and eternal salvation of sinners is preaching the Gospel. Of course, the implication is that these gifts should be received by faith. Because the Gospel is soteriological as it is Christological, it is foolish to impose a rhetorical limitation on "Gospel," saying that it is not truly Gospel until the phrases "for us" or "for you" are added. The saving factor "for us" is contained within the action of preaching Christ because "the Son of Man came . . . to give His life as a ransom for many" (Mark 10:45).

the substitute sacrifice, a propitiation, a ransom, securing eternal inheritance, winning for us that enduring fellowship with God.

The Gospel in the Old Testament is varied in expression. For example, the background to the atonement theology in Hebrews 9 and 10 includes vivid imagery—the Mercy Seat and the sprinkling of blood within the Holy of Holies on the Day of Atonement (Lev 16; cf. Exod 25:17–22; 26:34; 30:10; 37:6–9; Heb 9:7; cf. Heb 9:11–12). A preacher may describe this Gospel imagery. The Pentateuch yields rich Gospel theology. Begin with the *protoevangelium*, Genesis 3, move to the promise made to Abraham, Genesis 12, and include Deuteronomy 7, where Yahweh recalls for Israel that He has chosen them to be a people, His possession, a people holy unto the Lord, not because they chose Him, but because He loved them and redeemed them from the house of bondage (Deut 7:6–11). Proclaim the Gospel in terms of Old Testament typology that points to future reality, types—both persons and objects—Adam and the Second Adam, Christ (cf. Rom 5:12–14, 17); the bronze serpent and Christ raised up on the tree of the cross (Num 21:8–9; John 3:14–18). Add the many messianic prophecies and their fulfillment. The images of restoration and establishment are Gospel expression (Isa 51:9–11; 60; Jer 32–33; Zeph 3:14–20; et al.). The covenant idea is Gospel, teaching Yahweh's declaration to be faithful in His grace, forgiving sins, and giving assurance that He shall ever remain for His people the God of love (cf. Jer 31:33–34; Exod 24; Deut 7:6–11). And see the Gospel in the Psalms. How Gospel-rich is the Old Testament!

In addition, the biblical record of lives transformed proclaims the power of the Gospel. The Christians at Ephesus, who were once dead in trespasses and sins, were saved by grace and raised up with Christ to heavenly places (Eph 2:1–6). Indeed, St. Paul honored them as the Bride of Christ (Eph 5). Such transformation by the Gospel was evident earlier when Matthew was called by our Lord from a checkered life in the service of Caesar to be His disciple (Matt 9:9). Recall Zacchaeus (Luke 19:1–10), to whose house salvation came when Jesus entered, resulting in a flurry of restitution and resolve. After St. Paul's conversion, his life and ministry turned on the Gospel (Acts 9; 1 Cor 15:8–10; 1 Tim 1:13–17). These few citations from the Old and New Testaments alert the preacher to a wide variety of Gospel expression across the horizon of biblical theology.

Planned Preaching

Sermon development is spontaneous for some preachers. When a text comes to mind, they ruminate

Principle: Sermons best grow as they develop long term. Monday morning, next Sunday's sermon has been on its way for months. Now it matures toward completion the days prior to the preaching event next Sunday.

on the passage, organize a few thoughts, and get up and preach. For the majority of pastors, however, both long-term and short-term plans serve productive preaching. The two ranges, long and short, complement each other. Monday morning, a pastor should consult his long-term plan and focus on the preaching text selected earlier for sermon work leading to next Sunday. He does not scratch and pull and sweat to answer the question "What shall I preach next Sunday?" His long-term plan provides a quick start in sermon preparation.

A feasible plan divides fifty-two Sundays of a year, or Church Year, into four quarters, each containing thirteen Sundays. At the beginning of any quarter, the sermon texts and possible themes and titles, plus worship and music accessories, are in place for the upcoming Sundays. Preparation for this new quarter was accomplished during the weeks of the preceding quarter. The pastor works with a worship committee or staff to plan for Sundays the next quarter. The quarterly preaching plan may be configured in this manner:

One Quarter—3 Months	1st Comm./Staff Mtg.	2nd Comm./Staff Mtg.	Final Plan
April, May, June	2nd week in Feb.	1st week in March	March 31
July, August, Sept.	2nd week in May	1st week in June	June 30
Oct., Nov., Dec.	2nd week in Aug.	1st week in Sept.	Sept. 30
Jan., Feb., March	2nd week in Oct.	1st week in Nov.	Nov. 30

The pastor and the worship committee meet twice each quarter to develop a plan ready-made to begin the first Sunday of a new quarter. The pastor works with a repository of preaching and worship material for every approaching Sunday. For the sermon, he has on file exegetical work and notes assembled months earlier. He is working from a plan, and he will be prepared next Sunday.

Secondary Sermonic Material

Pastors may brighten their sermons with material that enhances listening without distracting from the text or the central idea of the sermon. The improper use of illustrations, excerpts from literature, examples from life and current culture may overpower or distract from the main message, yet a prudent use of supplementary material may prevent reducing the sermon to a drab lecture or vague discussion. The first Lutheran Hour preacher, Dr. Walter A. Maier, spoke in the genre of the times—World War II. Controlled reference to current events helped press home points of meaning from the Scriptures.

Getting the Sermon

Many homiletic configurations provide a path to the sermon.[136] Some homileticians question *construction* of the sermon, but sermon development in some form is both sensible and necessary. Numerous models are available, and most will include these three factors:

1. Discovery

Prayer

Text selection

Exegetical discipline	vocabulary of the text, grammar and syntax, both the general and immediate context, a first translation from the Greek or Hebrew, thought progression, word study of principle terms, comparison with other translations, listing of parallel passages, gathering insights
Doctrine	the teaching of the text, and wider implications of the doctrine
Meaning	a summary statement, expounding the text, what the text is about, what it means and teaches within the larger narrative of the Scriptures, how Law and Gospel are present in the text, the goal that the sermon may adopt
Support material	gathering of hearer-related material—narratives, illustrations from the Scriptures and from other sources such as literature, current events, and commentaries

2. Development

Prayer

Diagram of the text	subject/verb plus attending adjectives, adverbs, prepositional phrases; the diagram assists grasping the essentials of the text
Purpose	goal or aim of the sermon arising from the text and its meaning, implications for arrangement of the message flowing from the essential central idea or thought or theme or thesis

136 See Appendix 4, "Examples of Sermon Development." Give consideration to the expository development, which should be used more often and more effectively in Lutheran preaching.

Structure	outline—rhetorical/deductive, or inductive with track/stages or moves, expository development
Working brief	the body of the sermon in extended outline and detail, preceded by introduction, and followed by a conclusion
Writing and revision	First, second, third, and more drafts of the written sermon, reaching for conciseness

3. Delivery

Prayer

Preparation	absorption of meaning, fixing of expression, employing memory
	attention to emphasis, movement, pace, gestures
Dry run preaching	evening prior to or early morning of the preaching day
	final functional memorizing of the message

Hindrances to delivery

Fright vs. positive nervous energy

Feeble grasp of the sermon

Slavish use of manuscript instead of proper use (nonuse) of preaching outline, notes

Reading the sermon and absence of eye contact

Mannerisms that distract

Homileticians—teachers of the craft of preaching—affirm that the sermon is *not the sermon* until delivery of the message, the Word of God proclaimed and reaching the people. Then the sermon is complete. For this holistic enterprise, consider an additional indispensable rubric. Simply put, this rubric is ***PREPARATION!***

CHAPTER SEVEN

The Sacraments of the Church and the Conduct of the Church's Public Worship

Part I. The Sacraments

Introduction

Dr. Martin Luther remarked about the Sacraments instituted by Christ, "For every Christian ought to have at least some brief, elementary instruction about them, because without them no one can be a Christian."[137] Luther's counsel finds its way into catechesis preparing children and adults for the Rite of Confirmation. Normally, formal instruction ends there. How do Christians use the Sacraments ten or twenty years later? How much do they remember about the meaning and purpose of the Sacraments? Have perceptions been altered by many influences? This possibility suggests that a program of reinstruction about the Sacraments is imperative. Below is a guiding principle.

Principle: The practice of the Sacraments in the Church calls for continued and intentional reinstruction if Christians are to use these Means of Grace for the reason that they were given—the strengthening of faith and life by the Holy Spirit through the Lord's gift, the forgiveness of sins, which He offers in the Sacraments.

The Need for Continuous Instruction about the Sacraments

The meaning and the proper use of the Sacraments escape the devotional attention of many Christians. Nonuse of the Sacraments by inactive members is one reason for this loss. Others who use them are misguided by faulty perceptions. Pastors hear expressions such as these: "I think that I got my name by Baptism." "I am pretty certain that I was baptized, but does it really matter?" "I go to Communion when I need a lift in order to face the

137 Large Catechism. Fourth Part: Concerning Baptism, 1, *Book of Concord*, Kolb-Wengert, 456.

next week." "It feels good to be closer to God when I take Holy Communion." "I am a better person, I think, after I partake of the Lord's Supper." "Taking the bread and the wine at the altar cannot hurt anything." "I ought to be at the Table now and then. It is the least that I can do, and it will help somehow."

Topping misperceptions must be the approach by some Christians that the Lord's Supper is what they determine it to be. A young adult announced that he was leaving his Lutheran congregation to affiliate with a Methodist fellowship. When his Lutheran pastor cautioned that the Wesleyan congregation did not practice the Sacrament—confessing the meaning and acknowledging the blessing according to the Lord's institution of His Supper—he replied, "When I go to Communion and kneel at the altar in any church, I determine for myself what I am receiving, and I am quite happy with that." How many Lutheran Christians approach the Lord's Table with similar bravado contrary to Christ and His institution of the Sacrament? Again, it is imperative to shore up congregations by reinstruction in the meaning and the proper use of the Sacraments.

The Term *Sacrament*

The meaning of the term *sacrament* remains a curiosity for many Christians. To explain the term, we begin with the adjective *sacramental*, a veiled reference to notions of *sacred*. In the military, soldiers have a sacred calling and duty, according to dignitaries speaking on Memorial Day or Independence Day. The Latin term *sacramentum* held numerous meanings in the ancient world. It stood for the oath taken by soldiers in the armies of Rome. Allegiance to the emperor and undying loyalty in battle was bound by this *sacramentum*. The eminent British exegete Bishop Lightfoot thought that Pliny, in reference to Bythinian Christians, used the term *sacramentum* to signify their pledge of faithfulness taken at the time of Baptism.

Within the Church, ecclesiastical usage assigned the term *sacramentum* to things that were set apart as sacred—consecrated or dedicated—even things such as the Word of God, or doctrines. The Church Fathers Tertullian, Cyprian, and Augustine applied *sacramentum* in reference to certain Christian rites. Distinguished among these were the *rites* instituted and commanded by Jesus Christ: Holy Baptism and the Lord's Supper. These are the two great *sacraments* of the Gospel. Later, *sacrament* was applied to other religious rites and ceremonies. Thomas Aquinas opted for seven sacraments, a number affirmed later by the Council of Trent, 1545–1563.[138]

138 For background to the meaning of the term *sacrament*, see A. Plummer, "Sacraments," *Dictionary of the Bible*, vol. 4, ed. James Hastings (Edinburgh: T & T Clark, sixth impression. November 1909), 327–329.

The Marks and Number of the Sacraments

In Lutheran theology and practice, the number of the Sacraments is determined by their marks. In this regard, the Word of Christ is essential and absolute (Matt 28:18). The marks of the Sacraments are His command and promise. He commands, "Go therefore and make disciples of all nations, baptizing them" (Matt 28:19). Giving His Holy Supper to His disciples, He commanded, "Do this" (1 Cor 11:24–25). Add the promise, the forgiveness of sins. The directive to Saul of Tarsus was "rise and be baptized and wash away your sins" (Acts 22:16). Distributed in the Lord's Supper are His body and blood, given and shed for the remission of sins (Matt 26:28). Backing our Lord's command and promise as they relate to the Sacraments is His work of redemption, His atonement for our sins (Col 1:13–14; 1 Pet 2:24).[139] Indeed, the Sacraments are mystery, and they have been called the *mysteries* of the Church. By these understandings, ceremonies such as marriage, confirmation, and last rites for the dying are not classified as sacraments. They are human institutions, and humans have no authority or power to promise God's grace. Melanchthon states, "If we define the sacraments as rites, which have the command of God and to which the promise of grace has been added, it is easy to determine what the sacraments are, properly speaking" (Ap XIII 3). By this criterion, the Lutheran Confessions state that the Sacraments are Baptism, the Lord's Supper, and Absolution (the sacrament of repentance) (Ap XIII 4a).[140] Martin Luther called Holy Baptism and the Lord's Supper "promises which have signs attached to them," meaning sacred actions, employing elements—water, bread, and wine—as commanded by Christ and through which God promises grace and forgiveness of sins.[141] The Sacraments, moreover, remain in the Church's use as long as the command and promise of Christ avail, that is, to the close of the age.

Therefore, the true Church of Christ cannot be antisacramentarian, nor can church doctrine or practice manipulate them so that they have no sem-

139 If forgiveness of sins is paramount in the Sacraments, a blessing from the Lord's act of redemption, it seems proper to review for the people the doctrine of Christ's atonement for sins. Clear teaching and reinstruction about this work of Christ for us will sharpen focus on the Sacraments and discourage subjective perceptions about their meaning and significance.

140 The Reformer Philip Melanchthon expressed willingness to name the Rite of Ordination into the Office of the Ministry a sacrament, if the rite is understood with reference to the ministry of the Word. He explained, "For the ministry of the Word has the command of God and has magnificent promises like Romans 1[:16]: the gospel 'is the power of God for salvation to everyone who has faith.' Likewise, Isaiah 55[:11], '. . . so shall my word be that goes out from my mouth; it shall not return to me empty, but it shall accomplish that which I purpose'" (Ap XIII 11).

141 Luther's comment is referenced by Kolb-Wengert, 219n379. Dr. Hermann Sasse observes the Lord did not institute "the sacraments," but each particular rite. These have commonalities, beginning with Dr. Sasse's assertion that the sacraments are the Gospel. Hermann Sasse, "Word and Sacrament: Preaching and the Lord's Supper," in *We Confess the Sacrament*; We Confess series, 2; trans. Norman Nagel (St. Louis: Concordia Publishing House, 1985), 25–26.

blance to His Word of command or promise.[142] The Sacraments do not yield to private interpretation, and their recipients shall not redefine or reconfigure them. The Sacraments are strictly *dominical*. They are of the Lord. They are His Gospel Word. And therein we have confidence in their capacity to convey to us the grace of God. They are His designated means to give this blessing.[143]

The Right Administration of the Sacraments

The sacraments are *dominical*; therefore, they require careful handling by an ordained pastor. To His apostles, our Lord gave the command "to baptize" (Matt 28:19). Celebrating with them His Holy Supper, He said, "Do this" (Luke 22:19; 1 Cor 11:24b, 25; FC SD VII 80). A pastor baptizes in the name of the Holy Trinity or administers the Lord's Supper engaging His Words of Institution. Thereby, Christ our Lord actively exercises His power and gives His gifts (FC SD VII 75–76). Luther contended that continuing to the end of the world, Christ Himself effects the Sacraments administered through the instrumentation of the pastoral office and ministry (FC SD VII 77). The called pastor properly administers the Sacraments under the dominical rubric "As the Father has sent Me, even so I am sending you" (John 20:21b; AC XIV). The Church has always recognized there may be times when a layman must administer Holy Baptism, which the Church then confirms in the Rite of Public Recognition of Holy Baptisms, but no such "emergency" exists for the Lord's Supper.

---

142 Antisacramentarians are churches who either elect not to have sacraments or, in their teaching and practice, have sacraments that are unrecognizable compared to the Lord's institution and teaching. In the latter camp are many Calvinist and Wesleyan churches. One exponent of the Calvinist doctrine is the church historian Hugh T. Kerr. In his monograph *The Christian Sacraments: A Source Book for Ministers*, Kerr orients his discussion of the sacraments around the notion of symbol versus the Lutheran focus on the Word and institution of Christ. Like most Calvinists, Kerr acknowledges that Christ instituted the sacraments and that He is present in them. It is their accompanying explanations that cause concern. For instance, Kerr asserts that the mystery of the sacraments is related to nature, where things that are seen speak to the soul of man of things that are not seen. About the sacraments, he states, "God takes of the things of sense, using them as signs and symbols of things spiritual and invisible, and through them conveys Christ to the believer" (23). He adds, the sacraments become for us not only symbols but also seals that authenticate to us Christ and the benefits of the covenant, even as He speaks through the glory of the sunset or the murmur of the wind. For things become sacramental through the indwelling and blessing of the Holy Spirit (24). Kerr names these benefits of the sacraments: assurance is given, promises are vindicated, the Gospel is proclaimed, Christ is present (23). Notably absent is the blessing named by our Lord, the forgiveness of sins. Kerr emphasizes a total sacramental action within which the believer is party to a religious experience of the Sacrament, an experience in which God is actively at work. In the sacraments, where this religious experience is at its best, states Kerr, God the Father, God the Son, God the Holy Spirit is actively present (25). See Hugh Thomson Kerr, *The Christian Sacraments: A Source Book for Ministers* (Philadelphia: Westminster Press, 1944).

143 That Holy Baptism and the Lord's Supper are dominical, Luther attests in LC IV 6, and the Formula of Concord affirms with emphasis (FC SD VII 73, 74). In a parallel statement, the Formula reads: "But, as has been shown above, nothing can be a sacrament apart from God's command and the practice that he has ordained, as instituted in God's Word" (FC SD VII 108b; VII 75, 26, 43).

Faith—The Proper Use of the Sacraments

The Sacraments, then, are the Lord's doing, and the proper use of them is faith. They are *promissio*, the promise that God for the sake of Christ through these means forgives sins. This truth compels faith that can do no less than actively believe and trust the steadfast promise made in the Sacraments. Therefore, in regard to the Sacraments, Melanchthon corrects mistaken notions that faith is a mere attitude or frame of mind, a mood, sentiment, or feeling. Frankly, he discusses faith joined to its proper object when he counters the widespread notion in the Roman Church that the sacraments confer grace *ex opera operato* (by mere performance of the rite, faith or not). Melanchthon argues with St. Paul's example of Abraham (Rom 4:9ff.) and concludes,

> Thus we teach that in the use of the sacraments faith needs to be present—faith that believes these promises and receives what is promised as offered there in the sacrament. The reason for this is plain and well established. A promise is useless unless it is received by faith. But the sacraments are signs of the promises. Therefore, in their use faith needs to be present, so that anyone making use of the Lord's Supper uses it in this way. (Ap XIII 19–20)

The *promise* of the forgiveness of sins is compelling. Melanchthon clarifies further,

> We are talking about that particular faith that believes the promise being offered, not just a faith that in a general way believes that God exists but one that believes the forgiveness of sins is being offered. This use of the sacrament comforts devout and anxious minds. (Ap XIII 21–22)

Lest anyone reduce faith to a mental exercise, the Augsburg Confession shows that the energy of faith, believing the promise borne by the Sacraments, is awakened by the Word of the Gospel in these very Sacraments. The Confession puts in proper perspective both the gift of faith and the requirement of faith:

> Concerning the use of sacraments it is taught that the sacraments are instituted . . . as signs and testimonies of God's will toward us in order thereby to awaken and strengthen our faith. That is why they also require faith and are rightly used when received in faith for the strengthening of faith. (AC XIII 1, 2)

When instructing the people about the Sacrament of the Altar, the pastor exhorts the people to believe. Melanchthon appears to support such external exhortation to faith when he explains that taking the Sacrament in remembrance of the Lord is "to remember Christ's benefits and to receive them by faith so that we are made alive through them" (Ap XXIV 72). Again, Melanchthon states, "Such use of the sacrament, in which faith gives life to terrified hearts, is the New Testament worship" (Ap XXIV 71). When teaching the people to use the Sacrament, pastors will press them to say, "This we believe!" In repentance and faith, they acknowledge first their deplorable state before God as sinners, and second they recognize the will and mercy of God. Melanchthon caps our discussion about use of the Sacraments. He stated, "Now faith that recognizes mercy makes alive. This is the principal use of the sacrament, through which it becomes clear both that terrified consciences are the ones worthy of it and how they ought to use it" (Ap XXIV 73).

The Comfort in the Sacraments as Divine Revelation

When using the Sacraments, the people take comfort also in the truth that they are means whereby God reveals Himself and His grace to them. For instance, scheduled Baptisms in the Church may be announced in advance so that the people may anticipate this Sacrament the next Sunday. It is an occasion to rejoice that the Lord is with them on terms of His grace and mercy, and that by His Word He gives His Holy Spirit to another soul and brings that person to eternal life by this washing of regeneration.

Pastors instruct further that the Sacraments are "things as handed down from God" (Ap XXIV 68). External as they are, the Sacraments are God's present and transparent action here and now. This astounding truth captivates new inquirers and converts studying the Christian faith in the pastor's adult class. As Yahweh was present in the pillar of cloud by day and the pillar of fire by night among Israel in the wilderness (Exod 13:21–22), God is among His people in the immediate conduct of Baptism and the Lord's Supper. God acts for them in the present. He reveals His love and grace. He forgives their sins and seals to them His mercy. He desires that they be His people. God does all of this for them in the present use of the Sacraments. What greater support for their faith in God than now in the Sacraments? Here God is no longer *deus absconditus*, the God hidden in a shroud of mystery, but *deus revelatus*, God revealed, disclosed to the people, the God whom they may trust to be gracious for the sake of Christ. This *here* and *now* of God's self-revelation in the Sacraments invites childlike trust, firm and unwavering faith. Is this why Christians at death's door request the Sacrament? In His gift, the Sacrament, Christ sustains the hope to be with God as His saint for eternity.

Part II. Conduct of the Church's Worship

Normally, the pastor administers the Church's sacraments in the company of the worshiping congregation. What are his sensibilities in approaching this ministry? How does the liturgy focus on God's Word of salvation? How does liturgical form communicate the substance of *Gottesdienst*, the proper worship of God?

Sensibilities

A pastor rises early on Sunday morning for the event, *cultus Dei*, *Gottesdienst*, the congregation gathering in the house of God for worship.[144] He arrives at the church in the spirit of the Levites and priests who entered the ancient temple. There, God met His people in fullness of glory (1 Kgs 8:10–11), the place where God put His name (1 Kgs 8:29; cf. Jer 32:34). The Church is not an ordinary place, but the place where God has put His name in the persons of the baptized who assemble to call upon the name of the Lord. They are the living stones of the temple of God in this age. The Spirit dwells in them, and when they gather in the name of the triune God, the glory of the Lord fills the place (Rom 8:16–17; 1 Cor 2:9–13; 3:16–17; 6:19–20). Sensing the *holy* in this special house—Christ's people assembled for worship—the pastor goes about his morning tasks.

Lutherans hesitate to frame worship in terms of *locus* or *place*. With Luther, they affirm "that God gives no one his Spirit or grace apart from the external Word" (SA III 8, 3), but that external Word—hosted and proclaimed within the sanctuary—hallows this *place*. So the people erect houses of worship, honoring God with externals, the best and the most beautiful they can afford. Here, the cross of Christ dominates, the Word is central, the Holy Spirit is present, and Christ is among His people (AC XXVIII 8, 9). In this place, the pastor is no less moved than Solomon in the temple. He is in awe, as if standing in the temple complex named "The Lord Is There" (Ezek 48:35).

Salvation

The ambiance and adornments of this place point to a higher adornment. Melanchthon reminds, "The true adornment of the churches is godly, useful, and clear doctrine, the devout use of the sacraments, ardent prayer, and the like. Candles, golden vessels, and similar adornments are appropriate, but they are not the distinctive adornment of the church" (Ap XXIV 51). Yet the exter-

144 The phrase *cultus Dei, Gottesdienst* is a portion of the title of a pivotal work in the Lutheran tradition. See *Worship, Gottesdienst, Cultus Dei: What the Lutheran Confessions Say about Worship*, ed. James L. Brauer (St. Louis: Concordia Publishing House, 2005).

nal properties are significant. The pastor's eye is drawn to the altar. True, in the cultus of ancient Israel, the altar connoted sacrificial action. But in Lutheran sanctuaries, the cross over the altar conveys the truth that God has provided the final sacrifice, which is "the Lamb of God who takes away the sin of the world!" (John 1:29, 36; Isa 53:7, 12; cf. Heb 9:14, 26; 10:10). The altar, the lectern and pulpit, the font for Baptism speak what the hymnist wrote, "God Himself is present: Let us now adore Him." The pastor rejoices. He is ready to lead worship in this *place*. "This is the day that the LORD has made" (Ps 118:24).

SUBSTANCE

The external adornments—chancel, altar, lectern, pulpit, font—speak of the Gospel, the forgiveness of sins and salvation. They should suggest a liturgy or order of worship consistent with delivery of these gifts. A question for those who frame the order of worship is "How does order or liturgy focus on salvation substance central in Christian worship?" This is a question for those who adhere to traditional worship form and for others who reconfigure the church's historic liturgy.

The debates over this question in recent decades are beyond our reach. The so-called worship wars engaging entrenched traditionalists versus independent liturgical freethinkers are beyond discussion here. What shall we say? The best wisdom is to make certain that any order or liturgy contains what the Church has historically considered essential to retain the focus on *salvation substance*. We arrive at essential components that accommodate that substance. They are the following:

- ☐ Trinitarian Invocation
- ☐ Confession/Absolution
- ☐ *Introit*
- ☐ Reading of the Scriptures
- ☐ *Gradual*
- ☐ Preaching/Sermon/Exposition
- ☐ Creedal Corporate Confession of Faith
- ☐ Praise & Offering
- ☐ Prayer of All Kinds—The General Prayer
- ☐ Baptism and the Lord's Supper
- ☐ Benediction/Blessing

These components—in this or a similar arrangement—compose the form that honors the essentials of Christian worship. For Lutherans designing worship services, this salutary statement from the Commission on Worship remains cogent:

> Are there basic ingredients in a service that mark it as Lutheran? Yes. A Lutheran service is one that is built on the article of justification by grace through faith. It is a service that expounds the Word of God as both Law and Gospel. It is centered in the reading of Scripture and its exposition and the administration of the Sacraments. It follows the Mass form which was inherited from many cultures and peoples of the last twenty centuries. It is not culturally biased to one group. In fact, most of the material found in the Mass is a direct quotation of Scripture or paraphrase.[145]

Numerous Lutheran pastors do not accept the statements above that recommend essential components of the liturgy. They consider the traditional liturgy too limiting. Furthermore, they assert freedom to reconfigure public worship with forms that, in their view, are more palatable to modern diverse audiences at worship services. Understandably, they are quick to dismiss formality or informality with respect to worship form as a matter of casuistry.

Lest pastors be carefree in the exercise of freedom regarding worship form, we counsel, do not overlook subtleties in the relationship between substance and form. Give thoughtful attention to factors discussed above, such as salvation, sensibility, and ambiance. Add dignity, solemnity, reverence. If assembling in the name of the triune God places the congregation where God is present with His grace and mercy, let all figuratively remove their shoes, bow humbly before the almighty God, and remain so through the worship hour—His service of the Gospel to us, and our dedication to Him.

---

145 A statement issued by the Commission on Worship as a guide and discussion piece for the people and parishes of The Lutheran Church—Missouri Synod, Fall 1994.

CHAPTER EIGHT

The Ministry of Holy Baptism

Introduction

Dr. Martin Luther cited the gifts and blessings Holy Baptism grants: "It brings about forgiveness of sins, redeems from death and the devil, and gives eternal salvation to all who believe it, as the words and promise of God declare."[146] The pastor administering Baptism, one who is fine, moral, serious, and upright, as Luther prescribes, is keenly aware that the Spirit of God, through Word and promise with the water, effects regeneration, a sinner's new birth, a life glorifying God now, and in eternity life with the saints praising and serving God (cf. Titus 3:5–8). Grace poured over them through Jesus Christ, our Savior, sinners are made righteous and heirs in hope of eternal life, all by means of Holy Baptism.[147] Luther states what treasures these are: "For baptism is our only comfort and the doorway to all of God's possessions and to the communion of all the saints."[148]

This is a brief sketch of the grand new world our Lord instituted when He commanded "to baptize" (Matt 28:19). The kingdom of God's grace comes among us. Note how the New Testament customarily references Baptism in connection to those for whom the Sacrament is intended. It is proper, therefore, to open this discussion with a word about presenting children, youth, and adults for the Rite of Baptism. A larger discussion follows with theology addressing aspects of the practice of Baptism.

---

146 Small Catechism, The Sacrament of Holy Baptism, *Book of Concord*, Kolb-Wengert, 359.

147 Ibid.

148 Martin Luther, "The Baptism Booklet: Translated into German and Newly Revised," 9, Kolb-Wengert, 373. The biblical doctrine of Holy Baptism, also Lutheran understanding and practice, come together in a work by David P. Scaer, *Baptism* (St. Louis: Luther Academy, 1999). Also see Edmund Schlink, *The Doctrine of Baptism*, trans. Herbert J. A. Bouman (St. Louis: Concordia Publishing House, 1972).

Preparation for the Rite of Holy Baptism

The Practice of Baptizing Children

Interest and Care of the Congregation

Preparation for Baptism begins with initiatives by the congregation. Anticipating the Baptism of children or adults, the congregation prays that in Baptism the Holy Spirit may deliver them from the tyranny of Satan. To encourage prayerful anticipation of a Baptism, the pastor and church office alert the congregation in advance. The congregation prays for Baptism candidates, setting themselves against the devil with all their strength and demonstrating that they take the Baptism seriously. This is Luther's solemn instruction.[149]

The reference for Holy Baptism is our Lord's Baptism, celebrated by the Church the First Sunday after the Epiphany (Matt 3:13–17; Mark 1:9–11; Luke 3:21–22; cf. John 1:32–34). Following the Early Church, Luther considered this event at the outset of the Lord's public ministry to be the essential institution of Holy Baptism.[150] Also foundational are the Lord's death and resurrection, celebrated on Good Friday and Easter, as Romans 6:1–11 attests. The Gospel lessons read in the churches also attest to the dominical institution of Baptism. The Church's life is anchored in Baptism, so she carefully attends to those brought for this Sacrament.

Pastoral Care and Counsel for Parents of Children for Baptism

The pastor meets with prospective parents. Early in pregnancy, a Christian woman will appreciate receiving devotions and prayers prepared for her.[151] The pastor also briefly instructs about the Lord's institution of Baptism and its blessings. Parents want to know what the Sacrament will mean for their infant child. Scrolling forward, the pastor informs about Christian education—Sunday School, Christian Day School, and such, the follow-through after Baptism. He emphasizes parental example, living their Baptism in the home. He encourages family devotional life—the use of Scriptures and prayer—and taking the Lord's Supper together. The pastor may discuss the selection of Baptism sponsors. He counsels about the day of the Baptism and conduct of the rite. He informs how to contact him in case of an emergency requiring immediate

---

149 Martin Luther, "The Baptism Booklet," 2, 7, Kolb-Wengert, 372.

150 Hermann Sasse, "Word and Sacrament, Preaching and the Lord's Supper," 22.

151 Formerly, Concordia Publishing House provided a classic devotional piece, prayers printed on attractive cards, prepared by Dr. A. R. Kretzmann for expectant mothers. In lieu of these materials that may be out of print, the pastor may prepare such an exhibit and make it available either in print or online from the congregation's website.

Baptism. In one or two sessions, the pastor ministers to the family expecting a newborn candidate for Baptism.

Counsel with Baptism Sponsors

When possible, pastors counsel Baptism sponsors who are *parents in the faith*. The sponsors or godparents confess the faith expressed in the Apostles' Creed and taught in the Small Catechism. Formerly, in dire circumstances, primary care and nurture of a baptized child fell to Baptism sponsors. In light of that contingency, they would commit to rearing the child in the faith of its parents. Lutheran families, therefore, preferred Lutheran sponsors. It remains wise to select sponsors from among Lutherans in fellowship with the congregation's church body who commit to serve in every way consistent with the Lutheran confession.

The sponsors pray for a baptized child's nurture in the Word and Christian upbringing. At intervals, sponsors remind a child of his or her Baptism and its meaning. They mark special events in the child's life, such as birthdays, Baptism day remembrances, confirmation, and graduations. They may provide gifts that enrich the child's growing in Christian faith and life—pictures depicting the Lord or other Bible figures, crosses, jewelry comprised of Christian symbols, a Bible story book; later, a Bible, prayer book, Small Catechism, hymnal, even the Book of Concord. Sponsors, therefore, partner with parents in active care for the spiritual life of a baptized child. Looking to the day of Baptism, the pastor explains the rite to sponsors and secures their part in the ceremony.

Nurture of the Baptized Child

Baptism sponsors and parents must be intentional about nurturing the baptized child in the Word of God and all the nuances of truth, norms, and values consistent with God's Word. The holistic nurture of the child as a Christian precludes distractions such as cultural intrusions, sports programs, and extra school activities. A discipline, therefore, is recommended:

The Home

- Prayer—designate times in the family schedule for prayer—the Lord's Prayer, Luther's Morning and Evening Prayers, bedtime prayers, table prayers in Jesus' name
- Have devotions, designated time with the Scriptures—reading, explanation, application to life, guidance from God's Word
- Monitor children's images or perceptions of God; enrich with teaching from the Bible and Bible story books

- Bring attention to the Law and the Gospel when reading the Bible—the Law brings judgment to family life, and the Gospel gives forgiveness for Jesus' sake
- Saturate the home with Christian art and literature, videos, audio
- Provide catechesis—multilevel instruction for children, using Bible stories, Bible, the catechism
- Monitor and control influences from outside the home:
    - Television and the Internet
    - Social media
    - Organized sports
    - Family associates—neighbors, friends, acquaintances
    - Playmates
- Cultivate family relationships—"Heirs together of the grace of life" (1 Pet 3:7 KJV); baptized children and their God-fearing parents are those heirs of life
- Worship together as a family with fellow Christians in the local congregation
- Help the child to remember and to celebrate what God has done for him or her in Baptism, and to live life from this miracle of regeneration by the Spirit

The Congregation

- Cradle roll—accounting for children recently baptized
- Sunday School and Vacation Bible School
- Christian Day School
- Midweek School or released time arrangement
- Children's confirmation classes
- Youth groups formed by the congregation
- The congregation's larger ministry of Christian education
- The congregation, in all its life modeling the Baptism-life for its children

These lists point toward a culture of Christian faith and life with boundaries established by the Word of God. As the gap widens between Christian and secular in America, this distinctively Christian culture will require constant development and oversight that calls for interaction with baptized children—offering give-and-take in conversations, listening and answering questions, leading with good counsel from the Bible, framing rules but standing by with the forgiveness of Jesus, lifting up the fallen, meeting repentance with the Gospel, setting children on the right path again and again.

Preparation of Youth and Adults for Baptism

Expressed Desire for Baptism

Pastors work with unchurched youth, young adults, and older adults. Alert pastors sense when the time is right for Baptism. Through counsel and instruction, the Holy Spirit stirs within the heart a desire or readiness to be baptized. Philip instructed the man from Ethiopia. Stirring within the man was that desire for Baptism (Acts 8:29–39). This is quite typical. No constraint or pressure is evident. The pastor listens and senses eagerness; he is prepared to administer the Sacrament of washing by water and the Word.

Instruction Prior to Baptism

Principle: Adults who are candidates for Baptism should be instructed about the Gospel prior to confession of faith in Jesus Christ and receiving Holy Baptism.

The account of the Ethiopian man baptized by Philip suggests a guiding principle.

Normally, inquirers prepare for Baptism by studying the major doctrines of the Christian faith in a class conducted by the local pastor. This same class is for adults preparing for the Rite of Confirmation. Pastors attest that conversions occur in these classes as students focus on the major doctrines of the Scriptures. Of course, the theology of Baptism is essential. Learning the daily use of Baptism is also important. The baptized person bears God's name. That marks new identity. Though sin stalks the new person in Christ, turning back to Baptism in faith yields strength of resolve and the will to brace for the cost of living as a new person in Christ. Mini capsules of apostolic teaching accent the theology of Baptism and the new life that follows Baptism (cf. Rom 6:4, 11, 12–14, 17–18, 22–23; 8:4b, 5–8, 10–11; Col 2:12–15; 3:2–3, 5ff.).

The Essential Practice of Baptism

Officiants Administering the Sacrament

The Church's Called Pastors

Our discussion momentarily shifts from candidates for Baptism to administration of the Sacrament. C. F. W. Walther cites essentials for the practice of baptizing, the proper order (*ordnung*), beginning with the administrant, the rite, the formula, the application of the water.[152] A key question is "Who shall administer this Sacrament?"

152 Walther, *American-Lutheran Pastoral Theology*, 88–89, 97.

Principle: Baptism is God's action through water and the Word. He claims and receives to Himself the baptized into Christ Jesus. Administering the Sacrament whereby God acts, the Church calls trained and qualified pastors to exercise this public ministry.

Any Christian may baptize, but should they? A practice of Baptism that is free and open may lead to misuse of this Sacrament. That is why the Lutheran Confessors require that the Church conduct the Sacraments in good order, that is, "the sacraments are administered in conformity with the divine Word" (AC VII 2). Who is knowledgeable and able to fulfill this requirement? Again, all Christians may speak the Gospel and administer Baptism, but the Church wisely assigns the public preaching of God's Word and administering the Sacraments to the pastoral office.

Lay Christians baptizing is inadvisable when the Church's called pastors are available. A family may be sincere when they request that a lay Christian in their circle of friends baptize their child, but honoring such a request would conflict with the normal order. Of course, there are times of stress and extenuating circumstances that prevent normal procedure. When life is fragile—a premature newborn, an adult at death's door, and other emergencies beyond the reach of the pastoral ministry at the moment—a lay Christian may baptize, and should do so. This is why pastors train congregations to administer Baptism in emergencies. Just as the public at large is trained to give emergency first aid in the absence of physicians, lay Christians may be trained to baptize.

The Church's Baptism—Public or Private?

All Christian Baptisms, public and private, are Church Baptisms. Pastors conduct private Baptisms in hospitals, residences, and other venues. The reasons vary. Health issues are a factor. Or parents may request private Baptism for a severely deformed child or a child born out of wedlock. Public settings are uncomfortable for some adults. They desire private Baptism.

When a pastor baptizes privately, he reports the Baptism in a public worship service and elicits the church's prayers for the person baptized. He states that the private Baptism was attested by witnesses.[153] Similarly, the pastor makes the proper report when he learns of a private Baptism conducted by a lay Christian. This report, too, notes the presence of witnesses. Consider a frantic mother who fears for her child's safety and welfare and baptizes her child. No one witnessed the Baptism except the mother. In such an instance,

153 Witnesses attest that the Baptism was conducted properly according to the Lord's institution and command. Thus, on the basis of the testimony of witnesses, the Church recognizes and accepts the baptismal action as a public sign or Sacrament, according to Walther. See *American-Lutheran Pastoral Theology*, 96.

good *order* is served, according to Luther, when the pastor baptizes this child in public at a later time.[154]

There are *baptisms* that are not Holy Baptism. Antitrinitarian heretical fellowships may employ the language of Baptism, but their heretical confession negates the meaning. It is not Holy Baptism. Persons may profess self-baptism, which is outside the Church's order. It is irregular (cf. Matt 3:13ff.). Imitations of Baptism acted in a drama on stage are not Holy Baptism. Doubtless, in such a setting the Lord's command and Word are absent or trivialized. A child at play may pretend to be at church and "baptize" her doll. This is not Holy Baptism.

A child, however, may invoke the trinitarian Baptism formula and baptize a friend. Such an action may be dismissed as mock baptism, and wise parents counsel children not to imitate Word and Sacrament actions. However, if the child administering is a baptized believing Christian, and her playmate desires Holy Baptism, the action may be judged a valid private Baptism. This is one view. All rests on the power and efficacy of the Word, assuming that the Word and its meaning indeed were involved. If informed of such an incident, the pastor counsels both children. He instructs the "baptized" child. With parental consent, this child may be received into baptized membership of the congregation. There is no way to negate a valid Baptism, nor should anyone attempt to do so. Yet questions surround such a Baptism. Can the church be convinced that this sacramental action by children for children is proper? Were there witnesses who attest that the Baptism was conducted properly? Why was the pastor not consulted? In the light of many concerns, a young child baptized by a friend in the casual setting of *pretend* should be baptized publicly in the presence of the worshiping congregation.

Essential Components of the Church's Rite of Holy Baptism

The Rite of Holy Baptism contains the essential Word of Christ's institution, His command and promise. The rite has ten components:

1. The rite begins, invoking the name of the triune God. The name is everything—God, the authority to baptize, His name placed upon the baptized, the name that is substance to grace, redemption, sanctifying—and in that name the Spirit brings the baptized to faith in Christ, effecting rebirth, regeneration with the forgiveness of sins, new life, and eternal salvation. In this name, Baptism saves (1 Cor 6:11; Titus 3:5–7; 1 Pet 3:21; John 3:5–6).

154 Cited from Martin Luther, *Table Talks*, *Luther's Works*, Erlangen edition, vol. 59, 56ff. See Walther, *American-Lutheran Pastoral Theology*, 96. A church rite facilitates reporting of a Baptism. See "Public Recognition of Holy Baptism," in *Lutheran Service Book: Agenda*, prepared by the Commission on Worship of The Lutheran Church—Missouri Synod (St. Louis: Concordia Publishing House, 2006), 18–21.

2. The second essential component is the sober reminder that all are conceived and born sinful. They are under the tyranny of the devil, and they are objects of the wrath of God until delivered by Christ and claimed by Him to be His own. In the rite, the sign of the holy cross made upon the candidate's head and heart firmly declares that Christ's redemption and deliverance from sin is for us (Ps 51:5; Eph 5:6b; Rom 3:23; 7:7; 6:23a; 1 Cor 1:18; 2 Cor 5:14–15; Eph 1:7).

3. Baptism sponsors are theologically nonessential, but they are needed to support parents in their task of bringing up the baptized child in the nurture of the Lord. Publicly, the sponsors resolve to pray for the baptized child, to see that the child is in the company of the church at worship, to assure that the child is taught the Word of God, and to encourage life in Christ as a devout Christian.

4. The Word and prayer follow, usually reading the Gospel of Mark 10:13–16 and speaking the Lord's Prayer. When an adult is baptized, John 3:1–15 may be read. Another preferred reading is Romans 6:1–11. Petitions in the Lord's Prayer are appropriate. They call for hallowing God's name, implore that His kingdom of grace surely come, and request the blessing bestowed in Baptism, the forgiveness of sins.

5. Following the Lord's Prayer is the renunciation of Satan and repudiation of sin and eternal death—personally, verbally, publicly. This is an exorcism in the sense of victory, for such renunciation of Satan and his evil works is an affirmation stated in confidence that sin and death and Satan are conquered by our Lord Jesus Christ (Heb 2:9, 14–15; 1 John 3:8).

6. Having renounced Satan, the attention now turns to God in profession of faith, the words of the Apostles' Creed spoken by the candidate, by sponsors and parents on behalf of an infant. The Church comprehends that the *credo* is the faith into which the candidate is baptized. The congregation joins in this robust confession, everyone saying, "I believe!"

7. The pastor proceeds with the action of baptizing, a demonstrable external action engaged by the Holy Spirit. With shell in hand, or the hand cupped to administer an amount of water, the pastor pours water upon the head of the candidate, speaking his or her name, and then the words "I baptize you in the name of the Father and of the Son and of the Holy Spirit" (Matt 28:19). Such a moment,

such splashing, droplets everywhere—God in and around and above and below, God in it—this is the wonder of Holy Baptism!

8. The pastor brushes excess water away and places his hand on the candidate's brow, a gesture employed by Moses, Jesus, and Paul. The pastor speaks a word of prayer and blessing with the sign of the cross that God would keep this child, this adult, strong in faith to everlasting life (Num 27:18, 22–23; Luke 4:40; 2 Tim 1:6; et al.).

9. The congregation and the baptismal party all join together in prayer, thanking and praising God for His grace in Baptism this day, imploring continued Baptism blessings for the new person in Christ Jesus. Then the pastor adds a word, welcoming the baptized into the living fellowship of the Lord's Church.

10. Last, the pastor speaks the Benediction as the Spirit's seal upon all that God has wrought here this day.

Prior to conducting a Baptism, a pastor may review these ten essentials devotionally. They recall what a monumental event Baptism is. Surely, they serve as a primer for the pastor's spirited conduct of the Rite of Holy Baptism.

Reflections on the Rite of Holy Baptism and Emendations

Location of the Baptism Font

Pastors conduct the Rite of Baptism according to orders fixed in the official church Agendas. C. F. W. Walther urged pastors not to alter, add to, or subtract from the Agenda. If a pastor proposes alterations, he should confer with the congregation leaders.[155] In some instances, however, stated rubrics are clearly adiaphora, and may be altered. One such instance is the location of the Baptism font, at front near the chancel or in the narthex, the entrance to the nave. The latter has strong symbolic character—it conveys the notion of entrance by Baptism into the fellowship of the Body of Christ, but in some sanctuaries, the former location serves well. Surely some latitude is appropriate.

Reading of the Scriptures

The appointed reading from the Gospel of Mark 10:13–16 should be included to make the theological point that all baptized—whether infants or adults—come to the Sacrament of Holy Baptism as little children. In addition, particularly when adults are baptized, other readings may be included, such as from the Baptism narratives of the New Testament; for example, Nicodemus

155 Walther, *American-Lutheran Pastoral Theology*, 101.

(John 3:1–15); the Baptisms at Pentecost (Acts 2:37–39); the man from Ethiopia (Acts 8:34–39); the Baptisms of the households of Cornelius (Acts 10:44–48), Lydia (Acts 16:14–15), and the jailer at Philippi (Acts 16:25–34). Also, Romans 6:1–11, followed by Romans 6:12–14 and Titus 3:3–7, may be used.

The Baptism Prayer

In the Rite of Holy Baptism, the prayer following the mark of the sign of the cross calls for emendation. The lines in the Agenda read, "Grant that he/she/they be kept safe and secure in the holy ark of the Christian Church, being separated from the multitude of unbelievers." Is the latter phrase appropriate when conducting the Rite of Baptism in today's public worship services?[156] Among family and friends who attend a Baptism, there may be unbelievers. They are present because they were invited. The Church shall not go out of its way to stir in these persons a sense of rejection by ill-chosen words and phrases. Moreover, the Rite of Baptism is not about the *skandalon* of the Gospel. It is about the Spirit calling the baptized out of darkness into the light that is Christ our Lord. Recognize that here is a tacit call to those present who are not baptized believers. Any part of the rite and its spoken prayers that is out of character with this understanding may require amendment.

The Place for the Rite of Baptism in the Divine Service

It is custom to conduct the Rite of Holy Baptism at the beginning of the Divine Service in the narthex where the font is placed in many churches. Baptism is the Sacrament of entry into the kingdom of God and the beginning of new baptismal life. Is another arrangement possible? The font may be located in front at one side of the chancel. Then, could the rite be conducted within the Office of the Word, following the reading of the Scripture lessons? The Invocation, also the Confession and Absolution, remain in their place. The *credo*, the Creed, is spoken within the rite. The Baptism, therefore, is visible in the Divine Service.

The Baptized Child and Its Name

A rubric in the Rite of Baptism asks, "How are you named?" The question is put to the infant, awaiting response from the parents or sponsors. This rubric is unwieldy if the child is not yet named. Still, the pastor may baptize the child. Lest perceptions prevail that the Spirit gives the child its name, it is better to

156 The phrase is from Luther's "flood prayer," as it is called. According to Arthur Just Jr., the notion of separation expressed in this prayer is sound Lutheran theology. He frames Baptism in three steps, *separation, transition,* and *incorporation.* Arthur A. Just Jr., *Heaven on Earth: The Gifts of Christ in the Divine Service* (St. Louis: Concordia Publishing House, 2008), 172–173, cf. 154–158. Surely, *separation* properly understood may be expressed in a manner that does not stigmatize unbelievers who may be present as guests at a Baptism. Perhaps the phrase from Luther's prayer should undergo review and revision.

view the Sacrament as the giving of God's name to a child presented for Holy Baptism. To the question "How are you named?," it is preferable that parents or sponsors respond by speaking the child's full name. In large congregations where one hundred-plus infant Baptisms occur annually, first names of numerous children are similar, though the Agenda asks only for the first and middle names, omitting the surname. To distinguish a child from others in the congregation, the pastor asks for the child's full name in the presentation phase and he speaks the full name—first, middle, last—later in the rite when he baptizes the child.

Private Baptism

Conducting Baptisms outside the Divine Service—in emergencies or in private—the public rite may be abbreviated.[157] The pastor remains alert to requests for emergency Baptism. When conducting Baptism in health-care facilities, the pastor observes all prescribed procedures. Hospitals require hand cleansing, wearing of a gown, mask, headpiece, even shoe covering. The pastor cooperates and follows directions to the letter. Nurses and other medical staff are helpful, and these persons may serve as witnesses, even providing their name and address for proper recording of the Baptism in the church registry. A pastor should express sincere gratitude to these hospital personnel.

Some families request that the pastor conduct Baptism in their home. Observe that these occasions often develop as a party for family and friends. Is this a reason for declining to serve? The pastor will decide. Consider that a Baptism in the home may afford opportunity to socialize with unchurched persons—an open door to further witness and instruction. In these settings, pastors discover prospects for the Christian faith. There are persons present whom the pastor may lead either to church or to the pastor's class for inquirers.

Some congregations accommodate private Baptisms, either following the public worship service or at another time, frequently on Saturday morning. Families claim that such *off-hours* are compatible with an infant's feeding schedule, napping, and such. Sponsors and extended family coming from a distance is another reason for varied scheduling. These are less than cogent reasons for privatizing Baptism, which should normally be conducted in the presence of the worshiping congregation. Notable, however, are particular situations when Baptism in the public worship hour would be a source of misunderstanding either to members of the Baptism party or to the congregation. Private Baptism, for instance, may be preferable when a single parent presents for Baptism her

157 For an abbreviated order, the exhibit "Holy Baptism in Cases of Emergency" provides helpful rubrics. See *Lutheran Service Book: Pastoral Care Companion*, prepared by the Commission on Worship of The Lutheran Church—Missouri Synod (St. Louis: Concordia Publishing House, 2007), 21–22.

third child born out of wedlock. Parents and family of a seriously impaired child may be more comfortable with private Baptism.

The Use of the Element Water in Baptism

Application of Water

In the action of Baptism, the pastor applies water to the candidate. Water that is clean and clear serves well. The quantity of water is incidental, but application should be generous. The "waters of Baptism" is a familiar expression that excludes the use of any other element. Novelty reigns when well-meaning Christians suggest that soda or beer, milk or wine could serve, perhaps even pointing to the water content in such commodities. Baptism requires the use of water. C. F. W. Walther asserts that this Sacrament is falsified by usage of substitutes because true water is necessary for the essence of Baptism, since it is the washing of water with the Word (Eph. 5:26; John 3:5; Acts 8:36; 10:47).[158]

The Mode of Baptizing

Application of the water with the Word is possible in a variety of modes. Immersion, for instance, speaks the rich theology of Baptism—dying and buried with Christ in His death, and rising with Him in His resurrection to newness of life (Rom 6:4–11). For this reason, Luther favored immersion.[159] Practiced in the Early Church,[160] immersion is problematic today because numerous Baptist churches and Pentecostal bodies assert that immersion versus other modes of applying the water assures the efficacy of the Sacrament. Lutheran theology disagrees. The Spirit effects the efficacy of Baptism through the Word connected with the water in this sacred washing. The term βαπτίζω means "immerse" or "submerge," but it can also mean "dip" or "bathe." St. Luke reports that the Ethiopian and Philip both went down into the water and came up again (Acts 8:38–39). The Gospels, in Mark 1:9–11 and Matthew 3:13–17, portray the Baptism of the Lord by John in the waters of the Jordan River (cf. John 3:23).

Other reported instances of Baptism, however, do not suggest immersion. The Baptism of three thousand in Jerusalem on Pentecost is one instance (Acts 2:41). Several reports of Baptism in households—Lydia, the jailer of Philippi, the house of Stephanas—are weak attestation to the practice of immersion (Acts 16:15, 33; 1 Cor 1:16). And there is support for application of the water

158 See Walther's citation of Salomon Deyling in Walther, *American-Lutheran Pastoral Theology* (2017), 137.
159 Martin Luther, *The Babylonian Captivity of the Church*, in *Luther's Works*, American Edition, vol. 36, trans. A. T. W. Steinhauser and Rev. Frederick C. Ahrens and Abdel Ross Wentz (Philadelphia: Fortress Press, 1959), 68. See Arthur A. Just Jr., *Heaven on Earth*, 294n12.
160 Dr. Arthur A. Just Jr. has researched the early practice of immersion. At two locations—Kelibia in Tunisia and Ephesus—ancient baptistries demonstrate the prevalence of immersion. See *Heaven on Earth*, 164–166.

in modes like pouring or sprinkling liberally.[161] These are acceptable modes for baptizing. The water is not for cleansing the body and may be applied, therefore, to one member only. Connected to the Word, this water is for regeneration of the person.

The Baptism Formula

Principle: The Church properly uses the words commanded by Christ, for they compose the "Word" of the Baptism formula.

The Baptism formula—the spoken Word in the action of baptizing—is from the Lord's command. The pastor applies the water three times concurrent with the phrases naming the persons of the Holy Trinity. He speaks, "I baptize you in the name of the Father and of the Son and of the Holy Spirit." This formula, nothing more or less, is the New Testament Rite of Holy Baptism. The Early Church employed this trinitarian formula.[162] We discourage any attempt to alter this formula in the interest of modernizing either words or meaning. What purpose is served by the altered formula, "I baptize you in the name of the Creator, Redeemer, and Sanctifier"?

What's in a name? More than we realize for the person baptized in the name of the triune God. Consider the phrase "in the name," εις το ονομα in the Greek (cf. Matt 28:19; 1 Cor 1:13). At the same time, reflect on the word *baptize*, βαπτίζω. Souter notes, "When the preposition *eis* with a noun in the accusative case follows, it appears to indicate that through this ceremony the baptized person becomes the property of the person indicated after *eis*."[163] The riches of God's grace and the Holy Spirit in Baptism imply beyond doubt that God claims the baptized person as His own. The name of the Holy Trinity authenticates that claim. The name, therefore, affords certainty that a person is a child of God through Baptism. This can be of great comfort. Where God's

161 The external form of baptizing is indicated by multiple expressions: buried with Christ (Rom 6:3–4), allusion to immersion; the washing away of sins (Acts 22:16; cf. Eph 5:26); the outpouring of the Holy Spirit (Titus 3:5–6). These texts speak of the benefits of Baptism, and doing so, they may well reference the manner or mode of baptizing. Add the imagery suggested by being sprinkled with Christ's blood (Heb 10:19–22; see Exod 24:8; Heb 9:19–20; 1 Cor 10:2). See the *Didache* VII, 1–3; Walther, *American-Lutheran Pastoral Theology*, 89; Pieper, *Christian Dogmatics*, vol. 3, trans. Walter W. F. Albrecht (St. Louis: Concordia Publishing House, 1953), 257n8. Overarching this discussion of the mode of applying the water is Luther's pointed statements referencing God's external action in Baptism. See Luther's Large Catechism IV, 28–30.

162 See the *Didache* VII, 1, 3. Luther recalls that the apostles did baptize in the name of Jesus Christ (Acts 2:38; 10:48; 19:5), but he affirms that the apostles considered the trinitarian Baptism formula valid. Yet he comments that Baptism truly saves if only it is not administered in the name of man, but in the name of the Lord. See Luther, *The Babylonian Captivity of the Church* (LW 36:63–64). Further reflection suggests that baptizing in the name of Jesus, properly understood, is contiguous with the Holy Trinity by *synecdoche*. Recall that Peter's sermon on Pentecost, Acts 2:14ff., was itself a powerful testimony regarding the Father, the Son, and the Holy Spirit. See Pieper, *Christian Dogmatics*, vol. 3, 260n14. Also note that the Rite of Holy Baptism used in Lutheran churches today follows Luther's Orders (1523, 1526), where the action, baptizing, follows immediately after the *credo*, the confession of faith in the Holy Trinity.

163 Alexander Souter, *A Pocket Lexicon to the Greek New Testament* (Oxford: At the Clarendon Press, 1953), 46.

name is present, there God acts. Luther affirms that God's name is in Baptism, then life and salvation.[164]

Let no one presume to propose clever or cute changes to the Baptism formula given by the Lord. Such altering could generate uncertainty about the validity of Baptism conducted frivolously. What a mockery to baptize "in the name of the Mother, the Son, and the Holy Spirit"! How foolish it is to *jazz up* the Sacrament, tweaking the formula into cute words and phrases in order to be politically correct, relational, or relevant, expecting God to own such inventions. What Christ has ordained should stand.[165]

Candidates for Holy Baptism Revisited

Baptism of Adults

Why They Come for Baptism

Principle: The Lord placed teaching in close proximity to Baptism (Matt 28:19–20a). Therefore, instruction in the teachings of the Christian faith normally precedes the Baptism of children, youth, and adults.

Pastors instruct candidates for Baptism at the level of their capacity to learn. A basic principle abides.

There are persons in the immediate radius of Christian congregations who are silently waiting for Baptism. Reserved, silent, retiring, they are there—the youth who occasionally attends worship with his girlfriend; the middle-aged man with a serious coronary condition; the person who reflects, "I don't know that I was ever baptized"; the relative who attends an infant Baptism and muses, "Maybe that is for me too." A discerning pastor senses interest, curiosity, feelers with regard to Baptism. He acts, invites, instructs, and baptizes.

Paths of Instruction toward Baptism

The path toward Baptism is instruction, but the itinerary varies. Normally, instruction prior to Baptism covers the major doctrines of the Scriptures in a course of ten to fifteen class sessions. In critical situations, the pastor leads to Baptism quickly, and the larger instruction follows. For instance, a man suffering advanced coronary disease is traumatized by his sense of mortality. For him, the pastor counsels about the seriousness of sin and the certainty of sal-

164 Martin Luther, Large Catechism IV, 26–27.

165 Pieper summarizes, "We agree with those theologians who hold that the Matt. 28:19 formula of Baptism is the most fitting, the simplest, and the safest." Then Pieper quotes from *Prudentia Pastoralis*, a work by the pastoral theologian Deyling, who stated, "No doubt Christ had important reasons why He expressly mentioned the individual Persons in this formula of initiation and desired that we do likewise." Pieper, *Christian Dogmatics*, vol. 3, 261.

vation, baptized into Christ Jesus for the forgiveness of sin (Rom 5:12; 6:23; Eph 2:1–2; Acts 2:38; 22:16). In Baptism, the pastor counsels, God puts His name on us, claims us as His own, and points us to His gift of eternal life. The pastor asks, "Friend, do you believe in the Lord Jesus Christ? Do you wish to be baptized?"

In normal circumstances, there is value in giving instruction prior to Baptism. Candidates should comprehend the Christian faith that they confess in Baptism. But an alternate practice is Baptism first, followed by instruction. In either case, the catechesis is advisably thorough and comprehensive to the extent of the catechism's exposition of Christian doctrine. Unfortunately, in some churches, the catechesis is reduced to a quick single day of instruction and orientation to church membership. Surely, the Church's ministry can do better.[166]

Preparing the Young Child for Baptism

Preparing young children, ages 3 to 9, for Baptism is another itinerary. Analogies are helpful. For example, the pastor may refer to soap for cleansing. When a mother calls children to the dinner table, she asks them to wash their hands with soap and water. Baptism is God's washing away of sin by applying water with His Word from Christ, a Word that draws us into the Lord's taking away our sins on the cross. Baptism, then, cleanses our hearts and lives before God.

Instruction of a young child may include showing what will occur at the Baptism. This is best done in the sanctuary at the Baptism font. There, the pastor explains the rite. A child seven years or older may respond to questions in the rite, though parents and sponsors may speak the responses for a very young child. At some point in the pre-Baptism visit, the pastor may elicit from the child expressed faith in Jesus. All that God does in Baptism elicits faith in God's Word and promise.[167] At this pre-Baptism visit, a Sunday School teacher or Christian Day School teacher may be present to support the young child.

The Baptism of Infants

The Lutheran Confessional Stance

Infant Baptism is a long-standing practice in the Christian Church. Opposition to this practice is also long-standing. The Anabaptists who declared that the Baptism of children was useless proved to be a frustration to both Luther and Melanchthon. We understand that frustration. Uuras Saarnivaara states

166 Luther's Small Catechism treats major doctrines, the Law stated in the Ten Commandments, the Gospel in the Christology of the Apostles' Creed—Second Article—and Baptism, plus other chief doctrines. Dated, but still valuable for its presentation of Christian doctrine for adults, is the work by Oswald Riess, *What Does the Bible Say?: A Manual of Instruction for Adults* (Detroit, 1943).

167 Luther, *The Babylonian Captivity of the Church* (LW 36:64).

the view of the Anabaptists espoused by Baptists, Pentecostals, and others today. They assert that infant Baptism is without warrant, they say that there is no command in the Scriptures that infants should be baptized, and they deny that there is any clear example of the Baptism of infants.[168] Such assertions against infant Baptism—widely held in Christendom today—beg for a reasonable and convincing response from churches practicing the Baptism of little children. The Lutheran response follows.

The question of baptizing newborns, as Hermann Sasse pointedly asserted, is not a question simply answered historically.[169] It is not a mere practical, sociological question. The baptizing of infants is a theological question. Addressing the question as theological, observe that Lutherans are *pedobaptizers*, not only in practice, but in the strength of confession. The Augsburg Confession, Article IX, states: "Concerning baptism it is taught that it is necessary, that grace is offered through it, and that one should also baptize children, who through such baptism are entrusted to God and become pleasing to him. Rejected, therefore, are the Anabaptists who teach that baptism of children is not right" (1–3).

The importance of this confession is evident in pastoral care ministry to a young couple who wanted to join a Lutheran congregation, but refused Baptism for their infant daughter. Previously, they had their first child baptized. Then, relocated distant from any Lutheran church, they joined a nondenominational fellowship where they were schooled in the Anabaptist practice that denies Baptism to infants. Later, relocating again near this Lutheran congregation, they wanted to become members and enroll their oldest child in the Christian Day School. Only patient pastoral care could help this couple recover their Lutheran confession that little children invited by our Lord should be baptized (Mark 10:13–16).

In his reply to the Anabaptists, Melanchthon made two points. First, in the Church where Christ regenerates through Word and Sacrament, it is most certain that the promise of salvation also applies to children. He wrote, "Therefore it is necessary to baptize little children in order that the promise of salvation might be applied to them according to Christ's mandate [Matt. 28:19], 'Baptize all nations'" (Ap IX 2). Melanchthon argues, "Just as salvation is offered to all in that passage, so baptism is also offered to all—men, women, children, and

168 Uuras Saarnivaara, *Scriptural Baptism: A Dialog between John Baptstead and Martin Childfont* (New York: Vantage Press, 1953), 1.

169 That the practice of infant Baptism, first explicitly spoken of by Irenaeus (about AD 185), goes back to the time of the apostles, numerous authorities attest and support. Dr. Hermann Sasse has brought together historical references affirming the early and long-standing practice of infant Baptism in a succinct overview that serves the busy pastor. See Hermann Sasse, "Holy Baptism," *Letters to Lutheran Pastors, No. 4* (St. Louis: Concordia Publishing House, 1985), 38–39. Also see David P. Scaer, *Infant Baptism in Nineteenth-Century Lutheran Theology* (St. Louis: Concordia Publishing House, 2011).

infants. Therefore it clearly follows that infants are to be baptized because salvation is offered with baptism." Second, he argued that God's approval of the Baptism of little children is certain because God gives the Holy Spirit to those so baptized. For, if this Baptism of children were useless, as the Anabaptists teach, the Holy Spirit would be given to none, none would be saved, and ultimately there would be no Church (Ap IX 2, 3).

Martin Luther shared Melanchthon's frustration over the teaching of the Anabaptists, whom he named collectively the *sects*. Luther argues that the Baptism of infants is pleasing to Christ, and this is proved sufficiently by our Lord's own work (LC IV 49). Luther explained that God sanctified many who were baptized as infants and gave to them the Holy Spirit. God has confirmed their Baptism through the bestowal of the Holy Spirit. "But if God did not accept the baptism of infants," Luther argues, "he would not have given any of them the Holy Spirit—or any part of him. In short, all this time down to the present day there would have been no person on earth who could have been a Christian" (LC IV 50). Thus, Luther concurs with Melanchthon's argument. He is convinced that the very existence of the Christian Church, of saints and the fathers and the multitude of believers, most of whom were baptized as little children, shows that God approves of such Baptism through the gift of His Holy Spirit to the ones baptized down to the end of time. The opponents, therefore, must acknowledge that infant Baptism is pleasing to God. According to Luther, this is the strongest proof (LC IV 51).

Other Arguments Supporting the Practice of Infant Baptism

What God Promises in Baptism, Infants Receive by Faith

Integral to infant Baptism are the questions "Can infants believe? Can they receive the Holy Spirit and His gifts by believing?" (cf. Matt 18:6). Luther answers decisively: little children can believe. He explains, responding to another question, "Does the Gospel of John 6 refer to the Sacrament of the Altar?" Citing John 6:53, "Unless you eat the flesh of the Son of Man and drink His blood, you have no life in you," Luther argues, if these words refer to the Sacrament and sacramental eating as some assert, the Lord would condemn infants, all the sick, and all those absent or in any way hindered from sacramental eating, however strong their faith might be. But Christ is here speaking of faith in the Son of God, and by faith infants do eat the flesh and drink the blood of Christ without the Sacrament, partaking of them through the faith of the Church.[170]

170 Luther, *The Babylonian Captivity of the Church* (LW 36:19–20).

"Through the faith of the church" is the medium Luther employs when speaking of the faith of infants. This long-standing connection dates back to Thomas Aquinas and earlier to Augustine. How do infants believe? Luther explains:

> Here I say what all say: Infants are aided by the faith of others, namely, those who bring them for baptism. For the Word of God is powerful enough, when uttered, to change even a godless heart, which is no less unresponsive and helpless than any infant. So through the prayer of the believing church which presents it, a prayer to which all things are possible [Mark 9:23], the infant is changed, cleansed, and renewed by inpoured faith. Nor should I doubt that even a godless adult could be changed, in any of the sacraments, if the same church prayed for and presented him, as we read of the paralytic in the Gospel, who was healed through the faith of others [Mark 2:3–12].[171]

Luther focuses on the power in Baptism, which does not reside in the faith of the candidates, be they adults or little children. He shows that Baptism with or without faith is valid and true because everything depends upon the Word and commandment of God. In the Large Catechism, he explains:

> Everything depends upon the Word and commandment of God. . . . As we said, even if infants did not believe—which, however, is not the case, as we have proved—still the baptism would be valid and no one should rebaptize them. . . . We bring the child with the intent and hope that it may believe, and we pray God to grant it faith. But we do not baptize on this basis, but solely on the command of God.[172]

These passages from Luther suggest a rubric for the practice of infant Baptism. Simply stated, "Parents, bring your infant to the Sacrament. Believing, join with the faith and prayer of the Church for your child. The pastor baptizes the little one, and all are confident that by the Word and command of God connected with the baptismal water, the Spirit, washing and working, will impart to the infant saving faith."[173]

---

171 Ibid., 73n129.

172 Large Catechism IV 52, 55, 57.

173 Lutheran dogmaticians maintain persistently on the basis of Titus 3:5 that faith is produced in children through Baptism even though infants may not understand or perceive the movements of faith. Baptism, they argue, is the washing of regeneration; but regeneration cannot take place without faith. See citations from Gerhard and Chemnitz in the work by Heinrich Schmid, *The Doctrinal Theology of the Evangelical Lutheran Church*, 3rd ed., trans. Charles A. Hay and Henry E. Jacobs (Minneapolis: Augsburg Publishing House, 1889), 549.

Circumcision and Infant Baptism

Many proponents of the practice of infant Baptism see parallels between the Rite of Circumcision under the old covenant and the Rite of Baptism under the new. Beyond parallels, some theologians assert that infant Baptism replaces circumcision.[174] Dr. Hermann Sasse, however, judges that Baptism cannot be understood as the counterpart to circumcision, despite Colossians 2:11, for they are as different as the new covenant is from the old covenant, as Israel according to the flesh differs from Israel according to the Spirit.[175] Circumcision may be viewed as a *sign* that God chose Israel and separated them from nations who rejected Him. Similarly, Baptism may be understood as a *sign* of putting on the righteousness of Christ, and thus separating the baptized from the world, but Baptism is significantly much more than a sign. In the fullest sense, Baptism is a Means of Grace, of regeneration by the Holy Spirit. Note that St. Paul distinguishes Baptism as a circumcision made without hands, the circumcision of Christ that refers specifically to putting off the sinful flesh by Baptism into Christ's death and His resurrection, then rising to newness of life (Col 2:11ff.; cf. Gen 17:9–14, 21; 21:4).

Distinctions between circumcision and Baptism, however, do not lessen parallels and their implications for the practice of infant Baptism. Circumcision also held meaning beyond the notion of a sign. It brought internal grace—renewal of the heart to faith, love to God, and willing obedience to Him—to which faith responded.[176] By circumcision, God received Israel as His people in that covenant relationship marked by His grace toward them (Gen 17:11; Deut 7:9, cf. 6–11). This factor pressed the prophets to plead for circumcision of the heart that was indispensable for the Israelites as the true people of God (Deut 30:6; Jer 4:4; 9:25–26).

Oddly, the parallels between circumcision and Baptism are intertwined with their distinctions. On one hand, the Rite of Circumcision, after Abraham, was the entry into God's covenant for children in early infancy (Gen 17:9–14). In that covenant, they were sealed by God's love and grace to be His people, which they acknowledged by faith (cf. Rom 4:3, 11–12; Gal 3:27–29). On the other hand, Baptism in the New Testament age seals infants and declares them God's own people from infancy forward. Baptism is for infants the "circumcision of Christ" (Col 2:11–12), a circumcision without hands, that is, a burying

174 The Lutheran dogmatician Francis Pieper held that Baptism has supplanted the Old Testament sacrament of circumcision. He cites Abraham Calov, who stated, "Sacramentum baptismi christus surrogatum voluit circumcision," translated, "Christ wanted the sacrament of baptism to be the substitute for circumcision." See Pieper, *Christian Dogmatics*, vol. 3, 277.

175 Sasse, "Holy Baptism," *Letters to Lutheran Pastors, No. 4*, 44.

176 Saarnivaara, *Scriptural Baptism*, 5.

of the sinful flesh in Christ's death, and in Him and His resurrection a rising to God-fearing living.[177]

Infant Baptism—Jewish Proselytes and New Testament Families

Other practices in Judaism point to the Baptism of infants. Jewish zeal to win proselytes was well known in the first century. Baptizing these converts to Judaism was the common practice.[178] Converts came as families, and presumably the adults took their children with them into the covenant. Furthermore, infants abandoned by Gentiles were received by Jewish families who baptized and cared for them. If children of Gentile parents were cleansed of the uncleanness of paganism, the logic is, children of Christians are cleansed by Baptism from the uncleanness of original sin. They enter the kingdom of heaven.[179]

The New Testament cites the Baptism of οἶκοι, households. These reports do not specify age or gender of those baptized, but the term *household* is inclusive. The Old Testament manner of speaking refers to a man and his *household* or family—inclusive language. Furthermore, the term inferred not only immediate family but also house servants and their families. We surmise that in the households of Cornelius, Lydia, the jailer at Philippi, and Stephanas, Baptism was for everyone, including infants[180] (Acts 10:47; 11:14; 16:15, 31, 33; 1 Cor 1:16).

Jesus and the Children

Most telling is our Lord receiving children whom He blessed when they were brought to Him (Mark 10:13–16; Matt 19:13–15; Luke 18:15–17). Luke reports that Jesus received and blessed both βρέφοι (babes) and παιδία (children, about four to ten years old). The term βρέφος, according to Greek lexicons, has only two meanings:

1. An unborn fetus
2. A newborn infant

177 Andrew Das discusses how baptized infants become heirs of the promise just as infants in the Old Testament, by circumcision, became partakers of the promise God gave to Abraham. See A. Andrew Das, *Baptized into God's Family: The Doctrine of Infant Baptism for Today* (Milwaukee: Northwestern Publishing House, 1991), 68–69.

178 Saarnivaara, *Scriptural Baptism*, 7–8.

179 Ibid., 75. The rabbinic literature deals extensively with proselyte Baptisms among the Jews. See Alfred Edersheim, *The Life and Time of Jesus the Messiah*, vol. 2 (Grand Rapids: Wm. B. Eerdmans, 1953), 747.

180 Joachim Jeremias, *The Origins of Infant Baptism*, trans. Dorotheia M. Barton (Chatham, England: W. & J. Mackay, 1963), 25–27. Chapter 2 is devoted entirely to this subject. It is titled "The Baptism of 'Houses.'" For an appropriate use of the study by Jeremias on this subject, see Andrew Das, *Baptized into God's Family*, chapter 8, "The Baptism of Entire Families and Households," 79–91.

Obviously, the second meaning applies here. Jesus assures that the kingdom of God belongs to infants and children, and His words are sealed with the exclamation "Verily!" If Peter witnessed Jesus and the children, he may have recalled the incident later on the Day of Pentecost, when he preached about Baptism to the crowds in Jerusalem, saying, "For the promise is for you and for your children"[181] (Acts 2:39). That children are heirs of the kingdom is clear from our Lord's teaching that adults must receive the kingdom as a little child (Luke 18:17; Mark 9:35–36; Matt 18:1–6). Furthermore, our Lord welcomes the children, as He says, "Let the children come to Me" (Mark 10:14). When the children are brought to Him, He gives them the Kingdom, and they receive it in faith, the only way that the Kingdom is received by either adults or children.[182]

Original Sin—The Need for Baptism

Some theologians assert that infants by nature are members of the kingdom of God, and there is no need to interject Baptism as a means of getting them there. These theologians may deny the doctrine of original sin, claiming that a child is innocent from infancy through childhood until adolescence. When they deny original sin, they also deny that infants are in need of the grace of God. The Bible responds to this with severity (Eph 2:1–3; cf. Rom 5:12–14).

Infants enter this world with the sinful nature that is common to all mankind since the fall (Gen 3; Rom 5:12). This assessment does not come by observation, reasoning, or rationalization, but by divine revelation (Ps 51:5; Eph 2:1–3). The Church's Rite of Baptism literally mourns original sin at conception. Such infants, it cries, "would be lost forever unless delivered by our Lord Jesus Christ." There is no time or place or people where the devastation of the fall does not reach.

Conversely, this universal depravity that grips infants has met its match in Baptism—the drowning of the sinful nature in Christ's death, and the rising to newness of life in the power of His resurrection (Rom 6:4ff.). Though vestiges of original sin remain, the regeneration by the Holy Spirit through water and the Word signals release from the guilt of sin (Acts 2:38). In Baptism, the Spirit ends concupiscence—the love for sinful ways contrary to God's Word—and creates new impulses in the human being (Ap II 35). When the baptized infant matures and learns of this action of the Holy Spirit in his or her life beginning as a newborn, a Christian life springs forward: a Christian is made in Baptism.

181 These words from Peter's Pentecost sermon, directed to parents about the promise for their children, do not refer to descendants in future generations, but to children in the families addressed in the apostle's audience that day—infants and children baptized. Jeremias argues this point convincingly. See Joachim Jeremias, *The Origins of Infant Baptism*, 25–27.

182 Saarnivaara, *Scriptural Baptism*, 13.

Review: This lengthy discourse supports the Church's practice of baptizing infants. However, it will not convince anyone in the Anabaptist tradition that this practice is consistent with the New Testament. Defeating their arguments is not the purpose. Instead, beginning with a clear statement of the Lutheran confession, these points inform and encourage pastors and people who do baptize infants in their churches. They can be confident that infant Baptism is blessed by God because Baptism is His care and salvation that He intends all souls to have, including young children.

Regularizing Arrangements for Baptism

Parental Care for Infants to be Baptized

When Parents Are Christians

Christian parents take the initiative to have their newborn child baptized. They are in good company. St. Luke reports, "Now they were bringing even infants to Him" (Luke 18:15). Mary and Joseph brought the infant Jesus to the temple (Luke 2:22–23). Therefore, Christian parents arrange for their child's Baptism and they resolve that their child will receive nurture in God's Word. In England, parents enroll their sons in the elite schools of Eaton and Harrow the day the child is born. In the same way, Christian parents envision Christian upbringing for their child in the home, at church, and in school.

When Family and Home Are Unstable

Principle: The Church shall be generous with Baptism, for the Lord died and rose again to save all. His command to baptize is equally generous. He intends for all to be baptized (Matt 28:19).

Some households, however, do not have strong resolve to nurture a baptized child. The home may lack stability—some single-parent homes; two parents, one Christian, the other an unbeliever; or parenting shifted to grandparents. For whatever reason, the nurture of the child after Baptism is doubtful. In these instances, many pastors hesitate to baptize the child. Take caution: pastors shall not be stingy with Baptism, which the Lord intended for all. To assist unstable homes, the Church mounts an active ministry of nurture in God's Word. Two principles guide a pastor who faces irregular situations.

Irregular circumstances abound. For instance, natural parents or legal guardians request Baptism for a child, though they have no clue about the sacrament's meaning or purpose. This is not a reason to refuse Baptism, but it calls for patient instruction. In another instance, legal parents of a child are two lesbians or two homosexuals; they request Baptism for their adopted child. The informal curriculum in this home, however, is a relationship constituted contrary to God's Word. Shall the Church's ministry deny the child the Means of Grace because the custodial parents are unfit? Or is it possible that these parents may commit to raising the child in the Church—Divine Service, Sunday School, Christian Day School, catechesis, and confirmation? Then, by all means, baptize!

Surprisingly, declared unbelievers may want their child baptized. They are secular, but they yield to family pressure or the need for social acceptance. In Sweden, such parents want what is respectable for their child.[183] The pastor may arch his back and flatly reject a request from unbelievers for Baptism. Jesus said, "Do not give dogs what is holy, and do not throw your pearls before pigs" (Matt 7:6). Does His teaching preclude a pastoral response in this instance? Although the parents may be skeptics, agnostics, or atheists, the process of arranging Baptism for their child may offer teachable moments. Instruct the parents as is customary in planning every Baptism. Give the Spirit opportunity with these people (cf. Acts 16:14). Baptize their child and require that they raise their child within the orbit of the Church's teaching and life.

Principle: Instituting Christian Baptism, the Lord said, "Teaching them to observe all that I have commanded you" (Matt 28:20a). His intention is that all who are baptized should receive nurture and sound teaching—Christian doctrine according to the Scriptures.

Parents may be flippant and indifferent about the future nurture of their little one as a child of God. In light of a careless demeanor, shall the pastor baptize or refuse Baptism? A short answer is, baptize the child now and tend to parental deficiency later. For example, a couple registered their four-year-old in a Lutheran congregation's preschool. The husband was a bioscientist from Germany, holding a high position with a chemical company in America. On assignment, he travels the world, tending to agriculture in many countries. He met his wife in Mexico. They were blessed with a child, now four years old. For their second child, eight months old, they requested Baptism. The pastor agreed, and the Baptism was scheduled three months later on a Saturday morning when family from Germany and Mexico could be present. Though the parents were obviously lukewarm spiritually and ambivalent about becoming members of the church, the pastor honored their request and baptized their

183 Customs in Scandinavia still include church traditions. Though many secular parents profess unbelief quite openly, they view Baptism as the entrée into society. See Phil Zuckerman, *Society without God: What the Least Religious Nations Can Tell Us about Contentment* (New York: New York University Press, 2008), 8–10, 52.

child. By the first principle above, the pastor acted properly. Relative to the second principle, he had his work cut out for him. The challenge is to stay in touch with this young family and exhort, instruct, and train the parents to nurture their baptized children.

Nonbelievers typically refuse Baptism for their children, to the disappointment of Christian relatives. A devout grandmother is anxious about her granddaughter. This lady's daughter married an unbeliever and espoused the unbelief of her husband. Doubtless, the infant granddaughter in this family will not be baptized. Frantic, the grandmother sought the pastor and requested that he baptize the child in secret. The pastor refused. The child's parents had made a decision, and the congregation honors parental authority according to the Fourth Commandment. Furthermore, the grandmother shall not baptize the infant herself. She may not exercise authority in this matter. However, the pastor may serve as an advocate for the desperate grandmother. If not agreement from the parents, he may win permission to baptize the child. They may yield, saying, "Oh, all right, if it makes Mom happy, go ahead and baptize our daughter." Hopefully, the pastor may also win concession to receive this child later in Sunday School and worship services. Perhaps the parents may commit to both Baptism and nurture of their child.

Many homes are unstable, and parents may be clumsy at teaching the faith. Before pastors refuse to baptize children in such families, consider that the Word in Baptism is powerful. The work of the Spirit will not easily be diminished by unfavorable circumstances in the home. Further, observe Luther's practice. Minus perfect conditions, he concerned himself with baptizing foundlings.[184] So the pastor baptizes (LC IV 8, 23–25, 39)! But nurture beyond Baptism is imperative. Therefore, the Church tracks every baptized person even as we care for each member of our physical bodies (1 Cor 12:12–13, 25–26). An adequate program of catechesis that nurtures the baptized is a must.

Requests for Rebaptism

Baptism is as durable as God and His Word are faithful. Therefore, the Church does not rebaptize persons when it is clear that they have been baptized according to our Lord's institution and command. On the other hand, if a person's Baptism cannot be verified, for instance, adopted children or adults who cannot vouch for witnesses to their Baptism, these persons may be candidates

184 Walther, *American-Lutheran Pastoral Theology*, 96. In the year 2010, the City of St. Louis administered care for sixty-one infants left on the steps of public buildings—police stations and firehouses. In his day, Luther would see that such infants were baptized. When *foundlings* were discovered, he insisted that they be brought to the church and baptized if there was any doubt that they had properly received the Sacrament earlier. Doubtless, at that point there was no guarantee of future nurture and training for these baptized orphans. Still, Luther favored baptizing them.

for Baptism. Baptized persons, however, who attest to their Baptism but doubt its efficacy and for that reason desire the Sacrament should not be rebaptized. The pastor directs them back to Baptism and the Word, back to the *ship* as Luther describes Baptism, the solid ship that stays on course.[185]

Situations in the Practice of Holy Baptism

Anomalies

Principle: The Lord's institution of Baptism and the Early Church's practice indicate that normal use and application of water in connection with the Word suffice for valid Baptism. Resorting to extraordinary ways and means is not recommended in administration of the Sacrament.

Every imaginable procedure in administration of Baptism is afoot today. For instance, extrauterine Baptism, though uncommon, crops up in discussions. This bizarre application of the water to the exterior abdomen of the woman with child, presumably out of anxiety for the unborn infant, counters our Lord's command that clearly speaks simply of applying water directly in a normal manner to each candidate. This is not a valid Baptism and must not be done.

It is unusual, but parents bereft of their child, delivered lifeless from the mother, may frantically request the pastor's ministry at this critical time. They may request that the pastor administer Baptism to the child. Theologically, we comprehend that God has already acted and that the Lord's institution of Baptism is for the living (Psalm 31:15a; John 3:3–7). The pastor may gently affirm that God has now brought closure and that we are not alone. He remains with the family as our loving heavenly Father (Psalm 107:13–15, 28, 43). Thus, the pastor as caring shepherd ministers to bereaved parents, but he shall not baptize an infant now deceased.

Baptism in the Event of Infant Demise

Sensitive pastoral care addresses parents who suffer the loss of a child—stillborn or deceased at birth. In this time of grief, the pastor comforts the parents, explaining that God has His loving interest in this baby, and that their prayers for this child, also their intention to have the little one baptized, will not escape the attention of our gracious God. He will honor those prayers and those intentions. Moreover, our Lord instituted Baptism for renewal and regeneration of those born and living in this fallen age (John 3:3–7; Titus 3:3–5). Although God has intervened, He loves and cares and saves even when His action

185 Luther, *The Babylonian Captivity of the Church* (LW 36:61).

withholds opportunity to baptize. This child is Jesus' little lamb. Ministry to the beleaguered parents helps them to comprehend that the Lord who gives and takes life has brought closure, albeit sudden and devastating (Job 1:21). This is a time to let God be God and entrust all to His wisdom and mercy (Isa 55:8–9).

Principle: Consoling Christian parents burdened with a heavy cross—suffering the loss of a child at birth or the death of a child prior to opportunity for Baptism—the pastor's words and assurances remain within and do not extend beyond the clear words and promises of God (cf. 2 Cor 1:3–4).

When infant Baptism is prevented by untimely death, what shall a pastor bring to the bereaved parents and families? A pastor called to this delicate task should ask, "Under these circumstances, what would my wife and I want to hear from our shepherd?" Is it clichés, shallow rationalizations, and vague suppositions about what God is doing? No, we demand only the words and promises of God from His truthful Word. These are sufficient (Ps 116:1–4; 121; 117).

Pastoral care to the bereaved when a child dies unbaptized may be categorized as primary, secondary, and tertiary. Consider *primary* that the pastor directs bereaved parents and families to our God, a loving God, known for His grace and mercy in the face of Christ Jesus[186] (2 Cor 4:6; cf. 1 John 4:9–10). God's love is so near, so caring, so embracing that no sorrow or sadness can separate us from Him or His love (Rom 8:35–39). We cast care on our Lord, knowing that He cares for us (1 Pet 5:7). He includes their little one in His desire that *all* be saved (1 Tim 2:4; John 3:16; cf. Rom 8:27–39). To that end, God has given the preaching of the saving Word, Baptism, and the Lord's Supper. Still, He may elect to save, taking some to Himself outside His normal Means of Grace. In either case, He does not change, He is always gracious and all is well with His own. Therefore, we let go. We commend our child to the Lord, for in our family we know that whether we live or whether we die, we are the Lord's (Rom 14:7–8). In Jesus, we are together and shall be forever.

Secondary ministry to the bereaved upon the death of a unbaptized infant also moves toward closure.[187] Pastors may console based on familial connection cited in 1 Cor 7:14, "Otherwise your children would be unclean, but as it is, they are holy." The unbaptized child who died was a son or daughter of parents baptized into Christ. Thereby, this child was attached to Christians in

186 The opening sentences and the Scriptures cited in "Burial for a Stillborn Child or Unbaptized Child" serve well. They accent that God is love! See *Lutheran Service Book: Pastoral Care Companion*, prepared by the Commission on Worship of The Lutheran Church—Missouri Synod (St. Louis: Concordia Publishing House, 2007), 136ff.

187 Closure was exhibited when King David stated about his infant son who died, "Can I bring him back again? I shall go to him, but he will not return to me" (2 Sam 12:23b).

the home and to the larger fellowship, the Church. From conception, the child was in the orbit of the Lord's people, thus in the circle of the Lord's saving work. Luther's comfort for a bereaved Christian mother is poignant. He writes: "Let the mother not be angry with God, nor attempt to know the hidden judgment of God, but take comfort, her prayers for the child and deep longing for its Baptism will be accepted by God as an effective prayer."[188]

Certainly, *tertiary* in ministry to parents of an infant who dies without Baptism are rationalizations of doubtful value. Some pastors, however, find the following points useful. A woman with child participates in home devotions and attends worship and Bible class. Does her unborn child listen to the Word with the mother, and through that hearing does the Spirit work faith in the heart of the child (cf. Luke 1:41, 44; Rom 10:17)? This Christian lady also kneels at the Communion rail. She and her unborn child hear the Words of Institution and the words of distribution, "Take, eat, this is the Lord's body. Take drink, this is the Lord's blood." Consider the conjecture that when this mother communes, her unborn infant hears the Word and through her blood supply receives the body and blood of the Lord. Can such speculation provide consolation?[189]

Baptism of Handicapped Children

Hesitance to baptize because an infant is handicapped in some manner runs counter to the Lord's mandate that salvation is for all. So baptize all (cf. Matt 28:19). For instance, the newborn is diagnosed to be permanently deaf. Does the condition of deafness warrant forfeiture of Baptism? An affirmative answer goes against the larger discussion of infant Baptism above. No conditions or handicaps hinder the Holy Spirit, who brings a child to God's grace, ushering the child into the kingdom of God. C. F. W. Walther said that children in whatever state of health or form are to be baptized if they are alive.[190]

---

188 Martin Luther, "Comfort for Women Who Have Had a Miscarriage" (LW 43:247–251).

189 Other dubious consolations directed to parents who lost an unbaptized child are cited by Johann Georg Walch in his book *The Faith of Unborn Children*. Questionable are notions that the unborn are blessed through *scientiam mediam*, contingent knowledge, that is, whose faith God foresaw had they attained appropriate age, or that according to Revelation 20:12, the dead are judged by their works; but these children possess no works in reality so their judgment will be very light. Then, it is supposed that children prior to the Abrahamic covenant and the Rite of Circumcision were not lost. If circumcision was not "absolutely" necessary, the same would be true for Baptism. With respect to Baptism, Walch cites Augustine, "It is not the deprivation, but the contempt that damns." Thus, no charge can go against a child who cannot benefit from Baptism through no fault of its own. More problematic is another comment by Augustine, reportedly made about Matthew 11:21 in his discussion of degrees of glory (Dan 12:3), that because unbaptized children are marred only with original sin but not actual sin, they shall endure a very light damnation. These and similar notions may warrant mention, but hardly recommendation. See Johann Georg Walch, *The Faith of Unborn Children*, trans. Otto F. Stahlke (St. Paul, MN: Lutherans For Life, 1988), 8–10, 14.

190 Walther, *American-Lutheran Pastoral Theology*, 98.

Baptism of Human Clones

Questions about baptizing arise from unusual circumstances. Genetic science and/or human engineering may facilitate cloning human beings, though laws have been advanced in the United States that would forbid such a practice. But if the practice of cloning human beings develops in the future, the church's response may be that Baptism should be available to any living person.

Baptism of Unconscious, Senile, or Mentally Deranged Persons

Baptism of adults afflicted with dementia, Alzheimer's disease, or severe mental impairment, and those in a coma or even declared brain dead, tests pastoral judgment. Normally, adults are instructed in the Christian faith prior to Baptism. Diminished health, however, may preclude formal instruction. If a Christian family requests Baptism for a loved one in a state of severe disability and they attest that the person was not averse to Baptism, how shall the pastor respond? He will pose several questions. Is there precedent for such a Baptism in the New Testament? In these circumstances, do we reduce Baptism to a random churchly act? Will the action of baptizing trivialize the Sacrament?

These questions may lack specific answers. Observe that the family presents their loved one for Baptism—not just as family, but as the Church—the believing people of God. In faith and with prayers, they present a diminished or disabled person for the blessings of washing by water and the Word. When the request for Baptism is responsibly presented by fellow Christians, the pastor should baptize. In this instance, there is no *skandalon* of random Baptism.

The Practice of Baptism—Customs and Accessories

Intangibles

God's Name Put on the Baptized

Certain components, tangible and intangible, accompany the Rite of Holy Baptism. Intangible is the notion that in Baptism, the name of the triune God is placed upon the life of the baptized. Picture the saints as St. John saw them in that vision on the Isle of Patmos, the redeemed bearing the Father's name and the name of the Lamb on their foreheads (Rev 14:1). The trinitarian Invocation opens the Rite of Baptism, also every divine worship service, reminding that baptized Christians belong to God.

The Sign of the Cross

In the Rite of Baptism, the pastor makes the sign of the cross upon the forehead and the heart of the candidate. Walther explained this action threefold:

1. Testimony that the baptized is received into grace and regenerated to everlasting life only by the merit of Christ crucified
2. A reminder that the baptized child or adult has been received into the numbers of those who believe in Christ crucified
3. Testimony that the old sinful nature, the old man, is crucified with Christ[191]

The Laying On of Hands

The action of the laying on of hands has precedent in both the Old and New Testaments. Hands placed on the Levites designated them for service in the tabernacle (Num 8:10). The laying on of hands by the apostles signified consecration, divine blessing, or assignment to service (Acts 6:5–6; 8:14–17; 1 Tim 4:14; 2 Tim 1:6). Following the action of baptizing, the pastor places his hand upon the forehead of the baptized person and speaks the word of blessing.

The Exorcism

Luther retained exorcism within the Rite of Baptism from the Roman order that dated back to medieval times. We find it in Luther's rite, *The Order of Baptism Translated into German*, 1523, and modified in *The Order of Baptism Newly Revised*, 1526. In these orders, a number of exorcisms are expressed.[192] The 1523 Order identifies three:

1. "Depart thou unclean spirit, and give room to the Holy Spirit."
2. Salt is put into the mouth of the child as these words are said, "Receive the salt of wisdom. May it aid thee to eternal life. Amen. Peace be with thee."
3. "I adjure you, you unclean spirit, in the name of the Father + and of the Son + and of the Holy Spirit +, that you come out of and depart from this servant of Jesus Christ, Name. Amen."

Exorcism is not part of the Rite of Baptism, and Walther viewed it as ac-

---

191 Walther, *American-Lutheran Pastoral Theology*, 102.

192 Dr. Norman Nagel sorted out the exorcisms in Luther's two Baptism rites, 1523 and 1526. See Norman E. Nagel, "Holy Baptism," in *Lutheran Worship: History and Practice*, ed. Fred L. Precht (St. Louis: Concordia Publishing House, 1993), 273–276. Also see Luther, "The Baptism Booklet," Kolb-Wengert, 371–375.

cessory.[193] When engaged, exorcism should not be confused with deliverance from demonic possession of the body. In connection with Baptism, exorcism emphasizes the depth of human depravity and the great power of divine grace in Baptism, the Lord saving the baptized, freeing them from the dominion of sin and the tyranny of Satan and the finality of death. No longer bound to Satan, they are Christ's own[194] (cf. Heb 2:14; 1 John 3:8; Rev 20:10).

The Name Given to the Child in Baptism

Baptism gives no other name than the saving name of the triune God. The name parents assign to a child designates him or her as a recipient of God's name in the Sacrament. The question in the rite, "How are you named?" points to this designation. Earlier, we discussed the proper reply to this question.[195] When the names of candidates for Baptism may be misunderstood or confused, Fritz suggests that preceding the rite, the pastor may make an announcement, such as "There will now be baptized the child of Mr. and Mrs. Frank H. Smith."[196] A baptized child is heir to his or her Baptism name (*Taufname*). Therefore, parents should avoid novelty or oddity when naming children. Nothing should distract from the association between *name* and Baptism.

Tangible Accessories to Baptism

All external artifacts and accessories related to the Rite of Baptism should extol the power of the Word in Baptism and celebrate the work of the Holy Spirit. Therefore, none shall distract from the Word as the means whereby the Spirit does everything in Baptism. The recent rite contained in *Lutheran Service Book: Agenda* straddles both Luther's 1523 and 1526 Orders for Baptism. The Agenda limits externals to placing the chrisom cloth (white) upon the baptized child—sign of Christ's righteousness—and giving to the baptized the baptismal candle, signifying life in Christ, who is the light of the world. There is an additional rubric mentioned for the first of two Baptism rites in *Lutheran Service Book: Agenda*. It states that olive oil may be used in anointing to symbolize the sealing with the Holy Spirit for salvation (Eph 1:13–14), but the *Agenda* cautions: "The pastor should be careful to distinguish between the essential elements in each rite that constitute the sacrament of Holy Baptism . . . and the unessential elements of the rite that are ceremonial and symbolic."[197]

---

193 Walther, *American-Lutheran Pastoral Theology*, 103. Notably, a very brief form of exorcism in [for?] use today is found in "Holy Baptism—Alternate Form Based on Luther's Baptism Rite." It reads: "Therefore, depart, you unclean spirit, and make room for the Holy Spirit in the name of the Father and of the + Son and of the Holy Spirit." See *Lutheran Service Book: Agenda*, 13.

194 Norman E. Nagel, "Holy Baptism," 273.

195 See this work, pp. 134–135.

196 John H. C. Fritz, *Pastoral Theology*, 112.

197 *Lutheran Service Book: Agenda*, prepared by the Commission on Worship of The Lutheran Church—Missouri Synod (St. Louis: Concordia Publishing House, 2006), 1, 5.

In addition to other rubrics supplied by the Agenda, preparation for the Rite of Baptism may include incidentals such as preparing the font with sufficient warm water and accompanying hand cloths, posting church ushers on their duties, providing adequate voice enhancement for reading the rite, giving a certificate of a child's Baptism to the parents or giving a certificate to adults baptized, awarding Baptism sponsors with an appropriate memento that reminds of their responsibilities to the baptized child, and seeing that the Baptism is recorded properly in the church's registry.

CHAPTER NINE

The Ministry of Teaching the Christian Faith

Introduction

The pastor's principal teaching ministry is catechesis of youth and adults toward public confession of their faith in the Rite of Confirmation. Many pastors, however, lose interest in catechesis for children twelve or thirteen years old. They often delegate the instruction to others. To revive their interest, part 1 of this chapter reviews essential confirmation practice. The second part is preparation of adults for Baptism or the Rite of Confirmation.

Part I. Children's Confirmation

Highlights in the History of the Practice of Confirmation

The upbringing of God-fearing children began with the academy in the home that predated the synagogue and formal teaching in the Church. Parents imparted the Word of God to their children (Deut 5; 6:2, 4–7, 20–25; cf. 11:18–21). The curriculum was primarily the commandments and statutes of the Lord, and children learned to love the Lord and His Word (Deut 8:3; 11:1). Teaching children in the home is the first business of God-fearing parents, and they are assisted by catechesis in the Church.[198]

In the New Testament Church, the Lord's institution of Baptism with the command "teaching them to observe all that I have commanded you" prompted instruction toward Baptism and taking the Lord's Supper (cf. Matt 28:20), a practice that has become known as confirmation. Dr. Arthur Repp summarized, "After the candidates were baptized on Easter Eve, they were *confirmed* with chrisom, prayers, the sign of the cross, and the laying on of hands, and on

198 Luther held that no one should become a father unless he is able to instruct his children in the Ten Commandments and the Gospel so that he may bring up true Christians. See F. V. N. Painter, *Luther on Education* (St. Louis: Concordia Publishing House, n.d.), 119.

Easter morning they were permitted to make their first communion."[199] Confirmation was a bridge over the short interval between the two Sacraments.

The Eastern Church retained confirmation in close proximity to Baptism, but later in the West, Baptism and confirmation became distinctive rites. Confirmation was elevated to the status of a sacrament by the Council of Florence in November 1439, an action articulated in the papal decree *Pro Armenis*, issued by Eugene IV. The notion was common in the Church of Rome that Baptism gave the forgiveness of sins but the Holy Spirit was given in confirmation. Luther objected to this distinction with his vigorous assertion that the Holy Spirit, indeed, was given at Baptism, which needed no complement whatsoever. Further, Luther refused to recognize confirmation as a Sacrament, and this may explain why the Rite of Confirmation did not play a major part in Luther's thought and ministry. Catechetical instruction, however, was important for two reasons, both being the two Sacraments, Baptism and the Lord's Supper.

Luther's practice of confirmation was catechetical. The Sacrament of Baptism carried with it the obligation for parents and sponsors to ensure that the faith of a baptized child was nurtured by the Word. Furthermore, this nurture would enhance the hearing of sermons and Bible reading. Of great importance to Luther was instruction given to all Christians of all ages so that they could partake of the Lord's Supper in a worthy manner. Both of Luther's catechisms prepare students for taking the Sacrament.[200] Subsequent to Luther's practice, confirmation developed into multiple types identified by Dr. Repp in his work *Confirmation in the Lutheran Church.*

Types of Confirmation in the Sixteenth Century

Catechetical Type

Using Luther's catechisms in the home, parents instructed their children. When a child acquired sufficient understanding, parents and sponsors brought him or her to the pastor for examination in order to be declared ready for first Communion.

Hierarchical Type

The hierarchical type of confirmation is associated with Martin Bucer (1471–1551). In response to Anabaptists who rejected Bucer's practice of infant Baptism, asserting that he paid little attention to sanctification, he invoked two notable accents in the Rite of Confirmation:

199 Arthur C. Repp, *Confirmation in the Lutheran Church* (St. Louis: Concordia Publishing House, 1960), 13.
200 Ibid., 18.

1. Surrender to Christ in the form of a confession of faith.
2. Submit to the discipline of the Church.

Sacramental Type

Retaining elements of the Roman Catholic tradition, this type of confirmation is known for two accents:

1. With the laying on of hands, the Holy Spirit is given; this action is necessary to complete Baptism.
2. Confirmation conferred a new and fuller church membership not previously accorded in Baptism; this was based on the assumption that the Holy Spirit and full membership in the church with rights and privileges are conferred in the Rite of Confirmation.

Traditional Type

The Brandenburg Order (1540), prepared by Bugenhagen and approved by Luther, exhibits a fourth type of confirmation that attempted to retain the old order in a strict sense, but without Romanizing tendencies. It was drawn up as a reaction to those who had done away with confirmation altogether. Instruction, confession of faith, attestation to the Christian life of the child, and the prayers of the Church accompanied by the laying on of hands were the chief accents.

Confirmation, 1700–2000

Pietistic Type

The pietistic type of confirmation arose during the upheavals in seventeenth-century Europe. Theologically, it was a reaction to the period of orthodoxy and the decline of meaningful catechetical instruction. Two principal spokesmen advanced this type of confirmation. Philipp Jakob Spener (1635–1705) injected a subjective element marked by a renewal of the confirmand's Baptism vow in his or her experience versus a remembrance of Baptism as God's unilateral covenant of grace. August Herman Francke (1663–1727) of Halle carried personal experience of one's conversion further. He favored substituting for the Apostles' Creed the confirmand's confession of faith in his or her words. Dr. Repp observed that confirmation now became both anthropocentric and subjective in nature. It was an action initiated by the confirmand himself. The question "What does it mean to me to be a Christian?" supplanted the affirmation based upon the Scriptures, "This is the Christian faith, and this I believe and confess together with the entire church on earth."[201]

Rationalistic Type

Under the influence of Rationalism, confirmation grew in importance while Baptism was minimized. Dr. Repp observed that the sacramental emphasis of the sixteenth century now came into full bloom.[202] Congregational rights and privileges come not with Baptism but with confirmation when the catechumen joins the congregation. Then, confirmation took on social significance, that is, youth came of age with emphasis on the day of confirmation as an occasion for special celebration and gathering of family and friends. To arrive at this pinnacle, confirmands had to be older, and they endured rigorous instruction requiring memorization of vast amounts of Christian doctrine. In many churches of Germany, the principal curriculum was Dietrich's Catechism, a work comparable to a text in dogmatic theology. The Rite of Confirmation was elevated and embellished with numerous customs, such as the wearing of gowns, the tolling of bells at the moment of the laying on of hands, and the solemnity of the confirmation vow. Though incidental themselves, these customs undergirded confirmation as the principal event in the life of a young Christian, overshadowing Baptism in the confirmand's consciousness.

From History, the Substance of Lutheran Confirmation

Every church body and their congregations must articulate clearly the practice of confirmation. The Lutheran practice is framed principally by theology and less by historical precedent and accrued customs. The essential thing is instruction in the doctrines of the Word of God. Through this teaching, the Holy Spirit confirms students in their faith once given in Baptism, and confirmation instruction points students to the Lord's Supper, where they will receive the body and blood of the Lord. Note that the confirming action of the Spirit occurs not in the Rite of Confirmation but through ongoing instruction in many class sessions that leads to the rite.

The content of confirmation instruction is the Six Chief Parts of Christian Doctrine set forth in Luther's Small and Large Catechisms. The *Ten Commandments* hold students accountable in thought, word, and action. Failing in this accountability, students flee to Christ by remembering *Holy Baptism* into His saving death and resurrection, expounded in the Second Article of the *Apostles' Creed*, the teaching of the Gospel. The First and Third articles teach what it means to be redeemed and the reality of new life under God in His creation.

---

201 Arthur C. Repp, *Confirmation in the Lutheran Church*, 68ff.

202 Ibid., 77.

The *Office of the Keys* and *Confession* draws students to God's grace available in Holy Absolution, and the *Lord's Supper* brings assurance by the body and blood of the Lord given and shed for the forgiveness of sins. Finally, the *Lord's Prayer* reflects on the Law and the Gospel across the chief parts of doctrine.

This instruction prepares students for the Rite of Confirmation when they confess faith in the triune God, a confession nurtured by the Holy Spirit through God's Word. In Baptism, they became members of the Church; and coming of age, they act on this privilege in a congregation of fellow Christians. In the rite, they vow—they put off Satan and promise by God's grace to remain loyal to the triune God for life, and they pledge themselves to faithful use of God's Word and the Sacrament. As they kneel at the altar, the laying on of hands is a gesture of blessing sought in the prayers of the Church that the Holy Spirit keep them close to God's Means of Grace and staunch in faith in Christ our Lord.

Regarding one aspect of instruction directing students to the partaking of the Lord's Supper, the intent is to assure the following:

- Students discern the Lord's body and blood given in, with, and under the bread and the wine according to the Lord's Words of Institution, and received orally in taking the Sacrament (1 Cor 11:23–25).
- Students know and accept the special purpose for which the Sacrament is given by Christ, namely, the remission of sins (Matt 26:28).
- After confirmation, students approach the Lord's Table confessing Christ as their Savior and Lord, with focus on His suffering and death on the cross (1 Cor 11:26).
- Students are instructed and thus are able to examine themselves prior to coming to the Lord's Table. They are trained to use exhibits such as "Questions and Answers for Those Who Propose to Attend the Lord's Supper," attributed to Martin Luther.

Confirmation and First Communion

In traditional Lutheran confirmation practice, children were confirmed and took first Communion at age 13 or 14. But this practice has been challenged by the supposition that confirmation at early adolescence improperly delayed first Communion. Numerous congregations, therefore, adopted the practice of early first Communion for children ages 6 to 9. Later, these young children enroll for catechesis in Christian doctrine leading to the Rite of Confirmation. In rare instances, catechesis and first Communion are deferred to late teen years, 17 or 18, emphasizing maturity to better comprehend doctrine.

Obviously, the long-standing practice of catechetical instruction prior to taking the Sacrament is at stake. Luther insisted on instruction *before* taking the Lord's Supper. His catechisms—the Six Chief Parts of Christian Doctrine—serve this purpose. If instruction is reduced in order to prepare the young child for the Sacrament, what will the curriculum be? Certainly, the sixth chief part, the Sacrament of the Altar, is a must. Also required is instruction about our sinful nature, Christ and His redemption, Holy Baptism, and God's forgiveness of our sins. Then, a stable Christian home with committed parents is essential for teaching a young child. The pastor trains parents to instruct their children and to assist them with examination prior to each occasion they take the Lord's Supper. In the young child's future—perhaps several years—is catechesis leading to the Rite of Confirmation? Will children, already communing at an early age, settle for catechesis later? Will some opt out?

Instructors of Confirmation Classes

Involving parents in the instruction leading to first Communion or confirmation is common. In traditional confirmation practice, the pastor was the sole instructor. Congregations were content with this model. Pastors, however, delegate portions of catechesis of children to others. Church staff and some parents lead class sessions, and the pastor monitors the program. Another model leans heavily on the student's effort at self-learning. Instead of formal class sessions, each student engages numerous resources in a learning center and proceeds at his or her own pace under the guidance of supervising personnel. A family-oriented model enlists parents to catechize their children, who are in grades 6 and 7 when they take first Communion. In grade 8, the children gather for classes or small groups at the church or school. Observe that they commune together as they matriculate through the closing year of confirmation instruction.

Curriculum for Children's Confirmation Revisited

Change in confirmation practice today is especially apparent with regard to curriculum. Numerous pastors construct their own confirmation curriculum, and many of these models place student needs at center stage.[203] A re-

203 Change in confirmation practice and curriculum within the ELCA is the subject of a key essay by one of its own educators. See Kent L. Johnson, "The Changing Face of Confirmation," in *Confirmation, Engaging Lutheran Foundations and Practices* (Minneapolis: Fortress Press, 1999), 18–40. Sampling numerous models for children's confirmation from pastors of the ELCA during the 1990s, Johnson notes a shift in emphasis from doctrine to the social and psychological needs of the student. For a discussion of diversity in perceptions, that is, *confirmation*, *confirming*, and *confirmand*, see Stephan Goodwin and Lewis Grace, "What Are We Confirming?" in *Currents in Theology and Mission* 22 (June 1995): 206–209. Also see the reply to Goodwin and Grace by Theodore Jungkuntz, "Pentecost and Confirmation," *Currents in Theology and Mission* 23 (October 1996): 368–371.

minder is appropriate. The principal aim of confirmation instruction by Luther's standard is to immerse children in the catechism. Luther stated that the Ten Commandments, the Creed, and the Lord's Prayer should be learned word for word and recited at intervals during the day.[204] Today, we do a favor for children when confirmation class leads them into the catechism. Parents sometimes press pastors to abandon doctrine and to focus instead on topics that are pressing for teens, such as sexuality, dating, managing the social network, and invoking a Christian worldview. Respecting parental wishes, we ask, how beneficial is fixation on such topics if the child is not grounded in the central teachings of the Scriptures? Besides, a creative pastor will instruct from the catechism while fully aware of the present culture. Within the Six Chief Parts of Christian Doctrine, he integrates many contemporary subjects and addresses current issues and questions.

Teaching Children in Confirmation Classes

Readiness for Confirmation Class

Are parents, children, and the pastor ready for the first day of confirmation classes? Parents are challenged to encourage children and oversee their study of the catechism. Children will gain if they come to class with knowledge of the Bible, its major themes and its principal stories in God's unfolding plan of salvation. The pastor is ready when he is excited to bring the Word of God to a new class of children. He wants to bond with boys and girls as their shepherd. A wise veteran Christian Day School principal gently advised his young senior pastor that confirmation class is teaching *children* versus lecturing about theology. Instead of stumbling into the classroom ten minutes late with the old yellow notes in hand, a pastor is prompt and brings a well-prepared lesson. The lesson plan includes subject, aim or goal, and projected outcome in the learning and life experience of the children. Pastor, lighten up. You are about serious business, but getting to it with a sense of humor reaches children. Roll up your sleeves, toss the basketball and make a few baskets, or take your turn at bat on the ball field with your students during breaks in class sessions. Most important, pastor, ***love*** the children.

Decorum and Discipline

Decorum in the classroom benefits teaching and learning. At the outset, it takes a few minutes for the rowdy ones to have their hurrah. So be it. Then we settle down and focus on the task at hand. There must be boundaries for student behavior, and they must be enforced consistently. The lack of boundaries may explain why seminarians struggle with seventh-grade confirmation class.

204 F. V. N. Painter, *Luther on Education*, 121.

Discipline—correction of unacceptable behavior—is a challenge. When a student's behavior calls for correction, let the ministry of the Gospel be the last word. The pastor does not permit the offending student to leave until he or she has had a conversation. "What is happening? What is going on, Joe? Can you tell me? I want to understand. You know that disruption in class blocks the Lord and His Word. And that leaves an open door for Satan. Do we want that?" The pastor listens. Then he sums up. "Joe, if you know that your behavior today was dead wrong, this is a good word before you go home. The Lord Jesus loves you, forgives you; and I, your pastor, love and forgive. Let's try again next class. Okay?" This Gospel conversation sealed with an arm gently extended around the shoulders is pastoral care.

Teaching with Bible Narratives

Points of doctrine come alive when they are discovered within Bible narratives. The Bible story itself teaches the doctrine. For example, how does a pastor teach the Ninth and Tenth Commandments to show that covetousness is a root sin that blossoms into other sins? King Ahab's confiscation of the vineyard belonging to his neighbor Naboth is the lesson (1 Kgs 21:1–19). In this narrative, Ahab is gripped by covetousness, leading to his actions—destroying his neighbor's reputation, taking his life, and stealing his property—sins against the Eighth, the Fifth, and the Seventh Commandments. Here, the Bible itself does the teaching.

Memorizing Scripture and Catechism Teachings

Though memorization has all but disappeared in today's pedagogy, the Lutheran fathers valued memorizing Scripture passages and the catechism. Memorizing Scriptures and points of doctrine anchors the teaching from God's Word in the mind. Students may commit to memory the catechism's answers to key questions such as "Who is the only true God?" "Why was it necessary for our Lord to be true God, true man?" "Why do we believe in the real presence of the Lord's body and blood in the Sacrament?" Then, memorization creates a reservoir of Scriptures that support a Christian's witness to others. Memorized Scriptures and hymn verses bring comfort to a Christian later when life is difficult and short. Memorization is useful, so the pastor should assign memory work and hear the students' recitations.

Administering Tests

Testing students in confirmation classes is debatable. Accountability for learning is a useful device, but test results can thoroughly discourage a sincere student and fortify pride in a gifted, but careless student. Also, how shall we test for both cognitive and affective learning? There is no perfect test, but written exams can be utilized for review. Tests administered, graded, and returned to students should be discussed point for point. During the discussion, the pastor offers encouragement as well as right answers. He notes a student's poor performance in the manner of pastoral care. He permits every student to move on, as is fitting for him or her. Finally, the public examination of a class prior to the Rite of Confirmation is a long-standing practice and helpful review (Ap XV 41).

Part II. Adult Baptism and Confirmation

Teaching and Baptizing

Normally, adult converts to Christ come into the Church by teaching and Baptism. A fixed sequence—teaching followed by Baptism, or the reverse, Baptism followed by instruction—is elusive in the New Testament. It is clear, however, that the two are complementary. Thousands of persons were baptized in Jerusalem on Pentecost upon hearing the apostle Peter's preaching (Acts 2:41). Similarly, Peter's sermon preceded Baptisms at Caesarea (Acts 10:30–48). House Baptisms—Lydia, the jailer at Philippi, Stephanas—occurred with preaching and teaching by the apostle Paul (Acts 16:14–15, 33–34; 1 Cor 1:16). Interjecting a debate over so-called believer's Baptism—that is, whether or not faith precedes Baptism—is fruitless. The passage frequently referenced in this regard is Acts 8:12–13. Observe, however, the prime emphasis is that Baptism was linked closely to Philip's preaching the Good News of the kingdom of God and the name of Jesus Christ. Those in earshot reportedly believed and were baptized.

The Pastor's Class

Adults preparing for Baptism and others preparing for the Rite of Confirmation assemble in a learning environment known as the pastor's class. What the Bible teaches—the doctrines from creation to the end times—forms the substance of this course. These doctrines are the articles confessed in the Church's creed. Luther's Small Catechism serves as a reference. In one model, weekly class sessions run ten to thirteen weeks, one and one-half hours each. Some pastors, however, compact the teaching

Principle: Holy Baptism and instruction in Christian doctrine complement each other, and the Church normally administers Baptism to adults upon instruction; they should not be baptized into the Christian faith when it is yet unknown to them.

into four hours on a Saturday. Whether such a reduction is suitable and effective is a judgment call.[205]

When the class approaches completion, the pastor interviews each candidate for Baptism and/or confirmation. He is interested to know what the person has learned. Also, he seeks to know if the candidates are prepared to make public confession of their faith before the church and world. A debate continues over the timing of Baptism—at the beginning of the class, midway through the course, or at the close. Baptizing after completion of the pastor's class is an established practice, but a growing number of pastors hold different views. Clearly, Baptism at the close of instruction does not deprive of the Sacrament. Understandably, there are exceptional needs, like the person who enrolls in the pastor's class and for reason of ill health is anxious and desires Baptism now. The pastor acknowledges this urgent desire, prepares the person, and baptizes. This person pursues the remainder of the course and appears later for the Rite of Confirmation.

At the close of the pastor's class, there will likely be candidates for Holy Baptism and others for the Rite of Confirmation. In the public worship service, Baptism is at the beginning. The Rite of Confirmation follows the sermon, the offertory, and the general prayer. Adults baptized early in the service may join the class for the Rite of Confirmation. The Lord's Supper follows. The class communes at the Lord's Table with the larger congregation. Beautiful!

Several weeks after Baptism and confirmation, the pastor visits again with each candidate. He answers questions and clarifies what may be unclear to the recently baptized or confirmed person. This is an opportunity for the pastor to shepherd new members of the flock. He is assuring, encouraging, and supportive. These new Christians will be comfortable in the larger fellowship when they discover that they can be comfortable with their pastor.

Building the Pastor's Class

On January 1, the pastor sets the dates for two or three pastor's classes that calendar year. This was the practice of Dr. Guido Merkens, founding pastor of Concordia Lutheran Church, San Antonio, Texas, who baptized or confirmed one hundred adults every year. With dates set, the pastor takes the initiative to assemble these classes. He accepts assistance from the laity, but he does not depend on the congregation's evangelism ministry. Single-handedly, the pastor makes these classes happen. Three actions are required:

---

205 For a fair assessment and critique of much abbreviated "pastor's classes," see Jeffrey Gibbs, "Microwave Christians," *Concordia Journal* 22, no. 1 (January 1996): 9–11.

1. Identify and conserve prospects.
2. Cultivate the prospects.
3. Gather the prospects into the classes.

There is a method—simple, tried, and true—to identify and conserve prospects. They may be sorted and conserved by these categories:

- ☐ New resident in the community
- ☐ Visitor at worship services
- ☐ Inquirer
- ☐ Spouse of a member
- ☐ Relative of a member
- ☐ Friend of a member
- ☐ Lutheran for transfer to the congregation
- ☐ Acquaintance by official acts: Baptism, wedding, funeral
- ☐ Child attending or has attended Vacation Bible School
- ☐ Child or youth enrolled in Sunday School or Bible study
- ☐ Attends a small group in our fellowship
- ☐ Attends congregation events
- ☐ Attends congregation mission events

Identifying prospects with this instrument can be accomplished manually or digitally. The categories may be altered or adjusted for suitable use in particular settings.[206] Once prospects are identified, cultivate them aggressively. Stay in touch with them, befriend them, invite them to worship and to congregation events, show care for them. Finally, gather them into the pastor's class through personal contact. Help them to take the step and be present for the first class session. Send a letter or email ten days prior to this first class, and request a response; if a letter is sent, include a return postage-paid card indicating their decision to attend the class.

Conduct of the Pastor's Class

The conduct of the pastor's class begins with welcoming persons and making them comfortable. It is a psychological hurdle for newcomers to venture on the premises of church/school buildings for the first class. They need assistance, beginning with clearly marked buildings, hallways, and rooms. Ideally,

206 These categories were prepared in the late 1950s by the Rev. William G. Polack, pastor of Trinity Lutheran Church, Stockton, California. Pastor Polack adapted them from an exhibit by Luther W. Bekemeier, "Developing and Using a Prospect File," *Advance: Information for Church Workers* 5, no. 3 (March 1958): 2–4. Note: Prospects may also be identified and sorted ideologically: "nones" who abandon churches, humanists who seek spirituality without religion, agnostics who prefer to remain as doubters, professed atheists who do not believe in any god whatsoever, et al. These prospects may be categorized separately and cultivated in creative ways.

in larger settings, greeters are posted here and there to show the way. We assist the stranger with a cordial welcome in a nonthreatening setting. Helping all to be acquainted, setting out the course, introducing materials, giving cues about procedure and how the course will be taught puts newcomers at ease. The pastor will assist the class to feel at home in the facility—water fountains, restrooms, exits. Prepared refreshments that are set out in good taste—fruit as well as pastries, water, coffee, and soft drinks are a nice touch. While the pastor may be anxious to *get going*, ten minutes of relaxed orientation yields great benefits.

Curriculum and Learning Materials for the Pastor's Class

The pastor's class is about the major teachings (doctrines) of the Christian faith. Several other topics are integrated into the lessons:

- ☐ Introduction to Worship in the Lutheran Church
- ☐ Preparation for Taking the Lord's Supper
- ☐ Introduction to Christian Stewardship
- ☐ Helps for Personal and Family Worship, Devotional Life
- ☐ Instruction about Holy Baptism and the Rite of Confirmation

Need we emphasize the importance of providing students with materials? These may include a Bible, a catechism, a hymnal, a prayer book, and a workbook that sets out lessons for the course.[207]

When all members of the class are using the same version and edition of the Bible, references to books, chapters, verses, and page numbers are shared in common. Using the same Bible enhances students' attention to the Scripture text and facilitates reading in the class, though some persons may not wish to read aloud. The pastor asks for volunteers to read before he calls on class members to participate. The Bible and teaching materials may be available in digital format. In any case, the congregation finances and provides the materials for the pastor's class free of charge to the class members.

A recent work most suitable as a follow-up to the doctrine class, *Lutheranism 101*—second edition, by Concordia Publishing House, along with its associated workbook for the series, *Lutheranism 101: The Course*—second edition, will serve recent adult confirmands quite well.

---

207 A workbook formerly used by many pastors was titled *What Does the Bible Say?* by Pastor Oswald Riess, who revised this workbook later under the title *That I May Know Him*, still available at this writing from Concordia Publishing House. In both of these editions of Riess's workbook, the method is inquiry about a point of doctrine (that is, a question), answered with "The Bible says . . . ," followed with a conclusion, "From this we learn . . ." The method is lucid and leads the student.

Assimilation of New Converts into the Congregation

Bringing new members into the congregation begins at the close of the worship service when they were baptized and/or confirmed. An arrangement in the sanctuary or narthex that permits the congregation to greet the new members following the worship service is a first step. How fitting if the congregation had provided either a corsage or boutonnière to each new member for the occasion. In addition to receiving congratulations from the congregation, the new members will pose for a photo in the chancel or at another location on the church premises. Each member of the class receives a copy of this photo.

When the celebration of new Christians or new members is over, the pastor and congregation leaders point these persons to opportunities for Bible study and fellowship. In this regard, how expedient and helpful if the congregation assigns a sponsor to each adult confirmand! Experience has taught us that persons arriving at the close of the pastor's class do not want the class to end. So the sponsor points them to biblically based courses designed to train for discipleship:

- ☐ Using My Bible
- ☐ Worship at My Church
- ☐ Christian Family Life
- ☐ Telling the Gospel to Others
- ☐ Supporting Church and Ministry
- ☐ Living the Christian Life

Each of the topics may span several class sessions. The topics may be developed and taught by the pastor and others on the church/school staff. Gifted lay Christians can teach in this program. School teachers and other professional persons serve well. New Christians will profit from opportunities to continue in the Word.

CHAPTER TEN

The Ministry of the Lord's Supper

Prologue

Dominical Authority and the Sacrament of the Altar

Divine call, ordination, and office come together when a pastor consecrates bread and wine at the altar and distributes the Lord's body and blood to the people. The gravity is overwhelming! This is the culmination of schooling, learning, and training. The office—preaching the Gospel, administering the Sacrament—a privilege that is humbly received from the Lord and the Church (Ap XXIV 80).

In these sacred moments, standing in the pulpit and officiating at the altar, the pastor is a servant coming to Christ's people with holy words and holy things that He entrusts to the called and ordained minister. The preaching and the Sacrament are *dominical.* All is of the Lord.

The Instituted-Use Principle

Pastors, therefore, administer Holy Communion according to the Lord's institution. This is the *instituted-use* principle. Observe that the New Testament texts portray the Lord instituting His Supper, using the third-person singular pronoun "He" (Matt 26:26–28; Mark 14:22–24; Luke 22:19–20; 1 Cor 11:23–25). The Lutheran confessors assert, therefore, "Nothing has the character of a sacrament apart from the use [*usus*] instituted by Christ or the divinely instituted action [*actio*]" (FC SD VII 85). The confessors explain the *instituted-use* principle further:

Principle: Until the *parousia*, when the Lord has fellowship with His people in the new order, He hosts them in the present at His Supper, which He institutes, defines, and distributes—His true body and blood for the forgiveness of sins, the Sacrament administered by the Church's pastors in the name and in the stead of the Lord Himself (FC SD VII 21, 24, 54, 75, 77).

> The *usus* or *actio* (that is, the practice or administration) does not refer primarily to faith or to the oral partaking, but to the entire external, visible administration of the Supper, as Christ established the administration of the Supper: the consecration, or Words of Institution, and the distribution and reception or oral partaking of the consecrated bread and wine, Christ's body and blood.[208]

Because the Lord set the practice of the Sacrament—use, words, and action—novelty or experiment are not allowed. This applies to modernizing the Sacrament in various ways or framing its importance socially as a relational experience. Another distortion is privatizing the consecration, speaking the Words of Institution in a subdued and secretive manner as if the Sacrament was the exclusive province of the clergy. Proper rubrics call for clear and audible speaking of the words and plain, unadorned, nonsensational action when handling the elements in the Sacrament (cf. FC SD VII 79–82).

The *instituted-use* principle casts light on assisting with distribution of the Lord's Supper. Hundreds commune in services conducted for large congregations. Assistance in the distribution is necessary.[209] Lately, the Lutherans distinguish between the presiding minister who consecrates and the assisting ministers who distribute. Because the pastoral office administers the Sacrament—one holistic action of consecration, distribution, and reception—any who assist in this *one* action are doing so simply in an assisting role[210] (FC SD VII 80, 83–84). Because the pastoral office administers the Sacrament—one holistic action of consecration, distribution, and reception, as ordered by our Lord—only men should assist in the distribution of Holy Communion, preferably men serving as elders in the congregation.[211]

---

208 FC SD VII 86.

209 According to the Augsburg Confession, priests or deacons receiving the Sacrament possibly remained and assisted the officiating priest in the distribution (AC XXIV 37–38).

210 Enlisting a diversity of persons to assist with Communion distribution is widely practiced and popularly defended. In his unpublished essay titled "May Only Ordained Ministers Distribute the Body and Blood of Christ in the Sacrament of Holy Communion?" the Rev. Dr. Philip Secker distinguishes the *distribution* of the Sacrament from prerogatives of the pastoral office. Referencing AC V, Secker argues that the German phrase *zu reichen und handeln*, or the Latin *administrandi sacramenta*, refers not to *distribution* but to *administration* of the Sacraments. He concludes that *distribution* of the Lord's body and blood is not a distinctive role of the pastoral office, and other persons in the Christian community may rightly assist in the Eucharist. Selecting assistants for Communion distribution is a matter of pastoral judgment, but the Formula of Concord, not referenced in Secker's argument, brings clarification. The Formula cites Luther, who speaks of the body and the blood of the Lord "daily distributed through our ministry or office" (FC SD VII 77). Luther's comment prefaces the Formula's teaching that administration of the Sacrament, including the distribution, is a single entire action executed by the pastoral office (FC SD VII 83–84). Others involved in this one sacramental action—administration of the Lord's Supper—according to the Augsburg Confession, were priests or deacons who undoubtedly, besides receiving from the one officiant, also may have assisted him in the distribution (AC XXIV 37–38).

211 This is the counsel of the task force appointed by the president of The Lutheran Church—Missouri

The Sacramental Union

In the consecration, the Words of Christ unite with the bread and wine; He states, "This is My body," and "This is My blood." This sacred action composes the *unio sacramentalis*, or sacramental union. The meaning is that Christ, "when giving the bread, gives us simultaneously His body to eat."[212]

This mystery, though impenetrable, is the subject of inquiry that has led to three notable factors that have implications for the practice of the Sacrament among Lutherans.

1. *Inception*, the *Verba* engaging with the elements, bread and wine
2. *Duration*, the notion that the sacramental union extends beyond the *usus* and *actio* within the celebration of the Sacrament
3. *Termination*, the view that post-Communion or outside the use and action, the sacramental union does not prevail

Regarding the first factor, *inception*, observe that alert catechumens studying the doctrine of the Lord's Supper may inquire, "In the consecration, when do the bread and the wine become the body and blood of the Lord?" Normally, Lutheran pastors refrain from exploring the mystery, much less explain it. They simply invite inquirers to have faith in the Words of Christ whereby the Lord gives His body and blood with the bread and the wine in the Sacrament.

About *duration*, some Lutherans assert that the *reliquiae*, the remaining elements, having been consecrated, continue to be the Lord's body and blood beyond the Communion celebration. Proponents of this view argue that there is no word from Christ that indicates the consecrated elements are no longer anything but the Lord's body and blood even when the Communion service has ended with the Benediction. Certainly, this notion, *duration*, is part and parcel of taking consecrated elements from the altar post-Communion celebration to other settings, a practice that we reject. The practice of either the pastor or laypersons bringing elements used during the Communion service is not a sound biblical or Lutheran practice. There should be no separation of the distribution from the consecration.[213]

Synod. The task force advised, in order to avoid confusion regarding the Office of the Holy Ministry and to avoid giving offense to the Church, lay assistance in distribution of the elements in the celebration of Holy Communion should be limited to lay men. See "Guidelines for the Service of Women in Congregational Offices," prepared by the President's Task Force, January 2005 (St. Louis: The Lutheran Church—Missouri Synod, 2005), 21, distributed with *The Service of Women in Congregational and Synodical Offices: A Report of the Commission on Theology and Church Relations* (St. Louis: The Lutheran Church—Missouri Synod, September 1994).

212 A citation from N. Selneccer, *Vom bl. Abendmahl des Herrn etc.* (1591) BL. E 2 provided by Hermann Sasse, *This Is My Body: Luther's Contention for the Real Presence in the Sacrament of the Altar* (Minneapolis: Augsburg Publishing House, 1959), 103n53.

213 Roland Ziegler, "Should Lutherans Reserve the Consecrated Elements for the Communion of the Sick?" *Concordia Theological Quarterly* 67, no. 2 (April 2003), 131–48.

Related is the notion of *termination*, that the pastor's speaking of the Benediction at the conclusion of the Divine Service of the Sacrament brings closure to the sacramental action, and also the sacramental union in that setting. Then the *reliquiae*, the remaining elements, are either disposed of properly or stored, having no further use until engaged for another celebration of the Sacrament.

In regard to these factors, widely discussed and debated with respect to practice of the Sacrament, ultimately the Word of Christ and nothing else must prevail. Taking rigid positions and dogmatically insisting on certain practices as a result of speculation over the implications of the sacramental union must be discouraged. Luther would have nothing to do with such attempts to penetrate the mystery and manipulate practice of the Sacrament. Rather, Luther let God be God; and consistently he returned to the clear Word of Christ, the ground for his faith expressed in these words, "We maintain the bread and the wine in the Supper are the true body and blood of Christ" (SA III 6:1; FC SD VII 19, 77). Beyond this assertion, he would not speculate, nor would he advocate practice evolving from such speculation. The Formula of Concord echoes Luther: "Faith does not make the sacrament, but only the true Word and institution of our almighty God and Savior Jesus Christ, which Word is always powerful and remains efficacious in Christendom" (FC SD VII 89). The discussion prompts a guiding principle.

Principle: The best course for the Lutheran pastor, in the light of factors raised by consideration of the sacramental union, is to seek the clear Word of Christ and recognize that His Word does not address numerous issues raised about the significance of the consecrated elements in the Sacrament beyond their proper use and action—the consecration, distribution, and reception of the Lord's body and blood.

The Conduct of the Sacrament

Preparation

The Pastor

The practice of the Lord's Supper is first a matter of preparation. A man in Christ, the pastor comes to the Sacrament prepared to handle holy things for Christ. "Keep yourself pure," counsels St. Paul (1 Tim 5:22). The term is ʿαγνός, *hagnos*, and the sense is "Keep yourself in good ethical condition, be chaste, and ritually (ceremonially) fit and proper." In pursuit of his calling—preaching the Word and handling the Sacrament—the pastor is alert and vigilant with respect to his conduct and behavior (ethical) so that he remains conditioned in mind and heart for the ministry (ceremonial), engaging holy things.

The pastor is ready for this ministry. In his private devotion, he has prepared to take the Sacrament himself. Then he reviews the Communion liturgy and tracks details unfolding in the Divine Service. Prior to these preparations, he has attended to his person this day—clean and well groomed, clothing clean and pressed, vestments in top condition. How did Moses come to the mount to meet the Lord (Exod 19:3–6; cf. 19:10–11, 14)? On the morning of worship services, the pastor presents his best self to the Lord and for the people. He is a vessel fit for handling and dispensing holy things.

Principle: With diligence, the pastor prepares for the ministry of the Sacrament as one serving in the stead of Christ, attending to details so that nothing with respect to him or his person or the Table may distract or offend those who come for the Lord's body and blood in the Sacrament.

At the church sanctuary, the pastor sees that all is in order. The Communion vessels and accessories are in place and the elements are sufficient and ready. Is everything there—ciborium or pyx, paten, flagon and chalice, the veil and purificators, the spoon? Vested, the pastor takes on the stole and, if used, lays out the chasuble for conducting the service of the Sacrament. Before entering the chancel for the Divine Service, he washes his hands. Hygiene is important. No running water in the sacristy? A pitcher and basin, soap and towel will serve. If the pastor uses tobacco, his hands may require additional cleansing.[214]

The Elements

Preparation for the Sacrament includes attention to the elements. They are bread and wine. The Lord instituted His Supper at Passover. Likely, the elements were unleavened bread, ἄρτος, and the fruit of the vine, that is, wine, οινος (Matt 26:17–19, 26, 29; Luke 22:7–8, 18–20; 1 Cor 11:23–25). For bread, the base commodity—wheat, rice, or oats—is immaterial. Today, commercial businesses supply unleavened bread in the form of wafers for distribution in the Sacrament. The wine may be red, white, or blush. Color and viscosity may vary, but with certainty, the cup shall be genuine wine, and preferably of high quality.[215] Wine that is low grade in quality is hardly consonant with the gift

214 In the sacristy prior to the service of Holy Communion, an otherwise faithful and effective pastor reached for a bottle of floral spray left by morticians for freshening decaying funeral bouquets. The pastor rinsed his hands liberally with the sweet lotion in an attempt to cover the tobacco smell on his nicotine-stained fingers. He was a heavy smoker. *Kyrie eleison!*

215 Nonalcoholic "wine" should not be used. The product is pale wine. It may be a beverage with added chemicals and carbonation making it sparkling or effervescent. But it is not wine. Proper for the Lord's Supper is wine, the fermented beverage usually with less than 5% volume of alcohol, though that percentage may be higher. See the discussion "Is the 'Non-Alcoholic Wine' Really Wine?" Opinion of the Department of Systematic Theology—Concordia Seminary, St. Louis, Missouri, in *Concordia Journal* 17 (January 1991): 4–6. See the similar opinion offered by the Department of Systematic Theology, Concordia Theological Seminary, Fort Wayne, Indiana, in *Concordia Theological Quarterly* 45, 1 and 2 (January–April

that the Sacrament is. In some Christian communities, the single option is red wine to oblige the mental association with the blood of Christ.

Preparation of the sacramental elements includes respect for sensitivities of the communicants. To ignore claims of allergic reactions or to dismiss hesitance to imbibe alcohol in the least quantity is foolish. The pastor makes adjustments. Substitute breads—rice- or oat-based—may suffice for persons sensitive to gluten in wheat-based bread. These substitutes may be set alongside the unleavened bread for the consecration, yet such close association of the two commodities may be negative. Hypersensitivity to gluten reacts even to minuscule particles. For some persons with high sensitivity, private Communion may be in order.

Alternatives to the wine and its distribution—communing *sub una*, under one kind, the host only; using unfermented vacuum-packed commercial grape juice; intinction (steeping a corner of the bread in the contents of the chalice)—are unsatisfactory. While dilution of wine in large volumes of water is an accepted option, another procedure is possible. On Saturday evening prior to the Sacrament on Sunday, a pastor may press the juice from a cluster of grapes and filter it through a clean cloth, storing the residue in the refrigerator overnight. Supposedly, sufficient fermentation occurs so that the liquid qualifies as wine, but the fermentation is not strong enough to trigger a negative reaction in most persons who are sensitive to alcohol.[216]

The Action of Consecration

In the service of the Sacrament, following the prayers and the Proper Preface, the pastor speaks the *Verba* and directs these Words of Institution to the elements on the altar, the bread and the wine. This is the action of consecration.[217] The pastor speaks or sings the Words clearly and audibly so that the congregation hears and is included in this action of consecration and thereby edified and strengthened (FC SD VII 74ff., 79–82). Why do pastors sometimes speak these Words too rapidly or softly, and, quite frankly, flippantly? Pastor, speak or sing the Lord's Words of Institution accurately, slowly, deliberately,

1981): 77–80. Also see the article on this subject featured in *The Lutheran Witness* (April 1986).

216 This procedure is subject to technical scrutiny if the pastor wants accuracy with respect to alcohol content in the fermented product.

217 "Consecration," states Dr. Francis Pieper, "is correctly defined as the act whereby bread and wine are detached from their ordinary use and appointed to the use in the Lord's Supper, that is, are set apart to this end, that with the bread, according to Christ's promise, the body of Christ and with the wine, according to Christ's promise, the blood of Christ be received. We see from 1 Cor. 10:16 that consecration was in use already in the Apostolic congregation: 'The cup of blessing, which we bless (το ποτήριον εὐλογίας ο εὐλογοῦμεν), is it not the communion of the blood of Christ?'" Pieper, *Christian Dogmatics*, vol. 3, 366. Also see the extensive discussion of consecration by Gerhard contained in Pieper, *Christian Dogmatics*, vol. 3, 367n110.

sincerely—and enunciate clearly and loudly. While speaking the Lord's Words, the pastor may simultaneously touch the vessels containing the elements—the paten and ciborium, also the cup, the chalice or trays of glasses, and the base of the flagon. After touching, he makes the sign of the cross over the entire quantity of the bread, then over the entire quantity of the wine. This action is preferable to speaking the Words and making the sign over only one wafer and only over the chalice. When done slowly and deliberately, the action of the consecration is of great comfort to the people because they are assured that all the elements on the altar are brought into the Sacrament. It is helpful if the pastor speaks and signs, turning slightly aside, so that the people may observe this action. Of course, facing the congregation from a free-standing altar serves well.

When speaking the Words of Institution, the pastor may elevate the host and then elevate the chalice of wine. The words "Given and shed for you (*pro vobis*)" govern this notable action. The elevation of host and chalice is not directed to God as if the pastor were offering a sacrifice, the Romanist practice. To the contrary, the elements here are raised toward the people, that is, to show the Lord's gift *for you*.

It should not be considered that the elements initially placed at a distance, that is, on credence table or shelves attached to side walls of the chancel, are included in the consecration. To remove all concern, that supply, if used in the distribution, should first be brought to the altar, where the pastor pauses in the distribution and speaks the Words of Institution to these elements as well. Then they may be distributed to the people. The pastor takes the same action if and when additional elements are brought new from the sacristy to replenish a short supply during the distribution. To shrug shoulders and beg off, saying, "Oh, we don't have to go through all these motions," is simply unwarranted.

The Distribution and Reception

With the consecration accomplished, all is ready. The Lord invites people and pastor, "Come to Me." The people approach the altar—standing, kneeling. Bowing reverently, they honor their Lord and greet their pastor. He reciprocates, and he bows toward them. The distribution and reception follow immediately after the consecration.[218] The pastor gently places the host on the

218 The distribution following immediately after the consecration is the preferred practice. Dr. Norman Nagel emphasizes that the centrality of Christ's words is paramount (1 Cor 11:25; Luke 22:20). The Lord's words are the principal factor, but His words and the action of *giving* are closely aligned. Therefore, interjecting canticles and prayers between the two actions in the Divine Service may be a concern. Another matter of concern is the practice of bringing and distributing the consecrated elements to the sick and homebound persons at a distance by time and space from the actual consecration at the altar during the service of the Sacrament. The notion of *duration* notwithstanding, this practice, for reasons stated here,

tongue of the communicant. Receiving the host in the hands is also a common practice. In either case, communicants receive what is here and given in accord with the Lord's Words.[219]

Prior to distribution to the larger congregation, the pastors and assistants commune. The presiding pastor may commune himself. Then he communes the assisting ministers. The practice of the bishop communing himself dates back to the Early Church Fathers.[220] There is nothing amiss in the context of the Lord's Supper for the pastor to receive the elements from his own hand. This is not the "private mass" condemned in the Lutheran Confessions.

Congregations develop their own patterns of moving communicants to and from the altar. Whatever the arrangement, the Sacrament is not served by a hurried distribution. Partaking of the Lord's Supper is an event in a Christian's life. There should be brief but meaningful intervals as communicants approach the altar, receive, and return to their place in the congregation. In many churches, the "rush" is on. Pastors race with distributing the host, followed much too closely by distribution with the cup. Care must be taken not to rush through the distribution, the goal being to do all things in a reverent manner in good order.

In the distribution, the use of the chalice or common cup bespeaks the Lord's Church as one body partaking together of Him who is their common life and salvation. This is salutary. Nevertheless, the practice of distribution by individual glasses is widespread. Numerous congregations distribute by both modes. Hygienic concern over the common cup is difficult to alleviate, and the notion that the silver metal of the chalice fosters sterilization is specious. Regarding hygiene, note that the handling of individual glasses in the preparation and distribution offers no distinct advantage.[221] Furthermore, the disposal of plastic glasses post-Communion is unacceptable when communicants toss them in a trash container on their way back to the pew. The church can do

---

may be ill-advised. See Norman E. Nagel, "Holy Communion," in *Lutheran Worship: History and Practice*, ed. Fred L. Precht (St. Louis: Concordia Publishing House, 1993), 308–309.

219 Dr. Nagel observes that any gesture that overtly or tacitly suggests "co-participation" deflects attention from the Lord's doing to ours, and this is hardly faith's or the Gospel's way. He locates the origin of hand Communion with Karlstadt, a practice roundly discarded by Luther.

220 Describing the Communion liturgy from earliest time, Carl Volz notes that following the consecration, the bread and wine were given to all present by the assistants, the bishop communing himself and the other clergy first, in order to be an example to the flock. Volz draws from numerous sources, principally the *Didache* and the *First Apology* of Justin Martyr, also the *Apostolic Tradition* of Hippolytus of Rome, usually dated ca. AD 216. See Carl A. Volz, *Faith and Practice in the Early Church: Foundations for Contemporary Theology* (Minneapolis: Augsburg Publishing House, 1983), 100–102 (cf. AC XXIV 37–38).

221 The author recalls at his former parish the ornate set of individual silver chalices, forty to a tray. This mode of distribution to three hundred communicants in a single service proved challenging. From the tray, the pastor lifted a single chalice and put it to the lips of the individual communicant. It was impossible to avoid contact with facial parts. That this procedure was hygienic is indefensible. This mode of distribution was also extremely arduous.

better. The set of individual cups should be genuine glass, and a receptacle may be a table with a perforated top to receive them post-communing. Following the service, the altar guild may retrieve the glasses and rinse each individually in a container of clear water. Then the glasses are washed in warm soapy water, rinsed, dried, and stored. The residue in the container should be taken outdoors and poured on the ground. Closing this discussion, permit this note: the elements acquired and brought to the church building should enjoy storage appropriate to their use in the Sacrament. Storing these elements in a broom closet is unconscionable.

Reverent Handling of the Consecrated Elements—Post-Communion

Handling the consecrated bread and wine, the *reliquiae*, following the Communion service, we are about disposition of those elements, not disposal of them. According to Hermann Sasse, Luther was adamant that the consecrated elements post-Communion should be either consumed or burned.[222] Some pastors and altar guilds return consecrated elements to the ground, exterior to the church building. Another practice is to consume what remains and to take care not to consecrate more than is reasonably expected to be distributed. A pastor will wish adequately to instruct the altar guild not to set out too much. If during the distribution elements run out, it is a simple matter to bring more and consecrate again. Many unnecessary questions can be avoided simply by consecrating what is needed and consuming the hopefully very small quantities of consecrated elements that remain afterwards. But if not, elements which have not been consecrated should not be mixed with those that have served as host to our Lord's body and blood. Reverently either dispose of the host elements, or store them reverently until they are needed again next time.

Admission to the Lord's Supper

Christians—Baptized, Catechized

When administering the Lord's Supper in the way of His institution, to whom does Christ intend to give this Holy Supper with its blessings? Our initial inquiry cannot be "who is *not* to be admitted, who is to be excluded?" Pursuing this question may lead to severity in examination of those who wish to commune. Both pastors and congregations shall guard against denying the Lord's Supper to anyone to whom Christ wants to give it. In this regard, Luther had to warn against laxity in practice but also against legalism and unnecessary

222 Sasse, *This Is My Body*, 174n102.

rigor. Walther, too, cautioned against rigorous examination. He recommended a friendly interview of those who desire the Sacrament in order to reveal the state of their Christianity and to have an opportunity to state what the Lord's Supper is and why they wish to partake.[223]

Clearly, the Lord instituted the Sacrament for His disciples—first, the Twelve whom He named apostles[224] (Mark 3:14; 14:12, 17, 22–25). Who partook of the Lord's Supper following His ascension and then Pentecost eludes precise determination. Presumably, those communicants were both baptized and catechized. At least, the earliest record of Communion practice confirms this. St. Paul counseled those who were baptized into Christ about the Lord's Supper (1 Cor 10:15–17; cf. 1 Cor 12:13, 27; Eph 3:6), and his correctives against abuses of the Sacrament are sensible only if his readers at Corinth were also catechized (1 Cor 11:17–34). Beginning in the late first century and beyond, the practice was established that only baptized catechumens were permitted to partake of the Eucharist.[225]

Christians Who Examine Themselves

Christians who are baptized and catechized shall prepare themselves for the Lord's Supper. The apostle Paul frames preparation in this manner: "Let a person examine himself, then, and so eat of the bread and drink of the cup" (1 Cor 11:28). "Examine," that is, δοκιμαζέτω, the same term applied to prospective deacons, δοκιμαζέθωσαν πρῶτων, "And let them also be tested first" (1 Tim 3:10). The imperative mood emphasizes unqualified examination, beginning with "self" before God (First Table of the Law), then scrutiny of life with others (Second Table of the Law). Sin is there in abundance, and it must surface for what it is, the radical cleavage between the soul and God, between self and the needs of others.[226] In the Lord's Supper is forgiveness of sins, so sin must not be left to die, exhorts Luther.[227] This is the initial focus, not frivolous reasons for going to Communion. Sin and guilt dare not slip into oblivion, out of consciousness, to condemn quietly but painlessly with no further reckoning. "Apart from the law, sin lies dead" (Rom 7:8b). Examination prior to taking the

223 Pieper, *Christian Dogmatics*, vol. 3, 386–387.

224 Whether or not a larger contingent of "disciples" also gathered in the place where Jesus instituted the Sacrament on the night He was betrayed, Mark's Gospel states that Jesus came to that setting with the Twelve (Mark 14:17).

225 Baptism has ever been the entrée to the Lord's Table. Walther states, "Only he should receive the holy Supper who has already become a child of God through the washing of regeneration, holy Baptism, just as in the Old Testament only he could receive the Passover lamb who had already been received into the divine covenant of grace through the sacrament of circumcision." Walther, *American-Lutheran Pastoral Theology*, 109.

226 See Kenneth Korby, "A Form of Self-Examination based on the Ten Commandments," *Issues, Etc. Journal* 6, no. 1:12–16.

227 Cited by Pieper, *Christian Dogmatics*, vol. 3, 375n120.

Sacrament does not go easily. Time and attention to one's sinful condition and need places the terrified conscience under the Law (the Ten Commandments), where sin and guilt are painfully real. This reality must be faced in preparation for the Gospel in the Sacrament, the body and blood of the Lord given and shed *for you*, for the forgiveness of sins. Where examination leads, that is, to repentance, the Formula of Concord maps clearly:

> The true and worthy guests, for whom this precious sacrament above all was instituted and established, are the Christians who are weak in faith, fragile and troubled, who are terrified in their hearts by the immensity and number of their sins and think that they are not worthy of this precious treasure and of the benefits of Christ because of their great impurity, who feel the weakness of their faith and deplore it, and who desire with all their heart to serve God with a stronger, more resolute faith and purer obedience.[228]

Second, those who examine themselves inquire how they *discern* Christ and the Sacrament.[229] How is Jesus important to me? Is His importance first that He atoned on the cross for my sins (1 Cor 11:26b)? Do I now "remember" Jesus as I take the Sacrament (1 Cor 11:25b)? Do I desire that His body and blood seal to me the forgiveness of sins (Matt 26:28)? Posing these questions, the communicant discerns the Lord and distinguishes this Lord's Supper from other social eating and drinking (cf. 1 Cor 11:20–21, 28–29).

Third, those who wish to commune examine themselves to see if they are in the faith so that they partake of the Lord in His Supper in a worthy manner. About such preparation, Luther assures, "A person who has faith in these words, 'given for you' and 'shed for you for the forgiveness of sins,' is really worthy and well prepared" (SC V 9–10). Luther speaks not of idle, unconscious, nondemonstrable faith, but of alert and aggressive faith, believing intensely that it is the Lord's body and blood as He promises with His Word.[230] More than

228 FC SD VII 69.

229 Luther counseled that before a pastor admits persons to the Lord's Table, they give account of their faith and especially answer the question of whether they understand what the Sacrament is, what it benefits and gives, and what they want to use it for, that is, whether they can say the words of the Sacrament and their explanation by heart; and they indicate that they are going to the Lord's Table because they are plagued, on account of sins, with a burdened conscience or the fear of death or with any other assault of the flesh, the world, or the devil; that they hunger and thirst to receive the word of grace and salvation from the Lord Himself through the office of the minister so that they may be comforted and strengthened, as Christ has given and instituted it out of inexpressible love in this Supper with these words: "Take, eat, etc." Walther, *American-Lutheran Pastoral Theology*, 114–115.

230 Who receives power and benefit from the Sacrament? In the Large Catechism, Luther directs close attention to our Lord's Words of Institution and replies, "It is the one who believes what the words say and what they give . . . those to whom he says, 'Take and eat,' etc. And because he offers and promises forgiveness of sins, it can be received in no other way than by faith. This faith he himself demands in the Word

casual assessment of his or her relationship to Jesus, the communicant grasps the incarnate Lord of the Gospels. He or she wants and receives the Lord as He gives His body and blood "for you" in the Sacrament. In this examination, it is important to distinguish between worthiness and communing in a *worthy manner*, that is, a worthy use of the Sacrament. Some Christians mistakenly attempt to get themselves up for Holy Communion. They want to compensate for sin and guilt by falling back on perceived goodness and good works. In this way, they are comforted that they arrive worthy at the Lord's Table. But they do not so arrive, and they have taken false comfort. They are worthy only and entirely by a righteousness that is not their own, namely, the holy obedience and perfect merit of Christ (FC Epitome VII 20).[231] Some baptized Christians, however, who are worthy by Christ and His righteousness inadvertently or carelessly use the Sacrament in an unworthy manner. This can happen by thoughtless, casual, or routine going to the altar without first exercising the discipline of examination. Why does the apostle Paul address the Corinthian congregation in terms that are direct, if not stern? He says, "You come together . . . not for the better but for the worse" (1 Cor 11:17b; cf. 11:18–22). Preparation for the Lord's Supper is imperative: "Let a person examine himself"[232] (1 Cor 11:28).

Christians Who Intend to Amend Their Ways

Examination projects beyond the Sacrament to the faith-life strengthened by Christ and His gift of forgiveness of sins. The faith that receives the Lord's gifts in the Sacrament is faith that makes alive (Ap XXIV 73). "I have Christ and His blessed forgiveness, and how shall I live?" (2 Pet 3:11–12) This faith-use of the Sacrament helps Christians amend sinful ways and carry through with repentance as change for the better, the godly life. Melanchthon states, "Once a conscience has been uplifted by faith and realizes its freedom from terror, then it fervently gives thanks for the benefits of Christ and for his suffering"

---

when he says, 'given FOR YOU' and 'shed FOR YOU,' as if he said, 'This is why I give it and bid you eat and drink, that you may take it as your own and enjoy it'" (LC V 33–34). Observe how Luther dismisses other preparations—fasting, prayer, and the like—which have their place as external preparations involving the body but have no capacity to appropriate what Christ here offers in the Sacrament. He states, "But the body cannot grasp and appropriate what is given in and with the sacrament. This is done by faith of the heart that discerns and desires such a treasure" (LC V 37).

231 Explaining the proper use of the Sacrament, Melanchthon dismisses our works and also the notion that the Sacrament is a work *ex opere operato*, and presses communicants for faith that remembers Christ and His benefits and receives them, and thus are made alive through such faith that gives life to terrified hearts. This is impossible for any who plead their goodness and works. Melanchthon puts the matter clearly: "This is the principal use of the sacrament, through which it becomes clear both that terrified consciences are the ones worthy of it and how they ought to use it" (Ap XXIV 73b). That use is by faith that remembers Christ and claims the benefits that He provides in the Sacrament (Ap XXIV 71–73).

232 This is not to exclude a Christian who had no intention of communing and therefore did not prepare, but during the worship service discovers his or her need and wants the Lord's assurance by His body and blood. Certainly, this Christian may and should partake of the Lord's Supper.

(Ap XXIV 74). What does this faith quest for newness mean? Will it challenge the way we grow comfortable sinning? Will it mean turning a deaf ear and a blind eye and a stone heart to the temptations that keep us in their grasp? Will this faith involve new designs in our daily life that rise above the pitfalls in which we reveled in the past? To these and many more such inquiries, faith replies with a resounding yes!

Tools for Examination

Disciplines for the Individual Communicant

To recover the discipline of examination, the Church's ministry may provide a few notes for the individual communicant. The congregation's monthly publication or online newsletter may feature "My Holy Communion." Edited by the pastor, this spot may include penitential psalms and other Scriptures, as in 1 Corinthians 11:23–29. Paragraphs from Luther's catechisms treating the Lord's Supper also serve well. A pre-Communion message and prayer, and some or all of the "Christian Questions with Their Answers" for those who propose to go to Holy Communion, from Luther's Small Catechism, are edifying. Taken from those questions and answers are four points that are easily memorized. They compose the answer to this question, "What am I to think about and ponder when I approach the Lord's Table?" Think in this way:

1. My sins are grievous.
2. I look to the cross, for there Christ died for my sins.
3. Only Christ could make satisfaction for my sins before God.
4. Eagerly, I take His body and blood for the forgiveness of all my sins.

Conversations—Pastor and People

Also helpful are conversations that a pastor has with the people in many settings—homes, small groups, informal gatherings. Now and then, the pastor tactfully leads to a brief discussion of Holy Communion. He listens for questions that press for clarity about the Sacrament. Certainly, he converses about other subjects too. He is not a pastor who limits conversation only to the Sacrament; yet occasional discussion of the Lord's Supper can edify the congregation.

A logical setting for these pastoral care conversations is private Confession and Absolution. Someone may inquire if Confession/Absolution is necessary before Holy Communion. It is certainly preferable, and it provides opportunity to hear and learn more about the Sacrament from the pastor. Luther did not insist that all go to Confession before taking the Sacrament. For some Christians, once annually was sufficient, or once in a lifetime, or not at all.[233] Walther, however, upheld the value of private Confession prior to the Sacrament. He cited a passage from the theological faculty of Wittenberg in 1619:

> Private confession had been retained in order to give the pastor the opportunity to speak individually with people; to give people the opportunity to speak to the pastor about specific concerns or problems; and to apply God's grace and the forgiveness of sins for Jesus' sake individually to penitent sinners.[234]

Walther's counsel in this regard is representative of the practice set by the Lutheran Confessions.[235] He recognized, however, the difficulty of hosting large congregations for private Confession prior to each celebration of the Sacrament. Therefore, he counseled that short of private Confession, communicants should make confessional announcement to the pastor before communing.[236] In Walther's time, the people came to the pastor's quarters in small numbers—families and groups—to experience what private Confession was to accomplish on behalf of the individual communicant prior to the Sacrament. In later decades, extending to the late twentieth century, these sessions were known as Communion announcements.

In the twenty-first century, the practice of private Confession prior to the Sacrament and the practice of Communion announcements have largely disappeared from the sacramental ministry of the Lutheran Church in America. This development has handicapped pastors. In many congregations, pastors have little idea what is going on in the lives of the people—their temptations, sins, questions, doubts, misgivings, challenges to faith, and pressures on Christian life. Furthermore, many busy and distracted Christians retain only fragments of catechesis in the theology and practice of the Sacrament. What do they still possess of the meaning and purpose of the Lord's Supper? These conditions call for reinstruction about the Lord's Supper in brief refresher classes offered at various times. In addition, pastor-people conversations should be active and

---

233 Martin Luther, "A Christian Way to Go to God's Table," (1523), cited by Walther, *American-Lutheran Pastoral Theology*, 114–115.

234 *Consil. Witebergens.* II, 139, cited by Walther, *American-Lutheran Pastoral Theology*, 116.

235 See AC XXV 1: "Confession has not been abolished by the preachers on our side. For the custom has been retained among us of not administering the sacrament to those who have not previously been examined and absolved." Melanchthon extended the practice when he stated, "The sacrament is made available to those who wish to partake of it, after they have been examined and absolved" (Ap XXIV 1). He articulates the practice again: "Many among us celebrate the Lord's Supper every Lord's day after they are instructed, examined, and absolved" (Ap XV 40).

236 Walther, *American-Lutheran Pastoral Theology*, 116.

ongoing in every parish. We leave no stone unturned to assist the people toward meaningful attendance at the Lord's Table.

The Practice of Closed Communion

Closed Communion—A Christological Fact

Inclusive of Disciples, Those Who Believe in Jesus Christ

In twenty-first-century America, where toleration of all forms of human behavior is the norm, shall the Church's altars be as open as its sanctuaries? Or does the Lord's Supper—His institution and ordinance—signal criteria to be met when taking this Sacrament? Should pastors apply these criteria for the welfare of all who commune at the Lord's Table?

The Lord's teaching offers tacit but essential answers to these questions. From early times, the Church has embodied His teaching in the long-standing practice of closed Communion. It is surprising, however, that this practice is primarily about inclusion at Holy Communion and only secondarily about what must be excluded in order to confess Christ with integrity at His Table. It is all about Christ and His guests. Indeed, the practice of closed Communion is Christological.

Moreover, inclusion and confession complement each other as they apply to Christians coming together for the Sacrament. Look in on Holy Communion at a local Lutheran congregation. The first set or table of communicants approaching the rail following the pastor's action of consecration may be fourteen in number. Together, they honor their Lord. They bow, and, by the same gesture, they greet the pastor. All kneel at the rail to receive from the hand of their pastor with the bread and wine, the body and blood of the Lord, which they take orally in a sacramental manner.

Receiving what Christ gives, they confess Him and believe what He states in His Word, that is, all that the Scriptures teach of Him, capsulated within the phrases of the Second Article of the Nicene Creed. Further, Christ has affirmed and commended to these disciples the teaching of the Scriptures. Moses and the prophets and the psalmists had spoken of His death and resurrection; our Lord affirms these words of God, explaining all that happened involving Him from Good Friday through Easter (Luke 24:24–27, 44–47; cf. John 12:16; 1 Cor 15:1–4). Further, Christ gives to His apostles the Word from Him and the Father that endures forever; and confessing Him, the communicants believe His Word (Luke 10:16; John 12:47–50; 14:10, 26; 15:15b; 16:12–15; 17:8, 14a, 18, 26; 1 Cor 15:1–11; 1 Thess 2:13; cf. 1 Pet 1:24–25).

Noninclusive of Any Who Believe or Confess Other Than the Lord's Teaching

Principle: Caring for the people and attending to their privilege to be guests at the Lord's Table, the pastor knows them well. Also, he knows how they come—instructed and prepared—to partake of the body and blood of the Lord.

In the practice of closed Communion, confession and inclusion are complementary. The doors to the sanctuary are open to all for hearing the Gospel. The Lord's Supper, however, is open to those who confess Him and believe His Word as we have discussed here. This principle also marks any belief or confession other than what is expected of those included at the Table. It would be unconscionable for any to receive the Sacrament and simultaneously be in denial about the teaching or doctrines of Holy Scripture that the Lord affirms. Moreover, ignoring this distinction between those who should and should not partake at the altar can lead to the practice of *open Communion*, which alters the proper *koinonia* or fellowship at the altar. Retaining the distinction, also note that the *inclusion* principle as a complement to orthodox *confession* understandably dismisses heterodoxy from the Lord's Table. This we uphold and confess.[237]

The Practice of Closed Communion Compromised

The Counter Practice—Open Communion

Pastoral care and instruction may assist those who should not be at the Lord's Table to arrive at proper participation and partaking, but welcoming all such persons to the Lord's Supper without this pastoral attention is open Communion, a practice counter to closed Communion. In some congregations, preceding the Divine Service the pastor announces, "If you are baptized and confess faith in the triune God, you are welcome at the Lord's Table today." Some persons in the general audience, however, for reason of their present state of questionable confession or nonconfession, may accept the open invitation to their harm rather than blessing (cf. 1 Cor 11:29–30). This is risking much. The practice of open Communion, therefore, is not responsible administration of the Sacrament. Loose or permissive practice with regard to attendees at the Lord's Table veers toward *open Communion* and is subject to correction.[238]

---

237 In his monograph titled *Communion Fellowship: A Resource for Understanding, Implementing, and Retaining the Practice of Closed Communion in the Lutheran Parish*, Paul T. McCain gives guidance to the parish pastor who is earnest in practicing closed Communion. See *Communion Fellowship* (Fort Wayne, IN: Luther Academy, 1992).

238 See Matthew C. Harrison and John T. Pless, *Closed Communion?: Admission to the Lord's Supper in Biblical Lutheran Perspective* (Concordia Publishing House, 2017).

The Revisionist Practice—"Close Communion"

Seeking a mediating practice between closed and open Communion, some pastors believe that close Communion holds promise. The reality is that there can be no close Communion unless the practice is indeed closed. If *close* signifies friendly fellowship among those who comprehend the Lord's Supper loosely and partake for negligible reasons such as firming up relationships, what is accomplished? The fact is, the horizontal dimension—closeness to our fellows at the Lord's Table—occurs only when all who commune are in accord, confessing Christ, believing His Word, and participating in the Lord's action for what it is: the giving of His body and His blood in the Sacrament for the forgiveness of sins.

Observe furthermore, the term *close Communion* is relatively recent.[239] Undisputed is the fact that in the early centuries the Church practiced closed, not close, Communion.[240] Dr. Norman Nagel stated, "The freight of the term *closed communion* is there from the start."[241] He reminds that in the early fellowships the body and blood of the Lord were not given to persons who

1. did not receive and give the kiss of peace;
2. were not baptized;
3. had not made confession of faith; or
4. had not been absolved.[242]

Nagel cites the Large Catechism, where Luther stated, "For we do not intend to admit to the sacrament and administer it to those who do not know what they seek or why they come" (LC V 2).

Koinonia at the Lord's Table

The discussions that distinguish between closed and close Communion are essentially about a distinction between pew fellowship, inclusive of both congregation and visitors assembled for public worship, and altar fellowship, inclusive of those from the pews who have been instructed and are prepared to

239 Dr. Norman Nagel reported that research disclosed the term *close Communion* first in the *American-Lutheran* (November 1941), though John H. C. Fritz speaks of *close Communion* in his work, *Pastoral Theology* (1932), 130. See Norman Nagel, "Closed Communion: In the Way of the Law, in the Way of the Gospel," *Concordia Journal* 17, no. 1 (January 1991): 27–28. For background to the use of both terms, *closed Communion* and *close Communion*, see Paul T. McCain, *Communion Fellowship*, 19–20.

240 The *Didache* (AD 120–180) relates about the Lord's Supper, "Only those who had been baptized were permitted to receive." The *Apostolic Tradition* of Hippolytus of Rome, usually dated ca. AD 216, contains a report of a reconstructed Communion service, when, following the prayers for the emperor, the sick, and all others in need of God's help, prayers addressed to the Father in the name of His Son, in the unity of the Holy Spirit, "those who have not been baptized are excused, and the Eucharistic service begins." See Carl A. Volz, *Faith and Practice in the Early Church*, 98, 100.

241 Nagel, "Closed Communion: In the Way of the Law, in the Way of the Gospel," 22.

242 Ibid., 23.

receive the Lord's Supper in a worthy manner. The latter fellowship is *koinonia*, that is to say, those who commune and thus partake together of the Lord's body and blood (1 Cor 10:16). Not simply an individual action, each communicant in this *koinonia* participates with others in a public act of confession of the one Christ with and to one another.[243]

The extended implications of this *koinonia* are nothing short of wonderful and even beautiful. The individual Christian kneeling at the altar to receive the Lord's body and blood for the remission of sins should, indeed, focus intently on the Lord's suffering and death at the cross for him or her. No other subject should ever distract at this moment. Later, however, when communicants return to their places among the worshiping congregation, they may properly celebrate closeness with their fellow Christians. They have just been at the altar elbow to elbow, heart to heart, with others in a wonderful exchange that includes a sharing of burdens and also love, care, and support. Together, they live by Paul's poignant exhortation in 1 Corinthians 10:24, "Let no one seek his own good, but the good of his neighbor[!]" Because he viewed the Sacrament as a sign of this extended *koinonia*, Luther said, "As love and support are given you, you in turn must render love and support to Christ and His needy ones. . . . You must fight, work, pray, and—if you cannot do more—have heartfelt sympathy. . . . Here the saying of Paul is fulfilled, 'Bear one another's burden, and so fulfill the law of Christ' [Gal. 6:2]."[244]

Principle: From those sharing *pew* fellowship come the baptized ones to the *altar* in a fellowship of those who confess Christ and His Word, examine themselves, and in faith partake of what He gives in the Sacrament—His body and blood for the forgiveness of sins.

Koinonia at the Lord's Table—Jeopardized

The *koinonia* at the Altar, however, may be in jeopardy when confession of Christ and His Word are in any way diminished. This is a sad circumstance. To prevent any weakening of this confession, the pastor monitors the fellowship among those he has carefully instructed about the Lord's Supper and proper partaking of the same with fellow Christians. Certainly, he will note and address any confession that is inimical to Christ and His Word. Several examples come to mind.

243 McCain, *Communion Fellowship*, 12. Note that the term *koinonia*, in the New Testament, sometimes expresses correspondence between bread and wine and what the Lord gives by His Words of Institution, His body and blood (1 Cor 10:16). See the Smalcald Articles III VI 1: "We maintain that the bread and the wine in the Supper are the true body and blood of Christ" (cf. FC SD VII 77). See Martin Chemnitz, *The Lord's Supper*, 138–140.

244 Martin Luther, "The Blessed Sacrament of the Holy and True Body of Christ, and the Brotherhoods" (LW 35:50). This writing from Luther is a classic treatment of *koinonia* among those who are the Body of Christ, the Church, assembled at the Lord's Table.

1. For whatever reasons, a member of the congregation may have absorbed false teaching of one kind or another. As a result, he or she may even question the historicity of Jesus, including His sayings, miracles, death, and resurrection. Or the person may hold that there is no evidence for Jesus except for parts of His message. Misled as this person may be, the proper confession of Christ at the altar is at stake. Pastoral care for this individual is paramount.

2. Misperceptions of the Lord's Table occur sometimes. A communicant may anticipate less than what the Lord gives with His body and blood, the remission of sins. Affected by such a misperception, a person may seek the existential experience of encountering Christ or His presence spiritually. A person may view Christ and His sacrificial death as merely a salutary effect, or may await something of the energy of the Spirit or some other positive influence and nothing more. Holding these or similar misperceptions of the Sacrament, such a person needs gentle but pointed instruction or reinstruction from the pastor.

3. True *koinonia* prevails among those who firmly believe that they receive the remission of sins with the body and blood of the Lord. Some persons, however, conveniently set aside this truth. They formulate subjective notions of the Sacrament and its benefits. Usually, these same persons assert that Holy Communion is a matter of personal interpretation quite independent of the Lord's ordinance and institution, or they may press synergistic notions that grace comes in the Lord's Supper to those who cooperate and present themselves in the way of good conduct, as if their own perceived merit deserves the benefits of the Sacrament. Unwittingly, perhaps, they jeopardize the proper *koinonia* at the Lord's Table.

4. Some persons may believe that the Service of Holy Communion should host many teachings, confessions, and faiths. Thus, in their mind, they prefer to accommodate diverse views of the Lord and His Sacrament that compromise, abridge, reduce, or alter what the Lord and His Word declare. They would be comfortable with an open ecumenical Communion service. Again, such views compromise the *koinonia* articulated by the New Testament.

5. Some persons may desire to commune at the altar, even though they confess, believe, and teach other than the cardinal teachings of the Scriptures. For example, some professing Christians hold to the evolutionary view of beginnings, quite contrary to the scriptural teaching of creation, the act of God whereby He brought into existence all things and owns all things in the created order (Exod 19:5b; Ps 50:10–11). In our confession at the altar, we dare not diminish, much less ignore, Christ in the action of creation (John 1:3–5, 10; Col 1:16–20). Any belief or confession counter to this teaching of the Scriptures is a weakening of proper *koinonia* at the Lord's Table. Again, pastoral care is paramount for persons whose confession conflicts with the Scriptures.

Citing these examples whereby *koinonia* at the altar may be jeopardized, we are not pressing for a witch hunt to ferret out either distorted views or false beliefs that mistakenly are held by some persons in the congregation. The examples, however, urge the pastor to be vigilant as he cares for his people and how they approach the Lord's Table. Busy pastors, of course, are tested. Still, pastors will be alert to red flags and address them as necessary so that all who commune do so in the strength of that *koinonia* we enjoy as members together of our Lord Jesus Christ.

Pastoral Accountability at the Lord's Altar

Accountability as Pastoral Care

Principle: The pastor attends closely to all who approach the Lord's Table. When ministering to a person who should not commune, the pastor is a good shepherd who extends himself and reaches for the lost sheep. He seeks to rescue and restore that person in the love and care of Christ for sinners.

The pastor gives care to those partaking of the Sacrament because he is accountable for the flock gathered before the altar (1 Cor 4:1–2; 2 Cor 2:17).

This principle expresses Luther's statement that "we should know with whom it [the Sacrament] takes effect."[245] Elsewhere, Luther counsels, "Here I must not act in doubt, but be [reasonably] sure that the one to whom I give the Sacrament has laid hold of the Gospel and has true faith."[246] Again, a pastor responsibly accounts for those who come to the Lord's Table only through continuous conversations with the people about the Sacrament and formally through a discipline of instruction

245 St. L. XI:615, cited by Pieper, *Christian Dogmatics*, vol. 3, 385.
246 Cited by Pieper, 381–382.

and reinstruction combined with on-site preparation or examination prior to each Communion celebration.

Responsible Administration of the *Minor Ban*

There is the rare instance when the pastor does not welcome a Christian at the Lord's Table. Instead, he informs the party that he or she may not commune at this time. This temporary suspension from the Sacrament is known as the minor ban.[247] Having conferred with the church elders or consistory about the matter, the pastor imposes this suspension on a person who is blatantly unrepentant of public sins (Acts 20:28; 1 Cor 4:1–2; 2 Cor 2:17; 1 Pet 5:2–3; cf. 1 Cor 5:1–2, 13b; 1 Tim 5:20). Taking the Lord's Supper in this state is contrary to God's will and ordinance.[248] The *minor ban* is appropriate when nonrepentance for egregious sins mocks the forgiveness of sins for which the Lord died on the cross and here gives with His body and blood. Taking the Sacrament in this condition could place the person under divine judgment (1 Cor 11:27–29).

Pastoral Administration of the Minor Ban

Of course, the pastor is guarded before suspending a Christian from the privilege of the Sacrament. When admission to the Lord's Table is problematic, the pastor inquires, questions, counsels, and sometimes admonishes with a view to correcting and leading to repentance. Nevertheless, when hearts are unyielding, obdurate, or belligerent and unwilling to confront the sin or turn away from it, the pastor executes the minor ban. He advises a recipient of the ban that he or she is unprepared at this time to be at the Lord's Table. The pastor assures the person that he looks forward to the time of contrition and expressed sorrow for the sin. Then he may lift the ban and assure that Christ welcomes that person to receive His body and blood for the forgiveness of the sin.[249]

---

247 The *minor ban* is distinguished from the *major ban*, excommunication. For reason of callous nonrepentance, the Church excommunicates; that is, it declares the unrepentant person to be no longer a Christian.

248 Pieper's remark about pastoral duty and admission or suspension from the Lord's Table is pertinent. He states, "The thing that must be maintained is that the pastor is personally and directly responsible not only to the congregation, but also to God, with regard to the persons he admits to the Lord's Supper. Therefore the pastor has both the right and duty to suspend those whose admission to the Sacrament would be contrary to God's will and ordinance." *Christian Dogmatics*, vol. 3, 389. Also see AC XXIV 36.

249 Noteworthy is the candor and seriousness displayed by our Lutheran fathers when considering this pastoral action, the minor ban. Dr. Pieper reflects their earnest views. Should the pastor administer the ban justly and the congregation disagrees, seeking to reverse the suspension, Pieper counsels, "The pastor must nevertheless rather suffer removal from office than give the Lord's Supper to a person to whom, according to God's Word, he must deny it." *Christian Dogmatics*, vol. 3, 390.

Pastoral Care Vignettes in the Administration of the Lord's Supper

Visitors—Non-Lutheran—Desire to Commune in the Lutheran Service

Manning the Gate in the Divine Worship Service

The Lutheran pastor monitors Communion at the Lord's altar. As unpalatable as the term may be, the pastor is a gatekeeper (cf. AC XXIV 36). Persons of a different confession may wish to commune. The pastor receives their inquiries and counsels before admitting them to the Table. Otherwise, he may suggest that they remain in the pew or approach the altar with arms crossed over their torso and receive a word of blessing. He is at a juncture. He may decide either for the practice of *open Communion* or for *closed Communion*. What shall it be?

When the pastor surmises that visitors or strangers present in the worshiping congregation may wish to commune, he makes a brief and pointed overture at some pause in the liturgy. He shows that members of the congregation come to the altar not because they are *members*, or even members of The Lutheran Church—Missouri Synod, but because at a point in their lives as baptized Christians, they received instruction from their pastor about the nature of the Sacrament, the Lord's institution of it, the giving of His body and blood, and the proper manner to receive the Lord and His gifts. So the pastor states for the benefit of visitors, "Unless you have been so instructed by a Lutheran pastor about the Sacrament, it would be best for you to remain in the pew. If you wish, you may come forward to the altar, but please cross your arms and receive from the pastor a word of blessing. Later, let us have a conversation and arrange to instruct you. Then you may come to this altar and receive the Lord's Supper."

Now and then, however, a stranger will appear at the altar for the Sacrament. Does the pastor commune this person or pass by him? Does he converse with the person briefly at the Communion rail and then commune him or pass by him? To pass by a visitor at the Communion rail could arouse a deep sense of rejection, causing resentment and alienation. Consider, therefore, communing the person, and with urgency briefly invite him to meet following the service so that he may hear about what he has received. Or, electing not to commune, the pastor may speak a word of blessing to him. Still, not receiving the Sacrament, the person may exit and never return. The pastor will not have an opportunity to counsel and instruct this person about the Lord's Supper.

Manning the Gate in Private Conversation with a Stranger

When the pastor has an opportunity to counsel a stranger in private prior to the Divine Service, his conversation may be pointed and direct or more relaxed. The direct format may be four questions put briefly and promptly:

1. How do you come this day? How shall you approach the altar? Do you come sorry and contrite because of your sins? Is this your pressing spiritual need?
2. How are you thinking about Jesus today? At His Table, you meet Him. Do you believe and confess Him to be the Son of God and your Savior?
3. How do you view the Lord's Supper? Do you believe that with His Words Jesus gives His body and blood, which you receive orally?
4. What blessing do you anticipate? Is it the blessing that the Lord gives with His body and blood, the forgiveness of sins? Do you want this blessing?

The pastor may add, "If these issues raise more questions than we have time to address now, perhaps it would be best to defer taking the Lord's Supper until we have the opportunity for more instruction, the same teaching that our congregation receives before taking the Sacrament. Meanwhile, please worship today. You may come forward, but cross your arms at the rail and receive a word of blessing."

Or, in a relaxed manner, the pastor says, "We are here just prior to the service of the Lord's Supper. You desire to commune, and I am sure that you know that we should be on the same page. You are from a different church. You may have been taught differently about the Sacrament. We should talk about this." The pastor may add this concise counsel, "To belong to a church means to confess what that church believes and confesses. To commune at a church's altar is the highest expression of confessing oneness with what that church teaches."[250]

The pastor continues, "But we both recognize that our churches differ in teaching and belief, and differences matter when they concern the Lord's Supper. We would not serve you well if you communed at the altar of this Lutheran church today.

Principle: Persons who are communed are only those who know what the Lord's Supper is and have been properly instructed, examined, and are able to discern the real presence of Christ's body and blood under the elements of bread and wine.

250 This articulate counsel is offered by McCain, *Communion Fellowship*, 12.

Can we speak another time and offer the same instruction about the Sacrament that our congregation has received? For now, you are welcome. Yes, you may approach the altar. There, I will speak to you a word of blessing. Shall we leave it for now? Let us pray."[251]

Communing for Superficial Reasons

Monitoring the altar fellowship, that is, those taking the Lord's Supper, is primary pastoral care. We have noted how communicants may bring subjective attitudes, feelings, and emotions regarding Holy Communion and not focus on our Lord's suffering and death and His body and blood given and shed for the remission of sins. Vacuous opinions about the Sacrament can place one on the slippery slope toward unbelief, a posture marked by our Lord's words, "Whoever does not believe is condemned already" (John 3:18; cf. FC Ep VII 18). *Coming together* in frivolity and failing to distinguish the Lord's Supper from their partying, if you will, the Corinthian Christians were eating and drinking themselves to the judgment of the Lord (cf. 1 Cor 11:17–22, 29).[252]

Therefore, recovering the chief purpose of the Sacrament, the forgiveness of sins, is pivotal pastoral care for casual inattentive communicants (Matt 26:28). Luther's Small Catechism, in "The Sacrament of the Altar," captures this essential point, calling attention to the Lord's words "given for you" and "shed for you for the forgiveness of sins."[253] On the mark is Pieper's comment, "It must not be overlooked that the Lord's Supper is private absolution."[254] Frequent reminders of this purpose of the Sacrament, offered in fresh and winsome reinstruction, will assist persons who resort to subjective or negligible reasons for communing.

Communicants Charged with Public Sin

A Christian may fall into public disgrace through adultery, flagrant sexual

---

251 McCain notes, in *Communion Fellowship*, that when the Lutheran pastor declines to give Holy Communion to persons of another confession, it is not because he thinks that they are "bad people" or "not Christians." Nor is the practice judgmental, in the sense that he is condemning people. He emphasizes that the practice of *closeness* at the altar is our way of affirming what the Word of God teaches about the Lord's body and blood. Thus, practicing *closed Communion* honors and preserves the truth and power of the Sacrament.

252 Chemnitz, *The Lord's Supper*, 128–130, 134. Chemnitz views St. Paul's entire discussion about *eating and drinking* in the Sacrament in light of the Words of Institution (1 Cor 11:23–25), the particle ὥστε, *hoste* (1 Cor 11:27), linking the substance of the Sacrament to the action, partaking of the Lord's Supper. Perhaps unwittingly, in their socializing, the Corinthians lost cognizance of this connection. They did not distinguish the bread of the Lord's Supper, the body of the Lord, from other common bread, and thus they failed to recognize Christ's true presence and attribute due honor to Him. They did not eat and drink at the Lord's Table fittingly nor spiritually—that is, in a worthy manner—and they incurred judgment upon themselves. For the larger discussion of this point, see Chemnitz, *The Lord's Supper*, 133–134.

253 Luther's Small Catechism, "The Sacrament of the Altar," 7–8, Kolb-Wengert, 362–363.

254 Pieper, *Christian Dogmatics*, vol. 3, 385.

misconduct, embezzlement of funds, inflicting physical harm, and such actions. This same Christian accused of public sin may appear at the Lord's Table. How shall the pastor minister to him? Scandalous or criminal behavior does not in itself exclude a fallen Christian from the Lord's Table, but the pastor may advise private Confession and Absolution prior to taking the Sacrament. The integrity of confession and repentance is critical, and the pastor administers *tough love* in an effort to elicit integral facing of both reality and truth[255] (cf. Gal 6:7).

When a Christian is on trial in the courts for criminal action, the congregation shall be patient and show Christian love. Regarding Holy Communion for the accused, Pieper comments,

> Because the Lord's Supper is not intended for believers and unbelievers, but only for Christians, everyone who has made his Christianity doubtful for the congregation must, before he communes again, enable the congregation to become convinced that by God's grace he has risen from his fall.[256]

The pastor helps an accused person with a ministry of the Law and the Gospel, so that he or she may approach the Lord in true repentance and be received by fellow Christians partaking of the Sacrament.

Weak and Disconsolate Christians

Preparation for taking the Sacrament is agonizing for some Christians who believe that going to Communion presupposes a strong faith and a high degree of sanctity. On these counts, they judge themselves to be inadequate. Therefore, these distraught Christians postpone communing until they can demonstrate to their satisfaction a degree of fervency. Until they *arrive*, they say, "I don't know that I am ready to go to Communion. I don't know if the Lord will accept me."

Such sentiments are disabling. To these distraught ones, the pastor may commend the hymn "Jesus Sinners Doth Receive."[257] He counsels that sins and a gnawing sense of inadequacy will never yield to our own resolve, but God's abundant grace and forgiveness are up to the task (cf. 1 John 1:9; 3:20; cf. FC Ep VII 19–20). Luther counsels weak and disturbed Christians, "Let nothing keep you from the Communion."[258] There is help for sensitive souls. The pastor may cite Psalms 32; 51; 130. Review the Lord's ministry to such persons as the

255 Additional notes on ministry to suspected felons are found in chapter 11.
256 Pieper, *Christian Dogmatics*, vol. 3, 384.
257 *Lutheran Service Book* 609.
258 See Luther's extended counsel cited by Pieper, *Christian Dogmatics*, vol. 3, 387–388.

woman of Samaria (John 4:7–26), the woman caught up in adultery (though recorded in a disputed text, John 8:10–11), also His absolution spoken to Zacchaeus (Luke 19:1–10, especially vv. 9–10). The Gospel for the troubled apostle Paul is helpful (Rom 7:18–20, also vv. 24–25a; then 1 Tim 1:15–16 in the light of Rom 5:1, 6).

The Christian Plagued by Doubt

Other Christians want the Lord's Supper, but they harbor uncertainties and doubts. Their hearts plead, "I believe; help my unbelief!" (Mark 9:24). As long as misgiving and questioning have not hardened into heretical conclusions, the pastor has a viable ministry to these persons. It is vital to *listen* in nonthreatening venues, and a pastor both hears and addresses serious concerns in gentle, nonjudgmental conversation. If a Christian is weighed down by doubt and misgiving, the pastor may counsel as did Luther that doubting Christians should give themselves to God's Word, in faith and love, letting the Sacrament to others for the time being.[259] On the other hand, it may be time to thrust a doubting Christian into the powerful reality of the Lord's Supper for the ever-steadying gift of the Lord's body and blood, allowing the Spirit to have His way with the doubting heart. To Thomas and the other disciples who were unsteady in their believing, the risen Lord came rushing with the Gospel of the resurrection (John 20:24–29). Take leave for a moment from doubts and cling for dear life to the Gospel!

Communing Christians Embattled in Strife with Their Neighbor

Some Christians partake of the Lord's Supper even when they are hostile to fellow Christians. They partake of Him who loved us and laid down His life to deliver us from our sins. At the same time, they are loveless and unforgiving and impatient with their neighbor. This may call for administering the minor ban. Luther is candid when he states:

> God will not be gracious and forgive a man's sin unless he also forgives his neighbor. Besides, a man's faith cannot be sincere unless it bears this fruit, that he, too, forgives his neighbor and asks his forgiveness; otherwise man may not appear before God. If this fruit is missing, his faith and his first confession [his confession 'before God'] is also not sincere.[260]

Jesus instituted and gave the Sacrament to His disciples, and the mark of

259 See Luther's comment in Pieper, *Christian Dogmatics*, vol. 3, 384n134.
260 St. L. XI:585. Cited by Walther, *Pastorale*, 194, in Pieper, *Christian Dogmatics*, vol. 3, 385n137.

discipleship is love for one another (John 13:34–35). The corollary to saving faith in Jesus Christ is love for one another, just as He commanded (1 John 3:23b). Love is generic to the Sacrament.

Discouraging, then, are situations when two parties, both members of the same Christian congregation, go at it in continual conflict. Their welfare and the unity of the spirit in the larger fellowship are at stake. Parties to conflict should weigh and consider the extent that loveless behavior harms both them and their fellow Christians. Open expressions of anger, spite, malice—persons not speaking with one another—call for loving but firm admonition under the Law (cf. 1 John 3:10b–11, 14b–15, 23; 4:7–8). It may come to the point that the pastor addresses the minor ban to one or more of the combatants.

Ministering to parties in conflict, the pastor may engage methods of conflict resolution, and within the boundaries of the Sacrament itself, there are dynamics that are helpful toward mutual forgiveness and reconciliation of parties. Luther understood these dynamics, and he counseled that everyone in Communion fellowship shall take care not to give themselves to hatred or anger. "For this sacrament of fellowship, love, and unity," he wrote, "cannot tolerate discord and disunity. You must take to heart the infirmities and needs of others, as if they were your own. Then offer to others your strength, as if it were their own, just as Christ does for you in the Sacrament."[261]

Communing Persons Who Hold Heretical Beliefs or Convictions

Some Christians expect to commune even when they hold beliefs and convictions that are contrary to the teaching of Holy Scripture. They may assert, "I know what the Bible teaches, but I cannot accept its teaching about this or that subject." Again, their assertion presses the question "May a Christian who holds convictions contrary to the Lord and His Word approach the Lord's Table?"

Wanting to be charitable, the pastor may permit a Christian to commune, though he or she admits to heretical beliefs. That this person is baptized, the pastor reasons, trumps all other concerns. As a matter of confession, however, giving the Sacrament to those who espouse false doctrine is errant practice. Taking the body and the blood of the Lord is a public confession of faith, of belief in Christ and His Word (cf. 1 Cor 11:26b). Generic to this confession is Baptism into Christ, and please understand, Holy Baptism as confession of faith incorporates all that Christ is and teaches. Giving His commission to bap-

---

261 Martin Luther, "The Blessed Sacrament of the Holy and True Body of Christ, and the Brotherhoods" (LW 55:61–62).

tize, He also gave this charge, "teaching them to observe all that I have commanded you" (Matt 28:20). The confession of Christ in the action of taking the Lord's Supper embraces confessing the doctrines of His Word.[262]

A pastor works patiently with Christians who entertain views or adopt beliefs that are contrary to Holy Scripture. They may fixate on errant teaching advanced by people in sects, such as Mormons, Jehovah's Witnesses, or Pentecostals. Or they may be given to endless debate over open questions, which the Scriptures leave unanswered. Their fixation may conflict with the importance and meaning of the Sacrament. Others, confessing belief in the Bible, insist on fashioning its teaching or doctrine in light of their own understanding and experience. The pastor listens, counsels, and leads. In general, the pastor's pulpit and teaching ministries, always intentionally proclaiming sound doctrine, will serve his care of troubled individuals.

Communing Infants

Communing infants and very young children has become a practice among some Lutherans in recent years. This practice has no basis in Holy Scripture or the Lutheran Confessions or in the historic practice of the confessionally orthodox Lutheran Church. Infants and very young children, and for that matter those who are unconscious or otherwise incapable of self-examination and conscious discernment, are not to be communed either. [263] In some instances of mental impairment, such as Alzheimer's disease, persons may have moments of lucidity when they are capable of participating in Confession and Absolution, profession of faith (the Creed), and the prayers. If they are attentive to the Words of Institution, they may commune and receive the Lord's body and blood.

---

262 The totality of this confession is paramount. We have noted how unqualified belief in evolution is a belief that questions our Lord's active part in the work of creation and offends against a fundamental doctrine (John 1:3, 10; Col 1:15–16). (See p. 188.) Fundamental doctrines are revealed in the Scriptures, and they relate to saving faith, that is, faith in Christ the incarnate Son of God and His atoning work on the cross for forgiveness of sins. Nonfundamental doctrines, though disclosed in Holy Scripture, are not the foundation or object of faith insofar as it obtains the forgiveness of sins. The doctrine of the Antichrist is one such nonfundamental doctrine. Pieper explains the distinction between fundamental and nonfundamental doctrines. See *Christian Dogmatics*, vol. 1, 80–81.

263 Thus Walther, "Since according to God's Word everyone who would approach the Lord's Table should first examine himself and discern the Lord's body, it will not do to give the Lord's Supper to children incapable of examining themselves." Walther attributed the rise of the practice of communing infants in the early centuries to a misinterpretation of John 6:53 as referring to sacramental eating and drinking. Then he cites Luther's disagreement with the Bohemian Hussites on the practice of communing infants. Luther said, "I cannot side with the Bohemians in distributing the Lord's Supper to children, even though I would not call them heretics on that account. Furthermore, those who cannot examine themselves and therefore are not to be admitted to the Lord's Supper include also those asleep, or unconscious, those in the throes of death who are already deprived of the use of their senses, deranged people, and the like." For the statements by Walther and Luther and the accompanying discussion, see Pieper, *Christian Dogmatics*, vol. 3, 383n133.

The Sacrament Administered in Various Circumstances

Private Communion of Homebound Persons

The practice of private Communion is both legitimate and feasible.[264] In his discussions of the Christian Church, Luther emphasized the truth in our Lord's words, "Where two or three are gathered in My name, there am I among them" (Matt 18:20). For this gathering, though small, the Church's liturgy of Holy Communion is fitting. Here are some select components of this liturgy:

- ☐ The Trinitarian Invocation
- ☐ The Devotion (a brief message based on a text from the Scriptures)
- ☐ The Confession of Sins and Absolution
- ☐ The Apostles' Creed
- ☐ The Lord's Prayer
- ☐ The Consecration—Words of Institution
- ☐ The Distribution
- ☐ The Closing Prayer or Collect
- ☐ The Benediction

Bringing the Lord's Supper within the basic order of the Divine Service serves homebound persons well. Anchored in the Lutheran Communion liturgy, this order may be abbreviated or tailored to need. This ministry of private Communion is the pastor's work. When the numbers of persons needing this ministry abound, retired pastors may assist.

A pastor who is organized can serve as many as thirty homebound persons with Holy Communion each month. Five or six visits one afternoon a week, adding an afternoon the fourth week, will suffice. Absorbing as such a schedule is, the pastor will discover that he never tires bringing Christ's body and blood to the people. Their reciprocal welcome and response will be reward enough, because for them it is an event when the pastor brings Holy Communion.

The pastor honors this anticipation with attention to details. Communionware should be immaculately clean and the elements fresh. A folded napkin serves as a base for the paten and Communion chalice or glass. A small standing cross adds much. The pastor may wear a mini stole. Brief prepared devo-

264 Luther, and later Chemnitz, were sensitive to abuses when the Mass was celebrated for various reasons outside the Divine Service. This sensitivity undoubtedly influenced their views about private Communion for sick or homebound persons. It is understandable, therefore, that Luther would not rule out the practice of serving the sick with the *reliquiae*, the consecrated elements from the Eucharist. Nor did Chemnitz consider this practice abusive of the Sacrament. Therefore, we shall not look to either Luther or Chemnitz for support of the practice of private Communion. See Martin Luther, "Receiving Both Kinds in the Sacrament 1522" (LW 36:257) and Martin Chemnitz, *Examination of the Council of Trent*, Part II, 301.

tions, expounding and applying the Scriptures, are pivotal. These may be brief confessional addresses. When possible, the pastor and the homebound person may sing a few verses of a hymn. It is well if other members of the family participate and commune. When it is the pastor one-on-one with the person communing, the pastor may participate by communing himself. He should do this only if he is comfortable with the practice. Also, if he communes numerous persons in an afternoon, he may reconsider self-Communion at each location. At day's end, the pastor records these Communions. Later, he shares with the church elders the condition and welfare of the homebound congregation.

Mass Communion Services

Considering rubrics for celebrating the Sacrament in large settings, the primary concern is that each communicant partakes of the Lord's Supper in this meaningful way, the Sacrament *for you*. The Sacrament is not cast about herds of people. All who commune in settings such as conventions, conferences, and rallies should examine themselves in preparation for the Sacrament. Let each communicant in any setting approach the altar as a humble sinner looking to the Lord for forgiveness of sins.

The responsibility and oversight for a mass Communion service rests with one pastor. His congregation serves as host. It is proper that the consecration takes place at one *locus* or place in the auditorium. Then the consecrated elements are dispersed to several altars where the distribution occurs. Many persons approach the various altars, and the openness of the event may tacitly imply *open Communion*. Certainly, the public has access to the Sacrament in these large assemblies. Doubtless, pastors distributing cannot know all of the communicants. Therefore, good order suggests that all who desire to commune as attendees at a conference or convention announce to their home pastor their intention to commune well in advance of the meeting. If this rubric is in place early in the planning stage, perhaps months earlier, the pastor serving as celebrant may declare that those who previously announced to their pastor are welcome at the Lord's altar. Or the convention may provide opportunity for attendees to announce for Communion to a pastor on-site prior to the service.

Frequency of Celebration of the Sacrament in the Local Congregation

Celebrating the Sacrament in the local congregation, two questions pertain:

1. How frequently shall the individual Christian take Communion?
2. How frequently shall the Sacrament be offered?

The Lord's invitation attached to the Sacrament, "Do this," and the need for the forgiveness of sins mandate frequent attendance at the Lord's Table. A Christian who is absent from His Table for weeks, or even years, forfeits all that Christ wants that person to have in this Sacrament and certainly dishonors Him.[265]

Therefore, the answer to the second question, "How frequently shall the Sacrament be offered?" is emphatically, *frequently*! Offering the Sacrament four times a year—a practice by some Lutheran congregations up to the mid-twentieth century—was inadequate. It advanced the notion that the distance between celebrations of the Lord's Supper made congregations more sincere and earnest when they communed. The result was that, missing one of the four Communion services, a Lutheran Christian would not commune for six months.[266]

Many Lutheran congregations today schedule celebration of the Lord's Supper every Sunday. The Lord instituted this Sacrament, saying, "Do this in remembrance of Me" (Luke 22:19). The apostle Paul encouraged communing often, noting that in doing so, Christians proclaim the Lord's death until He comes (1 Cor 11:23–26). The Lutheran Confessions follow. The Augsburg Confession states, "Among us one common Mass is held on every holy day, and it is also administered on other days if there are those who desire it" (AC XXIV 34—Latin text). In the Apology, Melanchthon attests to the practice in Lutheran churches of celebrating the Mass on every Lord's Day and on other festivals (Ap XXIV 1). Recently, The Lutheran Church—Missouri Synod has reaffirmed this practice, urging member congregations to schedule Communion services every Sunday.[267] Some of the congregations comply by celebrating Holy Communion in every Divine Service on each Lord's Day.

This practice, however, is subject to scrutiny. Commendable as the practice of weekly Communion is, the policies that develop around the practice should take care not to create the impression that receiving Communion every Sunday is now some sort of a new law. Care must be taken to teach clearly on these

265 Liberated from papal commands and compulsion to commune, some Christians in Luther's time took the liberty to ignore the Sacrament altogether. The Reformer called them to their senses, pressing how the Lord desires that they commune, for it pleases Him. Thus, they shall not show contempt for the Sacrament. Martin Luther, LC V 34, 35, 52.

266 McCain links *infrequent* communing to a strain of pietism in the Lutheran Church. He advocates return to the historic every-Sunday celebration, which he asserts is the practice recommended by the Lutheran Confessions and by Martin Luther himself. See McCain, *Communion Fellowship*, 14.

267 In 1995, the Synod took this action: "*Resolved*, That the Lutheran Church—Missouri Synod in convention encourage its pastors and congregations to study the scriptural, confessional, and historical witness to every Sunday communion with a view to recovering the opportunity for receiving the Lord's Supper each Lord's Day." Res. 2-08A, "To Encourage Every Sunday Communion," *LCMS Convention Proceedings*: 59th Regular Convention (1995): 113. For a thorough study of the practice of every-Sunday Communion celebration, see Kenneth W. Wieting, *The Blessings of Weekly Communion* (St. Louis: Concordia Publishing House, 2006).

points so as not to create the impression that unless a Christian communes he is not actually worshiping, the unspoken stigma attached to one or another Christian who is uncomfortable communing in a particular service.

These factors—perhaps others too—subtly burden consciences. Lost is the liberty of the individual Christian to commune by personal decision, that is, according to need, desire, preparation, and readiness. The Lord's invitation to "Take, eat" and "Take, drink" is recast as pressure, and His word "Do this . . ." intensifies beyond His intention. It becomes a fierce, irrevocable demand in the perception of some conscientious communicants. The wise counsel of the late Rev. Dr. Alvin Barry comes to mind. Reportedly, this former president of the LCMS advised to regulate congregation Communion services rather than individual Communion practice.

The truth is, in some congregations where Communion in every worship service is the practice, little or no attention is given to factors such as examination, preparation, and readiness to partake of the Lord's Supper in a worthy manner. Can the Church restore Communion practice that stresses frequent but meaningful partaking of the Sacrament? This was the apostle Paul's paradigm (cf. 1 Cor 11:17–18, 26). Noteworthy, in the Large Catechism, Part V, Luther advances persuasive arguments for regular partaking of the Sacrament. Elsewhere, however, he denounces frequency of masses because the effect was insensitivity to the Christian fellowship in its various nuances.[268] He objected when substance and meaning of the fellowship fostered by the Sacrament was lost by many masses. In fact, Luther's discussions about the use of the Sacrament retain proper balance between frequency and meaning.

The Lutheran Confessions retain this vital balance. Note that the Augsburg Confession complements frequency with regular instruction of the people "concerning the holy sacrament, as to what purpose it was instituted, and how it is to be used, namely, as a comfort to terrified consciences" (AC XXIV 7). In the Apology, Melanchthon retains the proper balance when he affirms that among the Lutherans the Mass is celebrated not routinely but every Lord's Day for those who desire it after they have been examined and absolved (Ap XXIV 1). Thus, frequency of the Sacrament is combined with preparation and readiness to partake in a worthy manner. This is the challenge of the practice of the Lord's Supper in our time.

Lutheran congregations may adjust their Communion schedule in several ways. Where a single Sunday worship service is the schedule, a congregation may celebrate the Sacrament weekly; or it may designate two Sundays a

268 Martin Luther, "The Blessed Sacrament of the Holy and True Body of Christ, and the Brotherhoods" (LW 35:56–57, 65).

month for Communion services, adding Communion every fifth Sunday. Congregations holding multiple worship services on a weekend may designate one or two Saturday evening services a month and one service each Sunday morning for Holy Communion. Alternating Communion services among several worship hours week to week makes the Sacrament available each Lord's Day. Make an arrangement that strikes the proper balance: frequently offer Holy Communion but permit individuals freedom without constraint to avail themselves of the Sacrament in light of their spiritual need and desire.

Principle: Congregations and pastors arrange for Communion services, neither adversely diminishing the number of Communion celebrations nor increasing the number to a point that may be misconstrued as pressure or constraint and overriding the individual's decision to commune on the Lord's Day in accordance with need, preparation, and readiness to commune in a worthy manner.

CHAPTER ELEVEN

The Ministry of Private Confession and Absolution

Introduction

Recently catechized, a man became a candidate for Holy Baptism. Following the last session of pre-Baptism catechesis, he requested a word with the pastor in private. With broken voice, he related that for forty years he had carried a burden on his conscience. Confessing, he exclaimed in despair, "Pastor, I don't know what to do!" The pastor addressed him by first name and said, "In the name of Jesus, who died on the cross to lift from our hearts any and every burden, I declare to you His forgiveness of your sins. It's over, friend. Jesus has forgiven you, and He has told you so. Believe His Word. You are a free man. Now pull yourself together and be free from the burden that you have carried so long." The man stood up. Composed, smiling, he shook the pastor's hand. He said, "Thank you, Pastor! You will never know how I have been helped here tonight. Goodbye." He left a free man, a happy man. Never underestimate the power and blessing of the Absolution!

Confession/Absolution in the Church's Ministry

Regarding the Value of Private Confession

This true story highlights the Absolution. Nevertheless, in Lutheranism today, the ministry of Confession/Absolution has fallen into disuse. Numerous reasons are apparent. For instance, the Lutheran tradition sends mixed signals. On the one hand, private Confession shall be retained in the churches because of the Absolution, which is the principal part (AC XXV 13). On the other hand, the Confessors note that confession is not commanded in Scripture. The Church instituted this ministry (AC XXV 12). This statement, however, does not permit reducing Confession/Absolution to the status of an option because the distress of sin presses for opportunity to receive Absolution[269] (AC XXV 3–4).

269 Walther, *American-Lutheran Pastoral Theology*, 122.

Second, some pastors conclude that the general Confession administered in the public worship services is sufficient. Luther could not disagree more. In 1542, he signed a church order that opposed a general Absolution for a group prior to receiving them at the altar for Holy Communion.[270] Luther does not question the validity of the Absolution spoken to the confessing congregation, but he emphasized, "What is Absolution, other than the Gospel spoken to an individual person who thereby receives comfort about the sin he has confessed?"[271] Again, the Augsburg Confession states, "Confession [private Confession] has not been abolished by the preachers on our side. For the custom has been retained among us of not administering the sacrament to those who have not previously been examined and absolved" (AC XXV 1; cf. Ap XV 40b).

Principle: Luther states, "One should also not let anyone go to the holy Sacrament unless he has individually been examined by his pastor, whether he is prepared for the holy Sacrament. For St. Paul says in 1 Corinthians 11:27, that those who receive it unworthily are guilty of the body and blood of Christ."[272]

Many pastors, however, find Confession/Absolution for each individual prior to taking the Sacrament cumbersome. In large congregations, they face the logistical impossibility of examining hundreds of Christians who commune every week. Recognize, furthermore, that Luther also sensed the impracticality of close scrutiny of each communicant prior to each celebration of the Lord's Supper. He concluded that intense examination once annually may be sufficient for a faithful Christian.[273] He leaves much to the responsible and knowledgeable discipline pursued by baptized persons who have been properly instructed and who lead a proper Christian life and monitor their spirituality.[274]

Third, some pastors have grown cool to the practice of Confession/Absolution. It can happen that busy pastors become insensitive to the crisis of the soul. Perhaps they have not experienced another pastor speaking forgiveness to them in the name and stead of Christ, which is nothing less than the voice from

270 Ibid.

271 Ibid., 123. (Cf. AC XI 1; FC SD XI 33a, 37–38.)

272 Ibid. 111.

273 Ibid., 114–115. Luther cites essentials of the examination: communicants give an account of their faith, demonstrate that they understand what the Sacrament is and its benefits, recite the words of the Sacrament and their explanation, and indicate how they are going to the Lord's Table with a burdened conscience that is plagued on account of sins and fearful of death. He adds that such intense examination may be sufficient once annually for a faithful Christian.

274 Walther follows the sensible counsel of Luther. When Walther addressed the practice of *open* Communion, he was adamant, stating that the pastor shall admit no one to the Lord's Supper unless he or she has been individually examined (ibid., 111). In another passage, Walther considers the faithful worshiping congregation and offers this counsel: "It is not only not necessary to examine each person before each Communion (it is enough to do it from time to time, perhaps once a year), since the examination is not based on a law but on the needs of souls; in the cases of those who are known to be knowledgeable, upright, and proven Christians, the examination can be omitted entirely" (ibid., 117).

heaven absolving and speaking comfort and consolation (AC XXV 3–4; Ap XII 39b, 40–41). Have they forgotten the gravity of Melanchthon's teaching that Holy Absolution is a sacrament, albeit a sacrament of penitence (Ap XIII 3–4; XII 41)? May they remember that sin weighs heavily on consciences, that the Gospel of Christ and His forgiveness alone can lift this burden, that Christian pastors by virtue of their office have both authority and power to forgive sins in our Lord's name and see consciences liberated (John 20:23; cf. Ap XII 39–40). The following excerpt from Walther may be fitting:

> The theological faculty of Wittenberg wrote in 1619 that private confession had been retained in order to give the pastor the opportunity to speak individually with people; to give people the opportunity to speak to the pastor about specific concerns or problems; and to apply God's grace and the forgiveness of sins for Jesus' sake individually to penitent sinners (*Consil. Witebergens.* II, 139).[275]

The Practice of Communion Announcements

Somewhere between proper use of Confession/Absolution and outright disuse of the same is the practice of communicants—individuals or families or small groups—meeting with the pastor prior to the service of Holy Communion, a practice that Walther named confessional announcements, subsequently known as Communion announcements. When the practice was in use, the people came to the pastor's sacristy or office. During conversations, the pastor moved the discussion toward the Sacrament. Touching on the meaning and the blessings of the Lord's Supper, he was open to perceptions and questions that might surface. He accomplished instruction and examination; meanwhile, he was prepared to arrange a private conversation with a person who felt the need for private Absolution.

These ministries, private Confession or Communion announcements, were aided by several factors. The people were comfortable with their pastor. He was not aloof nor insensitive, certainly not judgmental. The pastor's demeanor was that of a servant, not a lord or master (Mark 10:42–45). He did not preach to the people. His primary discipline was careful listening. When he sensed that anxiety oppressed a troubled person, the pastor took initiative to come alongside and minister with love and compassion. In this regard, informal conversations with the people can develop into the ministry of Confession/Absolution. Formerly, pastors were alert to these occasions when the Gospel could be spoken with concern and empathy.

275 Ibid., 116.

The Practice of Private Confession and Absolution

Conducting Private Confession and Administering the Absolution

The pastor's conduct within the confessional is open for further comment. The account of our Lord's ministry to the woman of Samaria (John 4) is instructive for administering the confessional. In the manner of our Lord, the pastor is a friend. He permits the person to lead. What are the sins that oppress this Christian? He listens. He is not condescending. He does not ask, "Why would a person like you think such thoughts or do such things?" Confession is painful, and the pastor does not make it more so. He may ask for clarification of a point, but he does not require that the person enumerate sins (AC XXV 7–11). Nor does he explore for secret sins, as if to say, "Tell more, more" (Ap XII 110–112). If the confessing Christian hesitates to disclose hidden sins, the pastor does not go there. He may caution that those sins known only in one's heart should be confessed to God (cf. AC XXV 11). When persons assure the pastor that in the heart they have confessed hidden sins, the pastor obliges with the Absolution.

In the confessional, the pastor is neither severe nor lax. He does not intimidate with holier-than-thou judgment. Nor does he make light of matters, saying, "Oh, John, you are too hard on yourself. It's human to err. Everyone makes mistakes." No, the pastor faces sin for what it is. He draws the confessing person into the presence of God so that sin is clearly the serious offense deserving God's wrath and punishment. Persons come with burdened consciences. In the words of King David, they plead, "My sin is ever before me!" The pastor is there, feeling that pain (Ps 51:3). In these moments, he takes the lead and turns with the Absolution, "For the sake of His Son, Jesus Christ, God is gracious. And He declares what I now say to you, 'In the name of Jesus, your sins are forgiven.'"

If rumor has it that the person confessing has committed public sin, may the pastor bring up the subject, in Walther's terms, on the basis of the "common cry?" The pastor observes that suspicion of the sin is in the public domain. He asks, "What say you of this?" Pursuing the matter depends upon how the person answers this question. The pastor does not press or threaten. He shall not sear the conscience. He does not attach conditions to be met in order to prove sincerity of repentance. He encourages honest reflection. The purpose is not to grill or interrogate the person or force a confession. The purpose is speaking the Absolution to repentant sinners.

Framing the Confessional

The conversation within the confessional is unstructured, but a framework in the background may assist the pastor. Four specific helps are:

1. *Comfortable setting*, that is, helping a person to relax and know that he or she has a sensitive and caring pastor. Transparency is assumed, and leading with prayer is essential. Interjecting brief prayers during the conversation may assist the person to speak openly and freely;
2. *Clarification*, that is, what is the sin, what precisely is it? Behind the facade of excuses, diversions, and escapes, what is the core reality? The pastor's patient listening and pointed questions assist the person to sort things out and see them for what they are and then disclose and confess. A confessing person may get close to clear comprehension but then hesitate and retreat. The pastor does not press. He may suggest, "Another time, perhaps."
3. *Confrontation*, that is, seeing the sin for what it is, the ramifications or implications, adverse effects, the tragedy of it, and then the shame and the guilt over it before God, whose divine scrutiny breaks a sincere person and holds him or her accountable before God and also before others—family, peers, and so on.
4. *Confession*, that is, owning up to the sin, its enormity and its serious consequences, saying to God as did King David in the presence of Nathan the prophet, "I have sinned against the Lord" (2 Sam 12:13).

In the spirit of our Lord's words "Son, your sins are forgiven" (Mark 2:5), the pastor administers the Absolution in this manner, "Friend, what you have told, I have heard, and God hears. Now He speaks, so hear His good words. In the name and the stead of Jesus our Lord, I say to you, your sins are forgiven! You are free, and you may go in peace this day. This word of forgiveness is God's gracious speaking to you. Believe His good word, His grace and mercy." Alternate frameworks may also lead to the Absolution.[276] For example, in conversation, the pastor may ask key questions:

1. What happened? What has occurred? How were you involved?
2. What are your true feelings about what you thought, said, or did?
3. Are you sorry for your thoughts, words, or actions before God?

276 Beside the framework recommended here, another can be adapted from the paradigm set out by military chaplain Steven C. Hokena. It is comprised of four parts: Contrition, Confession, Absolution, and Amendment. See Steven C. Hokena, *Forgiveness Is a Choice* (St. Louis: Lutheran Hour Ministries, 2015).

4. Upon your sincere repentance, "Be absolved, forgiven, in the name of Jesus Christ! Your sins are forgiven! You are free!"
5. What are we going to do? Can you handle questions like these: "How shall I make amends?" "How shall I repair the damage?" "How shall I provide restitution?"

Some prospective users of this framework may object that the fifth point is accessory to the Absolution and hints that forgiveness is conditional, that it depends upon the good intentions of the confessing person. This is not true. The Absolution is *absolute* as is the grace of God in Christ. The factor of amendment following the Absolution, however, is inherent in true repentance, which includes a turnabout from the sin now forgiven.

The Seal of the Confessional [*Sigillum Confessionis*]

Stipulations

Whatever format private Confession takes, a pastor should never disclose a person's confession to any party. For that matter, strict confidentiality is the cardinal rule for any and all communication between pastor and people.[277] Whether it is a formal appointment with the pastor or a casual meeting and informal conversation, Christians expect that their pastor will keep confidences. Even the civil courts recognize and respect privileged conversation of the clergy—pastor and people—within the confessional. The pastor's obligation to strict keeping of the confessional seal is stated in the Rites of Ordination and Installation.

Principle: The Rite of Ordination cites critical pastoral functions, and it binds the pastor to confidentiality when it asks the candidate, "and will you promise never to divulge the sins confessed to you?"

Regarding private confession, Luther gave unconditional protection to the seal of the confessional, and he adhered to absolute confidentiality.[278] Protected conversation is also the principle governing pastoral care. Lay leaders or elders of the congregation may inquire how a pastor counsels a troubled person. The pastor may describe his approach in general terms, but he dare not divulge sensitive issues from his counseling ministry.

277 The confessional rests on the foundation of a silent contract between a confessing person and the pastor as confessor, one that the Church universally respects. Scripture passages that call for integrity in communication between parties in any venue may be cited. For example, see Proverbs 11:13, "Whoever goes about slandering reveals secrets, but he who is trustworthy in spirit keeps a thing covered."

278 Walther, *American-Lutheran Pastoral Theology*, 126–127.

Special Situations Involving the Confessional

The conversation within the confessional is protected, but a particular sin or offense disclosed by a confessing person may involve factors that cannot be ignored. When the confession is clearly criminal action for which a person may be apprehended and possibly indicted and convicted, the pastor must respond. If he suspects that a person is bringing such a serious matter, he may alert the person up front. If errant behavior was breaking the law, the pastor will press the confessing person to reckon with the authorities. In some jurisdictions, the laws may compel the pastor to report certain actions either to the authorities or to other professionals. Included may be instances of physical or psychological abuse, crimes categorized as felonies, and actions that cause great harm. At issue here is the tension between a pastor's first obligation to the seal of the confessional and his obligations to the civil order, its laws and regulations. The historic view is that the pastor keeps the confessional seal inviolate. Obvious behavioral aberrations, however, signal a need for the pastor to connect a troubled person either with the authorities or with specialists for care and treatment.

In some instances, the pastor may hesitate or even refuse to speak the Absolution. Consider several cases. The sin confessed is a felony, but the person refuses to right himself with the authorities and others impacted by his criminal actions. Possibly the pastor is dealing with impenitence. In a similar instance, a confessing person agrees to reckon with the authorities but refuses to be part of amends or restitution. Consider further, a person confessing felonious action seeks Absolution but threatens the pastor with harm if he ever reports the confessed felony to the authorities. Or a person confessing sinful action that brought harm to the community refuses to assure the pastor that he or she will never repeat the action. In these and related situations, the pastor reminds a confessing person that the Absolution is God's action, and expectantly, recipients of His mercy and forgiveness shall follow God's will in every aspect, beginning with right action and behavior under the civil law that is of God (Rom 13:1–5; cf. 1 Pet 2:13–17).

Related to this discussion is an instance when a person discloses to the pastor that he or she intends hostile or violent action that will ruin reputation, damage property, or threaten life or limb. Though the confessional is strictly confined to actual sins committed, the intentions of the heart gripped by darkness should be acknowledged and confessed. The pastor counsels a person inclined to violence to view proposed deliberate sinning for what it is in the eyes of God (Mark 7:18–23; 1 Pet 3:12; cf. Rom 13:8–10; Heb 6:1–8). If the pastor can move the person toward proper confession, he may speak the Absolution.

But the person must be sincere. He or she may not *misuse* the grace of God as encouragement to sin boldly, holding mistaken assurance that proposed evil actions are legitimate because God always forgives (Rom 6:1–2; cf. Gal 6:7–8). Short of sincere repentance and assurances from the person that he or she has canceled all intentions to do harm, the pastor shall inform the inflamed person that in view of what appears to be his or her insincere confession, the pastor hesitates to speak the Absolution.

Again, the tension is acute between retaining the seal of the confessional and constraint to disclose aberrant behavior to other professionals or the authorities for the welfare of the confessing person and the larger community. The fact is some sins disclosed to the pastor are egregious, requiring attention in other venues—counseling, therapy, and reckoning with the authorities. The pastor informs the person that the matter presented in the confessional must be pursued further. It is best when the pastor and the confessing person arrive at a common understanding of these issues. When that understanding is reached, the two parties may agree on how to proceed from that point forward.

Regardless, absolute protection of the confessional seal remains a requirement. Wilhelm Loehe asserts that breaking the confessional seal in any situation destroys the integrity of the pastor's ministry.[279] In that event, the confessing person no longer has a true and trusted friend. Loehe adopted Luther's absolute position, namely, when confessing to the pastor, we confess to God, and just as God hears and keeps all confessions secret, the matter dare not escape the pastor's strict confidence. Once a single instance of the broken seal occurs, the implications are negative. Congregations soon learn that their pastor *talks*. Then the ministry of private Confession is rendered quite useless, and the Church is deprived of an essential gift from the Lord. Proponents of this *absolutist* position defend the Office of the Holy Ministry and they argue fiercely for strict retention of the seal under any and every circumstance.

Procedure When the Confessional Is Tested by Aberrant Behavior

Communication within the confessional is between two parties. Both share a responsibility. The pastor's role and obligation is clear. The other responsible party is the person confessing sins. Of course, overseeing the confessional is God Himself. Again, some pastors argue that sins confessed to the pastor are confessed to God who keeps all things secret; therefore, whatever the matter,

279 See Wilhelm Loehe, "Simple Instructions in Confession," trans. Delvin E. Ressel. This writing is cited in *Una Sancta* 10, no. 2 (1951): 9 and is referenced in *The Pastor-Penitent Relationship: Privileged Communications; A Report of the Commission on Theology and Church Relations* (St. Louis: The Lutheran Church—Missouri Synod, September 1999), 6n8.

it shall ever remain undisclosed. Recall, however, that it is God who instituted the civil order for the maintenance of justice, that is, adjudication of criminal matters resulting in punishment of the evildoer (Rom 13:1–7). Surely we understand that God holds the Church and its ministry accountable to the state, whose function is to deal with persons who commit crimes. Therefore, we emphasize again that it may be necessary to urge some confessing persons to right themselves with the authorities.

True, the pastor is committed to the confessional seal, but the confessing person is also obligated to honor the seal in every respect. This is done when repentance is genuine. A person confessing sins may bind the pastor to secrecy regarding the felony that he or she has confessed. The pastor obliges that request and keeps the confessional seal. The Absolution, however, leads to newness of life that includes amendment of what is amiss, painful as this may be. It may come to this action—the confessing party takes the initiative to reveal his or her felonious behavior to the authorities and cooperates with the process of jurisprudence. The pastor stands with the person.

Furthermore, both parties in the confessional not only have responsibilities, they partner together in pursuit of the right course. Note how the Absolution itself orders things. The Word of the Lord forgiving sins stirs and brings about new life. Before the Absolution, the confessing person knows only trauma over concealing the crime and escaping from the law's demands. The Absolution, bringing forgiveness of sin and the righteousness of Christ, frees the confessing person from guilt to calmly come to terms with his or her obligations. This person has a partner, the pastor. Together, they keep the confessional inviolate, but in a quiet extended dimension. The Absolution follows upon contrition and confession. Then it leads to true repentance, bringing forth fruits of faith in the active life of the person confessing his or her sins (Matt 3:8; Gal 5:22–24; Jas 1:22, 25; 2:8, 14, 21–22). In this holistic private confession, the confessing person and the pastor are on the same page.

Observe further that the ministry of Confession/Absolution is a treasure to the congregation. Preunderstanding of private Confession by the congregation will benefit the individual when he or she needs the Absolution announced by the pastor. Advocating this vital ministry, the pastor informs the congregation that the confessional seal is absolute, but

Principle: The Absolution is cardinal pastoral care. Administering this gift of the forgiveness of sins, the pastor's commitment to the confessional seal is complemented by extended pastoral care that assists a confessing person toward repentance. The confessing person honors the seal by heeding guidance toward repentance and the life of faith enabled by the Holy Spirit through the grace of God given in the Absolution.

he teaches that persons who come to the pastor for Holy Absolution shall bear responsibility for their lives and actions under the grace of God in Christ. The pastor is there for both needs. By virtue of his office, he declares sins forgiven. Also he monitors and energizes with the Gospel the newness of life that comes with the Absolution. Individuals of a congregation so informed will receive the Absolution and partner with their pastor on the journey set out by true repentance.

Encouraging the Ministry of Private Confession and Absolution

Accessibility of the Pastor

There is reticence on the part of many Christians to avail themselves of the opportunity for private Confession and Absolution. Why do the people hesitate? The congregation trusts the pastor, but unwittingly he may foster the perception that he is too busy to bother with the troubles of the individual Christian. Pastors have a lot on their plates, but when they are with the people, their relaxed and patient demeanor will assure that they are available and ready to hear about concerns or sins that weigh heavily on burdened consciences. It is a matter of conveying to the people that the pastor is accessible. He may announce select times for confession, though opportunities frequently arise from informal conversations with the people.

Pastor's Use of Private Confession and Absolution

C. F. W. Walther was convinced that the pastor's readiness to administer Confession/Absolution depended largely on his use of the same. Certainly, one is better equipped to give what he himself has received. There is no standing rule, however, that requires a pastor to seek private Absolution from a fellow pastor on a regular basis. He must be comfortable with it. In times of theological controversy, it may be difficult for a pastor to seek out a brother pastor for the Absolution. Peace in the Church makes for trust among pastors, and mutual trust is essential for pastors to use this ministry of Confession and Absolution.

CHAPTER TWELVE

The Ministry of Altar and Pulpit Fellowship

Introduction

Through the twentieth century, altar and pulpit fellowship among Christian churches was the goal of ecumenical dialogue. Denominational leaders and theologians were the principal players. In the early twenty-first century, ecumenical dialogue and activity have shifted and expanded. Interchurch relations within communities involve a diversity of Christians and non-Christians. How Lutherans fit into the ecumenical scene today is the focus of this chapter.[280]

The subject of altar and pulpit fellowship includes numerous issues. Can a Lutheran pastor and his congregation have fellowship with clergy and congregations of other Christian churches or non-Christian religions? Is agreement in doctrine among participating Christians in joint public ministry a requirement? May confessing Lutheran pastors unite in public ministry with clergy of other confessions in weddings and funerals or memorial services, for example? How does the Lutheran pastor participate in community religious events and retain confessional integrity? May the Lutheran pastor move about in civic organizations and other venues that call for the presence of religion? What principles govern Lutheran participation in joint fellowship activities where unity is assumed across denominational lines?

280 The local Lutheran congregation practicing inter-Lutheran and interdenominational church fellowship was the subject of the document *Inter-Christian Relationships: An Instrument for Study; A Report of the Commission on Theology and Church Relations* (St. Louis: The Lutheran Church—Missouri Synod, February 1991). Earlier CTCR documents addressing church fellowship are *Theology of Fellowship* (1965), *A Lutheran Stance toward Ecumenism* (1974), and *The Nature and Implications of the Concept of Fellowship* (1981).

The Local Congregation—Matrix for the Practice of Church Fellowship

The Lutheran Quest for Fellowship with All Christians

Many Lutherans answer these questions, frustrated that confessing Lutherans are viewed indifferent and even hostile to church fellowship with other Christians. This supposition, however, is contrary to Lutheran tradition. Long-standing is sincere eagerness among Lutherans for fellowship with other Christians. Already in the sixteenth century, the Lutherans offered to settle disputes with Roman Catholic bishops and heal divisions that gave rise to the Augsburg Confession, AD 1530 (AC Preface 10–11). Fifty years later, the Lutherans expressed continued desire to celebrate oneness in Christ with both the Roman Catholic hierarchy and with Lutherans who had departed from some aspects of the Augsburg Confession. In 1580, they expressed their quest for unity in teaching and practice in these words:

> Rather we have a deep yearning and desire for true unity and on our part have set our hearts and desires on promoting this kind of unity to our utmost ability. This unity keeps God's honor intact, does not abandon the divine truth of the holy gospel, and concedes nothing to the slightest error. Instead, it leads poor sinners to true, proper repentance, raises them up through faith, strengthens them in new obedience, and thus justifies and saves them eternally, solely though (*sic*) the merit of Christ.[281]

When Christians from other traditions are also eager for unity and are open to dialogue with a view to resolving differences in doctrine and practice, Lutherans are ready for such discussions.

The Proper Understanding of Church Fellowship—*Unitas* and *Concordia*

Two terms in the Lutheran tradition clarify the nature of fellowship among Christians. They are *unitas* and *concordia*. The first term, *unitas*, expresses the spiritual unity of all Christians because of their shared faith in Jesus Christ by the work of the Holy Spirit through the Gospel. The second term, *concordia*, expresses what is external to *unitas*, namely, concord, the agreement among Christians who believe, teach, and confess the Gospel and its articles. Also known as doctrinal unity, *concordia* connotes peace and harmony among Christians because they publicly confess the same teaching, that is, articles of doctrine in accord with the Holy Scriptures.

281 FC SD XI 96.

The concepts conveyed by these terms, *unitas* and *concordia*, are biblical and confessional. When St. Paul greeted the Christians at Corinth, he addressed them, "Called to be saints together with all those who in every place call upon the name of our Lord Jesus Christ" (1 Cor 1:2). These Christians were the living expression of unity, oneness, that is, all in every place who say, "Jesus is Lord[!]" (1 Cor 12:3). Then, expectantly, the apostle Paul frames vibrant internal spiritual unity into external oneness, *concordia*, when he exhorts them to avoid dissension in their communal life and to be united in the same mind and judgment (1 Cor 1:10). He was moving the Corinthians toward *concordia*, peace and harmony, by resolving divisions in doctrine and practice. He wanted common understanding, teaching, confession, and practice consistent with their faith in Christ (*unitas*).[282]

The Lutheran Confessions engage the concepts, *unitas* and *concordia*. First, they celebrate the one faith in Christ that is true of believing and righteous people scattered through the entire world (AC Preface 11, also 4, 5; VII 1; Conclusion of Part One 1b; Ap VII and VIII 14, 16, 20, 29). Specifically, *unitas* expresses unity among those who receive the forgiveness of sins by faith in Christ, the saints who truly believe the Gospel of Christ and have the Holy Spirit (Ap VII and VIII 25b, 28). Second, the Confessions press for *concordia*. The Augsburg Confession was the attempt to unite Luther's followers and representatives of the Roman church in one, true religion, *concordia* (AC—German text—Preface 10, 11). In 1580, the Book of Concord was framed in accordance with the infallible and unchangeable Word of God, as the Lutheran confessors sought unity in teaching and practice among their own and with other Christians in both the Roman Catholic and the Reformed churches. The Book of Concord stands as witness to their efforts toward *concordia* (Preface to the Book of Concord 1, 16, 20, 21; FC Ep Intro. 4, 5, 6, 7; FC SD XI 95, 96; FC SD Basis, Rule and Guiding Principle 14, 15, 16).

Unitas and *Concordia* in the Life of the Christian Congregation

The biblical and confessional understanding of church fellowship—*unitas*, united in faith in Christ, and *concordia*, agreement in doctrine and practice—finds clearest expression in a congregation of Christians. They are one in faith in Christ and they show that faith in confession and teaching. Sharing in the faith in one Lord, *unitas*, there is continuous—sometimes agonizing—pursuit

282 Diversity in doctrine and practice among the Christians at Corinth is cited in detail by Dr. Jeffrey J. Kloha in his essay "The Lordship of Christ and the Unity of the Church," *Concordia Journal* 39, no. 1 (Fall 2013): 278–279. Dr. Kloha infers that differences among the Christians at Corinth, in many instances, were essential manifestations of a different "gospel," foreign to the faith in Jesus as Lord. Thus, different "gospels" were tools of Satan, destroying the unity and fellowship at Corinth.

of *concordia*, teaching and practice that is true to the Gospel and its articles in accord with Holy Scripture. The key player is the pastor who leads the congregation from *unitas* into proactive *concordia*, the external ministry beginning with preaching and teaching that addresses life situations involving a diversity of Christians who lay claim to one Baptism into one Lord and one faith in one God and Father of us all (Eph 4:5–6).

The pursuit of *concordia* is difficult. The Lutheran confessors faced this reality. Instead of concord, agreement, and peace, there were dissensions and religious disputes that caused divisions[283] (Ap XII 90; FC SD XI 94; FC SD 8, 9, 10, Basis, Rule, and Guiding Principle 19). Reaching for *concordia* today is equally difficult. Diversity in congregations—gender, age, vocation, ethnic origin—is complicated by diverse views and beliefs as well as doubts and misgivings. Though baptized into Christ (Gal 3:25–26; Rom 6:1ff., 22), Christians are vulnerable to temptations, misunderstanding of teaching, and distractions in the form of senseless disputes and heresies (2 Tim 2:16–18; 3:1–9). It is a daunting task to keep a congregation focused on the cardinal teaching of the Scriptures and its articles, the Gospel of forgiveness of sins in Jesus Christ.

Church Fellowship Beyond the Local Congregation

Concordia, an Earnest Pursuit

Church fellowship beyond the boundaries of the local congregation is more challenging for pastors. The same celebration of *unitas*, unity as one faith in Christ, is foundational. Then the pursuit of *concordia*, right teaching of the Gospel and its articles in accord with the Scriptures, must follow. Where do Lutherans fit in this pursuit? First, Lutheran Christians rejoice over oneness or unity with all Christians, and they deplore doctrinal disagreements and dissensions as well as disputes that cause division.[284] Second, Lutherans with other Christians seek *concordia* so that peace and harmony may result when all abide

283 The Lutheran confessors address numerous issues hindering *concordia*. Among these issues was commingling of the Law and the Gospel to the detriment of peace of conscience (FC SD V 27). Likewise, Melanchthon defends against philosophical and social ethics mixing with the Gospel (Ap II 43–44), and he pleads that the meaning of Law and Gospel, how they both differ and complement, be clarified for the comfort of sinners (Ap IV 3, 5–6). When opponents asserted that religious rites are useful for meriting forgiveness, or when they said that devotional acts account for righteousness, Melanchthon pressed for the peace and harmony that the truth of the Gospel guarantees without works or supposed merit (Ap XV 4–5). Melanchthon viewed aberrations in doctrine and practice foisted on the people by the opponents as destructive of the Gospel, doing away with the entire teaching of faith (Ap IV 81). In this manner, Melanchthon worked toward *concordia* in the context of the fellowship of Christians in the local congregations. For commentary on the difficulty of achieving *concordia*, see *A Lutheran Stance toward Ecumenism with Application for The Lutheran Church—Missouri Synod: A Report of the Commission on Theology and Church Relations* (St. Louis: The Lutheran Church—Missouri Synod, November 1974), 9–10.

284 See Ap XII 90; FC SD XI 94; preface to the Book of Concord 4, 5; Ap Preface 14–16.

by the true and correct doctrine, even though harmony in confession may come only with proper correction of teaching that is contrary to the Gospel.[285]

Inconsistency is often apparent when pastors and people engage in church fellowship beyond their local congregations. A pastor who vigorously pursues *concordia* in his congregation may be lax and accommodating in dialogue with peers from other churches. It is proper to be polite and civil, but in ecumenical discussions there is a need to be frank and integral.[286] This is vital because participants in these discussions are there to pursue *concordia* at the level of executing together the Office of the Ministry. Lutheran pastors cannot look the other way when there are differences in doctrine and confession. Nor can they remain silent participants in practice that follows upon teachings that are contrary to the Scriptures (cf. Ap Preface 14–16; FC SD XI 94–96).

Some Lutheran pastors are ready to abandon this hard road for the easy path of accommodation and compromise to achieve *concordia*. They are convinced that joint worship and teaching and related practices are possible simply on the basis of *unitas*. But Lutherans and others must recognize that properly celebrated *unitas*—unity in one faith in Jesus Christ—is not in itself *concordia*. It is, however, the base and the stepping stone to *concordia*, that common understanding of the Gospel and its articles, and common confession, teaching, and practice in accord with the Holy Scriptures.

For the Sake of the Gospel

Lutherans pursue *concordia* in dialogue with other Christians for the sake of the Gospel and that hearts may be led to Christ (cf. Ap IV 81–85). Thus, more is at stake than appears in this Lutheran statement: "The scope of ecumenical endeavors is nothing less than the attainment of full confessional unanimity throughout Christendom with respect to all articles of faith."[287] More precise, endeavors toward full confessional unanimity are for the sake of the Gospel, as hundreds of passages in the Book of Concord attest. Cited here is a sampling of concern for purity in doctrine in the interest of preserving the Gospel.

1. The Lutheran confessors caution against confusion of the Law and the Gospel, for such confusion will easily darken the merits and benefits of Christ, and that would rob Christians of the true, proper comfort against the terror of the Law on account of sin (FC SD V 27).

285 See FC SD Basis, Rule, and Guiding Principle 14; XI 94–96.

286 At a local ministerial alliance meeting—a gathering of clergy from numerous denominations—a priest from a large Roman Catholic parish related frankly that he could not engage in some practices proposed that day because he lived under constraints of Roman Catholic teaching and practice. He stated his position clearly and requested that all present understand. He had the respect of all in attendance.

287 "A Lutheran Stance toward Ecumenism," 10. The statement is in reference to FC SD X 31.

2. The Scholastics weakened the doctrine of original sin, asserting that the human psyche is neutral to sin, unless it is voluntary. This results in notions that feed a trust in human powers and obscures the knowledge of the grace of Christ (Ap II 43b–44).

3. The notion that justification is not by faith, but by the disposition of love as merit, prompted Melanchthon to respond, "Where does this end but with the abolition of the promise and a return to the law?" (Ap IV 109–110; cf. 81).

4. Melanchthon countered the suggestion that observance of human traditions merits forgiveness of sins when he stated, "For the opponents openly Judaize and openly supplant the gospel with the teachings of demons. . . . This obscures the gospel, the benefits of Christ, and the righteousness of faith" (Ap XV 4).

This sampling from the Lutheran Confessions shows that the pursuit of *concordia* always has the Gospel in sight so that souls may be led to Christ.

Concordia, Agreement in the Gospel, the Basis of Church Fellowship

It is essential for church fellowship at the level of the Office of the Ministry to confess agreement according to a correct understanding of the Gospel. The Augsburg Confession, Article VII, affirms this rubric. The translated German text reads, *"For this is enough for the true unity of the Christian church that there the gospel is preached harmoniously according to a pure understanding and the sacraments are administered in conformity with the divine Word."* In a strict sense, the correct understanding of the Gospel according to Augsburg Confession VII is the promise of the forgiveness of sins and justification through Christ, which believers accept and confess by faith. Some Lutherans, however, press this succinct understanding as a minimal basis for practicing church fellowship. The plea is that we have the Gospel and that is all that matters. Therefore, with any who call themselves Christians and affirm Jesus Christ, we are free to worship, preach, and teach jointly, no further questions asked.

Augsburg VII, however, is not license to engage in church fellowship on a minimal foundation. The Gospel, properly understood and preached, is the Gospel integral with other articles—the Article of God, which the Lutheran confessors say they teach *mango consensu* (AC I); the Article of Original Sin, which shows man's need for the Gospel (AC II); the Article of the Son of God who became incarnate and redeemed the human race (AC III), and so on. Dr. Herbert J. A. Bouman explained how articles of doctrine are integral to a proper understanding of the Gospel. He wrote,

> This does not mean that the specific *locus "De justificatione,"* considered by itself, is all that the Lutherans consider indispensable. Rather, they regard the entire *corpus doctrinae* as bound up inextricably with justification. All doctrines have their place in this doctrine. All doctrines stand or fall with the doctrine of justification.[288]

We understand, therefore, that agreement in the Gospel and its articles—the fundamental articles of the Christian faith—must precede engaging in joint public ministry of Word and Sacrament across denominational lines. This is proper *concordia*. Moreover, in the Lutheran view, when two or more churches practice altar and pulpit fellowship but are not united in confession of the Gospel or a pure understanding of it, that practice is *unionism*.

Principle: In joint execution of the Office of the Holy Ministry, delivering Word-and-Sacrament ministry, the Lutheran pastor is bound by rubrics drawn from the Lutheran Confessions that imply avoidance of unionism in every shape or form.

Joint Conduct of Weddings and Funeral/Memorial Services

A Lutheran pastor faces difficult circumstances when he is asked to participate jointly in a wedding or a funeral or memorial service with a Roman Catholic priest, a Protestant clergy person, or a spiritual leader of an independent nondenominational fellowship. We are speaking about joint public ministry when the Lutheran pastor and clergy of another confession do not share a common understanding of the Gospel and its articles. Some clergy make light of this matter because they view weddings, also funerals and memorial services, as mere ceremonies or functions.

In the Lutheran tradition, however, these minor services are the Church's worship, though not the Divine Service.[289] The Rite of Marriage, for instance, invokes the triune God in the invocation and at two other junctures, and calls

288 Herbert J. A. Bouman, "The Doctrine of Justification in the Lutheran Confessions," *Concordia Theological Monthly* 26, no. 11 (November 1955): 804.

289 Distinguishing weddings and funerals and memorial services from the regular and official services of Word and Sacrament conducted on Sunday for the Christian congregation begs the question inquiring about the nature of these so-called occasional worship hours. On the one hand, the Lutheran Confessions state that numerous ceremonies and church usages introduced solely for the sake of good order and the general welfare are in and of themselves no divine worship or even part of it (FC SD X 3, 8–9). On the other hand, Luther comments on the outward order of worship for the purpose that God's Word may exert its power publicly, that is, make holy the people in order that their work may be holy (LC I 93–94). The reference to *work* in Luther's comment may apply to marriage with the strong implication that the union between husband and wife be *holy*. Certainly, the services in question here are for the purpose that Luther advances, that God's Word may exert power. See Roger D. Pittelko, "Corporate Worship of the Church: Worship and the Community of Faith," in *Lutheran Worship: History and Practice* (St. Louis: Concordia Publishing House, 1993), 51.

upon the triune God for a divine blessing at the close. The rubrics call for reading the Scriptures, also exposition and proclamation of the Word in sermon or homily. The Mass or Holy Communion may be celebrated. Similar rubrics govern funerals and memorial services. The clergy officiating in these services vest and wear the stole, symbolic of the Office of the Ministry. And *concordia*, agreement in the Gospel and its articles taught by the Scriptures, is the essential overarching rubric.

The absence of *concordia* when exercising the Office of the Ministry with other clergy is problematic for the confessing Lutheran pastor. For instance, he is asked to officiate with a Roman Catholic priest in a wedding; more than likely the pastor and priest were asked to participate together in order to satisfy family concerns. The groom is Lutheran. The bride is Roman Catholic. Both are steeped in their respective faiths. Conduct of the Rite of Marriage by their pastor and priest, they reason, will bring families together, yet this arrangement is amiss and clearly outside the boundaries of *concordia*. One may thumb through Melanchthon's *Apology to the Augsburg Confession* and discover how disparate is the confession and theology of these two clergymen. The Lutheran pastor and the Roman Catholic priest, coming together in the Rite of Marriage, may appear to show compassion and deep care for good people of differing faiths, but genuine fidelity to God and His Word in both doctrine and practice is wanting. On the surface, fragments of compassion and care appear, but essentially this mixed public ministry may result in dismay, if not confusion, to any observant Christian.

Good counsel for the bride and groom heading toward a mixed marriage is to plan their wedding at either his or her church and let the conduct of the Rite of Marriage to the respective host pastor or priest. Some may object to this counsel on grounds that the arrangement forces one or the other—bride or groom—into heterodox worship. The objection deserves consideration, but it must be weighed in light of an arrangement that should not commingle public ministries. What it does reflect is the difficulty presented by the mixed marriage, a factor requiring extra love and patience on the part of both bride and groom. Still, the Lutheran pastor may offer to be present when the wedding or funeral or memorial service is set in a non-Lutheran church. He may bring a greeting, or he may make pastoral remarks and offer a prayer at a post-service reception or dinner. In like manner, when the public service—wedding or funeral or memorial service—is conducted in the sanctuary of the Lutheran congregation, the pastor or clergy serving persons and families of another denomination may be invited to offer remarks before or after the service, or at the reception or post-service dinner or fellowship.

Permit a postscript to this discussion of joint worship services. Whether the particular ministry is the Rite of Marriage or the orders for funerals or memorial services, the marks of the Church are paramount. Recall that the external marks of the Church are the pure teaching of the Gospel and the administration of the Sacraments in harmony with the Gospel of Christ (Ap VII and VIII 5, 20). In the joint service above, how shall these marks stand out when one participating clergyman—the Roman Catholic priest in this instance—espouses a confession that teaches that the forgiveness of sins is not received by faith alone but gained by merit through love for God prior to grace (Ap VII and VIII 21; XII 2; Ap IV in its entirety)?

Public Ministry in Venues other than Formal Altar and Pulpit Services

Participation of the Lutheran Pastor in Religious Events

Lutheran participation in ecumenical fellowship was debated following the attack on the Twin Towers in New York City on September 11, 2001, otherwise known as 9/11, and the Sandy Hook Elementary School massacre in Newtown, Connecticut, December 14, 2012. Clerics of Christian and non-Christian religions assembled after these tragic events in a show of care and concern for families of the victims. Rallies were staged at both sites and the clergy either led prayers or gave homilies or speeches. Concerns were voiced about the participation of Lutheran pastors. In these situations where doctrinal unity among participating clergy was nonexistent and prayers were offered to deities other than the true God, was Lutheran participation outright *unionism*?

Principle: Bound by his confession to preach, teach, and practice according to the Scriptures expounded by the Lutheran Confessions, a Lutheran pastor refrains from participating in mixed public ministry with clergy of heterodox churches or fellowships.

Some critics seized on the New York and Sandy Hook rallies, accusing participating Lutheran pastors of breaking with Lutheran confessional fellowship principles. When a city, a community, a nation, a world is hurting, shall we quibble over fellowship principles? In dire circumstances, can't the Church be dismissive of principles? It would seem so. Still, Lutheran pastors are who they are, confessing spiritual leaders in the Lutheran doctrine and practice. We cannot overlook the truth that participating Christian clergy in such events bring with them the Office of the Ministry. As holders and stewards of that office, Christian pastors are accountable first to the Lord of the Office (cf. 1 Cor 4:1–2; 2 Cor 2:17). Therefore, at these events every step must be taken in order to officiate in a God-pleasing manner, and the corollary to this mandate is avoiding any semblance of *unionism* or *syncretism.*

Wisdom suggests that Lutheran pastors, their congregations, and their ecclesiastical supervisors first grasp the larger picture. Lutheran Christians in America are not a culture unto themselves. They are part of the expansive social and cultural society impacted by mass tragedy when events like 9/11 and Sandy Hook happen. Tragic events of great magnitude will likely occur in the future, and religious people will come together. Advisedly, Lutherans should prepare a model for their participation in such gatherings and do so respecting both their Lutheran confessional identity and their place as members of the community.[290] An important detail in this preparation is the pastor's presence and his level of participation with other spiritual leaders who are there to comfort thousands of people.

Certainly, when the city or community gathers in behalf of stricken citizens, the Lutheran pastor wants to be present, and should be present, and will be present. He is a spokesman. He brings the sympathy, love, and tears of his congregation to those stricken by the tragedy. He brings the compassion of our Lord! It is proper that he take the podium to address the traumatized populace. His remarks may be phrased in this manner:

> We are here from St. John's Lutheran Church, your friends in this community, friends of those hurting terribly whom we include in prayers spoken in our homes and when our fellowship gathers for worship at St. John's. We are here today for you, and we seek ways and means to provide help and support. We stand by you. The Lord our God is faithful. He does not give up on you. The cross of our Lord Jesus Christ is the certain pledge that God loves you. In Jesus' name, God bless and keep you!

We may observe further that the Lutheran pastor's presence at such rallies is a matter of arrangement or logistics. He shall be present, and he can bring a greeting and word of comfort without participating in joint worship. Of course, he must secure a place on the agenda of the rally. He does this when he corresponds or networks with civic and religious leaders in advance. It is a conversation he must have early in his ministry in a community, and he must continue that conversation. Hopefully, civic and religious leaders will welcome his interest in bringing comfort and also respect his confessional stance in regard to leading joint worship in a pluralistic group. Having this dialogue in ad-

290 The substance of this insight was offered by Dr. Joel P. Okamoto, chairman of the Department of Systematic Theology at Concordia Seminary, St. Louis, Missouri, in a conversation about Lutheran presence at events expressing care for citizens traumatized by tragedies of massive proportion.

vance serves as reference if an event of mass tragedy occurs in the community. Particulars come together in a guiding principle.

Principle: Constrained by our Lord's love and compassion for the injured and the suffering, a Lutheran pastor will be present at public rallies when citizens gather out of sympathy for many who suffer great loss. When privileged to speak, he conveys God's love in Christ and the hope that all can have in the Lord who died and rose again. Regarding the worship aspect at these events, the Lutheran pastor is guarded for reason of confessional boundaries. He cannot participate in a regimen of homilies or readings or prayers framed as petitions to deities other than the triune God. Except for speaking at the podium, he takes a place with the general audience and declines seating with clergy on the platform.

This principle warrants further comment. Some will criticize that in terms of this principle with regard to gatherings at the time of mass tragedy, the Lutheran pastor is *there* and *not there*. This is not true. We have asserted that the pastor is there and should be there. We have counseled that he secure an arrangement that assures his presence in a manner that is respectful of his confessional stance. Of course, that stance involves some obligation to fellowship principles articulated by his church body. A pastor of The Lutheran Church—Missouri Synod is encouraged to bring an outpouring of love and care in settings where grief is the major shared experience. At the same time, the Lutheran pastor avoids any semblance of *unionism* or *syncretism* either by overt action or symbolic gesture. Securing integral participation may involve complicated negotiations with pan-leadership of the events. Again, some advance initiatives in this regard serve well.

Invitations to Participate in Joint Community Worship Services

In numerous instances, a Lutheran pastor is invited to participate in joint worship. The guiding principle is that where the Office of the Holy Ministry is in play, there must be agreement in doctrine among the participants, and this for the sake of the Gospel. Much is left to the pastor's judgment. For example, he may be invited to bring the sermon at a local congregation of a different denomination.[291] Or he may be invited to participate with other clergy in a joint ecumenical Thanksgiving Day service. His assignment may be to serve as lector or conduct the liturgy or lead the prayers, while the Methodist pastor brings the sermon. Responding to either of these invitations, the Lutheran pas-

---

291 It is well known in St. Louis that a former Lutheran preacher annually preached the sermon on Thanksgiving Day at a local Presbyterian church. This practice had been defended on grounds that the Lutheran pastor brings the Word, and that the governing priority is proclamation of the Gospel as a testimony to the truth (cf. 1 Pet 3:15).

tor must weigh and consider blending of confession at the level of the Office of the Ministry. If the various participants cannot vouch for *concordia* among them, it may be wise for the Lutheran pastor to withdraw and conduct Thanksgiving Day services in his own church.

Similarly, where baccalaureate services are still in vogue, the Lutheran pastor may be invited to lead or participate in the worship conducted for high school or college graduates. For reasons stated above, he is cautious, lest his participation lead to misunderstanding. Orthodox preaching and teaching may be of little effect when the public ministry is mixed with unorthodox or heretical confession and teaching. This reflection pertains also to an invitation to serve as speaker or to bring the invocation and closing prayer at graduation exercises of a local public school. Graduation ceremonies are commencement exercises and not public worship services, yet where prayer is engaged, participants are involved in prayer fellowship. This factor warrants serious reflection.

Generally speaking, The Lutheran Church—Missouri Synod views prayer with other Christians as an expression of *unitas*, unity in faith in Jesus Christ. Other Lutherans differ intensely and they avoid practicing prayer fellowship with heterodox Christians. Perhaps the incident at Thorn in Poland (1645) relates somewhat to this issue. At the colloquy between Roman Catholics, Reformed, and Lutherans, the president reportedly demanded that the Lutherans pray with the Roman Catholics and the Reformed parties. The Lutherans refused to do this on the basis of seventeen carefully crafted reasons. First among them was the simple, biblical, "the apostle forbids fellowship with darkness and the spiritual Babylon, 2 Corinthians 6 and Revelation 18."[292]

Participation in Assorted Fellowships

A Lutheran pastor participates in public events at his discretion. The setting and the arrangements, the other participants, and so on are factors to be considered. When the Office of the Ministry is involved, a pastor inquires, Is there doctrinal agreement among the participants in order to exercise the office with integrity? Then, the pastor may be asked to bring talks or lead in prayer at community gatherings or meetings of civic organizations. The pastor graciously accepts these invitations because they are opportunities to tactfully bring a witness to the Gospel of Jesus Christ.

292 Tom. G. A. Hardt, "The Confessional Principle: Church Fellowship in the Ancient and in the Lutheran Church," *Logia* 8, no. 2 (Eastertide 1999): 27.

Summary

Lutheran Christians are not isolationists. They exercise a long-standing practice, *cooperation in externals*, whereby they cooperate with many churches in projects that benefit members of the community. They also seek fellowship with other Christians in sacred things, *communio in sacris*. They rejoice over any initiative that leads to agreement in doctrine for the sake of the Gospel so that church fellowship may be implemented. They invite others to employ and engage the useful categories, *unitas* and *concordia*, to frame the basis of fellowship. In regard to public worship, the Office of the Holy Ministry is key. Lutherans pray our Lord's petition to the Father, that His disciples "may all be one," a petition following His earlier prayer, "Sanctify them in the truth; Your word is truth" (John 17:21, 17).

Principle: The pastor is called to serve the Gospel of Jesus Christ. When a request for his service affords opportunity to witness to the Gospel, the pastor makes time in his schedule to be present at community gatherings and meetings of civic organizations. He serves.

CHAPTER THIRTEEN

The Ministry of Pastoral Care and Counseling

Introduction

At the close of Holy Communion, two pastors brought the host and the chalice down the center aisle to an elderly man. He stood at the aisle next to his motorized wheelchair. The man suffered with advanced Parkinson's disease, and his head leaned forward and bent down. The first pastor reached his lips with the host. But the chalice was more difficult. The officiating pastor reached around the back of the neck and very gently touching the man's forehead, raised his face slightly upward so that he could also receive from the chalice. That touching gesture meant much to this man! Observing, what do you see? Quintessential pastoral care!

Do we need to explain? Look once again. A man overrides pain and stiffness to greet and honor His Lord. He is a bundle of physical suffering, and coming down from the altar is his Lord to touch him and nourish his spirit. The presence of the caring Lord in the Sacrament is unmistakable, and who bears the Lord's gifts to this Christian but His pastors? They have ministered at the altar for the congregation; but they have not forgotten. Here they are, coming to a disabled Christian with joy and confidence and hope—all that the Lord's body and blood in the Sacrament bear a hundredfold. The pastors, their care, the gentle touch, the help, and foremost the body and blood of the Lord Jesus, ministering to a soul crying out, "Lord, have mercy on me!" This is what you see. This is pastoral care in striking relief, and it is a picture that excels a multitude of words about pastoral care. You are a Christian pastor. You understand.[293]

---

293 This vignette is authentic. The Rev. Dr. Ronald R. Feuerhahn, professor emeritus of historical theology at Concordia Seminary, was worshiping with his wife the Second Sunday of Easter, 2014, at their home church, the Lutheran Church of the Reformation, St. Louis, Missouri. The officiating pastor was the congregation's shepherd, the Rev. David C. Pelsue, and the other pastor was guest preacher for the day, the Rev. Dr. Daniel Harmelink, director of Concordia Historical Institute, St. Louis, Missouri.

Prolegomena to Pastoral Care

Essential Pastoral Care

The root word, *pastor*, is key in pastoral care, referring to a protective and caring figure akin to shepherds, the keepers of flocks in an ancient agrarian setting. From this imagery, our Lord identifies Himself as the Good Shepherd (John 10:11, 14). He communicated pastoral care when He engaged this imagery and exhorted Peter, "Feed My lambs. Feed My sheep" (John 21:15b, 17). Peter did not forget. Later, he exhorted pastors, "Shepherd the flock of God that is among you, exercising oversight" (1 Pet 5:2). Thus pastoral care—the care for God's people—is generic to the pastoral ministry and is *dominical* and *apostolic*. It is care brought by undershepherds of Christ.

The ministry of pastoral care is as prophetic as it may be therapeutic. From the Office of the Ministry, the pastor proclaims and applies the Word of the Lord to the baptized in their need—anxiety, disappointment, dysfunction, waywardness, and such—but also when they celebrate victories, satisfactions, and joys (Rom 12:15). Care as therapy helps troubled persons toward emotional wellness and maturity whereby they may help themselves. There are needs, however, that defy the ablest human resources, when only the words and promises of God suffice. One example is the conscience seared by guilt on account of sin, a need that is met sufficiently only by Holy Absolution spoken by the pastor, thus by the authority of Christ (John 20:23). This understanding dates back to the Early Church when the Absolution was the mainstay of pastoral care expressed in later centuries as *Seelsorge*: care, even cure, of the soul.[294] Pastoral care in this instance dispenses God's grace and mercy in the gift of the forgiveness of sins.

Principle: Under Christ the Good Shepherd, pastoral care ministry is distinctively *dominical*, that is, pastors employ the Gospel of the Lord. Doing so, they use the Scriptures as they minister to the needs of the flock. This holds true also when therapy or therapies and/or their components assist the Christian pastor's care ministry.

---

294 The Rev. Dr. A. L. Barry, former president of The Lutheran Church—Missouri Synod, stated, "There is no better context for *Seelsorge* than in the act of private confession and absolution. . . . This private, one-on-one application of the office of the keys is indeed the capstone of pastoral care. Wherever and whenever the *Seelsorger* is proclaiming the good news of new life, hope, forgiveness, peace with God and all the other aspects of the good news there is real and genuine pastoral care going on." A. L. Barry, "The Echo of the Hammer," in *The Noble Task: A Letter to the Pastors of the Lutheran Church—Missouri Synod* II, no. 2 (Reformation 1998), 3–4.

Theology and Therapy in Pastoral Care Ministry

The question remains, how may theology and therapy together serve pastoral care ministry?[295] According to numerous pastors and counselors, the answer to this question is found in the program, clinical pastoral education. Two paradigms are at work in this program, a clinical view of man and a theology of man. Many practicing counselors lean heavily on the clinical view. In its more intense form, the clinical view operates with assumptions that leave God *in absentia* because theological assumptions are quite unnecessary when the potential for self-understanding and self-direction is latent in the psyche of the patient or client without reference to God or the supernatural. For some practitioners, however, religion is both recognized and utilized in the therapy.

The other paradigm is theology, the teaching of God revealed in His prophetic and apostolic Scriptures, the Holy Bible. Theology poses a distinctive understanding of man. Yes, he was created by God in the image of God, but tragically fell from this state and is afflicted with sin and all the negative effects of sin in mind, body, and spirit (Gen 1:26–27; 3:14–24; Rom 5:12; 8:7–8, 19–23; cf. Ps 8:4–9). The hope for fallen man is not in his own self-developed potential, important as this factor is, but in Jesus Christ through whom there is no condemnation for sin, but redemption from it, leading to a new life by the working of the Holy Spirit and ultimately to eternal life (Rom 8:1, 9–11; 3:23–26; 5:18–21; 6:22–23). Ministering with this theology, the pastor teaches and applies the Scriptures as they show man's condition, speak to that condition, and offer guidance in view of that condition. The pastor also wisely resorts to the behavioral sciences for assistance in comprehending the nature and the extent of dysfunction or maladjustment in persons. The question is "Can the pastor avail himself of this assistance—without adopting radical assumptions and operations of a strict clinical view of man or setting aside the Scriptures—and simply engage in clinical practice of a sort?"[296]

---

295 *Therapy* is a term used here in a broad sense to signify both the understanding of man and the remedy of his dilemma from knowledge provided by the behavioral sciences, and doing so quite independent of theology. It is probable that in some settings the practice of pastoral care has gone nontheological and is wholly engaged with psychology and psychotherapy. Widespread among practitioners of therapy, however, is the notion that clients or patients who are religious are thereby served well by religion. Or, when therapy-oriented pastoral care engages theology, it can be clearly the pragmatic use of religion. See, for instance, Russell L. Dicks who viewed religion as faith in a power greater than self, asserting that religion seeks not only to establish faith in God, but it seeks to build hope—hope of many kinds—that the world in which we live is creative, that one's fellow creatures are trustworthy, that life is worthwhile. Russell L. Dicks, *Principles and Practices of Pastoral Care* (Englewood, NJ: Prentice-Hall, 1963), 36.

296 Engaging theology realistically, we add that pastoral care is not alone a ministry of sin and grace—to the neglect of the ganglion of trouble and difficulties internal to the human psyche, to say nothing of the impact of negative external factors. The wise pastor attends to acquiring aptitudes and skills pertaining to such factors as the counseling relationship, empathic listening, assessment (intra- and extra-psychic factors), clarification, intervention, recognition of mental illnesses (bipolar disorder, clinical depression, schizophrenia, paranoia), and directive and nondirective counseling.

Pastoral Care in the Way of the Prophet

Preferably, insights gained from therapy assist the use of theology in pastoral care. What therapy contributes by way of observation, clarification, analysis, and assessment is complemented—and sometimes completed—when theology contributes the Word of the Spirit. The pastor acknowledges what is observed, receives what is clarified and analyzed, and supports assessment. This is skillful care ministry. We hasten to add, however, this care ministry is prophetic in a special sense. The insights of therapy in hand, pastors bring a clear and certain Word of God with regard to a person's struggle, fear, anxiety, pain, guilt, trouble. They provide good counsel framed by the words and promises of God. When skillfully administered, this prophetic model of pastoral care supports persons in their search for resolution of their difficulty.

The partnership of theology and therapy described here will be questioned. Acknowledging this, we observe that a major assumption governs how theology operates in pastoral care. Who better mirrors and discloses the condition of the heart than God who created the beings that we are? The Scriptures disclose most every thought, impulse, and passion common to the human psyche.[297] Note the abundance of Scriptures—addresses, overtures, counsel, exhortations, direction—that apply to the human condition. More often than not this prophetic disclosure is framed as the Law with its complementary response, the Gospel. Exposure, judgment, and censure are bold, but grace, forgiveness, and blessing are poignant. Sense the gravity in the exclamations from Psalm 38:9: "O Lord, all my longing is before You; my sighing is not hidden from You." In desperation the psalmist, presumably King David, cries out, "But for You, O Lord do I wait; it is You, O Lord my God, who will answer" (Ps 38:15).

When ministering to parishioners, a pastor engages the Scriptures, but not in simplistic or overbearing use of the Bible. Certainly, this spiritual ministry requires skill; it does not preclude engaging therapy in counseling troubled persons. The Scriptures, however, are always in the background when a pastor reflects and responds to a person's needs. When appropriate, he offers direct and helpful counsel from the Word of God. This ministry is prophetic in nature and character. This is pastoral care.

The Pastor's Role in Pastoral Care

The pastor ministers to persons one-on-one, but he cares for all persons in his congregation. His goal is that none are lost. He is concerned that each Christian in his care be sustained in his or her faith in Christ and that each one

297 The Psalter and the wisdom literature of the Old Testament, principally the books of Proverbs, Ecclesiastes, and Job, address the human condition. So do the addresses of Jesus in the four Gospels, also the Book of the Acts of the Apostles, and the remaining epistolary literature of the New Testament.

meets life's challenges as a new person in Christ (Rom 6:4–11; 2 Cor 5:17–19; Eph 3:14–19; Phil 1:27–30; 2:12–16; 3:20; Col 1:3–14; 3:1–10). Thus, his pastoral care ministry is distinctly soteriological. In this regard, as a shepherd under Christ (John 10:11; 1 Pet 5:2–4), he is accountable to both the Lord and the Church for the souls in his care (Acts 20:20–21, 27, 31; Heb 13:17; cf. Jas 3:1; Ezek 34:7–16).

Principle: Open to gaining knowledge from the behavioral sciences that elucidate the human condition, the caring pastor relies on divine discernment of malady and implied resolution of the same indicated directly or tacitly by the speaking of God in the Holy Scriptures.

When the pastor cares for others, he does so as a *whole person.* This means that he knows himself. He comprehends his background and upbringing, his strengths and weaknesses, also his hang-ups where he is uncomfortable and emotionally vulnerable. He is realistic about his gifts and abilities, the level of his emotional and spiritual maturity, his physical strength and stamina, his capacity for pain, and his capacity to bear with the pains and struggles of those he serves. He lives daily by the grace of God in Christ Jesus, forgiven, redeemed, restored. He rises from his Baptism to meet the challenges of the pastoral ministry. He lives among his people as a partner with saints and heirs together of eternal life (Phil 1:1, 5; cf. Eph 1:16–18; Rom 8:17). Thus, the alert pastor has it together as he cares for others.

Pastoral Care Described

A description of pastoral care closes this opening discussion.

> *Pastoral care is the care the pastor gives in the way of proper distinction between the Law and the Gospel, according to the Scriptures, for the total welfare of each member of the flock or congregation, giving special attention to the maturing of each Christian in faith and life, and ultimately his or her peace with God (eternal salvation) through faith in our Lord Jesus Christ.*

This description sets forth the salient theological parts of pastoral care. It is shy on the therapy parts of care, though the phrase "for the total welfare of each member of the flock" infers that beneficial contributions from the behavioral sciences in the practice of pastoral care and counseling are paramount. The theological parts, again, appear in this diagram, moving from left to right:

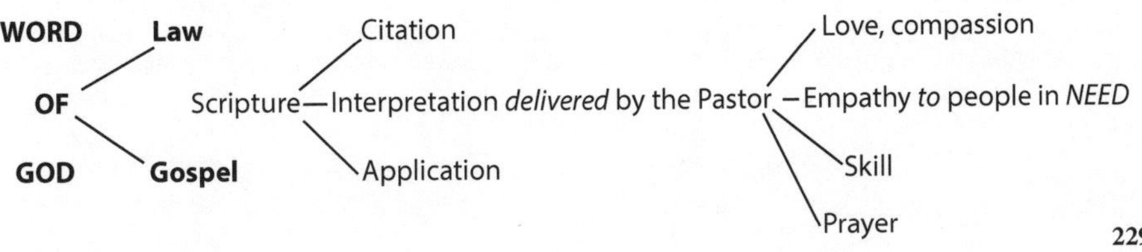

The Practice of Pastoral Care

The Care of Families

The pastoral care of families is essential in caring for a Christian congregation. Our Lord visited in homes such as Simon's in Capernaum (Mark 1:29–31), the home of Mary and Martha in Bethany (Luke 10:38–42; cf. John 11:1–5), the home of Zacchaeus the publican (Luke 19:1–10). If a pastor cannot reach all the homes in his parish, surely he can reach those whom he knows are hurting. Broken and dysfunctional homes are a priority.[298]

When the pastor visits a home, he arrives as a friend. He is human. A bit of humor in the exchange of greetings breaks the ice. The family welcomes the pastor and he is comfortable. They offer a cup of coffee or tea, a glass of wine. The pastor relaxes. His mind veers away from the press of his professional schedule. This family is at home with him. Perhaps for the first time they learn that their pastor is a man of God with whom they can freely converse. What may surface in the conversation are subjects such as decisions the family is facing, curiosity about the church's teaching or policies or practices, or compelling moral issues. The visit helps the pastor to know this family. Here are fifteen factors about a family he is visiting:

1. Ethnic and social background
2. Occupation, economic circumstances
3. Marital concord/discord
4. Emotional maturity—temperament
5. Physical surroundings—house, home
6. Family life, stable/unstable
7. Needs, wants, ambitions of the family, that is, family priorities
8. Faith and spiritual maturity, knowledge and ownership of teaching, doctrine

---

298 *The Lutheran Witness* published a letter written by a pastor who advocated that his colleagues expand their work schedule to include calling on member families in their homes. His letter received mixed responses. One brother pastor replied that most of a pastor's day spent in home visits is a remnant of a former age when people had simple needs and expectations from their minister. He opted for equipping and motivating church elders and small-group leaders to cultivate caring relationships. In this way, these persons would multiply the pastor's ministry of care for families. These initiatives are commendable. Do they, however, excuse a pastor from caring for families in their homes? See Leroy H. Pralle, "Paying a Call," *The Lutheran Witness* (March 1994): 23. Responses to Pralle's letter appeared in *The Lutheran Witness* (May 1994): 20.

9. Family worship and devotions—use of the Bible and the Means of Grace
10. Talents and abilities of family members
11. Whereabouts of children and their activities, interests, aspirations
12. Fears, frustrations—what troubles the family
13. Particular burdens, grief, sorrows
14. Prejudices
15. Perceptions of the congregation, the church, the ministry

The pastor listens to the family for their story. In the course of a visit, he may bring a specific accent or emphasis—the practice of Holy Communion, the family altar, Christian vocation, stewardship of treasures, taking advantage of Christian education offered by the congregation, the youth ministry, and so on. The pastor prays with the family before leaving their home.

Pastoral Care of the Sick and the Afflicted

The Ministry of Healing in the Scriptures

The ministry to sick and afflicted persons is major pastoral care. The Bible teaches that God is proactive, disciplining His people, sending affliction; but He is equally proactive bringing healing and health to them. Ancient Israel could expect affliction when they broke His covenant and refused to keep Yahweh's commandments and statutes (Lev 26:15–18; Deut 28:58–61; Ps 107:17; cf. Mic 6:13), but sparing the people of deadly illness was Yahweh's blessing upon the faithful (Exod 15:26; Jer 30:17; cf. Isa 38:9–20; Hos 6:1; 1 Cor 10:13). Yahweh attended to the health and the well-being of Israel and the welfare of those who honored His people (cf. 2 Kgs 5:1–14).

From the outset, our Lord's ministry brought healing with the Gospel of the kingdom. In Capernaum, He healed Simon's mother-in-law (Mark 1:29–31). That evening, "He healed many who were sick with various diseases, and cast out many demons" (Mark 1:34; cf. Mark 3:10; Luke 4:36; 5:15; also Matt 4:23–25; 8:16; 14:34–35). Jesus manifested His glory as the Son of God, attending to affliction and infirmities of the body, mind, and spirit. He extended His compassion when He commissioned His twelve disciples to a ministry of mercy. They cast out demons and anointed with oil many who were sick and healed them (Mark 6:7, 12–13; cf. Luke 10:9). This ministry of mercy reached into the apostolic age when John and Peter spoke a word of healing in the name of Jesus Christ of Nazareth and a forty-year-old man, lame from birth, stood up and walked into the temple praising God (Acts 3:4–8; 4:22). Healing actions by the apostles were demonstrable (Acts 5:16; 9:36–43; 14:8–10; 16:18). St. Luke reports that God did extraordinary miracles at the hands of the apostle Paul (Acts 19:11–12; cf. Acts 28:7–10).

Whether or not the gift of the miracle of healing is generic to the Office of the Ministry beyond the age of the apostles is much debated. Notable is the absence of a recorded mandate to exercise the gift of healing given to apprentices under the apostles, for example, Timothy and Titus. A claim to possess the gift of healing is unusual in light of the sparse mention of this gift by the New Testament relative to the public ministry of those who immediately followed the apostles; but the practice of attending to the sick with the Word and prayer, also anointing with oil is evident, and the power of the Absolution is present (cf. Jas 5:13–16). Certainly, the Church is open to receive gifts of the Spirit, including healing, as the Spirit wills (1 Cor 12:9), but any claim to gifts that are similar to the endowment of the Christians at Corinth should be validated by testing for sound teaching according to the Scriptures (1 John 4:1; cf. 1 Tim 4:16a; 2 Tim 3:14–17; 2 Thess 3:14; Rom 16:17).

The Reality of Affliction—Discipline of the Christian Life

The touch of God's healing is real and the need for this gift is acute. In spite of sensational initiatives by technology to extend life, sickness and death take their toll, yet affliction and the curse of death are occasion for God to serve the good of His people. Affliction underscores for Christians the apostle Paul's realistic axiom "For we walk by faith, not by sight" (2 Cor 5:7). Suffering and grief are sometimes an enigma. Even the ultimate affliction and suffering endured by our Lord—the cross—is shrouded in mystery, except for the clear intention of the Father that the Son should be the supreme sacrifice in order to redeem the world from sin and the wrath of God (cf. Isa 53:4–5, 10). Yes, the Christian who is baptized into Christ looks to the cross and knows the certain and enduring forgiveness of sins and assurance of salvation. All else is mystery, though God explains that He treats His own as a father chastens and disciplines the children he loves (Heb 12:3–11; cf. 2 Cor 12:7–10).

The heavenly Father administers discipline to His people so that they may share in His holiness and reap the peaceful fruit of righteousness (Heb 12:10–11). Beyond this interpretation by the Scriptures, we lack clear explanation of affliction. We dare not resort to clever rationalizations in view of our lack of understanding. The enigma of suffering compels Christians to be patient under the grace of our faithful God (Jas 1:12; 5:10–11; 2 Cor 12:9–10; cf. Job 40:3–5; 42:1–6). Conscious of God's gracious discipline, so difficult and painful and mysterious, the Christian lifts up his or her heart to the Lord, and the pastor comes alongside the afflicted Christian to focus on the cross and the grace of our Lord Jesus Christ (Ps 50:15; Matt 7:7; Ps 46:1; Jas 5:16b).[299]

Pastoral Care of Those Burdened with Affliction

The ministry to the sick and afflicted begins with a durable assumption. The afflicted Christian has heard the Gospel of his or her salvation, believes on the Lord, and is sealed with the Holy Spirit who is the guarantor of our inheritance until he or she possesses it to the praise of God's glory (Eph 1:13–14). Awaiting possession of that inheritance is nothing short of a struggle of faith. The afflicted Christian feels like one stranded at sea in the darkness—anxiety, depression, despair, doubt, even unbelief. Though a pastor may not be so forward to say that an afflicted Christian is under the attack of Satan, he knows that the onslaught is real. The evil one deceived our first parents (Gen 3:4; cf. 2:15–17) and he is eager to take unfair advantage by attacking the afflicted person when he or she is down (1 Pet 5:8).

These tensions make the pastor's ministry to afflicted persons difficult. Still, his ministry is promising because "the word of the Lord remains forever" (1 Pet 1:25). The pastor comes with that Word. Reflect that our Lord countered the attack of Satan with the Word of God. Then the devil left Him, and the angels ministered to Him (Matt 4:1–11). How important then, is the ministry of the Word when afflicted Christians are vulnerable to attacks by Satan! Can pastors do less than come with that Word and steel up Christians against the onslaught of Satan? This is the pastor's work.[300] This is pastoral care (Rom 15:4; Eph 6:11, 17; Titus 1:9a; 2:1; cf. 2 Tim 2:24–26; 1 Pet 5:2–4).

During ministry to the sick, nondirective conversation is useful. Listening is important. Hearing the patient—even asking the patient—and exploring with the patient his or her reaction or response to illness is sound practice when exercised skillfully. Proceeding in this manner may forge the way and prepare for using the Scriptures to bring the comfort of the Gospel. The pastor should approach the sick with the Scriptures in an appropriate manner—not

299 According to the theology of the cross, God and His working by means of affliction may not be visible to sight or senses as our Lord's suffering on the cross is in many respects shrouded in mystery. In spite of all that is hidden and mysterious, God's Word and promise are clear; He works through affliction in the Christian life according to His good and gracious will clothed in His precious promises (Ps 86:5–7; Gen 45:4–8; 50:20; Rom 8:18, 26; 1 Cor 10:13; Heb 13:5b; et al.).

300 Spare the Church of pastors who do not visit the sick, or visit only seldom, and then hesitantly. Spare the Church of pastor-clinicians who hesitate to open the Bible and read God's Word and then apply this Word to the sick and the suffering. The notion that sharing the Scriptures with the sick is much too directive, top down, and repressive of emotions that need to surface is countered directly by the texts cited in this discussion. The healthy venting of emotions and feelings is certainly warranted; but lest we forget, catharsis here calls for comfort and encouragement that only God's Word can give to the faithful Christian (cf. Rom 15:4).

long and drawn-out passages—but well-chosen helpful selections, verses that bring assurance. That assurance is abundantly available, for St. Paul exclaimed that God, "who did not spare His Son but gave Him up for us all" (Rom 8:32), surely loves and cares for us when we are ill.[301]

If the use of the Bible in ministry to the sick remains simplistic or puerile in the view of some pastors, consider this vignette: a woman came to the pastor's office after hearing that he had accepted a Call and was leaving her church. Seven years earlier, the pastor had visited her in the hospital. His visit was memorable for her. She faced major surgery. The Bible passage he read and personalized to address her anxiety left a lasting impression. Years later, just days before he left that parish, the woman related, "Pastor, you don't know how much your devotion helped me get through the experience of surgery when you visited me in the hospital."

The Pastoral Call—Devotion and Prayer

When a pastor visits the sick in health-care facilities or at a patient's home, his entrée sets the stage for his ministry. When visiting at the home, an advance phone call is a courtesy. In a health-care facility, a gentle knock on the door, a smile and greeting, in some instances a word—"Hello, I'm Pastor Jones"—may help patients receive the pastor. In the conversation, the pastor may bring forward a pocket edition of the New Testament and Psalms or a Bible. Christians know why the pastor is visiting and seeing the Bible in hand confirms their expectations. He leads into the devotion, "What good words does our Lord have for us today?" He may read a portion of Scripture, reflect briefly, and conclude with a prayer, lifting the concerns of the patient to the God of all grace. He follows with the Lord's Prayer and perhaps a word of blessing.[302]

During prayer, the pastor may hold the patient's hand *gently* or touch the wrist or forearm. When ministering to Simon's mother-in-law, Jesus "touched her hand" (Matt 8:15). His action was sensitive, not prescriptive. Touching need not always accompany prayer. For medical reasons, it may be discouraged. Some patients are *untouchable*, that is, the slightest contact may trigger pain or risk infection. The alert pastor respects these sensitivities. Good counsel suggests that touch in the hospital room should not be the first contact with a person.[303] Good hygiene suggests an antiseptic for hands, but never applied in the presence of the patient who was just served by the pastor's ministry.

301 For a selection of Scriptures that apply to common anxiety reactions to illness, see Appendix 5, "Caring for the Sick—Response to Anxiety."

302 Christians in the Lutheran tradition, and probably Christians everywhere, want to pray the Lord's Prayer.

303 This recommendation is from the Rev. Bill Jensen, former student at Concordia Seminary, St. Louis. Spring 2009.

A pastor may be called to minister to strangers who may be unbelievers. Concerned family or friends make the request. Here, the pastor wins the opportunity to minister. He does not force pastoral ministry on the patient. A pastor *offers* devotion and prayer. A patient may flatly refuse this offer, saying, "I don't want that." The pastor complies. He conveys best wishes. He may say that he will pray for the patient. He adds, "I hope that we may meet again some time." Then he leaves as a friend. On the other hand, if the patient is receptive, the pastor may focus on clear Gospel passages with a brief explanation, witnessing to God's grace and care for the patient's welfare. Passages may include: Psalm 23; John 10:11–14, 27–30; John 6:37b; 1 John 1:9; Romans 5:1; 3:23–24; John 3:16; Psalm 51 (select verses). The pastor follows up on receptive patients during and after convalescence.

Three Factors in Ministry to the Sick

Three factors assist a pastor's on-site close observation and preparation for ministry to the sick. *First*, the patient's *physical condition* calls for assessment and understanding. What is the nature of the illness or injury? This information is not always at hand. A pastor may not be informed by the patient, the family, or the medical team. Does he probe? He will not press the patient, but he may inquire with family or at the nurses' station. In this regard, what medical personnel may communicate about a patient's condition or treatment is limited by government regulations such as the *Health Information Patient Privacy Act* (HIPPA). Nevertheless, available information about an illness and prognosis for the patient's recovery contributes to pastoral care. Unless the need is acute, he does not consult the physician.

Second, what is the patient's *emotional state*? How is the patient handling the illness? Accepting? Or is he or she resigned to what appears inevitable? Is the patient dejected, fearful, feeling punished or threatened? Some patients are deeply concerned about how their illness impacts the immediate family. Is the patient content, confident, hopeful? Or is the patient concealing hidden anxiety, defeat, or resentment? What is the patient's perception of the prognosis?

Third, is the patient *spiritually at peace*, or greatly distressed? In the light of this affliction, how does the patient view self and God? Does he or she ask the "why" questions? "Why is this happening to me? Why is God treating me this way?" Is the patient uneasy about sin and guilt? Is there a conflict raging in the patient's mind and heart—peace versus anger, trust and hope versus doubt, certainty versus questioning, determination to get well versus giving up to despair? Does the patient trust God, hope in God, express confidence in the Lord's love and care?

Seasoned pastors consistently engage these factors—*physical, emotional, spiritual*—when ministering to the sick. They are offered here with brief comments to assist pastors in framing conversations and devotions that apply the words of Scripture in a Gospel-centered ministry to the sick. The pastor will not always be on target addressing the patient's need. Accurate targeting is not absolutely required, but some reflection in terms of these three factors will spare the pastor from seeming prosaic, superficial, or even disengaged when visiting and ministering to the sick.

Decorum in Health-Care Facilities

A wise pastor considers decorum in hospitals and other health-care facilities. A physician outlined decorum issues for prospective pastors during a pastoral theology class at Concordia Seminary. He was Dr. C. R. Montz, member of the seminary's Board of Regents. The doctor made these points:

- *First*, show up! Show that you care about the patient. Should the patient be out of the room or otherwise indisposed, leave a business card with a note and promise that you will return. Then, *return*!
- *Second*, conversing with a patient is a discipline, both verbal and nonverbal. Maintain stance so that mutual eye contact is comfortable for the patient. Strive for eye contact that levels the playing field.
- *Third*, arrive for the visit dressed the part of a professional, not in sneakers or casual wear, like, "I was off somewhere else and just *had* to interrupt my important venture to be here in the hospital with *you*." Avoid giving the impression that you are on the run or that visiting today was an afterthought. Dress in a manner conveying to the patient that this visit was important enough for you, the pastor, to be up for the occasion.
- *Fourth*, ask, "Can I do anything for you?" Be prepared to be an advocate for the patient within reason, at least to this extent, that you may politely report the patient's need or desire to the front desk or the nurse in charge.

Decorum is about many factors. Two of them are pastor-readiness for ministry to the sick and patient-centered relationship. A pastor refrains from dragging into the sick room. Is he overextended? Then he should take five, have a coffee in the hospital coffee shop, or relax and regroup in the chaplains' lounge. His best preparation may be solitude somewhere for a devotion and prayer.[304]

---

304 Visiting between twenty and thirty patients in hospitals spread over a large metropolitan area, the author discovered that interjecting these few minutes for his own stability now and then over the long afternoon assisted him to minister to individual patients with attention to their particular needs.

When the pastor is up emotionally and spiritually, his visit shows promise. He enters the room to converse with the patient, not to preach at him. He permits the patient to lead. If it is light conversation, the pastor lightens up. When the patient is serious, the pastor listens and responds seriously. A strict *nondirect* approach can make the patient uneasy, suspecting that he or she is being analyzed. Similarly, the overly *direct* approach may reduce the patient to an object of pity—so it seems to the patient. Both approaches are cruel treatment. When the conversation is patient-centered, the pastor answers questions, even questions that seem to be trivial, like, "What is going on at church?" But the pastor gently moves toward core ministry for the patient. His visit is brief.

Ministry to Desperately Ill Patients

The greatest challenge is ministry to the patient for whom wellness is no longer an option, humanly speaking. Still, our care for terminally ill patients is a Law and Gospel ministry. Hush! Be aware that the Law is already boisterous and forceful when a patient deals firsthand with mortality. Be *generous* with the Gospel! Share Scriptures that convey the warmth of God's love and the assurance that God cares so much that His plan for us is eternal life through faith in our Lord Jesus Christ. Recognize that answers to the *why* questions are out of reach. Not *why* but *how* shall this illness be a tool for both God and us, strengthening the bond between both parties? Was not this the understanding whereby St. Paul dealt with his thorn in the flesh (2 Cor 12:7–10; cf. Rom 5:1–5; Heb 12:1ff.)? We take comfort knowing that the goodness of God to help and to heal is a direct derivative of the Gospel (Rom 8:32; cf. Matt 9:1–8; Mark 6:54–56). Whatever God has in mind for us, He is in control. His goodness is calling the shots and we are going to be all right.

Some pastors pare back prayers for *healing* in behalf of the terminally ill. One explanation for this decision is that time has come to wrap the patient in the theology of the cross and counsel toward submission to the will of God. Is there a better way? Though it is true, God is sparing with explanations for His will, the pastor still leads the terminally ill patient in fervent prayer to the throne of the God of all grace. Yes, the pastor persists, he prays for healing! It is a persistent prayer, not a foolish prayer (cf. Matt 15:21–28). It is a prayer, not for fleeting pleasure and passion (Jas 4:3). It is an earnest prayer for the life that God has given. Should we not pray about what He has given, "If the Lord wills, we will live . . ." (Jas 4:15; cf. 2 Kgs 20:1–6a)?

When the going is tough, does God want us to taper off with prayer and slink away when the outcome is predictably dark? The Canaanite woman reported in the Gospels pleaded her daughter's case with Jesus (Matt 15:22, 25,

27). Persistence marked the prayers of the psalmists (Ps 55:16–17; cf. Ps 57:1–2; Ps 61). Hezekiah prayed in the face of sickness unto death (Isa 38:1–6). Desperate and urgent, the centurion pleaded with Jesus in behalf of his paralyzed servant (Matt 8:5ff.).

What encourages such persistence? The invitation of God to "call upon Me in the day of trouble" (Ps 50:15). Certainly, it is invitation and more! It is the ground of hope in the resurrection of Jesus Christ from the dead, witnessed and reported resoundingly in the Scriptures (1 Pet 1:3–9; cf. Rom 15:4). Prayer with a desperate patient honors the greatness of God and takes the path of unyielding faith that, in life or death, we are the Lord's (Rom 14:7–9; cf. Ps 102).

Pastoral Care in Various Circumstances

Ministry to Patients in Intensive Care Units

Care for patients treated in areas other than the general hospital calls for varied approaches. When visiting patients in intensive care, the pastor identifies himself at the nurses' station and indicates the patient he wishes to see. His ministry combines limited conversation, brief Scripture reading, lucid Gospel, and prayer that may incorporate Gospel words. The pastor stays briefly, but he may return often, perhaps once a day. Always, he yields to the medical team.

Ministry to Families and Friends of Critically Ill or Injured Persons

The waiting rooms adjoining Intensive Care Units are scenes of trauma, anxiety, and grief where families wait out specialized care for a loved one. How does the pastor approach traumatized families? He gathers them for devotional words that may relate three points. *First*, the pastor acknowledges the situation. "The illness is serious, the injury is severe. We do not know the outcome, and we prepare for any unknown change in our loved one's condition." *Second*, where may we turn? We are Christians, God's people. We know where to turn. We lift up our hearts to the Lord (John 6:68; Ps 50:15). He calls us to cast all our care and fear and anxiety on Him. He cares for us (1 Pet 5:7). We may kneel with our Lord at His prayer desk and plead that God would spare us from this hardship (cf. Luke 22:41–44). *Third*, before we call, our gracious God answers. "God is our refuge and strength, a very present help in trouble" (Ps 46:1). He is the Lord of hosts, and from Him comes our help (Ps 46:11). He promises that nothing in this time and in these circumstances shall ever separate us from His love and care (Rom 8:37–39). He says, "I will never leave you nor forsake you" (Heb 13:5; cf. John 3:16). So we can confidently say, "The Lord is [our] helper; [we] will not fear" (Heb 13:6). Shall we pray? With words such as these, the pastor supports traumatized families. He leaves but returns later to be with them.

Ministry to Patients in Mental Health Units

Pastoral care reaches for patients suffering emotional or mental illness. The pastor acquires permission to visit a mental health patient, and he approaches the patient as a friend. He is there to listen and to support Christian faith and hope. He is not there to supplement psychotherapy or to interfere with it. He brings supportive Scriptures and prays with the patient. Restless patients may plead that the pastor arrange for their release from the hospital. The pastor hears the plea, but he suggests that the best course is to have confidence in the care and to follow procedures outlined by nurses and doctors. The pastor shall not get between the patient and the psychiatric care. Sometimes, a pastor may assure a patient that he stands with him or her and will visit again. Any tangible evidence of real abuse of the patient should be reported. The pastor may relate that a patient is feeling uncomfortable with the treatment. The medical staff will respond.

Ministry to Patients in Ob-Gyn Units

The pastor is careful to secure access to patients in obstetrics and gynecology units in advance by phone or cyber communication. On site, a nurse accompanies the pastor to the patient. If the lady has given birth, giving thanks to God for seeing her through this time and gifting with a child is appropriate. The phrases of Psalm 63:7 are helpful. The pastor points the mother toward Baptism of the newborn, encouraging that arrangements for Holy Baptism be made. His stay is brief and he closes with prayer that the parents may raise this little one as God's child.

Technology provides prenatal information, and it may prevent the shock of learning at birth that a child has severe handicaps. When ministering to traumatized parents in these circumstances, the object cannot be to heal the hurt. Instead, the pastor's ministry draws parents to the child, preparing them to accept reality and then give love and care. There may be initial revulsion against the handicap. Parents are conflicted over the instinct to love but also to reject. A sensitive pastor helps them beyond this point. God loves this child and wants the little one to be His child through Holy Baptism. The pastor is on solid ground when he alerts the parents to discover in the future that God has given special gifts to their child. They will see a loveliness that God bestows on their son or daughter. These blessings will come to light. Then acceptance and bonding will be certain and permanent.

Other Pastoral Care Ministries

Ministry to AIDS Patients

A pastor's ministry may reach people in dire circumstances, such as persons who have acquired HIV. A stigma attaches to the person who acquires a sexually transmitted disease. Bearing the stigma may erode self-esteem and foster a sense of rejection that begins within the home and family and extends to other social circles. Anxiety may lead to behavior modification—rejection of caregivers, friends, lovers—mild paranoia, withdrawal; or the opposite, overt clinging with a need for constant reaffirmation. The person may sustain losses—employment, financial security, status, connections, and relationships. All are devastating. Depression is common, leading to such things as diminished power of concentration, disorientation, memory loss, speech or visual dysfunction, and loss of motor control. An extreme reaction may include suicidal thoughts and intentions.

Beyond empathic gestures, the pastor's ministry to persons who acquired HIV through sexual indiscretion—homosexual behavior, fornication, adultery, or other sexual perversions—moves at the right time and moment to Confession of sins and Absolution. Speaking the Law toward contrition and eliciting from the person a plea for God's mercy is initial care (Ps 51; Luke 18:13), but the Gospel moves out in front and leads with God's grace and mercy and forgiveness of sins, with an accent on God's *acceptance* of those He has forgiven for the sake of Christ. Acceptance is the special need presented by persons who suffer disease as a result of sexual sins. Consider these Scriptures: John 6:37; Romans 8:1; John 3:16–18, especially verse 18; Romans 5:1–2, 6; Romans 3:24–25; Romans 8:32–35, 37–39; 1 John 1:5–9; Revelation 1:5–6; 1 Peter 2:24; Psalm 23; Psalm 121; and the text John 8:10–11, although disputed, conveys the truth of our Lord's compassion for sinners, His Absolution, and surely His *acceptance* of forgiven ones. Speaking and pressing the Gospel, the pastor and the larger congregation are challenged to continue giving love and care, accepting and reaffirming the person who has been forgiven and restored by our Lord Jesus Christ.

Ministry to Persons Caught in Dependencies

The pastor's ministry to persons with known dependencies—alcohol, drugs, tobacco—serves three actions: *acknowledgment* of the dependency, *treatment* of the dependency, *recovery* from the dependency. He assists a person to recognize and acknowledge the grip of addiction. Furthermore, habitual indulgence that brings harm to the body offends against the Lord who bought us with a price (1 Cor 6:19–20). Clearly, the Scriptures denounce overuse of alcohol, the inebriate condition (Isa 5:11; Rom 13:13; 1 Cor 6:10; cf. Titus 2:3). The pastor does not conceal these judgments. He is candid with persons about substance abuse that destroys the strength of the will and robs self-control. Beware, self-imposed abuses render one unprepared for the end time (Luke 21:34).

Pastoral care moves beyond confrontation and warnings to frank reminders that a baptized Christian stands at the entrée into newness of life (Rom 6:4, 11; cf. Rom 12:1–2; Eph 4:20–24). Addressing acknowledgment in terms of admission to dependency, then Confession followed by the Absolution, the pastor moves the person to the second step, *treatment*, facilitated by professionals—physicians, psychiatrists, psychologists, treatment centers, et al. Pastors and congregations recommend a network of these reliable resources.

Recovery, the third part of addressing dependencies, poses a larger ministry. The pastor is the pivotal party because normally he is closest to persons recovering from dependency. He inquires about their welfare and assures them that he is available and stands with them. Relapses occur that dismantle therapy and recovery. Walking with these persons is a test of patience, but the pastor is there for the fallen. Congregations are wise to develop support groups that provide access to professional help and other resources from which the community at large benefits.

When recovery is stable, some congregations publicly celebrate reaching this milestone in a rite or other means of gathering around a former addict or abuse victim. These events may help to strengthen a person who has good reason to celebrate God's care and blessing. The downside is that public celebration of recovery may inadvertently pressure a person to stay healthy. Such pressure can be uncomfortable. Planning public recognition of recovery should involve consulting the professionals who have cared for the person.

The Ministry of Crisis Intervention

A pastor may be drawn into crisis situations that call for special care. According to Gerald Caplan, a respected expert in crisis theory and management, a crisis arises out of some change in a person's life space that produces a modification of his relationship with others and/or his perceptions of himself.[305] Two types emerge, the developing crisis that occurs as the result of a long succession of factors affecting a person's status and image, and the situational or accidental crisis effected from some unexpected external cause. The latter prompts this brief discussion of crisis and intervention.

---

305 The reference to Caplan is cited from David K. Switzer, *The Minister as Crisis Counselor* (Nashville: Abingdon Press, 1974), 44.

A familiar tool for effective crisis intervention is the A-B-C method:

A—achieving contact with the person caught in crisis and acquiring the facts surrounding the problem

B—boiling down the problem to its essentials and focusing closely to the exclusion of extraneous concerns

C—coping actively with the situation, that is, assisting a person's initiative to draw on available resources and address the problem[306]

The A-B-C method at work is illustrated by initial steps of care afforded a young mother whose husband answered a knock on the back door of their home after 10:00 p.m. He announced upstairs to his wife that he was stepping out shortly. A few moments later, she heard two shots. She rushed downstairs and outside to discover that her husband was lying on the ground. Police came and an ambulance rushed him to a hospital emergency ward, where he was declared dead on arrival.

The pastor of this couple with three children arrived at the hospital about 10:45 p.m. The wife was in a state of shock. At that moment, the first step was to connect this stricken lady with trusted individuals and then seek clarification from authorities about what had happened. Second, it was established that the shooting was a homicide, and immediate arrangements were made for care of the family that night and the days following. Third, coping was a long process after the young husband's funeral, starting with grief counseling that dealt with long-term loss and helping the widow and children heal. The pastor stood by at each of these three steps of crisis intervention. He was especially needed for the long term.

The Ministry of Intervention When Persons Contemplate Suicide

The need for intervention is most acute when a person telephones or texts the pastor and declares an intention to commit suicide. Wouldn't it be helpful if these communications reached only the iPhone or iPad of counselors trained in suicide prevention? The fact is, pastors who are not trained in this specialty are often the ones receiving such messages. What is the pastor to do upon receiving such a call? He listens and helps the person work through suicidal feelings. Working quickly and buying time are critical. As a helper, the pastor is caring—interested, concerned, and stable. Keeping the conversation going, the

306 The A-B-C method of crisis intervention is variously expounded by these works: Howard W. Stone, *Crisis Counseling*, rev. ed. (Minneapolis: Fortress Press, 1993); David K. Switzer, *The Minister as Crisis Counselor* (Nashville: Abingdon Press, 1974); and Romaine V. Edwards, *Crisis Intervention and How It Works* (Springfield, IL: Charles C. Thomas. Second printing, 1979).

pastor may interject, "Why do you want to take your life?" Or, better phrased, the question may be "What do you mean when you say that you intend to take your life?" When the precipitating stress is out in the open, the person may be ready for alternative actions posed by the pastor. "What would help solve this problem other than taking your life?" Hopefully, the person gives thought and replies, "Okay, that is one possibility." The pastor responds, "What else may solve it?" If the troubled person gives thought to alternatives, he or she may move beyond the critical moment of contemplating suicide, thus allowing time for help to arrive. Romaine Edwards reflects on this point, "The client must be forced back out of the box he has worked himself into, concluding that suicide is the answer or a good answer to his problem."[307]

At some point, the person contemplating suicide may be open to accepting a *contact* that will arrive and remain close to the person. "You are probably alone. Is this right? It could help if someone was with you. Do you agree?" The *contacts* may be police, fire fighters, paramedics, family members, a friend, or a neighbor. If the person is known to possess a weapon, engage the police. At some point, the pastor will seek to elicit from the troubled person a jointly-agreed-upon plan whereby the person takes the opportunity to explore deep feelings with a psychotherapist. The bottom line is, every announcement of intention to take one's life is treated with utmost seriousness.

Ministry to Incarcerated Persons

Over three million persons are incarcerated in the United States. Some are members of Christian congregations, or they may be relatives or friends of congregation members. Is the pastor obligated to care for these persons? Consider our Lord's reply to John in prison (Matt 11:2–11) and His reference to the last judgment, "I was in prison and you came to Me" (Matt 25:36b). The apostle Paul welcomed those who came to him while he was a prisoner in Rome (Acts 28:30b). Luke was with him there (2 Tim 4:11). Therefore, revise the question. How shall the pastor care for imprisoned persons?

The pastor reserves time for prison ministry. Though others may have forgotten a prisoner and moved on, the pastor does not forget. If the prison is distant, he may engage local pastors to visit, but normally the pastor himself travels every two months to visit the prisoner. There, he observes the rubrics of the prison—visiting days, regulations, rules about what may be shared with inmates, and so on. He keeps apprised of changes in prison visitation policies.

The pastor comes as a friend, perhaps the only trusted friend the prisoner has. Although he avoids discussion about an inmate's sentence, term, or re-

307 Edwards, *Crisis Intervention and How It Works*, 45.

lease, the pastor may hear admission of wrongdoing. He helps to frame guilt as repentance before God, and he speaks God's forgiveness of sins in Christ. The incarcerated person has been judged, but God is gracious and forgiving. The pastor, too, accepts this person. He may bring the Sacrament. He shares the Scriptures, and he aids the prisoner to avail himself of God's Word. Therefore, the pastor provides a Bible, hymn book, prayer book, catechism, and devotional literature as prison regulations permit. Most important, he prays with the prisoner. These pastoral visits mean much to prisoners. Loneliness stalks the person behind bars. If visiting is not possible, the pastor corresponds regularly with the prisoner either by surface mail or email.

Ministry to Persons Caught Up in Conflict

Christian fellowships are not immune to internal conflict. This is why the apostle Paul cautioned the Galatians to be careful not to bite and devour one another, for through love they are to serve one another (Gal 5:13, 15). Unloving attitudes, words, and actions may surface, marring fellowship. Then conflict flourishes. Striving for Christian love in a congregation will go far to prevent hostilities that fester into continuous conflict.

Aiding prevention of situations that implode into serious conflict is the pastor's watchfulness and intervention when he observes or senses bad feelings in the congregation. He works to bring hostile parties together to interact, discuss, confess, and forgive. At junctures, he may introduce other caregivers who have special expertise in conflict resolution.[308] All of this takes both time and timing. A pastor may expend huge amounts of energy working to resolve conflicts. This ministry is a personal investment of Christian love.

Ministry to the Dying

The Pastor Belongs at the Side of the Dying Christian

Pastoral care ministry takes many turns. There is a time to die, says the writer, and the dying Christian is fortunate whose pastor is close by (Eccl 3:2). Pray that the pastor does not arrive at the bedside of the dying Christian kicking and screaming—hesitant, anxious, uneasy, or afraid. This is an existential moment for the pastor. If ever he wanted to be an effective pastor, this is a time when he wants to get it right. It is because we are poised on the threshold of eternity.

When visiting the dying, pastors sense that they are entering uncharted waters, so to speak. It seems that dying persons are a few steps ahead. How shall

308 See Ken Sande and Ted Kober, *Guiding People Through Conflict* (Billings, MT: Peacemaker Ministries, 1998).

we follow and gently enter their close world? Observe that a pastor may not be the dying person's choice. It is said that the dying finally look to one individual to accompany them—a family member, a faithful caregiver. How does the pastor fit in this group? How shall he be welcome? If the pastor has been close and brought Christ's Word and Sacrament through weeks or months or years of ministry to dying persons, he will be recognized as their pastor and welcomed in these last moments. The pastor's desire to be there is important, also what he brings belongs there; and he may be confident that God will honor and bless his ministry to the dying person.

The Pastor's Ministry to the Dying—A Ministry of the Word

Pastor, do not permit a sense of inadequacy to overtake you. Relax. If ever pastoral ministry was not about *us*, it is ministry to the dying. The Lord steps forward with His Word and comfort, so step aside. Approach the gravely ill or injured with the Gospel and its power to handle death. With a Word, our Lord put off Satan (Matt 4:1–11; Luke 4:1–13). Death is merely Satan's trump card, so he thinks, to dominate and enslave us. But Christ is risen! By the indomitable event of the Lord's death and resurrection, He defeated Satan and death (Heb 2:14–15; 1 John 3:8b; cf. Eph 1:20–23; Rev 20:9–10). Jesus turns dying and death to victory—the resurrection of the body and the fashioning of that body gloriously as God chooses to do (1 Cor 15:23, 38, 49). Pastor, let the plain Word of this Gospel speak for itself.

Medium for Communicating the Word to the Dying

Pastor, you are on the winning side, so come to the dying without emotion, but with sincerity, and make the Gospel clear and plain. How do we go about this ministry? One model is "Commendation of the Dying," a special rite contained in *Pastoral Care Companion*.[309] There is much to be said for reading this formal rite, but long passages can be taxing for the gravely ill, and the tone can be cold and distant. Is a more direct and gentle delivery possible? Consider an alternative approach that surely is consistent with what the Lord wants for the dying person:

> Yes, we are very ill. This we know. And where shall we turn? We lift our eyes and heart to Jesus. He died on the cross for our sins. In Jesus, we are forgiven, and we have peace with God. God is no stranger, He is our heavenly Father. Jesus will take us to heaven to

309 "Commendation of the Dying," a liturgy prepared for ministry to a Christian at impending death, in *Pastoral Care Companion*, prepared by the Commission on Worship of The Lutheran Church—Missouri Synod (St. Louis: Concordia Publishing House, 2007), 81–94. When death is imminent, consult the same volume for the exhibit titled "Ministry to the Dying," 234–246.

> be with God our Father in the very rooms or mansions Jesus has gone to make ready. Jesus is the one for us. We believe, we cling to Jesus, and we shall rest in Jesus.

At death's door, every Christian is entitled to hear the name of Jesus. Pastor, come with plain and clear "Jesus talk, Jesus words." An anonymous source summarizes:

> The emphasis for the dying expressed in simplest terms is:
>
> 1. Jesus loves you and died for you (Rom. 5:8; John 3:16).
> 2. Jesus bore your sins! (1 Pet. 2:24; 3:18).
> 3. Jesus rose again to be a living Savior and so can be your Savior now and the Lord of life who gives you eternal life now. Believe on the Lord Jesus Christ! He will welcome you to heaven when God calls you.[310]

Questions Concerning the Faith of the Dying

Questions abound for the dying Christian and for those who have lost a loved one. Not least is the question of a dying person, "Will I keep my faith in Christ?" A Christian receives that fateful word from a physician, "Your illness is terminal. You have four, maybe six, months to live." Those months are painful. The mind soars in every direction. The person dealing with terminal illness may ask, "When the going gets tough and the pain is unbearable and I am so alone, will I keep the faith?" These patients put their questions to the pastor. He turns to God's Word. The Scriptures answer without wavering, "Who are kept by the power of God through faith unto salvation ready to be revealed in the last time" (1 Pet 1:5 KJV). We may fall to pieces, but the Spirit shall keep us in that faith in Jesus unto salvation (John 20:31). Again, the Lord takes the initiative and takes the reins. What we cannot do, He does. "And I am sure of this, that He who began a good work in you will bring it to completion at the day of Jesus Christ" (Phil 1:6).

So we let go. We shall not rely on our own power and strength, which come to nothing, but trust in Him who continues His good work in us by His Holy Spirit until the Lord comes on the Last Day. This is also the assurance for Christians who question whether or not a deceased loved one kept the faith. "Did she believe at the end, did she keep the faith?" A God-fearing man asked this question about his wife who died of cancer. The answer is "kept by the power

310 "When We Face the Dying." Authorship unknown. This author shared this document with students in pastoral theology classes at Concordia Seminary, St. Louis, Missouri.

of God" (1 Pet 1:5 KJV). What a complete and powerful answer! The Lord does not forsake His own baptized Christians. He keeps them in saving baptismal faith unto the end.

Ministry to Those Who Grieve

Many losses are suffered in a lifetime, but none as poignant as the loss of a loved one. The grief that follows has many nuances—sorrow, regret, guilt, despair, depression—to name a few. Joseph and his brothers and their families mourned for Jacob, the Israelites mourned for Moses and later for Samuel (Gen 50:10; Deut 34:8; 1 Sam 28:3). The poignant scene at Bethany is captured in the report "Jesus wept" (John 11:35). Grief in the wake of death is common, and it is no less difficult for grieving Christians today.

The pace of living in the twenty-first century, the distraction of technology, and recent customs such as hasty cremation abbreviate and trivialize time for grieving. We move on, perhaps, too swiftly. The special need of the bereaved was honored in the Old Testament by assigning a time to grieve (cf. Deut 34:8; Gen 50:3; 2 Sam 1:12). This practice was wise. Carrying unresolved grief into the future is unhealthy. Thus, a caring pastor walks with the grieving at their pace long after the world has moved on. He schedules pastoral attention for each grieving family—to listen, to reflect, to offer sound words and the promises of God. Following the funeral or memorial service, a pastor may minister at intervals: one week, two weeks, a month, three months, six months, a year—with visits or contacts on anniversaries, birthdays, or other meaningful times in memory of the deceased.

The journey from grief to acceptance and adjustment is arduous. Helping persons make their way, the pastor may find useful five recognized stages of grieving:[311]

1. Denial—This is a period of rejecting or not believing that loss has taken place. It is often characterized by a sense of numbness, shock. "This can't be happening to me."

---

311 A respected source for understanding these five stages of grieving is Elisabeth Kubler-Ross, *On Death and Dying* (New York: Macmillan, 1969). Stages of grieving appear in Granger E. Westberg, *Good Grief: A Constructive Approach to the Problem of Loss* (Rock Island, IL: Augustana Press, 1962). To view grief and healing firsthand, see Gregory Schulz, *The Problem of Suffering: A Father's Hope*, rev. ed. (St. Louis: Concordia Publishing House, 2011). A succinct guide for ministry to those who mourn is Richard C. Eyer, *Pastoral Care Under the Cross: God in the Midst of Suffering*, rev. ed. (St. Louis: Concordia Publishing House, 2014), ch. 8, "At the Foot of the Cross: Mourners," 107–115. Useful are two works by Kenneth C. Haugk, *Don't Sing Songs to a Heavy Heart: How to Relate to Those Who are Suffering* and the four-part work *Journeying through Grief*, both from Stephen Ministries in St. Louis, Missouri, 2004. The authors, Haugk and Schulz, write from their own grief experiences.

2. Anger—Surfacing is deep-seated rage over what is happening. Random anger is projected in all directions—toward parents for letting the person down, also doctors, hospitals, friends, teachers, self, even God. It may be essential to experience and express anger, but in appropriate ways. "Why me?"

3. Bargaining—Grieving persons attempt to exchange something they are willing to do or give up for something they want to keep. They deal with someone who is in control when they are not. Bargaining here is an attempt to postpone or fix up the inevitable. It is also a time when grieving persons are vulnerable to unrealistic guilt feelings. "If only . . ." or "What if . . . ?"

4. Depression—When we cannot cope, life is out of control, we are overwhelmed. This happens when the reality of loss sets in. Depression may manifest itself as highs and lows, and keeping balance is a challenge. Again, it is a time when we are vulnerable to serious distraction—turning to drugs, alcohol, or even suicide. "What's the use?"

5. Acceptance—At length, grieving persons learn to live with changes in their lives. They arrive at a time when they no longer dwell on the past and begin to look forward to their tomorrows. "I thought I would never feel like moving on."

For healthy recovery from the loss of a loved one, psychologists stress the importance of passing through each of these five stages of grieving. The journey is not easy or pretty, and the grieving person will go forward one stage to another, then in reverse, then forward again. We cannot program a straight course to acceptance and closure. Wherever a pastor finds the person on this journey, he connects the bereaved to the Gospel promises in the Scriptures. God's Word assures the person that he or she does not walk alone. Along the way, it is healthy for grieving persons to share their story—events, circumstances, feelings.

Ministry and Care at Life's End

Critical decisions regarding the manner or limitations of medical care accorded a person who is terminally ill may rest with the immediate family, and they may consult with their pastor. Shall they authorize end of life by removal of life support, *pulling the plug*? In another instance, a family may become uneasy after authorizing removal of life support from a loved one and they consult with their pastor, seeking affirmation. Related to this subject is the person or family developing living wills, advance directives, and such. How shall these documents conform to Christian ethical norms? They seek the pastor's input.

When counseling families who are dealing with end-of-life issues, the pastor references two unfavorable options:

1. Taking life hastily or recklessly by lethal procedures imposed on a person, an action known as euthanasia
2. Extending life unduly when a person is in *death work*, that is, the body systems are failing, thus creating burdensome suffering and pain[312]

The first option—directly and forcibly taking life—is killing. This we shall not do. "You shall not murder" (Exod 20:13). The Lord gave life, the Lord takes life away (Job 1:21). The second option referenced above, prolonging life against every indication that body systems are shutting down and the person is in the throes of dying, may cause excruciating pain and extend suffering. This we shall not do.

End-of-life situations are difficult, and discerning them with clarity in order to make sound ethical decisions defies even the best intentions of Christian families. When there is viable life to sustain and nurture, then life support is the appropriate option. This is also true for persons perceived to be in a persistent vegetative state.[313] Even in these instances, the question prevails, how may the family show Christian care without aiming at killing, but also without causing burdensome suffering? Codes set by state law and followed by health-care institutions may direct physicians to press for ending the life of a terminally ill person, but removing support when life is viable may be the unfavorable action of euthanasia.[314] When pressed to determine a course for a dying loved one, what is the family to do? An alternative to euthanasia may be moving the patient elsewhere, to special hospice care or to other institutions that provide continuing palliative care.

---

312 These two options are discussed at length in the document *Christian Care at Life's End: A Report of the Commission on Theology and Church Relations* (St. Louis: The Lutheran Church—Missouri Synod, February 1993). For further refinements of these two options, see John T. Pless, *Mercy at Life's End: A Guide for Laity and Their Pastors* (St. Louis: The Lutheran Church—Missouri Synod, 2013), 12–15.

313 Yale University professor David Gelernter argued the case for continuing care of Terri Schiavo in the state of Florida in 2003. Mrs. Schiavo was facing death-by-starvation when her husband ordered her feeding tube removed. Gelernter's spirited concern was directed at the law that required action by the Florida legislature before the state's governor could override Michael Schiavo's decision to end Mrs. Schiavo's life.

314 A seventy-year-old woman suffering from acute pneumonia was on a respirator. The device was in use for several days. Her daughter informed the pastor one morning that she and her brother would report to the hospital and authorize removal of the respirator from their mother. The pastor suggested that they should be certain that their mother's life was no longer viable, that clearly, she was dying. Following a conference with physicians, they decided to leave the respirator in place another day. During the next twenty-four hours, their mother showed improvement. She overcame pneumonia, recovered, and lived another five years.

Pastors enter the game when end-of-life decisions affect both the patient and the family.[315] When approaching a decision or after a decision has been made and the family members are not in agreement, the pastor counsels that the gravity of the situation shall not fracture the family. We make critical decisions within a fallen creation subject to futility (Rom 8:20–21); we are part of that creation and its futility. "Consequently, we should not necessarily expect in our limited human wisdom always to be able to come to decisions with which all thoughtful Christians agree."[316] We are rescued and placed within the company of those baptized into Christ, and togetherness in Christ brings stability. We shall not fall apart, and our family shall prevail.

When a person expires in a health-care facility, the family may be approached for permission to harvest organs from the body. This request may come when no advance directive had been given by the deceased. Postmortem use of human body parts for medical use may stir sensibilities, but where the practice is legal, there is no objection on theological grounds.

Procedures are usually in place to guarantee that the action of gathering organs from the body happens after death occurs, not before.[317]

Ministry to Chronically Ill Persons

Illnesses, disabilities, and abnormalities beyond the ability of modern medicine to resolve may impact individuals with physical, mental, and emotional suffering. There are several constants at work here. The affliction is constant, but no more so than the constant love and mercy of our Lord (2 Cor 1:3–4; cf. Eph 2:4–7; Ps 86:5–7; 100:5). Then, the pastor ministers to chronically ill and disabled individuals faithfully, that is, *constantly*. His faithful attention and dependable care is testimony to the faithfulness of God. In many instances, the pastor communes these persons every month in their home or residence. The faithfulness of God caring for them is sealed in the Sacrament. What is more constant than our Lord giving His body and blood for the enduring blessing of the forgiveness of sins?

---

315 The hospital resident physician determined that life support should be removed from a man dying of cirrhosis of the liver. The patient was divorced. His former wife was not involved, but two adult daughters agreed with the physician. The man's mother, however, disagreed intensely. A conflict occurred. It was late at night. The pastor counseled that all get a night's rest and return to address the matter the next morning. Reluctantly, the resident physician agreed to that delay. During the night, the patient expired. His mother was thankful and expressed her deep feelings in these words: "Pastor, we did not kill my son! The Lord took him! Thank God!"

316 "Christian Care at Life's End," 13. The authors of this document counsel further, "Any decisions made in this highly complex area, and any actions taken that may later appear to have been wrong, have been redeemed by that forgiveness which is available to all who put their trust in the work and merits of mankind's Savior and Redeemer," 62.

317 Dr. Robert Weise, professor at Concordia Seminary, St. Louis, Missouri, provided this information in 2013: http://www.donatelife.net/facts.html.

In this ministry, time spent with chronically ill persons is vital. Conversation is important. These persons are eager to be included; therefore, the pastor shares news about the congregation, compares notes on mutual acquaintances, and refers to current events of interest. Sports may be of interest to some persons. These asides in conversation during visits with the chronically ill or disabled persons keeps them in the loop and conveys a sense of inclusion and belonging that are part of *koinonia*, or fellowship.

Ministry to the Elderly

Christians also need that sense of belonging when advanced age isolates them from the mainstream of society, congregation, and even their own families. An aging gentleman reflected, "This getting old is not for sissies." He referred not only to the discomfort of steadily decreasing physical strength, agility, and mental sharpness, but to the manner in which the elderly are perceived by everyone else. When, either by verbal or body language, young people react negatively to *age*, they effectively consign their elders to the status of unwanted. Elderly adults simply want to be persons like everyone else. They seek to maintain the worth and dignity of personhood. They are denied this honor when the major premise is "But you are old!"

A young pastor is somewhat handicapped when it comes to older persons. He cannot be one of them, but youth notwithstanding, he cares for the elderly. He brings the Gospel to them, perhaps unaware of how meaningful the grace of God and divine forgiveness and the hope of eternal life may be to persons of advanced age. The pastor cannot bridge the age gap, but the Word that he brings to them reaches across the divide and touches hearts with the glory and the love of God that we know in the face of Christ Jesus (2 Cor 4:6). A note about pastoral leadership: the pastor's right attitude and actions toward elder Christians lead the congregation to respect and honor the aged among them (Lev 19:32).

Moreover, the laity is a tremendous resource for ministry to elders. Suppose that in the congregation, there are leaders who have made a mark in industry or government or education or sports. What if one of these accomplished people took time to visit, affirm, and comfort an otherwise isolated aged fellow Christian? How meaningful would such a ministry be to this elderly Christian! How wonderful when such care helps the elderly toward consciousness of God's love and care. Congregations should build a reserve of resources and caring individuals who can brighten the lives of aging fellow Christians.

Losses and limitations loom large for aging Christians. They lose longtime friends or even close family. Their once active, full life is gone. Status and position, a comfortable home, freedom to travel and enjoy are only memories. Life is diminished to a fraction of what it once was. Limitations fence them, and there is no escape. As limitations increase, so do complaints in the conversation of the elderly. Dr. Richard Eyer remarks, "Pastors can be helpful to the elderly by acknowledging complaints of personal loss and not trying to comfort them by talking them out of their grieving but walking with them through it."[318] The challenge is to move older Christians from *doing* to *being* in aging.[319] The pastor, says Eyer, helps the grieving elder person look to God, who is there to be loved and to love as He does in Christ Jesus.[320] Thus, the pastor grows in his ministry to elders, a ministry that is far more significant than *cheering up* the old folks. Recognize that superficial efforts to *cheer up* miss the mark with elder persons who are in pain or who otherwise are out of sorts for any number of reasons. For these elder Christians, the Gospel is help, and this is the unique opportunity for the pastor.

What a blessing in the Christian community when older adults bond with the young, and they with the aged! To the young, old Christians give a living witness to the abiding faithfulness of God (Ps 9:9; 33:20–22; 36:5; 37:39–40). When an aging Christian has confidence that the God who redeemed us in Christ cares for us every step of the journey, expressing such faith to the young is a powerful witness (Rom 8:32). This is accrued wisdom that young people should not overlook or neglect. Richard Eyer stresses that the Christian life with its deepening reserve of wisdom begins to develop during spiritual childhood. It continues to develop with passing of the years.[321] This suggests that the young and elders are not strangers, but fellows, because wisdom accrues through youth and adulthood, and it matures in the elder Christian. When the young realize that wisdom is developing in their own life's journey, they may be disposed to honor and love the elderly. There is much to be garnered for both young and old through intergenerational ministry.

As the years lengthen, life ebbs to a close. The Lord has His hand in this (Job 1:21). It is a good thing. As limitations exceed coping, ailments diminish joy, the five senses fail, and solitude overtakes the aged, the need for light from above is paramount. The sense of mortality is heavy because of the burden of sin (Ps 31:10, 14; 38:8–18; cf. Ps 31:21–22; Ps 51). The aged Christian prays not only in the present darkness, but for the long night, "In peace I will both lie down and sleep; for You alone, O LORD, make me dwell in safety" (Ps 4:8).

---

318 Richard Eyer, *Pastoral Care Under the Cross: God in the Midst of Suffering* (St. Louis: Concordia Publishing House, 1994), 84.

319 *Engaging the Aging: Walt's Words*, ed. Walter Schoedel (St. Louis: Lutheran Senior Services, Fall 2015).

320 Eyer, *Pastoral Care Under the Cross*, 84.

321 Ibid., 81.

Therefore, the pastor's ministry draws the advanced aging Christian to Jesus, the Savior at the cross. Jesus is there before they call for Him. The pastor brings Scriptures that seal these assurances to them. He fixes their attention on things eternal, and the Sacrament he celebrates for them lifts up eyes and heart to the Lord and His heaven that He prepares for them. Keeping eyes and heart fixed on Jesus becomes the mainstay of the pastor's ministry to the very elder Christian (Heb 12:2).

Ministry When Confronting Demonic Possession

Jesus commanded His followers to perform exorcism in His name. He commissioned the Twelve Apostles (Mark 3:14–15 and Matt 10:1; Mark 6:6–13 and Matt 10:7–8; Luke 9:1–6) and the seventy disciples (Luke 10:17–20) for this ministry, to cast out demons from those physically possessed. Then why is the modern church hesitant about exercising this ministry of exorcism in the present age?

Notably, references to exorcism in the Lutheran Confessions refer not to deliverance from physical possession but to rubrics contained in Luther's Rite of Holy Baptism, advanced in his Baptismal Booklet (SC, 373, 374). Other reasons for hesitance to engage in exorcism are uncertainty whether or not a person is, indeed, a victim of demonic possession and the lack of a specific verbal formula for confronting the demon.

In regard to the first difficulty, distinguishing demon possession from other pathologies, C. F. W. Walther cites Johann Quenstedt's indicators of a demon. Further, Walther cites Luther's counsel that a person possessed by a demon should be met with fervent prayer and confidence that speaking the exorcism in the name of the Lord Jesus Christ, the demon will flee. How helpful this counsel may be is left to pastors who confront this phenomenon.[322]

322 Walther, *American-Lutheran Pastoral Theology*, ed. David W. Loy, trans. Christian C. Tiews (St. Louis, MO: Concordia Publishing House, 2017), 344–345. See, Darrell Arthur McCulley, *The House Swept Clean: a Biblically Balanced Pattern for the Diagnosis, Exorcism, and Pastoral Care of the Victims of Demonic Possession* (self-published), 2002, and Eric Sorensen, *Possession and Exorcism in the New Testament and Early Christianity* (Tűbingen: Mohr Siebeck), 2002. About spiritual warfare, see Robert H. Bennett, *Afraid: Demon Possession and Spiritual Warfare in America* (St. Louis, MO: Concordia Publishing House, 2016) and the account of spiritual warfare in the Lutheran Church of Madagascar, *I Am Not Afraid: Demon Possession and Spiritual Warfare* (St. Louis, MO: Concordia Publishing House, 2013).

CHAPTER FOURTEEN

The Ministry with Regard to Marriage, Divorce, Remarriage

Introduction

Sexual life in twenty-first century Western culture is marked by four notable developments: *First*, the lifestyle of open promiscuity among the young; *second*, increasing popularity of cohabitation, a man and a woman living together sexually prior to marriage or in place of marriage; *third*, a high percentage of marriages ending in divorce; *fourth*, societal toleration and approval of deviant sexual behavior. These cultural developments are eliminating traditional sexual boundaries and are destabilizing the divine institutions of marriage and family. How, then, shall Christians marry and live as God's people in these times?

Marriage

Marriage—Matrix for the Family

"Family" refers to numerous arrangements of communal living. The Scriptures sharpen the focus. "God settles the solitary in a home" (Ps 68:6). Individual life under the Creator is life with fellow creatures. This design appears first as the unique closeness of a man and a woman to each other and to God (Gen 1:27; 2:22). Male and female were created in the image of God and brought to each other by God, and He gave them the command and physical capability to "be fruitful and multiply" (Gen 1:28).

The first humans were not alone. They were blessed with children (Gen 4:1–2, 25). Family was launched. The Fourth Commandment orders life in the family. It reads, "Honor your father and your mother" (Exod 20:12). Luther regarded this Fourth Commandment as pivotal for life together in the same household and as the backbone of civil authority and order and social welfare (LC I 141, 142). The Lutheran Confessions assert that the family is a divinely ordained order of creation, a part of the *bonae creaturae Dei et Ordinationes divinae*, good creations of God and divine orders (Ap XVI 1b). The family—parents in the Lord exercising authority over their children and the children loving and honoring father and mother—is a true, holy, good institution that flows out of the Gospel (Ap XVI 5). Marriage and family are distinctly *dominical*, of the Lord.

Marriage—The Sexual Union of Husband and Wife

Though society perceives marriage in diverse ways, God sets forth the unalterable understanding that marriage is the sexual union of one man and one woman bonded to one another for life (Matt 19:4–6; cf. Gen 1:27; 2:24; Eph 5:31; 1 Cor 7:2–4).[323] This sexual union, one man and one woman in marriage, is the standard for human sexual relations. God blesses the sexual union only within marriage—the union of one man and one woman marked by enduring love, permanent commitment, and excluding all others, a publicly declared and transparent union. The Bible describes this marital union. A man finds a woman he loves. She loves him. He leaves father and mother, as does she. He cleaves to her, and she to him. The two become "one" (Gen 2:24; cf. Eph 5:31; Mark 10:6–9). Outside of marriage, the monogamous union of one man and one woman, the Scriptures brand sexual relations as sin; this includes fornication, adultery, and perversion[324] (Gen 2:18–24; 4:1, 25; 39:7–12; Exod 20:14; Matt 5:27–28; 5:32; 19:9; 1 Cor 6:18; Heb 13:4; Lev 20:13; Rom 1:26–27).

It cannot be overemphasized that the Scriptures teach that marriage is the monogamous sexual union of *one* man and *one* woman (Matt 19:4–6). Because it is ordained by God, marriage is honored in the Church as holy matrimony. The referent is that sacred union of *one* Christ and His *one* Bride, the Church (Rev 21:2; cf. Matt 9:15; Mark 2:19; Luke 5:34–35; John 3:29; Eph 5:21–22; Rev

323 One segment of the popular television program *Dr. Phil* illustrated the diversity of understanding of marriage in twenty-first-century America. The host marked a demonstrable trend in society—going from monogamous marriage to open marriage. See the *Dr. Phil* show, August 7, 2012. Note that same-sex marriage is unknown in the Holy Scriptures, where the sexual union of a man with another man or a woman with another woman is judged unnatural and contrary to God's creation of male and female and is summarily condemned as an abomination (Rom 1:18–27; 1 Cor 6:9–10; cf. 1 Tim 1:9–10; Lev 18:22, 29–30; 20:13, also Gen 19:5, 24–25). Summarizing the teaching of the LCMS in response to legal recognition of homosexual marriage, Dr. David Adams notes, "God has created marriage for three reasons: (1) to meet the need of mankind not to be alone (Gen. 2:18); (2) to provide through procreation for the continuing life of humankind (Gen. 1:28); and (3) to curb the inclination to sinfulness in a fallen world (1 Cor. 7:2)." Dr. Adams observes that the essential nature of homosexual relationships violates two of these three reasons for which God created marriage and cannot be what God calls marriage, and Christians may not endorse them as such. David L. Adams, "The Challenge of Homosexuality: What Is at Stake?" *Concordia Journal* 31, no. 3 (July 2005): 224.

324 The monogamous sexual union of one man and one woman in marriage is buffeted by the secular culture. Note the testimonies of numerous participants in the Jerry Springer TV production *Baggage*, who attest to sexual relations with scores of different partners, and witness the disdain expressed by some participants who spurn any relationship with a professed "virgin" of the opposite sex.

18:23). This is how the apostle Paul addressed the Church at Corinth: "I feel a divine jealousy for you, since I betrothed you to one husband, to present you as a pure virgin to Christ" (2 Cor 11:2). The Church, the one Bride, says the apostle Paul, is betrothed to one husband. The numeral is interesting. The texts cited above in discussion of marriage typically employ singular nouns as the antecedent and use singular possessive pronouns, for example, *his* wife, or *her* husband (Gen 2:24 [Eph 5:31]; Gen 4:1, 25; Mark 10:6–9; Rom 7:2–3). Observe the same usage in the ancient rubric that granted a furlough to the newly married young soldier, "He shall be free at home one year to be happy with *his* wife whom *he* has taken" (Deut 24:5 italics added). Marriage, therefore, is the union of two and only two, *one* man and *one* woman.[325]

Marriage—The Constituting Factor

Others consider this description of marriage deficient. Theologians continue to ask, "What constitutes marriage according to Holy Scripture?" Their question draws more commentary than is possible to document.[326] The mutual love, husband and wife, has been cited as constitutive. The consent given freely by each partner to be married is cited. Others cite the *copula carnalis* (sexual union) as constitutive. We have shown that the New Testament recognizes the essential physical union of husband and wife (Matt 19:4–6; Mark 10:6–9; 1 Cor 7:2; Heb 13:4; cf. Eph 5:22–33). The rubrics for this intimate life of baptized Christians in marriage are explicit. The apostle Paul writes, "For this is the will of God, your sanctification: that you abstain from sexual immorality, that each one of you know how to control his own body in holiness and honor, not in

325 That polygamy is reported among the ancients does not in any way abridge the principle of monogamous heterosexual marriage, a principle enunciated by our Lord when He appealed to the order of creation in which male and female, created by God, were brought together in the one-flesh union (Matt 19:4–6; cf. Mark 10:6–9). Furthermore, biblical discussions of the fracture of marriage by divorce or in the event of death are stated in reference to the union of one man and one woman (Matt 19:7–9; Rom 7:2; cf. 1 Cor 7:10–11). Paul exacts faithfulness from pastors and deacons in their marriages as husbands of one wife only (1 Tim 3:2, 12; Titus 1:6). In each instance, these church leaders are referenced as husbands, that is, "one woman's man," and their wives are to be a "one man's woman" (cf. John 4:18). The biblical teaching is clear. Marriage is a heterosexual union of one man and one woman unto one flesh, enduring for their entire life together. Cf. Erwin L. Lueker, "Marriage in the New Testament," unpublished essay contained in notes distributed by Prof. Harry G. Coiner to classes at Concordia Seminary, St. Louis, Missouri, titled "Christian Marriage and Family Life" (1960), 6–7.

326 This question should not be confused with a related inquiry, what place has marriage in the temporal order (AC XVI, XXVIII)? By human right and arrangement through the instrument of the state, marriage has legal status, and performance of the Rite of Marriage in the Church is a juridical action by human right (AC XXVIII 29). Thus, it serves as a means for society to pronounce the marriage final and binding when it is publicly declared. The state's interest in marriage, states Dr. Frank Beckwith, professor at Baylor University, is threefold: (1) Exclusivity—one man and one woman in a private and permanent union; (2) Conjugality—sexual power to bring children into existence; (3) Permanence—provision of security for children growing to maturity. As such, marriage viewed by the state must in some way be solemnized and enforced by the wider community. View the interview of Dr. Frank Beckwith by the Rev. Todd Wilken, archives of *Issues, Etc.*, August 28, 2014.

the passion of lust like the Gentiles who do not know God" (1 Thess 4:3–5). In the marital union of Christians, there is no place for unnatural lust, perversion; however, the two spouses have freedom in marriage to share one another. The wife, not the husband, is lord over his body; and the husband, not the wife, is lord over her body (1 Cor 7:3–5). Husband and wife, therefore, shall not deprive each other. Also, the instruction directed to the husband that he should dwell with his wife according to knowledge may apply to the intimate life in marriage (1 Pet 3:7 KJV).[327]

What constitutes a marriage? Luther approaches the question with a transcendent construct of husband and wife integrated with the redeemed in Christ. The Reformer saw the constitutive element, not in love alone, nor in consensus, nor in sexual union. Important as these factors are, Luther accents the couple's relationship to Christ, which means that their marriage is God's order for them, for their family, and for the community of humanity touched by their marriage and family. This factor is, for Luther, constitutive. Prof. Harry G. Coiner integrated Luther's view in this summary: "Marriage, as interpreted by faith, is the total commitment of one man and one woman to each other in a uniquely divinely ordered relationship comprising mutual consent, love, sexual union, and fidelity not only to the partner but to God's whole created order (*institutio divina*)."[328]

Marriage: Headship and Submission

Principle: The Holy Scriptures reserve sexual intimacy for the marital union of one man and one woman. This final and irrevocable teaching is complemented by universal honor and respect for sexual relations only within marriage. All persons in the Christian community commit to this principle by leading a chaste and decent life in thought, word, and action.

A Christian husband and wife, though members together of Christ's Body, have concrete marital roles. The biblical framework for these roles is often designated by the terms *headship* and *submission*. These terms are misunderstood and resisted both in the culture and the Church.[329] The feminist movement is particularly sensitive and resistant to the teaching that the wife submits to her husband who is κεφαλή, head, just as the Church is subject to Christ as head[330] (Eph 5:22–24).

327 Lueker, "Marriage in the New Testament," 7.

328 Harry G. Coiner, "The Christian Theology of Marriage" (unpublished essay distributed to students at Concordia Seminary, St. Louis, Missouri, 1960), 4.

329 Hostility toward headship/submission surfaced numerous times in the author's premarital counseling sessions. In one session, arriving at this phrase in the traditional Rite of Marriage, "love, honor, and obey," the prospective bride resounded immediately, "Don't say that. I don't want that." Her emphatic assertion was in reference to the word *obey*. And her fiancé chimed in, "And I don't want her to say those words."

330 While discussing the place of men and women in the Church, the apostle Paul instructs, "But I want

Because they comprehend their transcendent metaroles as members together of Christ their Redeemer, Christian husbands and wives honor the headship-submission principle. When the apostle Paul instructs, "Wives, submit to your own husbands, as to the Lord," he also instructs, "Husbands, love your wives, as Christ loved the church and gave Himself up for her" (Eph 5:22, 25). The wife's submission is possible only when her husband knows and exercises his headship role. He does this best when he learns from study of the four Gospels how Christ loved the Church and gave Himself for her. The wise husband does likewise for his wife. He discovers nuances of Christ's love that are instructive for his behavior toward his wife. Without taking these initiatives, he turns into a tyrant, and his wife is paralyzed. She will resist and fight him.

The difficulty is not headship and submission, which God designed for the happiness of both spouses in marriage, but the fall into sin that ruins husbands and wives for the order and structure that God ordained. Trust God, there is a blessing for husband and wife in the order He has established, but now it comes with a heavy burden.[331] With the fall came the curse. God said to the woman, "In pain you shall bring forth children, yet your desire shall be for your husband, and he shall rule over you" (Gen 3:16 RSV). To the man God said, "Cursed is the ground because of you; in toil you shall eat of it all the days of your life; . . . In the sweat of your face you shall eat bread till you return to the ground, for out of it you were taken; you are dust, and to dust you shall return" (Gen 3:17–19 RSV).

We underestimate the impact of this burden for both husband and wife. The husband rules as he loves and cares for his wife and family; and it is burdensome oversight, costing him energy and life. The wife submits, looking to the headship of her husband, for her desire is to him; but this form of self-denial, if not self-deprecation, is a pressing burden. In the temptation, the woman asserted her independence. Now the wife is bound by fixed attraction to her husband that seems almost compulsive. Furthermore, it is useless to instruct the secular mind about this burden, for it is borne only by couples who know and commit to headship and submission "as is fitting in the Lord" (Col 3:18–19). This involves two factors: as the Church submits to Christ as Lord and as

---

you to understand that the head of every man is Christ, the head of a wife is her husband, and the head of Christ is God" (1 Cor 11:3). The apostle Peter refers to Abraham and Sarah as an example of headship and submission in marriage (1 Pet 3:6).

331 Discussing the headship-submission principle, Dr. Larry Christenson observes that the Bible teaches a *subordination* of the wife to her husband. This subordination, Christenson asserts, is grounded upon the creation. "Adam was formed first, then Eve" (Gen 2:7, 18–23). It is further grounded upon the fall of our first parents: "Adam was not deceived, but the woman was deceived and became a transgressor" (1 Tim 2:13–14). Christenson points out that as long as he stood alone, Adam was not deceived. Christenson concludes, "After the Fall, upon each was laid a particular burden." Larry Christenson, *The Christian Family* (Minneapolis: Bethany Fellowship, 1970), 39.

Christ loved the Church (Eph 5:24–25). Thus, in marriage, both spouses as Christians submit to Christ, each taking up the role God has assigned to them (cf. Eph 5:21).

The challenge for Christian couples is to seek the blessing God has invested in marriage by pursuing the roles He ordained for them. That blessing is elusive partially because marriage is a mystery akin to the mystery of Christ and His Bride, the Church (Eph 5:32). A vivacious woman, talented, accomplished, and assertive, may yet show respect for her husband, a man who is steady and stable but reserved in demeanor. She shows how much she needs his stable temperament and rational guidance. She submits to him, and his undying love for her fulfills her.

In the book *Equal Marriage*, Jean Stapleton and Richard Bright show that marriage is more than the union of persons who are each one-half of the relationship.[332] Much less is it a union of a two-thirds person and a one-third person. Marriage is the union of two whole persons! This insight leads to an observation. Referring to marriage, the essence of the mystery, as the Scriptures teach, is that two whole persons can find their roles and discover that two disciplines complement each other—headship/love and submission/respect—for their mutual fulfillment and happiness. Living the mystery, husband and wife work things out in mutual love, honor, and respect. A couple living this mystery is in for all the volatility and bombast of close-knit life. So they are best attuned to Christ and His love. How wonderful if they prepare together, confessing mutually known failings, only to rush to the Lord's Table for His blessed forgiveness of their sins, together! And then they try and try again.

Marriage and Family—Procreation

In marriage, the possibility is always vibrant that husband and wife may become parents. All the pleasure seeking in sex notwithstanding, the deepest expression of love is enacted in view of procreation. Does every sexual encounter between husband and wife require intent to bring a child into the world? No, but sexual relations in marriage should never occur in denial that this purpose is paramount in the act of making love. It is possible that a couple becomes selfish. They may overtly thwart God's purpose of procreation that resides in their marriage (Gen 1:28). This is not to conclude that all family planning or delay in reproduction should be branded as thwarting the will of God. Most Christian couples, however, know the difference between salutary delay and crass, selfish denial. They know their own hearts. In the face of pressure from within their

332 Jean Stapleton and Richard Bright, *Equal Marriage* (Nashville: Abingdon Press, 1976), 14.

marriage or from societal influences to *control* and even thwart God's purposes, this excellent counsel is offered by the late Dr. Erwin Lueker:

> The New Testament is in harmony with the Old Testament view that children are a blessing (Mark 10:30; John 16:21; Gal. 4:27; Luke 1:7ff.; Heb. 2:13) and makes the bearing and rearing of children a woman's sphere of duty, dignity and privilege (1 Tim. 2:15; 1 Tim. 5:10, 14). Instead of presenting legalistic rules on family size the New Testament goes to the heart. Young women are to be taught by the older women to like children (Titus 2:4, 5). The proper attitude toward children would correct evils connected with the propagation and rearing of children. These truths are not changed by the fact that children increase wretchedness in days of calamity (Matt. 24:19; Luke 13:29).[333]

For all the challenges, the cost, the inconvenience, the anxiety, the taxing time spent, the drain of energy, the changes in daily living, the burden of care, and the need to be vigilant that is associated with bearing and rearing children, they are a blessing from God and they are His divine intention for marriage. In ancient Israel, the devout woman Hannah, at length from marital union with her husband, Elkanah, gave birth to a son, Samuel (1 Sam 1:19–20). How beautifully this mother exults in the Lord and attests what the psalmist affirms, "Behold, children are a heritage from the LORD, the fruit of the womb a reward" (Ps 127:3; cf. 1 Sam 1:19–20; 2:1–11). There is no other way whereby the world may move forward with the vigor of youth and vitality of minds and bodies applied to the general welfare of the human race than through the birth of little children who are given by God to well-intentioned parents in marriage.

Detractors from Christian Marriage and Family

Homosexuality

The Church in the World of Normalized Homosexuality

This paradigm—marriage, parenting, children—is anchored in God's creation, but it has many powerful detractors. The ascending influence of the Lesbian–Gay–Bisexual–Transgender (LGBT) movement in Western culture challenges traditional morality pertaining to sexuality, marriage, and family. The vigorous push for societal approval of homosexuality was crowned by the decision of the Supreme Court of the United States on June 26, 2015, *Obergefell*

333 Lueker, "Marriage in the New Testament," 6.

v. Hodges, to legalize same-sex marriage. A decade earlier, Dr. Robert Weise observed, "The fact is the gay agenda demands a fundamental shift in the way we've thought about sex and morals for a very, very long time."[334]

The Church's Response

In America, homosexual life and same-sex marriage are here, and they form part of the fabric of twenty-first century culture.[335] The Church marches into this century on a narrow path, bordered by extremes on each side—overreaction and under reaction. Harboring subliminal disdain for the homosexual community is one extreme that is fired by prejudice and discrimination contrary to Christian love. Equally reprehensible is the other extreme of complete tolerance of homosexual behavior that is contrary to the Word of God. Both reactions are unbecoming for Christians.

The Church proclaims that the Gospel of Jesus Christ is gender and race neutral. Homosexuals and lesbians are *coming out* in the churches. As members of Christ by Baptism, they have put on Christ, and diverse Christians—heterosexual or homosexual—are members of one another, εν χριστώ, in Christ (Gal 3:26–28). No one can gainsay this because it is the Spirit's doing (1 Cor 12:12–13; cf. Eph 4:4–7). The Gospel knows only sinners and declares them redeemed in Christ Jesus. Hence the Church, the Body of Christ, is race, gender, and sexual orientation neutral.

The Judgment of Christ and the Church

That said, a parallel position is irrevocable. Neither the Gospel nor the Church nor Jesus Christ are *deviant behavior* neutral.[336] Clearly, homosexual acts are contrary to the Word of God and severely judged by that Word. Persons, εν χριστώ, in Christ, refrain from these sins that dare not be tolerated in the Christian life nor condoned in the fellowship of the Church. The Scriptures emphasize that sexual deviants are thrust outside the kingdom of God. Lest Christians who uphold what the Bible teaches in this regard be accused of homophobia, recall that the Scriptures are incisive in their judgment against homosexual sin (Rom 1:24–27; 1 Cor 6:9–10; cf. Lev 18:22; 20:13). God's judg-

334 Robert W. Weise, "Christian Responses to the Culture's Normalization of Homosexuality," *Concordia Journal* 31, no. 3 (July 2005): 234

335 Ibid., 247.

336 That the four Gospels do not record a specific word from Jesus condemning same-sex relations cannot be turned into an argument that our Lord was either indifferent or approving of such deviant action, nor that His apparent silence essentially represses the fierce judgment against homosexual behavior cited elsewhere in the Scriptures. Jesus did not mention other deviant behaviors—bestiality (Lev 18:23; 20:15–16), incest (Lev 18:6–18), or the abuse of people with physical disabilities (Lev 19:14)—a factor that does not indicate that He would tolerate or even affirm such behaviors. This is the first of a number of salient rebuttals to the argument above, set forth by Tom Eckstein, "The Silence of Jesus," *The Lutheran Witness* (October 2013): 4–5.

ments are no less severe about adultery (Exod 20:14; Lev 20:10; Rom 7:3; 1 Cor 6:9; Heb 13:4b) or about fornication, illicit sex relations outside of heterosexual marriage (1 Cor 6:18; Matt 5:32; Acts 15:29; Eph 5:3; 1 Cor 6:9; cf. Deut 22:28–29).[337]

The Church's Care for Homosexuals and Lesbians

Deviant behaviors can be temptations. No Christian is sheltered from the darkness of the fallen age. Therefore, all Christians should find refuge in the fellowship of the Church. The local congregation serves as that safe place. Not only must the Church observe the distinction between homosexuality as a sexual orientation and outright overt homosexual behavior, it must act in accord with that distinction. One big step is to avoid ill-founded assumptions and uncharitable labeling of homosexual persons. In verbal and nonverbal language, we emphasize our common denominator, *simul justus et peccator*, that we are all sinners, but then all are justified for the sake of the righteousness of our Lord Jesus Christ and His propitiatory sacrifice of Himself on the cross for our sins (Rom 3:21–28). For the sake of Christ, God justifies both heterosexuals and homosexuals on the ground of faith in Jesus (cf. Rom 3:30). In this action of justification, our Lord sets His Church on a level playing field by means of the Gospel. It is a level playing field, especially with respect to homosexuals. Thus, closure to numerous sensitivities over sexual orientation in the Christian community comes with the Gospel truth that God is our gracious God to one and all (cf. Rom 3:28–30).

Accompanying Care, Restraints and Constraints

Every Christian is constrained to manage his or her sexual life in accord with the Sixth Commandment as explained by Luther, to lead a chaste and decent life in word and action (cf. 1 Thess 4:3–4). This begins when all respect the *locus* where God placed sexual intimacy, within the boundaries of marriage (Gen 2:24; Matt 19:5–6; cf. 1 Cor 7:2–4). Nothing shall extricate sex from within the confines of marriage. This divine principle has a corollary, namely, the practice of *abstinence* by the unmarried. The exhortation for the single unmarried heterosexual person is "flee from sexual immorality" (1 Cor 6:18). Add the caution "let everyone who names the name of the Lord depart from iniquity" (2 Tim 2:19b). The heterosexual Christian who is single abstains from sexual intimacy because as one baptized into Christ, his or her body is the temple of the Holy Spirit (1 Cor 6:19), and that entire person—body and soul—was

337 Exegetical studies and interpretation of these and other passages from the Scriptures addressing illicit sexual behavior are legion. The publication by Dan O. Via and Robert A. J. Gagnon, *Homosexuality and the Bible: Two Views* (Minneapolis: Fortress Press, 2003), posts an extensive bibliography in order to facilitate in-depth study of Scripture texts addressing these matters.

bought with the price of Christ and His precious blood (1 Cor 6:20; cf. 1 Cor 6:13b).

This same teaching is for the Christian homosexual person. Again, pointedly, the teaching is *abstinence*. Not only fornication and adultery but also homosexual relations with persons of the same sex are forbidden (1 Cor 6:9–10; 1 Tim 1:8–10; cf. Rom 1:18, 26–27). The Old Testament Scriptures are unsparing. God views homosexual relations as abominable acts that defile individual perpetrators, a defilement that carries over to society and tarnishes the nation tolerating such behavior (cf. Lev 18:20, 22, 24–30; 20:13).

Abstinence is not easy. The burden of sterling Christian life is heavy for single persons. Suppose they desire to marry. Often a heterosexual Christian may not be able to marry or may be unsuitable for marriage, and a homosexual Christian may not be joined in marriage with a person of the same sex.[338] Unfortunately, Christian congregations may be indifferent to the pain endured by single persons caught in this dilemma. How may the Church minister to them and support them?

Taking notice of the singles population in the congregation is a start, and we must be done with shock, prudery, and quiet self-righteous condescension with regard to singles in our churches. Assuming the lead, pastors are there to receive persons as they are, to give them time and counsel and friendship.[339] Pastors listen. More, they agonize with persons who are struggling against fierce temptations. Pastors lift eyes to the cross of Christ, to the saving realities that transcend momentary passion. If Christians fall, their pastors empathize with disappointment, the regret, the guilt, the sin. They are prepared to offer the Absolution, the forgiveness of sins, and cleansing and restoration in Christ. Pastors send absolved persons away with the peace of God that heals the broken heart. Now and then a pastor must be *in their face* with the Law's fierce demands. The pastor speaks God's "No" to fornication and homosexual acts. But he is there, and they know it. He is there for them with God's "Yes" in Christ, God's "Yes" to them for Jesus' sake.[340]

---

338 The extended discussion whether or not the Scriptures recognize same-sex marriage follows in the next chapter. Here the discussion is about the tension between desire to marry and the necessity of single persons to practice abstinence in order to lead a chaste and decent life.

339 Jesus received people as they were—the woman at the well in Samaria (John 4), Zacchaeus the despised tax collector (Luke 19), the Syrophoenician woman who had no Jewish pedigree (Mark 7), the desperate woman who touched the hem of the Lord's garment (Mark 5), the professional and accomplished, but sorrowful, centurion (Matt 8). Jesus met them, received them, blessed them. Therefore, the Church cares and ministers to heterosexuals and homosexuals alike. For an approach to care for persons with same-sex attraction, see the article by Jeni Miller, "10 Minutes with . . . Daniel Puls," *The Lutheran Witness* (October 2013): 6–7. Ms. Miller references the work by clinical psychologist, Daniel W. Puls, *A Christian Perspective on Homosexuality* (St. Louis: Concordia Publishing House, 1996).

340 For additional background, see four articles published in *Concordia Journal* 31, no. 3 (July 2005). "The Challenge of Homosexuality: What is at Stake?" by Dr. David L. Adams; "Christian Responses to the Cul-

Cohabitation

A second major detractor from marriage is the common practice of cohabitation. That a man and a woman who are not married share bed and board has become fashionable. "Everyone is doing it!" is the plea. Christians caught up in cohabitation, also known as *being in a relationship*, often seek validation in the community of faith for their choice of lifestyle. How shall the pastor and the congregation respond?

The Christian community must see cohabitation for its true identity, distinctive altogether from marriage, and in its raw form, simply planned fornication. Some Christians want to be tolerant. They cite commonalities between cohabitation and marriage, but when it comes to the matter of mutual commitment, there is no comparison. At best, couples in a cohabiting relationship may say, "We are together as long as the arrangement pleases each of us." How does this statement stand alongside the marriage vow to love and honor in sickness and in health, for better or worse, until death do us part?

The Anglican divine David Easton exposes the inadequacy of cohabitation when he describes marriage as "the commitment which a man and a woman make before witnesses to remain faithful to one another, both as sexual partners and in mutual support, until death do them part."[341] Easton notes further how marriage and cohabitation have their own different standing. Cohabitation is a private arrangement with no legal standing . . . whereas marriage is a public declaration that has the backing of law, which is to say that a cohabiting man and woman shall inevitably see that their relationship is not just their business and no one else's but is of wider concern.[342] Some may view cohabitation as merely another *form* of marriage, but the Australian Lutheran theologian Hebart Friedemann puts this to the test. He states, "If the cohabiting relationship be regarded as another 'form' of marriage, then the prohibitions attached to

---

ture's Normalization of Homosexuality" by Dr. Robert W. Weise; "The Local Congregation Approaches the Issues: Lutheran Responses, Sin, Sex, and Civil Silence" by Dr. Joel D. Biermann; "Where Is the Holy Family Today?: Marriage a Holy Covenant Before God—The Biblical Role of Man and Woman" by Dr. Louis A. Brighton. Also see LCMS.org—"Frequently Asked Questions, LCMS Views—Marriage/Human Sexuality," specifically, "What is the LCMS response to homosexuality?" Also, see the LCMS document, "Ministry to Homosexuals and Their Families."

341 David Easton, "Pastoral Issues Arising from CoHabitation," *The Rutherford Journal of Church & Ministry* 12 (Winter 1994): 11. To those who press that consent to live together is sufficient in the eyes of God, Easton explores such a plea in the context of Genesis 2:24. He expounds this passage. "Marriage is first exclusive ('a man . . . his wife'); secondly, publicly recognized ('a man will leave his father and mother'); thirdly, permanent ('united to his wife'); and fourthly, consummated by sexual intercourse ('and they will become one flesh')." He follows with this rhetorical question in reference to marriage, "How does cohabitation fit into the scheme of things?"

342 Ibid., 12. In America, following *Obergefell v. Hodges*, who knows if at some time cohabitation will be granted legal status?

marriage in the area of adultery and divorce must apply too."[343] Are cohabiting persons willing to submit to these restraints?

Setting marriage and cohabitation alongside each other, the latter has no credibility in view of the Church's understanding of marriage described in the Scriptures. In fact, the blunt judgment is inescapable that in most instances cohabitation is open fornication, and Christians who stubbornly choose to remain in a cohabiting relationship commit deliberate sin that is a hazard to their faith and hope in God. This is the only charitable response the Church can give (cf. Heb 3:12–15).

To elder persons—widows and widowers—who desire to live together and avoid punishing financial penalties attendant with marriage, and therefore request that the pastor and the Church publicly bless their choice for cohabitation, the Church's mandate must be "do the right thing; get married." The same mandate applies to young persons who are cohabiting. Set the date for your wedding—this weekend or two weeks forward—go to separate residences, and in the meantime refrain from sexual intercourse, showing true repentance and the fruit of absolution for the sin of fornication. Come together at the Lord's altar, get married under the blessing of God, and receive the respect of the Church that prays for your happiness.[344]

Fornication and Promiscuity

A third detractor from marriage is the current sexual revolution that has led people to sully their lives by fornication. An anxious mother procures birth control for her twelve-year-old daughter who is at the threshold of dating. "You never know," the mother reflects. Reportedly, inside the athletes' compound at the 2012 Olympic Games in London, *protection* was openly available to service casual sexual relations. Universities schedule *sex weeks* as campus events. If these reports are indicators, our culture is defined in part by open sexual activity outside the boundaries of marriage. It is fornication.

How *in your face* are the apostle Paul's exhortations, "Flee from sexual immorality" and "Keep yourself pure" (1 Cor 6:18; 1 Tim 5:22b; 2 Tim 2:22; cf. Phil 4:8; 2 Cor 7:1). Either the Church awakens to the roar of the apostolic

343 Hebart Friedemann, "What is Marriage Today? Problems and Perspectives," *Lutheran Theological Journal* 31, no. 2 (August 1997): 63.

344 Many pastors and counselors will be critical of this *rush-to-marry* program for cohabiting couples. They question whether persons sharing bed and board are therefore candidates for marriage. This factor, they contend, must be explored in counseling sessions before conducting the Rite of Marriage for the couple. *Not a rebuttal, but a response*: consider the matter once again. Two people have been living together, and they shall continue to do so, except that a faithful pastor calls their cohabitation to account. Perhaps they should forsake fornication and get married. Of course, premarital counseling is in order. Counseling cohabiting couples toward marriage, a pastor will find useful the Concordia Tract by the Rev. Dr. Matthew C. Harrison, *Second Thoughts about Living Together* (St. Louis: Concordia Publishing House, 2005).

counsel, or it practices soft toleration of sexual indiscretion that diminishes marriage for young Christians. Is it time to develop an ongoing program of sexual ethics in the local Christian congregation? Can we challenge young Christians to strive for chastity so that later they bring to marriage a person worthy of the investment of another life who becomes their spouse (Rom 6:3–4, 11, 15–19; 12:1–2; 1 Pet 1:13–16)? Of course, the Church retains the parachute for the young person who has fallen—the pastor and parents with whom he or she may speak freely and from whom the forgiveness of sins is announced and assured.

The path of *safe sex* often leads to *sorry sex*. The Church, however, can set the young on a higher path that leads to happy and fulfilling marriage. Some possible steps along the way:

1. Dating as clean fun
2. Growing a relationship with a favorite person
3. Acquaintance with his or her family and vice versa
4. Helping one another
5. Deepening romance and love
6. Sharing aspirations and goals
7. Moving toward engagement
8. Marriage

Divorce

Divorce Happens

A fourth detractor from marriage is divorce. It is shattering. Divorce leaves its mark on spouses who separate, and it can leave children at sea—either denying them the close and loving care of parents, or essentially making them orphans. Indeed, divorce frequently confirms the aftermath of the fall. It exhibits selfishness, belligerent stubbornness, bitter hostility, infidelity, and other sins that press against a happy marriage. This is painful also for the Christian pastor.

Furthermore, divorce displaces spouses and fractures their circle of family and friends. It dismantles the identity of husband and wife and uproots them from the place where God had bound them as one (Matt 19:6). The devastation affects others. Family and friends lose connection with the divorced couple. This citation marks the toll on relationships:

> As a stone cast into a pool makes ripples far and wide from its point of impact, divorce of a Christian couple effects and damages people and relationships far beyond the persons involved in the divorce itself. This includes . . . personal relationships with: God, their children and families, their brothers and sisters in the faith at the local congregation, their friends and co-workers, neighbors in the community, and any who would look toward them as examples of Christ and the Christian faith.[345]

C. S. Lewis observed how the sundering of the relationship between man and wife is not to be considered lightly. It is not like the dissolution of a business partnership, but rather like a painful amputation or mutilation of a living body.[346] Understandably, God exclaims, "For I hate divorce" (Mal 2:16 RSV). A marriage ended by divorce dismantles what God made with His attending blessing (Gen 1:28; 1 Pet 3:7; cf. 1 Cor 7:17; AC XXIII 18b–19; Ap XXIII 9–12, 46b; LC I 206–207).

Divorces in the Christian congregation call for intense pastoral care. In large parishes, however, divorce frequently finds the pastor before he learns about a broken marriage. He is caught unaware. Mary and Bill were married eighteen years. One Sunday morning, Mary exited one of the worship services, arm in arm with John. "Good morning, Mary! Where is Bill?" "Oh, Pastor, Bill and I were divorced three months ago. I want you to meet John. Could we make an appointment with you, Pastor? John and I want to be married. We will be honored if you do the ceremony." Learning about divorce by *surprise* disarms the pastor's ministry to persons in broken marriages. The pastoral care burden is great.

Divorce and Adultery

Divorce frequently violates the Sixth Commandment, "You shall not commit adultery" (Exod 20:14). On the one hand, the sin of adultery, the act of unchastity, πορνέια—living in the one-flesh union with a person other than one's spouse, a one-night stand or long-term affair—breaks a marriage. A legal decree of divorce may follow. On the other hand, when a married person divorces his or her spouse for a cause other than unchastity, this action puts away the one divorced from the marriage and marks him or her an adulterer or

345 The Rev. Christopher L. Cole, "Pastoral Theology Exercise: Divorce and Planned Repentance" (unpublished paper prepared for a pastoral theology class at Concordia Seminary, St. Louis, Missouri, September 26, 2003), 6.

346 C. S. Lewis, *Mere Christianity* (New York: Macmillan, 1955), 82, cited by Rev. Hans Trinklein in "Planned Repentance and the Pastor's Role" (unpublished paper submitted for a pastoral theology class at Concordia Seminary, St. Louis, Missouri, Spring 1995), 12.

adulteress, that is, one bearing the stigma of being outside the marriage where he or she belongs (Matt 5:32).

Divorce—End Result of Desertion

Divorce may follow not only adultery but also marital desertion. Refusal to engage in sexual relations in marriage when no health impediment is apparent is desertion. Also, a husband's growing attraction to a woman other than his wife may be desertion. There may be no indulgence in sexual relations, but the attention he gives to the *other* woman destroys the loving relationship with his wife. In a more blatant instance, a husband launches into unreasoned tirades at home. He destroys furnishings, effaces walls, shatters windows, throws things, and takes knives and hammers in pursuit of his wife and children. They fear for their lives. Such extreme actions—physical abuse, tyrannical behavior—is desertion as surely as if the errant husband had left the premises and never returned to support and care for his wife and family (cf. 1 Cor 7:15).

Divorce Permitted?

The adverse actions of adultery and desertion raise the question "Is divorce ever permitted?" May a Christian in good conscience seek a divorce? Normally, pastors direct this inquiry to our Lord's words known as the *exceptive clauses*. Divorce, our Lord teaches, is always contrary to God's will, except when a spouse threatens the marriage by his or her behavior, committing adultery, that is, the spouse has indulged in illicit sexual relations, πορνέια, with a person outside the marriage (Matt 5:32; 19:9).[347] In this instance, the spouse offended by the adultery may initiate one of two actions. First, he or she may hear apology, contrition, and repentance from the errant spouse and then forgive and be reconciled again in Christ. The matter is ended, and the marriage continues, advisedly with the support of marital counseling. Second, the offended person may seek a divorce in the wake of adultery committed by his or her spouse. Though Christians will forgive and strive to save the marriage, it can happen that after being offended by her husband's act of adultery, a wife cannot receive

347 By the *exceptive clauses*, Jesus does not categorically approve of divorce. Nor is He creating an easy path to divorce with a good conscience. His words "except on the ground of sexual immorality" (Matt 5:32) recognize the radical offense that adultery is. By singling out this one radical offense, He emphasizes that divorce for any other cause is contrary to God's will and should not be named among God's people. But did not Moses grant to men in ancient Israel the privilege of procuring a writ of divorce, putting away their wives? Jesus acknowledges that it was so not because it was pleasing to God but because of the hardness of hearts of men desiring to put away their wives for negligible causes. For God's will was otherwise from "the beginning." The writ or certificate of divorce helped to regularize the status of a wife put out of her marriage by the arbitrary action of her husband (Deut 24:1–4; Matt 19:8; Mark 10:2–12; cf. Gen 1:27; 2:24). The Lord's teaching is consistent with the word that Yahweh spoke, "For I hate divorce" (Mal 2:16 RSV); and the *exceptive clauses* notwithstanding, He presses for the permanence of the marital union, which means that married persons belong nowhere except in their marriage.

him back in intimate relations. She cannot live with him in the way of a wife. She may procure a divorce.

Formerly, theologians designated the offended spouse the *innocent* party and the offending spouse the *guilty* party in marriages injured by adultery. Hardly do such black-and-white distinctions prevail within marriage. Certainly, a loving and devoted spouse can be abandoned by adultery committed by the other person. Although the *innocent* spouse procures a divorce, the pastor counsels self-examination for any overt action or subtle attitudes that may have been difficult or distasteful for the other marriage partner. It can happen that a wife's unloving disposition drives her beleaguered husband to another woman. In marital difficulties, there is often sufficient cause for both marriage partners to repent.

There is adultery, breaking a marriage by acts of πορνέια, unchastity. Is there also a subtle form of emotional adultery? And does this constitute ground for divorce? A wife has had enough of her husband's roving eye and flirtation with other women. Discovering his intimate text messages to another woman is the last straw. No sexual relations have occurred between the husband and the other woman, but his wife is incensed. Her perception is that her husband has committed adultery. Believing this, she pleads that our Lord's words are an indictment of her husband's attention to another woman. Jesus said, "But I say to you that everyone who looks at a woman with lustful intent has already committed adultery with her in his heart" (Matt 5:28). The offended wife claims that she is a victim of *emotional adultery*. She wants a divorce. Adultery as lust in the heart can be a precursor to illicit sexual relations, but the action of adultery that Jesus addresses in His *exceptive clauses* is explicit unchastity, πορνέια, illicit sexual relations outside of marriage.[348] A husband may dally with attention to another woman, or pursue his fantasies with pornography and essentially desert his wife. The misbehavior may deteriorate into a state of malicious desertion, but it cannot be labeled adultery in the terms Jesus uses in His *exceptive clauses* where actual πορνέια is the sin in question.

348 *The Bauer Greek-English Lexicon of the New Testament* defines πορνεία, *porneia*, as prostitution, unchastity, fornication, every kind of unlawful sexual intercourse. Usage of the term in the New Testament reflects this definition. *Porneia* is the designation for the man in Corinth who was living with his father's wife (1 Cor 5:1). Addressing immorality (*porneia*), St. Paul references a man who joins himself to a prostitute as one who becomes one body with her (1 Cor 6:16). Further, he employs *porneia* to cite conjugal relations outside of marriage compared to proper relations within the marital union (1 Cor 7:2–3). In other texts, the term is cited as one of a number of sins of the flesh (Gal 5:19; Col 3:5). The specific action of *porneia*, sexual immorality or fornication, is action not to be named among the saints (Eph 5:3). Distinguished from evil thoughts, the actions—adultery (*moicheia*) and fornication (*porneia*)—signify engaging the body in illicit sexual relations labeled as sin with roots deep within the heart (Matt 15:19; Mark 7:21). For an extended discussion of the uses of *porneia* in the New Testament, see *Divorce and Remarriage: An Exegetical Study; A Report of the Commission on Theology and Church Relations* (St. Louis: The Lutheran Church—Missouri Synod, November 1987), 24n51.

Besides adultery, is desertion that damages a marriage ever ground for divorce? The apostle Paul addresses a specific circumstance of a mixed marriage when one partner is a believer and the other partner is an unbeliever. He states that if the unbeliever wants to separate—to leave and not return—the abandoned Christian spouse is not forever bound to this marriage that is no longer viable (1 Cor 7:12–15). Until such radical departure, Paul counsels the believer to remain faithful to an unbelieving marriage partner for reason of the positive influence the Christian may bring (1 Cor 7:12–14, 16). The situation may deteriorate, especially if the unbelieving partner has no scruples about commitment to the marriage. The teaching "But if the unbelieving partner separates, let it be so" (1 Cor 7:15a) addresses desertion, stark abandonment by an errant spouse.[349]

Abandonment may take forms other than physical absence from the marriage and home. Uncontrolled rage, volatile temperament, threatening harm to one's spouse or children, emotional abuse that goes unchecked, unrestrained pursuit of alcohol and drugs, or persistent and deliberate and intentional dysfunction that impairs life in the home certainly burdens a Christian who tries to keep a marriage together. There is subliminal behavior that may precipitate physical abuse so that the family lives in a constant state of insecurity. When emotional abuse flares into destructive actions, it can be termed desertion. Advisedly, we describe desertion or abandonment as the departure and/or persistent refusal of a spouse to continue to fulfill his or her marital responsibilities and duties.[350]

---

349 Some persons who are eager to be out of their marriage with a good conscience may rationalize abandonment by their spouse, when, in fact, this is not the case. They have not been deserted or abandoned. Desertion is not physical absence necessitated by military service or business obligations. Nor is it separation imposed by illness, disability, or insanity, none of which constitute willful and persistent refusal to continue in the marriage. Conflict in the marriage is both disappointing and disruptive, but it is not malicious desertion. Imprisonment of one's spouse, though taxing and burdensome, is not desertion, though felonious actions leading to incarceration may have been foolish and harmful to the marriage. Frigidity or impotence that develop unexpectedly are not desertion *per se*, but they are conditions that should be addressed medically in the hope of a cure. Though sex in marriage is not obligatory, it fulfills a compelling need. Therefore, couples afflicted by sexual impairment should address this matter seriously.

350 This is our understanding of desertion by way of inference from the apostle Paul's discussion in 1 Corinthians 7:12–16. Note that some Christians read this passage in an extremely literal manner. They assert that the situation addressed by the apostle is a marriage between a believer and an unbeliever. Therefore, they reject any application of this passage to the dysfunctional marriage of a Christian to a Christian because neither spouse is an unbeliever. The apostle cites the mixed marriage in his example, but surely not to the exclusion of other failing marriages when desertion is apparent. It happens that some professing Christians abuse and ultimately desert their Christian partner in marriage. Shall a Christian spouse remain bound to a fractured marriage just because his or her abusing and deserting partner is an errant Christian and not a professed unbeliever? This reasoning cannot be the teaching of 1 Corinthians 7:12–16. And desertion surely happens also in marriages where both spouses are unbelievers.

Remarriage

Introduction—The Current Practice of Remarriage of Divorced Persons

Remarriage of divorced persons is a common practice in the Lutheran Church and is referenced briefly in the Lutheran Confessions. The Treatise on the Power and Primacy of the Pope, 78, reads, "For the traditions concerning spiritual relationship are unjust, as is the tradition that prohibits remarriage of an innocent party after divorce."[351] But requests for remarriage also come from divorced persons who were guilty of adultery and from others who recklessly abandoned their former marriage for petty reasons—not adultery, fornication, or malicious desertion. The Church Fathers dealt with similar situations. This may explain the diversity of opinions among them:

> Clement of Alexandria allows for the right of putting away for adultery, but counsels continence. Tertullian says, "You shall not put away your wife except for fornication, and [Holy Scripture] considers as adultery a remarriage while the other separated person survives." Origen states that there is one exception to this seemingly absolute prohibition of divorce, namely, the clause in Matt. 19:9, and regards divorce and remarriage as permissible. Notably, St. Augustine teaches that no remarriage is ever permitted, thus setting indissolubility as a norm in the Western Church. He permits a separation *a thoro* [*sic*] *et mensa* (separation from bed and board) in cases of *porneia*.[352]

Identity and Place Following Divorce

Divorces occur in the Christian community, and pastors walk closely with a Christian whose marriage ended. Through ongoing contact with a divorced person, frank discussions may include acknowledgment of sin followed by repentance and opportunity for the Absolution. Thus, the pastor helps divorced persons heal in the aftermath of marital turmoil and failure. When remarriage is probable, pastoral care assists a person to do what is right in God's eyes.

Remarriage of divorced persons depends somewhat on candid under-

351 Regarding the prohibition to remarry, the editors of the Kolb-Wengert edition of *The Book of Concord* note that the Church Fathers based their position forbidding remarriage after divorce on Matthew 5:32; Mark 10:11; Luke 16:18. *Book of Concord*, Kolb-Wengert, 343n69.

352 Harry G. Coiner, "Those 'Divorce and Remarriage' Passages (Mt. 5:32; 19:9; 1 Cor. 7:10–16) With Brief Reference to the Mark and Luke Passages," *Concordia Theological Monthly* 39, no. 6 (June 1968): 373n23. The limited excerpts here are cited from an extensive list of citations of the Church Fathers in this article regarding remarriage.

standing of their present place or stance. The pastor assists a divorced person to consider, "Where am I, and where do I belong at this time in my life—in regard to my former marriage, and in light of God's Word? What must I as a Christian consider with reference to my future decisions?" The apostle Paul's counsel is "Only let each person lead the life that the Lord has assigned to him, and to which God has called him. This is my rule in all the churches" (1 Cor 7:17). He follows with counsel for both single and married persons (1 Cor 7:25–27, 36–38). His words imply that a reality check following divorce is wise.

Counsel with Regard to Remarriage

Short of adultery or fornication committed by their former spouse—ground for procuring a divorce—a person out of his or her marriage for negligible reasons may still belong in that marriage (Rom 7:2; Matt 5:32; 19:9). The only other circumstance that may thrust a person out of their marriage is desertion on the part of his or her spouse who willfully refused to fulfill responsibility and duty in the marriage (cf. 1 Cor 7:12–16). In any case, considering the prospect of remarriage, a Christian now divorced will be candid and honest: "Where am I, where do I belong? In another marriage, in my former marriage, remaining single? How may I avoid the pitfall of committing adultery by an ill-advised decision concerning remarriage?"

A Christian who procured a divorce on ground of their partner's adultery or malicious desertion may remarry. Divorce for other reasons is occasion to pause. Is the former marriage reparable? If the former spouse is remarried or refuses to be reconciled or has died, it is not possible to return to that marriage. The Church does not prohibit remarriage when doors are closed to the former marriage and the divorced person has repented of sins, received forgiveness in Christ, and is determined to show the fruits of repentance in a contemplated new marriage.

In rare instances, however, the door to the former marriage remains open. The former spouse is ready and eager to take back the one who divorced him or her, but this person has moved on emotionally. Still pressing, however, are questions for this divorced Christian. "Where do I belong? If, indeed, I do belong in my former marriage, how shall I address this factor?" A pastor brings forward the apostle Paul's counsel for a woman out of her marriage where she rightly belonged. He stated, "The wife should not separate from her husband (but if she does, she should remain unmarried or else be reconciled to her husband), and the husband should not divorce his wife" (1 Cor 7:11). A strict interpretation of these words constrains the divorced person to either return to the former spouse because that is possible, or remain single.[353] Furthermore, the pastor shall not remarry divorced persons when they belong in their former marriage and the door remains open to them. Conducting the Rite of Marriage in this instance may throw the divorced person and his or her new partner into adultery (Matt 5:32; 19:9; Rom 7:2–3; cf. Mark 10:11–12; Luke 16:18).

Can this be the final word? Face this situation: a divorced person belongs in the former marriage, but he or she refuses to return and wants to remarry. The person cannot remain single and continent. Temptation to fornication is severe. He or she needs to be married. How does the pastor counsel this person? What is the better course—going it alone and dealing feebly with the weakness of the flesh in the face of temptation, or remarrying and pursuing a chaste and decent sexual life? Possibly Paul's words apply at least indirectly to remarriage of this person when he stated, "But if they cannot exercise self-control, they should marry. For it is better to marry than to be aflame with passion" (1 Cor 7:9 RSV).[354]

Remarriage—Planned Sin and Planned Repentance

Remarriage may be a means to respectability sought by persons who know that aggressively procuring their divorce—rejecting the wishes of their spouse, ignoring the pastor's counsel against the action, flouting the teaching of the Bible—is contrary to God's will. Yet they go forward with the divorce, an action they know is sinful; and later they plan to feign repentance in order to retain good standing in the congregation. In these instances, pastors have no alternative except to confront callous impenitence with severity. They caution, "Do not be deceived: God is not mocked" (Gal 6:7a; cf. 1 John 1:6, 8). When King David planned and executed the tryst with Bathsheba, the Scriptures report this searing judgment, "But the thing that David had done displeased the Lord" (2 Sam 11:27b). This thing that a Christian is doing—either planning

353 Another interpretation of 1 Corinthians 7:11 is that the apostle Paul may have stipulated a temporary unmarried state. But this could only be for the purpose of discovering initiatives toward reconciliation and reconstruction of the failed marriage where the separated wife should then return. A Lutheran woman came with a request to join a new congregation. She also requested to be remarried in the near future. Fifteen years ago, she divorced. At that time, her pastor counseled her to remain single and never remarry. This, he said, was her only option as a Christian under the teaching of the Lord's apostle. Now she has fallen in love and wishes to marry. Her conscience was bound by the counsel given by her former pastor. But she wants to marry, and needs to be married. How shall the pastor respond?

354 One may press this person to remain single regardless of the struggle with temptation, but the Lutheran father Ottomar Fuerbringer sided with Luther who reportedly stated that vice and sins should be punished by other means but not by a hindrance to marry, which would only produce new sins. The example given is David, having committed adultery with Bathsheba, he was still permitted to marry her, although God punished him in other ways. Citing this example, an added comment states, "Neither has the church the right to punish the adulterer by prohibiting marriage (1 Cor. 7:9; 1 Tim. 4:1–3) unless the state prohibits it." "Summary of Doctrinal Writings on Marriage—Mo. Synod," supplementary reading for a class in pastoral theology at Concordia Seminary, St. Louis, Missouri, 1960.

wrongful divorce or planning later to appear repentant—does not please the Lord.

When a person is planning wrongful divorce and *planned repentance*, the pastor should ask, "Do you really want to do this? Do you want to make a shipwreck of your faith?" (1 Tim 1:19; cf. Heb 3:12–14). The pastor continues, "Think about who you are and to whom you belong. Know this from the apostle John's word, 'No one born of God makes a practice of sinning; for God's seed abides in him, and he cannot keep on sinning because he has been born of God' (1 John 3:9). John remarks further, 'Whoever does not practice righteousness is not of God' (1 John 3:10)." This counsel is severe, but a pastor owes any Christian contemplating deliberate sinning a stern warning against apostasy (Heb 6:4–6; cf. Heb 10:26–27). The pastor stands by with the Gospel of God's love for sinners and His forgiveness, but he can offer this good word only when genuine repentance comes from a sincere heart.

Rubrics for Remarriage

Divorce and remarriage are complexities, but the pastor is clear and forthright when he states the implications of biblical teaching for remarriage. He also insists on honesty and sincerity from all parties involved. He is alert to any sign of *planned repentance*. And he informs disingenuous persons, what they relate to the pastor about marital issues is spoken before God, who knows the heart. Let there be transparency and honesty! The words bear repeating, "Do not be deceived: God is not mocked" (Gal 6:7; cf. Acts 5:1–11; Heb 10:26–27; 1 Cor 5:5; 1 Tim 1:19–20; 2 Kgs 5:25–27).

When counseling divorced persons in light of God's Word regarding where they belong and also with respect to where they want to be in their life, a pastor may remarry when the divorced person has reckoned with three parties:

1. GOD: Repentance for behavior and actions that offend against God and His will. This could mean procuring a divorce or concurring in a divorce action when neither unfaithfulness nor desertion were the issues. The reasons for divorce may have been frivolous or negligible and the divorce hasty. Also, the person repents for his or her actions that contributed toward dissolution of the former marriage, especially if he or she must account for behavior that provoked their former marriage partner to fornication or desertion (Rom 3:23–24; 1 John 1:9; 2:12). The repentant person has seriously considered remaining single according to the apostolic exhortation (1 Cor 7:11; cf. Rom 7:3).

2. SPOUSE: The divorced person seeking to remarry has forgiven his or her former spouse and has received forgiveness from him or her. The two are reconciled as Christians and share peace in Christ. The party seeking remarriage gives evidence that he or she has fulfilled all obligations to the former spouse and family. This includes agreements to continue financial support.

3. SELF: The person who wants to remarry recognizes his or her involvement in the breakup of the former marriage and has taken steps to remove and/or correct factors such as attitudes, outlooks, behavior, and habits that may have contributed to failure of the former marriage. The person seeks proper understanding of Christian marriage and demonstrates clearly that he or she is a good candidate for another marital relationship.

Preventing Divorce

Putting the brake on aggressive steps toward divorce, the pastor's general pulpit ministry directs proclamation to families, most of whom are dealing with marital difficulty of one kind or another. Can we cultivate a somewhat stronger family-directed pulpit ministry? In addition, the Church assists Christian couples to mirror their marriages—trouble, dysfunction, failure—in the light of ideal marriage that God intended for them. This process can be therapeutic, but its strength is surely theological. A couple discovers that their marriage has hit new lows—unresolved conflict stoked by tensions and verbal abuse, sexual dysfunction resulting in incompatibility, miscommunication, and so on. Facing these realities is uncomfortable and potentially devastating. Close attention, candid assessment, and, quite frankly, hard work is required. For starters, the pastor challenges the couple to regroup and seek the *high ground* together. Call it *Holy Ground.*[355]

The appended exhibit, Appendix 6 "Holy Ground—Returning to the Lord's Altar," consists of three stories or narratives. The first, "His (God's) Story," is marriage as God intended it to be. The second, "Our Story," relates troubled and dysfunctional marriage. The third story, "Our Future (God and Us)," activates upon comparison of the first and second narratives. These three scenarios featured in "Holy Ground" focus on the present realities, review the essentials of Christian marriage, and point to restored life together in the future.

In conversation, the pastor begins with either "His Story" or "Our Story."

---

355 See Appendix 6, "Holy Ground—Returning to the Lord's Altar." This exhibit can serve as a discussion guide during initial phases of counseling those in a troubled marriage. Also, consult the article by the Rev. Scott Bruzek, "Marriage as Holy Ground," *Logia* 6, no. 2 (Eastertide 1997): 17–22.

The latter is a story of how the couple is either coping or not dealing with their difficulties in a positive manner. "His Story" is the rehearsal of God's vested interest in the couple, His love for them, His design and plan for their marriage. The stories unfold. Soon it becomes apparent that for a long time the couple has taken wrong turns in the road. Now, the move is toward creating a collaborative plan of action, "Our Future (God and Us)." There are choices—a choice of direction, a choice of initiatives, or a choice of helps. The choices press for decisions and firm resolve: "We can do this!"

This exhibit of three narratives is not a counseling track, but it may intervene and halt the rush to divorce. It places a couple on a trajectory for counseling. The pastor may offer his own expertise or direct them to professional counselors. In any case, the pastor follows through. He is convinced that God's grace and forgiveness of sins in Christ can dispose of all that is ugly and point the couple to what is beautiful, stable, and secure. Thus, a troubled marriage may be reclaimed and renewed. Our resolve is crystal clear, "Save the marriage!"

Mixed Marriages

The marriages most likely to encounter difficulty are mixed marriages.[356] For instance, a young woman who was baptized and confirmed in a Lutheran congregation returns from college at Thanksgiving to set the date for her wedding in spring the next year. She meets with the pastor and discloses that she has fallen in love with a Muslim man. The two will marry, and she is there to plan her wedding. How shall the pastor respond to this request when a Christian wants to marry a non-Christian? Shall he agree to conduct the wedding?

The Scriptures compel the pastor to be guarded with respect to the counsel he provides and regarding a wedding that sends a Christian into a mixed marriage. Upon entering the Promised Land, the children of Israel covenanted to only worship and serve Yahweh (Deut 7–8; cf. Lev 20:22–26). They were commanded to separate from the Canaanites, a people who worshiped and served other gods (Josh 23:6–8). Intermarriage was forbidden. Young men in Israel could not marry daughters of the Canaanites; the daughters of Israel were not given in marriage to the men of Canaan (Josh 23:12–13). Add to these prohibitions Ezra's strict word against syncretism by marriage in later centuries (Ezra 10).

These strictures were in keeping with Abraham's command that his servant not take a woman among the Canaanites as wife for his son, Isaac (Gen 24:3).

---

356 Formerly, the term *mixed marriage* referred to the marriage of two Christians of different denominational identity. A Lutheran married to a Methodist comprised a mixed marriage. Today, the term usually connotes the marriage of a Christian to a spouse who professes to be a non-Christian.

Isaac, in turn, directed his son, Jacob, to seek a wife not among the Canaanites but from the house of Laban, his brother-in-law (Gen 28:1–2). The reason for this radical separatism is clear. Yahweh explained, "For they [the Canaanites] would turn away your sons from following Me, to serve other gods. Then the anger of the LORD would be kindled against you, and He would destroy you quickly" (Deut 7:4). These Scriptures containing strict prohibition against mixed marriage are written for our learning (Rom 15:4; cf. 2 Tim 3:14–17). They imply that Christians today advisedly shall not marry persons who worship other gods or claim no god at all. Christians should seek life partners among fellow Christians.[357]

The New Testament also instructs about mixed marriage. The apostle Paul asks the rhetorical question "What portion does a believer share with an unbeliever?" (2 Cor 6:15b). He provides the obvious answer in verses 14–15: "Do not be unequally yoked with unbelievers. For what partnership has righteousness with lawlessness? Or what fellowship has light with darkness? What accord has Christ with Belial?" Going against these strictures by entering a mixed marriage could place the Christian in jeopardy. In such a marriage, a Christian's confession of Jesus could be silenced. This shall not be, lest our Lord not confess him or her before the Father in heaven (Matt 10:32–33).

It is true that a Christian may witness to the unbelieving spouse in a mixed marriage with positive outcomes (1 Cor 7:12–14). At Corinth, the apostle Paul addressed the marriage of a Christian and an unbeliever, but his counsel should not be misconstrued as apostolic favor for mixed marriages.[358] The difficulty for the Christian in these marriages is apparent in light of the apostle Peter's reflection on Christian marriage, "Since you are joint heirs of the grace of life, in order that your prayers may not be hindered" (1 Pet 3:7b RSV). This is not the situation in a mixed marriage where even prayer may be repressed.

Again, Christians should seek marriage partners who are also Christians.

357 Some point out the caveat that in a few instances Israelites found spouses among pagan societies and nations. The sons of Elimelech and Naomi, Mahlon and Chilion, married women of Moab, a nation devoted to other gods (Ruth 1:4; cf. 1:15). In Judah, Boaz took Ruth the Moabite as his wife, though doubtless at that time Ruth had pledged loyalty to the God of Israel (cf. Ruth 1:16). Against the counsel of his parents, Samson married a wife from the nation of uncircumcised Philistines (Judg 14:3). Queen Esther presumably became wife to King Ahasuerus (Esth 2:16–17). There is more to these instances of intermarriage than meets the eye. In the case of Samson, the Lord used the alliance, seeking occasion against the Philistines (Judg 14:4), and the Lord's interest in the captive Jews was in the works when Esther became the Queen of King Ahasuerus. Ruth became ancestress to the Messiah (Matt 1:5). However, these mixed marriages should not be viewed as exceptions to earlier prohibitions, nor should they be understood today as implicit permission for Christians to engage in marriages with non-Christians.

358 The apostle Paul addressed current mixed marriages at Corinth (1 Cor 7:12–16). The Christian spouse should hold together the marriage to an unbeliever. A positive outcome could occur, the conversion of the unbeliever. So the Christian spouse quietly but steadily lives out Christian life and example to that end. This said, it is also clear that the apostle, dealing with existing conditions in Corinth, is not recommending mixed marriages.

This seems to be Paul's counsel for a Christian widow who sought remarriage. Do so, Paul advises, but "only in the Lord" (1 Cor 7:39). Is he saying, "Marry whom you will, but be certain that the husband you take is a Christian"?[359] Is the apostle's counsel an extension of his principle "Do not be unequally yoked with unbelievers" (2 Cor 6:14a)? Philip E. Hughes observes that the apostle Paul undoubtedly has in mind marriage and other venues where Christians function relationally—civil service, the courts, public worship. Hughes comments:

> The negative injunction of course carries with it the opposite and positive implication, that believers should be equally harmoniously yoked with fellow-believers, so that in marriage, Christian service, and public witness they may walk and work worthily of the Lord. True Christian partnership is that which exists between (to use another Pauline expression) *genuine yokefellows*, and that can apply only to those who already are one in Christ Jesus.[360]

We may assume, therefore, that the apostle Paul's stricture against bonding with unbelievers in numerous venues sharpens rather than clouds the caution against mixed marriage.

The Prospect of Mixed Marriage and the Christian Wedding

The prospect of a Christian marrying a non-Christian calls for comment. First, does the Christian home and congregation instruct and guide young Christians about the risks in a mixed marriage? Review again the instance of the young college girl returning at Thanksgiving to meet with her pastor and set a date for her marriage to a Muslim. What nurture did this young Christian receive during preteen and teen years about dating non-Christians and long-term relationships of this kind?

---

359 In the passage, 1 Corinthians 7:39, does the phrase, μόνον ἐν κυρίω, only in the Lord, restrict the widow who wants to remarry? Does it forbid her to marry a non-Christian? In an absolute sense, does the phrase forbid any Christian from marrying a non-Christian? Certainly, the caution is vivid. Whatever marital decision a Christian makes will respect his or her union with Christ, never placing that union in jeopardy. In his Greek grammar, Moulton takes the preposition ἐν in an extended local sense to denote, *in the sphere of*, especially of God [and] Christ. Prof. David Vallesky favors Moulton's rendering of the phrase and concludes: "It would be too restrictive of the phrase *en kupiw* to make the claim that Paul is telling this Christian widow that she may not under any circumstance marry a non-Christian." But the counter question is, should the widow indeed marry a non-Christian, and how does she do this, ἐν κυρίω? See David J. Vallesky, "Exegetical Brief: Does 1 Corinthians 7:39 Forbid a Believer to Marry an Unbeliever?" *Wisconsin Lutheran Quarterly* 94, no. 4 (Fall 1997): 295.

360 Philip E. Hughes, *Commentary on the Second Epistle to the Corinthians* (Grand Rapids: Wm. B. Eerdmans, 1962), 245. Some interpreters assume that 2 Corinthians 6:14a, "Do not be unequally yoked with unbelievers," sheds light on 1 Corinthians 7:39 in regard to marriage of a Christian to a non-Christian, making 1 Corinthians 7:39 absolutely restrictive of such a marriage. Again, Prof. David Vallesky takes issue with this view. He observes, "A study of the context of 2 Corinthians 6:14 . . . makes it clear that the 'yoking' Paul is talking about there is not marriage but religious fellowship." David J. Vallesky, "Exegetical Brief: Does 1 Corinthians 7:39 Forbid a Believer to Marry an Unbeliever?," 295.

Second, when a young Christian is dating a person who is a nonbeliever, the pastor may gently intervene. As her spiritual shepherd the pastor may counsel a young woman somewhat in this manner:

> You and Jim, we see you together frequently. Can some of this time together be an opportunity to invite him to know the Lord as you know Him? When Jim knows how important Jesus is to you, he will be attentive. Obviously he cares about you. Perhaps you may lead him to a point when he inquires about Jesus Christ and His Word. Our pastor's class is open and welcoming to persons like Jim. The two of you may attend. It could be a journey for both of you.

This conversation impresses upon the young Christian that dating can lead to a long-term relationship, which must include Christ and His Word. This is paramount for a Christian. If it is clear that the non-Christian is uninterested, a pastor may tactfully address implications for the young Christian. "Where is your relationship going without God and His Word? Can this be good for you? Is it possible that you are heading into stormy seas? Are you prepared for that? Surely, you want God's blessing for a life together that you may be planning." This guarded but pointed conversation is sound pastoral care for a young Christian who is dating a non-Christian person.

Third, if a mixed marriage is in the offing, the pastor is cautious not to alienate affection, but with candor he counsels a Christian, in this instance, the college girl planning a wedding and marriage to a Muslim:

> Jill, you seem so happy. I like that. You are one of our finest—a baptized young Christian woman, loyal to Jesus, your Savior, as Mary and Martha were devoted to Him. I am privileged to be your pastor. I am glad that you are here today. Now, where shall we go with this matter? What direction should our conversation take? What guidance do you think is appropriate for your pastor to provide, for your welfare, your good, your blessing?

The young woman may react. This is not why she made the appointment with her pastor today. She just wants to set her wedding date. The pastor notes that weddings are entrée to marriage, a major step that she takes as a Christian. She was baptized into the Lord's death and resurrection. His cross is her life, her pride, her belief, her confession. College life may have marginalized the marks of her faith, but she is here at her church with her pastor. Shall he not remind her that in all our ways we honor Jesus Christ as Lord and Savior?

Will she be free to do this in the marriage she contemplates? Will she be free to make decisions for herself and her family, hard decisions in the light of our Lord and His Word?

Fourth, in this instance, the pastor obliges the request and agrees to conduct the Rite of Marriage for the young Christian woman and her Muslim fiancé. Many pastors will disagree with this decision, but this pastor has decided to marry the couple, provided they agree to comply exactly with the counsel he gives in this manner, including compliance with five stipulations in their marriage:

1. The Christian shall be free to pursue her faith. She confesses Jesus, and nothing in the marriage dare challenge or pressure her to alter or abandon her steadfast confession of Jesus (Matt 10:32–33).
2. Spiritual nurture and upbringing of the children shall be exclusively Christian. Children born to these parents shall be baptized as Christians and educated in Christian teaching only (Sunday School, Christian Day School, the Rite of Confirmation).
3. The Christian parent and the children shall be free to worship publicly at church, and privately in the home, using the Bible in their devotions.
4. The Christian shall be free to send dollar support to Christian institutions—her church, the Christian school, Christian charities.
5. The wedding shall be the Christian Rite of Marriage exclusively, and the pastor will offer a brief explanation about assembling in the Christian house of worship in the name of the triune God as part of the Rite of Marriage.

Both the Christian and the non-Christian parties must comply with these five points before the pastor honors their request for a wedding.

A wedding for a couple destined for a mixed marriage requires some alterations in the Rite of Marriage.[361] The non-Christian party shall not speak the name of the triune God in any part of the rite. Following the reading of the Scriptures, the questions put to both bride and groom may be omitted.

361 These alterations apply to "Holy Matrimony," the rite in *Lutheran Service Book: Agenda*, prepared by the Commission on Worship of The Lutheran Church—Missouri Synod (St. Louis: Concordia Publishing House, 2006), 64–65. We acknowledge the need for such alterations alludes to the complication of hosting nonbelievers as participants in a Christian service, the Rite of Marriage. The sanctuary of the Christian house of worship is the place where the Lord our God chooses to make His name dwell (Deut 12:11), yes, the place where the new Israel assembles ostensibly to serve the Lord and cleave to Him (Deut 13:4). Thus, the apostolic word continues to overshadow these arrangements, "What portion does a believer share with an unbeliever?" (2 Cor 6:15).

Giving the bride in marriage may be uncomfortable for Christian parents. It may be omitted. When speaking the wedding vows, omit the phrase "according to God's will." The wording for the exchange of rings may be reduced, saying: "Receive this ring as a pledge and token of wedded love and faithfulness." The words pronouncing the couple to be husband and wife may stand, omitting both the concluding reference to the Holy Trinity and the words of Matthew 19:6. The pastoral blessing may be omitted. The prayer following the pronouncement should be a general prayer making reference to the couple. The Lord's Prayer and the Aaronic Benediction may stand.

Making these alterations to the Rite of Marriage raises critical questions: "Why are we doing this? Why are we conducting a wedding that sends a young Christian into a mixed marriage? In light of the Scriptures cited and discussed earlier, is this practice essentially indefensible?" The answer is a judgment call that each pastor must make. He may follow the discussion here, consult elsewhere, and make his decision.[362] The whole matter appears in this treatment of pastoral practice because requests to conduct weddings toward mixed marriage are common. How may the pastor best care for a young Christian woman in these circumstances? The present discussion cites one approach in the hope that she will be a fervent and loving witness to her husband in the way of 1 Corinthians 7.

Remarriage to a Stepfamily

Remarriage into a stepfamily usually involves stepparenting of children that one or both spouses bring to the marriage. The complexities of the stepfamily are numerous. Couples dating toward remarriage in these instances are advised to seek professional counsel.[363] The pastor, too, is a source for counsel and wisdom.

The husband and wife in a stepfamily will determine parenting of their children. Does the biological parent of children on one side have primary parental responsibility? Will supervision of children of both parents in a stepfamily be fair and consistent? The fair and equal distribution of provisions for all the children is another factor. Conflicts will occur in a stepfamily and the parents must be prepared to resolve differences and settle disputes.

362 The pastor may consider Luther's adamant opposition to the papal impediment known as "disparity of religion" that forbade marriage to an unbaptized person, either simply or on condition that he or she be converted to the faith. He cites Patricius, a heathen man married to the Christian Monica, mother of St. Augustine, and asks, "Why should that not be permitted today?" (LW 36:100).

363 For comprehensive and sensitive counsel from a Christian perspective designed for couples marrying into a stepfamily, see Ron L. Deal, *Dating and the Single Parent* (Minneapolis: Bethany House Publishers, 2012).

The stepfamily can be *family* at worship, and the children have equal opportunity to hear God's Word in Sunday School or in other classes. The pastor can assist the stepfamily to fit in and take advantage of Christian education. He shows interest in spiritual life in the home. A pastor may shepherd the stepfamily so that the Gospel of forgiveness and love in Christ prevails when conflicts occur. Establishing a family altar is a discipline that the pastor may introduce and teach. In the beginning, he makes numerous visits to the home and leads the devotions for the family until the father and stepfather can assume that leadership.[364]

364 See the exemplary devotions for a stepfamily, Margaret Smith-Broersma, *Devotions for the Blended Family: Living and Loving as a New Family* (Grand Rapids: Kregel Publications, 1994).

CHAPTER FIFTEEN

The Conduct of the Christian Wedding

Introduction

A prospective bride and groom visit with the pastor to plan their wedding. Their immediate interest is the wedding, but he is looking to their marriage. Because the Rite of Marriage proclaims and teaches God's design for a man and a woman in marriage, this chapter about the Christian wedding also treats preparation for marriage.

The Marriage-Friendly Congregation

Nondirective Factors

Long before this appointment with the pastor, the couple profited from a marriage-friendly congregation. They discovered ideals within a fellowship of solid Christian marriages. As children, they saw husbands and wives model Christian love at family life gatherings and congregational events. These occasions were often capped with dinners and table talk and conversation when husbands and wives enriched the children. A child from a broken home may attach to a Christian man who is a strong father figure or to a Christian woman who is a caring mother. Children gain from fellowship with families that model stable homes.[365]

Direct Initiatives

In addition to informal positive influence, a congregation serves the young with intentional preparation for Christian marriage and home. At their church,

365 Children and adults in casual conversation around a table in the church hall—the exchange of thoughts and words, the give-and-take, the speaking and listening, the humor, the fun, the laughing, the serious moments, the affirming of truth and values, the sharing in praise of God, prayer, the promises given and fulfilled—children absorb from Christian adults what it means to be devoted to Christ as His baptized ones, how rich the Word of God is for maturing lives, and how the Spirit blesses God's people.

preteens, teens, and young adults participate in workshops and classes that enrich their vision of Christian marriage. The subjects include dating, long-term relationships, sexuality within marriage, roles of husband and wife, vocation, engagement, spiritual oneness in marriage, and many more. The instructors and leaders are qualified persons from the laity as well as pastors and the church staff. When a congregation intentionally prepares the young for marriage, it alerts the community that the home is the foundation of society.

Premarital Counseling

Arrangement

The pastor's premarital counseling may be framed in a number of ways. There is much to be said for the Roman Catholic model, known as the *Cana Conferences*, group counseling with a number of couples as a precursor to counsel with individual couples. A popular marital counseling program used by hundreds of Lutheran pastors is titled, *Prepare/Enrich*.[366] A pastor uses reliable resources and arranges his counseling in two or three or more interviews.[367]

Principle: Pastors conduct the Rite of Marriage for couples only after premarital counseling. Normally, pastors refrain from impromptu weddings without counseling, though exceptional circumstances may prevent the opportunity for premarital preparation. In rare instances, the pastor marries a couple when they appear with proper licensing from the state.

Content of Premarital Counseling

Many pastors begin marital counseling by inviting a couple to develop an agenda of subjects they are comfortable discussing with their pastor. Their selections may include some basic topics that a pastor and a couple can explore together.

- In the Presence of God—Theology of Marriage, Family, and Home
    - "In the presence"—the spiritual tie that binds two as one
    - Consciousness that marriage is God's institution
    - Married partners, creatures serving in God's creation
- Love in Marriage
    - Intellectual and emotional ingredients in a relationship

366 See www.prepare-enrich.com. Also recommended is Zoe Score at www.zoescore.com.

367 See Appendix 7, "Premarital Counseling Sessions," for a sample arrangement of three interviews, or, if necessary, reducing the counseling to a bare minimum of subjects in a single-hour interview. Counseling sessions described in the appendix may differ from the contents for premarital counseling here.

    - Intimate life—mystery, giving/taking, both love and pleasure
    - The private enriching experience of "oneness"
- Roles in Marriage—Headship/Submission
    - Each partner's "place" and "role"
    - She is my wife; I love, care for, support, protect her always
    - He is my husband; I love, respect, and honor him, and I yield to his loving oversight
- Conquering Conflict
    - Anger, but never rage
    - Mercy, patience, understanding, forgiveness—the "Christ" way
- Communication
    - Fidelity, trust, transparency
    - "Determined" monogamy, faithfulness
    - Timing is everything when discussing difficulties
    - Equal time—listening and speaking
    - Contributing to healthy communication
    - Courtesies—civil behavior day-to-day
- Homemaking
    - Our "dreams" for a home
    - Our realistic capability to make a home
    - Business—finances, managing money, saving assets
- Children/Family
    - Two servants of God in His creation
    - God's design for our place in His active, continuing work of creation
    - Contraception—pros and cons
    - Childbearing and child-rearing—parenting
- Keeping the Marriage Lively and Challenging
    - Special time *for us*
    - Up and out of daily routine
    - Mixing up our ventures and adventures
    - Striking out for new horizons
- Marriage "in the Lord" (1 Cor 7:39b)
    - In marriage, two people *in Christ* by Baptism
    - At home, "God talk"
    - The special opportunity—worshiping together
        - Regular week-to-week presence at church for worship and Bible study
        - Sacred moments together at the Lord's Table

        - Taking *big issues* to God and His Word, followed by prayer
        - Pointing to things eternal
- Marriage and society
    - Building high the walls of morality around our home
    - Keeping out the tawdry, the unlovely, the impure (Phil 4:8)
    - In society at large, it is always "I am married"; then, it is "we," "my wife and I," "my husband and I"
    - Fending away temptation and the tempter

The Outline for Premarital Counseling Expanded

In the Presence of God—Theology of Marriage, Home, and Family

Pastoral counseling of couples toward marriage taps into the marvelous and mysterious working of God. He made them male and female and He redeemed them for a sanctified life. Coming together to be one in marriage is the matrix of a home and then a family (Eph 5:31; cf. Gen 1:27–28; 2:24). Only God could prepare this venture for them. They begin the journey, confident that marriage is where God wants them to be. They commit their way to the Lord and trust Him as they commit to each other (Ps 37:5). Marriage is God's extraordinary plan for them.

Formerly, pastors began reading the Rite of Marriage, "We are gathered here in the presence of God to join this man and this woman in holy matrimony." That phrase, "in the presence of God," is foundational. All facets of Christian married life flow from it: love, fidelity, choosing a residence, making a home, vocation, providing, sharing, serving, forgiving, restoring, accepting, generosity, civility.[368]

Love in Marriage

If the pastor has led, exploring the theology of marriage, he may pass the lead to the couple when he asks, "What do we mean when we say, 'I love you'? Can three concepts—*eros, philia, agape*—be components of love in marriage? How do they interact, and what balance among them is appropriate? Which are decidedly Christian expressions of affection?"

The pastor may proceed with other lead questions. Is lovemaking also love-giving? In intimate life, is there place for both giving and taking, for love and pleasure? Counsel here is less instruction about *what* and *how* as it is to enrich and ennoble. The Lord spoke about sex in marriage when He stated,

---

368 Stirring sensibilities to the sanctity and loveliness of Christian marriage is the winsome small volume, titled, *In the Presence of God*, by Otto W. Toelke. This devotional booklet for those newly married first appeared in 1961 and remains a classic today, published by Concordia Publishing House, St. Louis, Missouri.

"and the two shall become one" (Matt 19:5–6). The physiological dimension of sexual union is transcended by *oneness* when each partner discloses self to the other, both embracing the other self and being embraced. They find themselves in private mystery, a sanctuary where each knows and is known in a way that is completely fulfilling to both. Mindful of this beautiful mystery, lust fades away. The pastor counsels, "Husband, discover and fulfill the needs of your wife; and wife, be intent on fulfilling the needs of your husband." Knowing each other in this way is unselfish, and it will always be beautiful.

Roles in Marriage—Headship/Submission

Principle: When husband and wife determine behavior and action within marriage "out of reverence for Christ," the two spouses—subject to one another—discover the wisdom of the husband's headship, in the Lord, and the wife's submission, in the Lord. The pattern is set in Christ, who loved the Church, and the Church is subject to Him (Eph 5:23–25).

Mystery surrounds the union of a man and a woman in marriage and part of that mystique is the way spouses complement each other. It is significant that a man who finds a wife, finds a good thing (Gen 2:18, 20b; 8:18; 23:2; cf. Prov 18:22; 19:14); and a woman who is with a man in marriage likewise discovers goodness. It was God's design to bring the woman to the man as a helper (Gen 2:20b–22). St. Paul describes this complementary relationship further as headship and submission (Eph 5:22–24). The husband leads with oversight and care for his wife, and she looks to his headship with respect. The immediate context, Ephesians 5:21, reads, "submitting to one another out of reverence for Christ." The exhortation applies to life in the Church and to life in marriage as well. In the Lord, the wife is not independent of her husband, and he is not independent of her (1 Cor 11:11; cf. Gal 3:26–28). Mutual love, honor, and respect is the construct for life in marriage.

Conquering Conflict

Conflict is a reality of close living in marriage, but awareness shared by both spouses that their life together is hidden with Christ in God will temper intensity and lead to resolution of the difficulty (cf. Col 3:3b). Living by the Spirit, there is the will in both hearts to "put to death" all that is divisive and ugly when conflict is out in the open (Col 3:5–10). Making friends *quickly* with your accuser, as Jesus counsels, is a first step toward constructive resolution (Matt 5:25). Embattled spouses may benefit by reading several apostolic exhortations aloud, and doing so together. These Scriptures are helpful: Galatians 5:16–17, 22–24; Ephesians 5:15–17, 20; Colossians 3:12–17, 18–20; Romans 12:9, 14–19, 21; 13:11–14. Preface this good counsel with St. Paul's topic sentence, "I appeal to you therefore, brothers, by the mercies of God" (Rom 12:1). By the Gospel of our redemption in Christ Jesus, a Christian couple strives to prove in their behavior toward one another what is the will of God for them, that is, all that is "good and acceptable and perfect" (cf. Rom 12:1–2).

Communication

In marriage, husband and wife can prevent conflict by good communication, which has two couplets, transparency and openness, faithfulness and trust. The latter couplet is foundational. Fidelity builds trust so that marriage partners can be free to express their feelings in open dialogue. Fidelity that preserves a platform for dealing with conflict is about keeping the Sixth Commandment, "You shall not commit adultery" (Exod 20:14; cf. Matt 5:27–28). Infidelity destroys trust, and conflict thrives.

Further, communication in marriage benefits from sensible timing. There is a time for every good gesture. Candor and honesty will happen at a time when both spouses are prepared to deal with differences and seek workable solutions. Pose the question "Is this a good time to have this discussion?" Perhaps another time would serve better. Seeking the high ground, a couple may establish ground rules—patience and understanding, also forgiveness. Time for cooling it—allowing *give* and *take* to happen—is constructive communication. Listening thrives when emotions are in control.

Communication benefits from other factors. First, maintain healthy tension between *intimacy* and *privacy*. Both husband and wife need private time. Mutually honored, this principle will not threaten the marriage. Second, resist the drive to reform. Cease analyzing and scrutinizing the other person. By all means, do not keep records on your spouse. Forgiveness knows no such accounting (cf. Matt 6:14–15). Third, minister to one another with the seasoning of civility. In this house, we do not use the "F" word! Nor do we resort to coarseness. Here, we are courteous. We show appreciation and we give compliments. We surprise each other with special favors. We go out of our way to please and to be pleasant. Fourth, we are visible and transparent. Each of us is free to be open with our feelings, and we are more ready to discuss and resolve than to do battle in conflict. Instead of giving the quiet *treatment*, we bring strong feelings to the surface and deal with them. Fifth, when one says, "I am sorry," we respond not with aloofness or rejection but as Christ has forgiven both of us. We forgive and the matter is settled.

Homemaking

Couples aspire to have their own home. Pastors, however, remind that *home* is more than material assets—land, property, house, accessories. Home is their life, also the altar they build, that is, their attention to the Word of God, prayer, and speaking to each other their faith and trust in God. Further, their extended dwelling is with God's people in His house on the Lord's Day (Ps 26:8).

Children/Family

The decision to have children or not, family planning, scheduling the birth of children at the right juncture in marriage, or delaying that prospect, are powerful drivers. Thus, the pastor calls attention to the Creator's purpose for marriage. Husband and wife are His servants. They fulfill His active work of continuing creation, and they attend to this without delay. Bringing the man and the woman together in the beginning, God said to them, "Be fruitful and multiply and fill the earth" (Gen 1:28). The preface to this mandate is "God blessed them." Children are God's blessing to husband and wife (Ps 127:3–5; 128:3–4; Gen 4:1, 25, cf. Gen 15:5–6; 16:1a; 17:15–16; Mark 10:13–16).

Marriage is the matrix for childbirth and family. Sexual power to bear children is not entirely a private matter. It is named *procreation*, meaning, as David R. Mace reflects eloquently, "creation for and on behalf of another—and the other is God Himself."[369] In this way, marriage is *dominical*. Having children is of the Lord. The question is, Shall married couples fulfill God's purpose, or shall they thwart God's purpose and will? Either children are desired as God's blessing—the love of husband and wife for each other blossoming into shared love for a child born of their flesh and blood—or the prospect of children is perceived as an impediment to secondary goals, one kind or another. This is not to trivialize valid concerns a couple may have, but happiness in marriage results when God blesses with children who require love and self-sacrifice.

For couples struggling with infertility, the pastor advises seeking the best medical care for this condition. He reflects with them in the light of Sarah's apparent infertility and Hannah's persistent wrestling with God in prayer for the blessing of a child (Gen 16:1a; 1 Sam 1:9–20). The outcome may be that a couple cannot have a family. Then, a pastor may counsel a childless couple toward adoption. The Lord may use them to provide love and care for a child in need of a Christian home.

369 David R. Mace, *Whom God Hath Joined*, rev. ed. (Philadelphia: Westminster Press, 1973), 17.

Keeping Marriage Lively and Challenging

Great effort attends to keeping marriage alive and interesting and enriching. The basic requirement is time for just *the two of us*, time to be out and away from daily routine, time to be together in new and fresh settings, time to pursue recreation together. Mix up the activities. Return to tried and true ones, but strike out for new pursuits—the ski trip in the mountains, the spot in the islands, a drive to stores in the next town, the sports event, or the evening dinner at a new restaurant. Pastors point couples to fresh and new experiences, outings from which they return, saying, "That was fun!" Or just quiet time at home may be a fresh experience. The weekly night out—date night—has helped couples keep the marriage lively. Pastor, put this question to a couple: "How do you plan to gain time *for us*?"

Marriage "in the Lord" (1 Cor 7:39b)

Two Christians in love will live as "heirs of the grace of life" (1 Pet 3:7 RSV). At times they will engage in *God talk*, the conversation that transcends sports, politics, or news clips and reflects on what the Scriptures say regarding many issues that cross their threshold. Though all thumbs at first, they gradually seek to know how the Lord is speaking. They check the Bible. What does God's Word say? A study Bible and a Bible dictionary help, as does the catechism and the hymnal. The Christian couple reflects and interprets life—family, society, church, culture—in the light of the Scriptures. They refer difficult questions to their pastor. They walk with the Lord as did the disciples going to Emmaus (Luke 24:15). In this way, marriage is "in the Lord" (1 Cor 7:39b).

The Christian couple worships at the Lord's house on Sundays. They cherish sacred moments together, kneeling at the Lord's altar for the Sacrament. Later, they will discuss the pastor's sermon. Together, they study and learn in Bible classes. This connection with God's Word and Sacrament every seven days helps them with some of the critical decisions they must make between Sundays, such as elective major surgery, home purchase, and schools for the children. They turn to the Scriptures for counsel, and they pray for wisdom to arrive at God-pleasing decisions.

In premarital counseling, the pastor demonstrates devotional life in the home, formerly named the family altar. He places a Bible in the hands of the groom and requests that he turn to a passage such as Luke 10:38–42. The young man reads the passage. What is the Lord doing? What does He mean by pointing out that Mary chose the one thing needful? Is that one thing needful for this husband and wife? If the devotion includes a psalm, the groom hands the Bible to his bride. She reads Psalm 119:129–136. Then the pastor asks the groom to lead the three in prayer. The couple may be all thumbs at this discipline. Perhaps they may try again prior to the next counseling session. The pastor recommends resources—a study Bible, a Bible reading program, possibly the devotional work from The Lutheran Church—Missouri Synod titled *Portals of Prayer*. He shows and demonstrates use of devotional works.

Marriage and Society

Marriage is a husband and wife in society—often as individuals—but always the husband married to her and the wife married to him. In America's jaded culture, pitfalls and temptations abound. A couple takes the offense, which means building a solid defense. In public, the assertion "I am married!" is such a defense. Frequently, Christians are caught up in unsavory circumstances. Standing firm in one's self-identity, "I am married!" fends off temptations. The Scripture admonition fortifies. James 4:7b reads, "Resist the devil, and he will flee from you[!]" In every encounter, a faithful married person asks, how does this situation, conversation, discussion, activity contribute to the strength of my marriage? Outside our house and home, I am never without my spouse. At all times, it is the *two of us*. Then, acquire this discipline at home. Build high the walls. Keep out all that is impure, unlovely, or tawdry (cf. Phil 4:8–9). Christians monitor television, literature, computers, and iPads, even the guest list when hosting parties.

Conducting Premarital Counseling

The pastor conducts premarital counseling in a manner that permits the couple to discover what is appropriate for them. This approach proves more effective than top-down directive counsel. The pastor does not lecture the couple. In the give-and-take of conversation, he interjects counsel and wisdom from the topics addressed above. The rapport between pastor and couple is important, therefore, some pastors take sixty seconds at the outset to tell about themselves and their calling. This self-disclosure sets the tone. The couple relaxes. They sense that the pastor receives them as they are. They freely convey their concerns and needs.

What develops is a relationship of trust. The couple looks to the pastor for leadership and wisdom instead of waiting nervously for what he might say that is judgmental of them or their lifestyle. Gradually, pastor and couple reach an understanding that welcomes insights from the Scriptures and from long-standing Christian marriage in the church. Opportunity for revised thinking and modified feelings occurs spontaneously. In the course of counseling, a pastor may administer questionnaires or inventories, but inept use of these devices can stultify the rapport we seek. Frankly, some pastor-counselors have abandoned the use of such instruments because rather than shedding light, they raise anxiety, which is detrimental. Take a cue from Bruce Rowlinson who frames the pastor's role in this ministry as that of a *coach*. He stresses the importance of a warm and trusting relationship established in premarital conversations with a couple. This growing relationship—pastor and couple—offers a secure step to a deeper relationship with the Church and her Bridegroom.[370]

Preparation for the Christian Wedding

Candidates for Holy Matrimony

The biblical teaching about marriage determines candidates for the Church's Rite of Marriage. The rite is for the marriage of *one* man and *one* woman joined by God in holy matrimony that is ordered by our Lord as it was in the beginning (Matt 19:5–6; Gen 1:27b; 2:24; cf. 1 Cor 7:2). Today, same-sex couples claim this same Rite of Marriage. They are supported by the Supreme Court decision that struck down bans on same-sex marriage in various states, thus giving homosexuals and lesbians the right to legal marriage in the United States.[371]

Same-sex marriage receives no support from the Word of God. The Church's Rite of Marriage, therefore, must be denied to same-sex couples. This is not about discrimination or contempt for homosexuals and lesbians. It is about the prohibitions against sexual relations of any kind outside of marriage for heterosexuals, sexual relations specifically cited in the Bible (1 Cor 5:1–2; 6:18; cf. Col 3:5–7; 1 Thess 4:3–7; 1 Tim 1:10). The apostolic warning is that those who disregard these prohibitions against immorality also disregard God (1 Thess 4:8).

This warning extends to the sexual union of persons of the same sex (cf. Jude 7). By engaging in same-sex relations, they forfeit the kingdom of God and trade that life in God for God's judgment (Lev 18:22; 20:13; Rom 1:18, 24–27; 1 Cor 6:9–10; cf. Gen 19:1–11, 24). When God created man and woman, He ordered their sexual relations to be the only proper relations, and only within marriage where the two become one flesh as husband and wife[372] (Gen 2:21–24; Matt 19:4–6; cf. 1 Thess 4:3–4).

370 Bruce Rowlinson, "Premarital Pastoring," in *Weddings, Funerals, and Special Events*, The Leadership Library, 10 (Carol Stream, IL: Word Publishing, 1987), 56.

371 The matter of same-sex marriage was argued before the Court on April 28, 2015, and decided on June 26, 2015, in the judgment rendered in case no. 14–556, Obergefell et al. v. Hodges, director, Ohio Department of Health, et al. A responsible response to this judgment is that from the office of the Rev. Dr. Matthew C. Harrison, president of The Lutheran Church—Missouri Synod. It is titled "Synod President Responds to SCOTUS Same-Sex Marriage Ruling," (June 27, 2015).

372 Affirming the single *locus* or place for sexual relations in the marital union and affirming the Church's refusal to conduct the Rite of Marriage for same-sex couples, the Rev. James Chinery stated, "God's Word forbids any sexual activity outside of a marriage between a man and a woman. Hearing and obeying God's Law in regard to sexuality . . . means that we cannot place God's blessing on something His Word clearly condemns." James Chinery, "Finding Home," *The Lutheran Witness* 132, no. 3 (March 2013): 15.

Furthermore, biological parenting cannot happen from sexual relations among homosexuals or lesbians. Same-gender parenting, though legal, has no standing within the natural order, and children raised in homes of same-sex parents are deprived of the benefits of both male and female parental influence. More tragic, they are denied the benefits of childhood with their biological parents. Heterosexual relations of husband and wife, however, are the precursor to parenting that is constituted within God's institution of marriage where He empowers procreation (Gen 1:28; cf. Ps 127:3–5; 128:3–4).

By taking this position, the Church faces pressure energized by the government to conduct weddings initiating same-sex marriages. Therefore, Christian congregations should refuse to conduct weddings for same-sex couples and clearly articulate this practice in their legal constitutions registered with the government. If pressures mount to the contrary, the Church should consider giving up the state's authorization for pastors to conduct weddings as a civil action. Then, Christian couples shall seek the civil ceremony from state officials, followed by the Rite of Marriage in the Church that solemnizes their civil union under the Word of God. This policy would counter pressure to conduct weddings for same-sex couples, and it would reserve the Church's Rite of Marriage for heterosexual couples only. The wording in the current Rite of Marriage may be retained except for omitting the marriage pronouncement, or rephrasing it in the past tense: "Joined in marriage by civil authorities, we affirm you as husband and wife, seeking for you the blessing of the Father and the Son and the Holy Spirit."

Readiness to Conduct Weddings

Pastors who conduct thirty-plus weddings annually may find themselves in a state of *wedding malaise*, especially if they conduct wedding rehearsals too. The same is true of many pastors whose wedding schedule is more limited. Every wedding, however, is a unique event in the lives of couples, their families, and friends. Pastors, therefore, owe enthusiastic attention to weddings. The pastor's eagerness to participate in joy and happiness at weddings serves well.

The Wedding as the Worship of the Church

Apostolic Exhortation

Weddings and their accoutrements are diverse, and the plethora of customs can prove frustrating. Numerous factors—current practices, institutional protocol, individual preferences, to name a few—complicate the conduct of the Christian wedding. The apostolic word regularizing the use of spiritual gifts in the Church at Corinth also applies to weddings in the Church today: "But all things should be done decently and in order" (1 Cor 14:40).

Sorting Out Numerous Variables

This diagram shows the complexity of input from four principal sources in the planning of weddings:

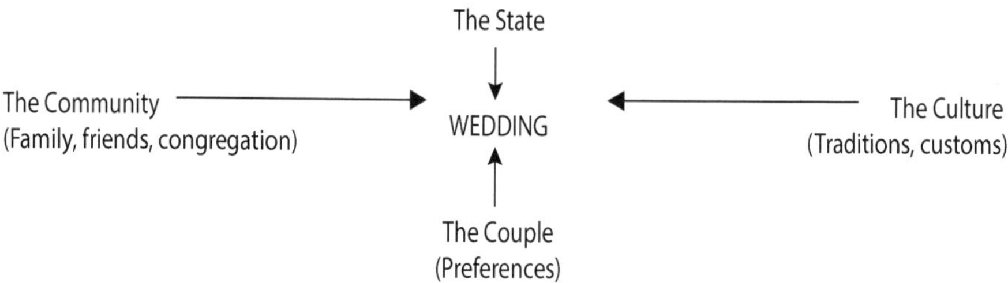

The state regularizes the wedding as a legal public rite so that the couple is received by society as married. The community, comprised of family, friends, congregation, neighbors, and more, brings expectations. The culture has powerful influence. The Church within the culture determines that the contents of the Rite of Marriage shall be distinctively Christian. Finally, the couple has their own expectations for *their* wedding.

The Wedding as the Church's Worship

Distinctively Christian, the Rite of Marriage invokes the name of the triune God five times—Invocation, exchange of rings, marriage pronouncement, prayers, and Benediction. The Scriptures are read and expounded in a homily. Also, the Eucharist may be celebrated. A called and ordained pastor shall conduct the rite.

Collectively, the parts of the rite compose the Church's worship and should be respected and conducted as worship. Some may distinguish the Rite of Marriage from the formal worship of the church. Luther asserts that the outward order of worship serves the purpose that God's Word may exert its power publicly, the Word that makes the people holy in order that their work may be holy.[373] The *work* framed by this rite is holy marriage.

Principle: When conducted as the Church's worship, the Rite of Marriage gives the wedding identity and character. The rite has boundaries within which various practices, customs, and traditions are properly reserved and retained to the glory of God.

373 Large Catechism I 93–94.

Music and Musicians for Weddings

For a wedding, the choice and selection of music—prelude and postlude, processional and recessional and interlude, solo or congregation singing—is fitting for the occasion. The wedding, we submit, is the worship of the Church. This principle below is advised.

Principle: Music for the church wedding is consonant with the public ministry that delivers the Gospel of Jesus Christ from the Word of God engaged for the occasion. Music selections should draw the wedding party and all in attendance to honor and hear the Word of God with hearts receptive to the Holy Spirit's working through the Word.

Music for weddings, therefore, is commonly similar to the church's music for divine worship services on Sunday. This working principle rules out secular or subjective music that lacks consonance with the Church's worship.[374] The Church offers a vast repertoire so that pastors and church musicians may assist couples in choosing sacred music. The musicians—organists, soloists, guitarists, ensembles—advisedly are personnel who possess a sense for the sacred and who render music that is edifying to the worshiping congregation.

When counseling couples, pastors and church musicians have wrestled with two music selections requested frequently. They are the Wedding March from Richard Wagner's opera *Lohengrin*, requested for the processional, and Felix Mendelssohn's music from the Shakespearian drama *A Midsummer Night's Dream*, selected for the recessional.[375] For generations, these pieces have been part of Americana. When a bride has focused on the Wedding March since childhood, she is not likely to alter her preference even when she is shown how ill-suited music from Wagner is for a Christian wedding. The better course is to oblige her request and prevent a serious conflict. The matter is settled, however, if the congregation prohibits secular music for church weddings.

Preaching at Weddings

When a pastor asks to include a brief sermon or homily in the Rite of Marriage, some couples reply, "Absolutely not!" Perhaps they expect that the

374 Modern ballads, love songs, rock music, rap, and such should be reserved for the wedding reception. Music in the Church honors God and the Gospel of Christ. Recall that the object of worship—and the wedding is the Church's worship—is not the *bride* or the *couple* or even a vague notion of *love*, but the triune God from whom couples seek a blessing for their life in holy marriage.

375 Wagner composed the Wedding March for Lohengrin, the central character in the opera so named, a figure from the world of spirits. The opera contains intrigue, mistrust, evil powers, and even false gods. When Wagner first heard that his Wedding March was used in church weddings, reportedly he laughed. Mendelssohn's march from *A Midsummer Night's Dream* is music composed to accompany the farcical and comical wedding for two animals.

preacher will say something that may embarrass them or their guests. Or they want to spare themselves of a message that is poorly prepared, such as they have heard at other church weddings. Nonetheless, the pastor can override their concerns by explaining that the Word of God proclaimed to the important state of marriage and family can edify them and their guests. When based on a text of the Scriptures and preached sensitively in a friendly style, the brief message or homily belongs in the Rite of Marriage.[376]

At weddings, the *overhearing* factor is poignant. The brief sermon or homily is heard not only by the bride and groom, the bridal party, and families, but also by a larger gathering of hearers in attendance. Careful listeners in the audience are eager to receive a helpful word from God for their own lives. Therefore, the pastor should refrain from citing divorce statistics and harping about marital failure. Reference to sin and repentance shall point to the counter truth that in Christ Jesus there is grace and forgiveness, the Spirit's power to get on with life. Point all to God's will for a stable and happy life within His order for their lives.

Marriage Vows

Marriage vows expressing the covenant a couple makes in the presence of God and the public should be spoken as they appear in the Church's Rite of Marriage. If a couple proposes alternative marriage vows, the pastor will request to see the words and compare them with the Church's wording in the formal rite. He guides the couple to say what they should say when speaking these solemn promises. He counsels against wording that suggests a tentative commitment or in other ways compromises the commitment that a man and a woman make before God and hold fast in marriage.

Prior to the marriage vows, the rite contains this question for the bride, "Will you submit to him as the Church submits to Christ?"[377] The reference is to the groom. In former editions of the rite, the question contained the phrase "love, honor, and obey." Whether the term is "submit" or "obey," some brides object to these terms. Frequently, their partners support their objection. This presents a teaching moment in premarital counseling, beginning with clear exposition of Ephesians 5:22–33. If the pastor is unable to persuade the couple to express the biblical headship/submission principle, this question, "Will you submit . . . ?" may be omitted.

---

376 Suggested Scripture texts for wedding addresses are found in these works: Paul W. Nesper, *Biblical Texts* (Columbus, OH: Wartburg Press, 1952); and *Sermon Texts*, ed. Ernst H. Wendland (Milwaukee: Northwestern Publishing House, 1984).

377 See *Lutheran Service Book: Agenda*, 68.

The Nuptial Eucharist

When the Lord's Supper is celebrated with the Rite of Marriage, it is not for the couple only but also for the bridal party, the families, and the larger congregation. All partaking of the Sacrament should prepare to approach the Lord's Table.

Principle: No less than other celebrations of the Eucharist as part of the divine service, those who commune at a wedding shall approach the Lord's Table in repentance for their sins, in true faith in Christ their Savior, and in conscious anticipation of receiving His body and blood for the remission of sins. Thus, all who commune have examined themselves as directed by the apostle Paul (1 Cor 11:28–29).

Such preparation is problematic, and the oversight of preparation is equally difficult. How can the pastor know that guests at a wedding are truly worthy and well prepared to partake of the Sacrament?

Setting boundaries will prevent a situation of *open Communion*. This can be done by inserting a printed card with the wedding invitation that informs guests that the Lord's Supper will be celebrated. They may respond to an insert that is similar to this sample:

At their wedding, Jim and Jill desire to partake of the Lord's Supper.

Guests who are members of congregations
of The Lutheran Church—Missouri Synod

Are invited

To partake of Holy Communion with Jim and Jill.

Make your intention to commune known in advance
to the Pastor of St. Mark's Lutheran Church.

Call the church office at (555) 555-5555.

When celebrated in a wedding service, the Eucharist follows the Rite of Marriage. At that time, the pastor may repeat publicly the invitation to commune. He announces that those guests who are members of congregations of The Lutheran Church—Missouri Synod and have previously announced their intention to partake of the Lord's Supper may join the bridal party at the altar and receive the Lord's body and blood.

Because the celebration of the Lord's Supper in an open assembly is problematic, the couple may elect to commune together the Sunday prior to their wedding as an alternative. Communing in this manner with the Church is preferable to private Communion, but private communing is a common practice. For example, the couple and their close families may commune either immediately prior to the wedding or following the service before departing for the wedding reception. Hosting the bride and the groom alone in the sacristy for private Communion is discouraged. In this setting, they may be distracted from the meaning and purpose of the Sacrament.

Protocol

State Laws and Local Ordinances

> **Principle:** The bridal couple, the pastor, and the host congregation carefully observe all state laws and local ordinances that apply to the conduct of weddings.

Weddings are civil actions and most states and counties in America regulate their conduct. Government offices oversee acquisition of marriage licenses and their proper disposition after a wedding. Regulations apply to engaged couples anticipating marriage and to clergy conducting the Rite of Marriage. Stipulations may require a couple to observe health regulations before the civil authorities will issue a marriage license. The pastor may need formal authorization to perform marriages. Normally, proof of one's ordination is sufficient, but some states require a thorough background check. Upon ordination or installation, the pastor promptly acquires the necessary authorization to conduct weddings.

In view of these rubrics, the pastor insists that he must have the wedding license in hand a day prior to the wedding. Further, after the wedding service, the pastor and witnesses sign the official documents. Portions of these legal papers must be returned to state offices. In some counties, the bride and groom must also sign the papers. The pastor attends to this matter promptly, and he sees that the marriage is recorded in the church books.

Decor

Floral arrangements as well as other decorations and accessories in the church sanctuary should be displayed according to established boundaries. Without boundaries for what is tasteful and appropriate, outlandish decor may result. Normally, the bride makes these arrangements. She inquires about the church's policies and coordinates with floral directors to prepare the sanctuary for the wedding.

Photography at Weddings

Technology enables recording a public wedding without intrusion during the Rite of Marriage. Many guests take photos on handheld devices. Professional photographers generally inquire with the pastor about boundaries for photography in the church sanctuary. Prior to the wedding service, pastors and photographers discuss the list of scheduled photos. The pastor may request that post-wedding photos that include him be early on the schedule. Aisle photos—processional and recessional—and a moratorium on photos during the Rite of Marriage is a reasonable arrangement.

Wedding Rehearsals

Wedding rehearsals may progress smoothly or they may be a nettling frustration. For starters, the wedding couple sets the rehearsal at a reasonable time when the bridal party and others can be present. Assuming that the pastor leads the rehearsal, he asks that all assemble in the rear of the church sanctuary. He welcomes the party and makes introductions, including the organist and the musicians. The bride and groom may comment briefly.

Then the rehearsal may unfold in this manner. First, take the bridal party to the chancel, show where each person will stand during the wedding, and share pertinent notations. Second, the bride and her entourage retreat to the narthex while the groom and the groomsmen stay in the area off the chancel. Rehearse the processional without the music and then again with musical accompaniment. Demonstrate walking down the aisle, meeting at the chancel steps, spacing or timing for each participant, and so on. When the group is stationed in the chancel, review the order for the wedding and the particulars of the Rite of Marriage. Give instructions about the close of the wedding service, and rehearse the recessional once, followed by formation of a receiving line in the narthex, if so arranged.

Rehearsals make for orderly and beautiful weddings. A rehearsal that runs smoothly should take no longer than thirty minutes. The pastor leads the rehearsal. A wedding coordinator or consultant may offer suggestions at intervals during the rehearsal. The pastor works directly with the wedding party and partners with them. He puts them at ease and shows that he cares that the wedding goes well.

Wedding Receptions

The apostolic exhortation to "rejoice with those who rejoice" (Rom 12:15) applies indirectly to joyful events in the Christian community. Weddings are occasions for the pastor to share joy and happiness with God's people. Why forgo this opportunity? Of course, if the pastor has three weddings on a Saturday—late morning, mid-afternoon, evening—he has some juggling to do. Still, he makes a point to be present at each reception and mix among the people as a friend. Disregarding wedding receptions is unconscionable unless the arrangement is by invitation only and the pastor is not invited. This may be the case when wedding couples are not members of the congregation.

When the couple is from the congregation, the pastor is usually welcome without a formal invitation. At the reception, the bride and groom look to the pastor to offer the invocation prior to the wedding dinner. Entertainment follows. The pastor monitors his imbibing, and he does not dance with any woman other than his wife. If she is not present, it is best for him to remain alone. At some point, he may graciously thank the bride and groom or her family and depart. He need not remain until the end of the reception.

Honorarium

For his effort in this ministry of the Christian wedding, the pastor may receive and should accept an honorarium from the couple or the family. Weddings are earnest work, so the pastor deserves a thoughtful honorarium. So do others: organists, soloists, instrumentalists, custodians. For these auxiliary personnel, the congregation may set fees. The congregation may set a minimum honorarium when the pastor serves couples outside the membership. In service to couples from the congregation, no such fee is set because weddings are the pastor's ministry. Weddings, however, entail considerable time and effort for the pastor. Therefore, a generous honorarium is right.

Private Weddings

There is more demand in recent years for small private weddings. The private wedding is comprised of the bride and groom, witnesses—best man and maid of honor—family, and a few friends. Normally, the total number of persons is thirty or less. These small weddings are preferable in instances when one of the partners was divorced, in cases of physical disability, or when pregnancy is involved. Economics may also be a factor. For the small wedding, a rehearsal may not be necessary. Private weddings may be conducted without music accompaniment.

Gifts for the Couple

Couples married by a Christian pastor should receive a marriage certificate, which they may cherish as a keepsake. The congregation provides this certificate. Upon receiving a formal wedding invitation, the pastor and his wife may provide a gift for the couple. It may be a memento that they customarily provide for all couples the pastor marries. The memento may be a cross or other wall decoration that helps to celebrate Christ as the unseen guest in the home. Or it may be a devotional piece such as the booklet mentioned earlier in this chapter, *In the Presence of God*. Or the memento may be an audio or video recording of the wedding ceremony, a lasting memory provided by the congregation. These gifts need not be expensive.

CHAPTER SIXTEEN

The Conduct of the Christian Funeral or Memorial Service—Ministry to the Living, Care for the Deceased

Introduction

The inescapable reality, death, is occasion for the Church's ministry. Death is as frequent as birth and rebirth by Holy Baptism. Someone quipped that since the fall, the death rate has remained the same: one per person. How shall the Church care for those who die? What is the Church's ministry to mourning survivors?

Ministry to the Living

Our Lord's Ministry

The Gospels depict Jesus ministering to people in death's shadows. He arrived at Bethany for Mary and Martha who grieved for their deceased brother, Lazarus[378] (John 11:14–27). Approaching the village of Nain with His disciples, the Lord met a funeral procession. He ministered to the grieving mother and widow (Luke 7:11–17). Again, Jesus went with an anxious father gripped by pain, losing his twelve-year-old daughter (Matt 9:18–19). The risen Lord consoled grieving Mary Magdalene (John 20:11–18). Jesus modeled for the Church and its pastors a ministry of care and empathy, a ministry in every respect *dominical.*

---

378 How telling is the secular dismissal of our Lord's power over death! In her article reporting on a Football Hall of Fame celebrity, the Rev. Aeneas Williams, pastor of the Spirit Church in St. Louis, writer Lilly Fowler referred to this pastor's recent Sunday sermon. "Williams," she wrote, "used the biblical story of the *death of Lazarus* as the text for his message" [emphasis ours]. How clever was the cynical denial. Surely Ms. Fowler was aware of the truth of the John 11 text, *the raising of Lazarus.* See *St. Louis Post-Dispatch,* September 7, 2014.

Initial Pastoral Care when Death Occurs

When a death occurs in the congregation, the pastor reaches out to the surviving family. He is there, and the Gospel is present. He greets the surviving family and friends, "Let not your hearts be troubled! You believe in Jesus, who rose, defeating death." Shortly, the pastor reads a brief selection from the Scriptures—John 10:14–15, 27–28; or John 14:1–6; or 1 Corinthians 15:1–4—then he leads in prayer, bringing deep feelings of loss to our Father in heaven. He closes with, "Peace be yours!" (cf. John 14:1, 6; 11:25–26; 14:27). The pastor leaves after this initial ministry. The family tends to phone calls, emails, and text messages, and makes decisions.

After his initial visit, the pastor meets again with the family to discuss arrangements for a funeral or memorial service or a simple private graveside committal. Both family and pastor coordinate with morticians.[379] Some families request that the pastor accompany them to the mortician's office. Decisions about choice of casket, vault, burial plot, and such are the purview of the bereaved. A pastor inclined to assist in these circumstances may gently reflect and advise. Subtly and tactfully, he may intervene if morticians or their representatives exert sales pressure on the family.

Extended Ministry to Grief-Stricken Persons and Families

Assisting a grieving family is the beginning of a journey. The pastor stays with the family for as long as it takes to regroup and get on with their lives. Not invasive or bothersome, sensitive pastoral care gently persists.[380] A caring pastor assures mourners that the God and Father of our Lord Jesus Christ comforts them (2 Cor 1:3–4a). This delicate ministry, we believe, can be the παράκλησις, consolation, of the Spirit. Staying in contact with grieving families, a schedule of visits following the funeral is helpful: two weeks, six weeks, three months, six months, a year after a loved one died. On anniversaries or birthdays when memories are poignant, the pastor may phone or send an email or text message. "Our pastor remembers. He cares."

Understanding the grief process assists a pastor's ministry. In her book *On Death and Dying*, Elisabeth Kubler-Ross outlines five stages of grieving:

---

379 In large parishes, the pastor may not hear of the death of a member until he receives a call from the mortician who has the surviving family in the office. Date, time, and place for a funeral or memorial service are decided in that conversation. The pastor may ask that the family visit his office or meet with him at their home in the next hours.

380 Following the death of his wife, a widower had to meet each Wednesday morning at the pastor's office. The man could hardly function, and these Wednesday sessions continued for a long time. Later, the man managed to travel. After an overseas trip, he did not require close care any longer. Through it all, the pastor remained constant. He was there for this troubled man.

1. Denial
2. Anger
3. Bargaining
4. Depression
5. Acceptance[381]

Grieving persons pass through these stages, but frequently they move ahead, regress, and then regroup and move forward again. It is a process of adjustment, accepting loss and moving on. The pastor is alert to steps along the way and adjusts his ministry to the family. His empathic response includes skillful sharing of the words and promises of God from the Scriptures. In addition, grief support groups provide the opportunity to express pain and discomfort among empathic listeners. Also, being there for others is a reciprocal ministry.

The Funeral or Memorial Service

Background and Purpose

The funeral service and the memorial service are intentional ministries to grieving persons and families. Normally, the remains are present at funerals but not for a memorial service. Usually, the interment precedes the memorial service that celebrates a life that was. In both of these services, the emphasis is on God's gift of eternal life through our Lord Jesus Christ (Rom 6:23b). In life or in death, we are the Lord's (Rom 14:7–8). "Blessed be the name of the Lord!"

Ambiance

Funerals and memorial services are less somber than in former years, but how celebratory should they be? Christians do not grieve in hysterical ways as do those who have no hope (1 Thess 4:13), but they do grieve, and they are entitled to do so. Thus, *celebration* shall not override grieving, as if grief is emotional weakness or lack of faith. A solemn tone that strikes a balance between grief and celebration is desirable. A bit of humor may ease emotional intensity, but hilarity is out of place.

Attention to ambiance suggests that funeral decor should not interfere with furnishings and artifacts in the chancel. A modest number of floral pieces is sufficient. Displays—photo remembrances and other memorabilia—belong in the narthex. If a paschal candle is used, it should be centered at the chancel steps or placed inside the chancel. Later, it may accompany the cross to the grave site.

381 For a brief description of each stage of grief, see Appendix 8, "Grief and the Sense of Loss."

Conduct of the Funeral or the Memorial Service

Planning the Service

The family may participate with the pastor in planning the funeral or memorial service, or they may leave all arrangements to the pastor. A service in the church sanctuary is preferable, though some families select the mortuary chapel. Others prefer a service at the grave site or within the columbarium. Families make special requests with regard to music, readings, Scriptures, sermon texts, and more. The confirmation verse assigned to the deceased is often the choice of sermon text.

Leading to the Service

In the time leading to the service, the pastor is available to the bereaved family. He visits at the wake held either at the mortuary or church. Some pastors make it a practice to be with the family at their first viewing of the remains. They draw the family together for a brief devotion. The pastor may read verses from the Gospel of John (John 20). Jesus appeared to His confused and grieving disciples and said, "Peace be with you." Those words are true comfort as only Jesus the risen Lord and victor over death can say them. We share that peace, and we pray.

Prayer for the mourners is also a ministry of the congregation. Is it possible to restore the custom of making a formal announcement of the death of a Christian in the worship service followed by a prayer? This announcement informs the congregation about the visitation and the place and time of the funeral or memorial service. If the funeral was in the past midweek, the pastor makes the announcement *post-facto* and speaks a special prayer, something more than a brief reference to the deceased among a host of terse petitions within the prayer of the church.

Rubrics for the Service and Other Customs

Preliminary to the Service

General rubrics serve the conduct of funeral and memorial services. When the remains are brought to the church, the pastor may conduct a brief liturgy, titled "Entrance of the Body into the Church." For preservice visitation, the casket is open in the narthex. At the beginning of the service, the pastor leads the closed casket and the bereaved, processing into the sanctuary. The pall, a white or purple linen covering with a large cross embroidered in the center, may be placed over the casket upon arrival at the church, or following visitation and prior to the procession.[382] When there is no procession and the casket is positioned at the chancel steps, the pall may be placed after seating of the family and just prior to the Invocation.[383]

The casket is often placed at the chancel steps parallel with the altar, but the rubrics call for positioning the casket perpendicular to the altar, pointing the feet toward the altar, with an exception for a deceased pastor, whose casket is pointed head first toward the altar. When it is time to close the casket, the family retreats to private quarters where the pastor has a devotion and prayer. Afterward, they assemble in the narthex for the procession into the sanctuary. The casket should remain closed during the service. If the casket is open, much of the comfort of the Word can be lost. This is true especially in mortuary chapels when, following the Benediction, all in attendance file by the open casket. Wrenching indeed!

The Service

The service begins with the Invocation and Prayer and Remembrance of Baptism, which are spoken from the narthex just prior to the procession. If sound enhancement is not available, these parts are best spoken at the altar after the procession. Following these preliminaries, the pastor steps to the lectern and speaks the Salutation prior to the Office of the Word. The Salutation is a strong saying comprised of verses that read:

> Grace to you and peace from God, our Father, and the Lord Jesus Christ.
>
> Unto our God, who alone has immortality, be honor and power both now and evermore.
>
> Our help is in the name of the Lord, who made heaven and earth.
>
> Like as a father pities his children, so the Lord pities them that fear Him. For He knows our frame; He remembers that we are dust.
>
> Blessed be the God and Father of our Lord Jesus Christ, the Father of mercies and God of all comfort, who comforts us in all our affliction, so that we may be able to comfort those who are in any affliction, with the comfort with which we ourselves are comforted by God (2 Cor 1:3–4).

---

382 See the rubrics for the funeral service in *Lutheran Service Book: Agenda*, 117ff. or *Lutheran Service Book: Pastoral Care Companion*, 110ff. The present discussion follows the order in these sources with allowance for some variation.

383 Note: Following the service and the recession, the pall is removed in the narthex prior to placing the casket in the hearse or the conveyance vehicle.

When the pastor plants his feet at the lectern and speaks this Salutation confidently, his stance and his speaking set an emotional tone that helps the assembly focus attention on the Word. It is a moment of stability when emotions run high.

Following the Salutation and prior to Scripture readings, the pastor may read a chronology of the life of the deceased. This reading may include: date of birth, parents, date and place of Baptism, confirmation, marriage, plus a few remarks about an exemplary Christian life, closing with mention of the time of death, age in years, months, and days. Mention of survivors includes members of the lineal family by name. Reference to aunts, uncles, nieces, nephews, cousins, and the like is best left in the generic mode to avoid unintended omissions or mistakes.

Today, the chronology is frequently replaced by a eulogy, sometimes multiple eulogies spoken by members of the family or friends. Has this practice exceeded reasonable boundaries? At one funeral, the daughter of the deceased gave a eulogy that exceeded twenty minutes. We are reminded that the eulogy, a subjective tribute to the deceased, has been discouraged in Lutheran funeral practice. When it is done, one member of the family should deliver the eulogy that stays within strict time boundaries so that it does not distract from the Office of the Word. The giving of multiple eulogies by several persons is discouraged.[384]

The Office of the Word—Scripture reading and the sermon—follows next. In place of the lessons appointed for Sunday, Scriptures that proclaim the Lord's resurrection and support belief in the resurrection of the body and eternal life are preferred sermon texts. The sermon expounds a Scripture text in a winsome manner so that the family may remember this text when they remember their loved one and take much comfort from this Word of God. Preaching at funerals and memorial services proclaims the Gospel. Thus, the sermon shall not be an extended eulogy, though the deceased is certainly remembered and referenced in the message. Admirable as his life may have been, God's mercy to a fallen sinner is the Gospel accent (1 Tim 1:15). Lutheran preaching avoids somber discussion of life and death, tear-wrenching sentimentality, and accents that are purely moralistic or humanistic. Sermons that argue against grieving or frame grief as guilt and imply weak faith are damaging. "Jesus wept" (John 11:35).

384 Supreme Court Justice Antonin Scalia paid a compliment to Dr. James C. Goodloe in regard to a funeral conducted by Dr. Goodloe at Grace Covenant Presbyterian Church. In his letter, Justice Scalia remarked, "But even in Christian services conducted for deceased Christians, I am surprised at how often eulogy is the centerpiece of the service, rather than (as it was in your church) the Resurrection of Christ, and the eternal life which follows from that." Chambers of Justice Antonin Scalia, "Letter to Dr. James C. Goodloe," September 1, 1998. In the Lutheran funeral or memorial service, discard the eulogy and exalt the risen Lord and His gift of resurrection and eternal life.

A sermon that reminds of God's promises serves well. More than a homily that embodies scattered reflection, the sermon speaks the central truth of the Scripture text and unfolds with structure that is evident, yet subtle. There is a point to discern, comfort to take, and a treasured word to keep. The sermon has its own structure, but it may include a number of recommended components.

1. Get in touch with the mourners, the family and friends, at the outset, possibly citing a shared experience with the deceased.

2. Focus briefly but gently on the reality of death.

3. Celebrate the goodness and faithfulness of God that is evident in Holy Baptism and countless blessings enjoyed during the life of the deceased.

4. Lead bereaved persons to peace with God and the hope of everlasting life through faith in Jesus Christ who is our sin-atoning Savior and the resurrection and the life (Rom 5:1; 8:1; John 11:25).

5. Draw mourners together before the living Lord who bonds us with the saints in glory.[385]

Other parts of the service are the prayers, the music, and the closing Benediction. Instead of a general prayer of the church or lengthy litanies, it is best to speak specific petitions prayed for the mourners. Petitions for them arise from the Word brought by the sermon. The pastor prepares this prayer that expresses hope of the resurrection of the body and eternal life with God through our Lord Jesus Christ. The same strong Gospel dominates the music. The somber hymns in the death and burial section of former church hymnals are questionable. Easter hymns are fitting, so are hymns that confess the faith in Jesus Christ. These may be old classic hymns or contemporary pieces. The music proclaims the Gospel. Some orders close the service with an exhortation to live in the strength of the Lord who is the life and the light of all. The Benediction concludes the service, followed by the recession.

In place of the lengthy regular church orders, this simple and dignified order of service may be suitable for funerals, especially when attendees are few.

---

385 This modified configuration of sermon components originates from a paradigm recommended by Robert G. Hughes, *A Trumpet in Darkness* (Philadelphia: Fortress Press, 1985), and set forth by Donald L. Deffner, "Proclaiming Life in Death: The Funeral Sermon," *Concordia Theological Quarterly* 18, no. 1 (January 1994): 5–24. Note: These components of a funeral sermon do not compose a sermon outline, which proceeds from exposition of the sermon text. They may enrich parts of the sermon bringing comfort of the Word to the mourners.

Preservice music

[*Seating of the family, pallbearers*]
Chimes [*One chime tolled seven times slowly*]
Invocation [*trinitarian Invocation or prayer of invocation at the altar*]
Prayer at the altar
[*Sentences or Psalmody, ending with the Gloria Patri*]
Salutation read at the lectern [See the Salutation above, page 305.]
Chronology of the deceased, read at the lectern
Reading of the Scriptures
The Apostles' Creed
Hymn or solo
The Sermon
Hymn or solo
The Prayer
The Lord's Prayer
The Benediction
Recession

The pastor leads the recession and accompanies the remains to the hearse. He stands aside at the door of the hearse until the remains are secured within. Then he travels to the cemetery or columbarium where he leads the procession to the final place of rest. The pastor attends to these details with dignity.

The Committal

Description

At the place of interment, the pastor speaks the committal, the Church's formal rite committing the body of a deceased Christian to God for His keeping until the return of our Lord Jesus Christ. It is a rite for those who gave evidence that they were confessing Christians. They cannot speak, but the committal expresses their enduring faith in the risen Christ and His promises (John 5:24; 6:27, 39–40, 44, 47, 54; 11:21–27). This special rite is also for the mourners and it gives them a living hope by the resurrection of Jesus from the dead (1 Pet 1:3–9). The committal is thoroughly Christological and soteriological, also eschatological. In the moments of interment, the great truths of the Christian faith coalesce and give meaning to the words *Requiescat in pace* (rest in peace).

Procedure

The pastor stands at the head of the grave, unless it is obstructed by the vault apparatus. In that case, he stands at the foot of the grave. When all are assembled, the mortician signals to begin. The committal service opens with the trinitarian Invocation and proceeds through the parts to the actual committal words, followed by prayer, the Lord's Prayer, and the Benediction. While speaking the words of committal, the pastor may pour a small quantity of earth or sand upon the casket, possibly making the form of a cross. Or he pours a small amount of earth three times, marking the three phrases of the trinitarian committal. If the casket is draped with the US flag, either he omits this gesture, or he turns aside a corner of the flag, places the earth or sand, and returns the flag in place. Military honors may follow the Benediction.

The close of the committal and departure from the site is a sensitive moment. Funeral directors announce that the assembly may return to their cars. At that moment, the pastor may move and speak a personal word of greeting or blessing to each of the mourners seated before the casket and those standing directly in back. Beginning with the first person, he shakes hands and speaks, "The peace and comfort from our risen Lord be yours," or a similar saying. Following his gesture of pastoral care to each of the mourners, the pastor steps aside and permits the family to pay their last tribute, regroup, and leave the site. Needless to say, idle chatter in these moments is inappropriate. Let the family have this time undisturbed and undistracted. Whether or not the pastor remains beyond dispersal of the people is a matter of judgment. In some communities, the pastor is expected to remain and witness the closing and sealing of the burial vault. A rubric in the committal rite states that the pastor remaining signifies the eternal presence of Christ with the departed.

Wording of the Committal

The words of the committal signify that the Christian dead are joined with Jesus Christ. The speaking of these words is a grand privilege of the Christian pastor, and hearing these words is a blessing to those who mourn. The words read:

> We now commit the body of our brother/sister (name) to the ground/its resting place/the deep: earth to earth, ashes to ashes, dust to dust, in the sure and certain hope of the resurrection to eternal life through our Lord Jesus Christ, who will change our lowly bodies so that they will be like His glorious body, by the power that enables Him to subdue all things to Himself.[386]

386 *Lutheran Service Book: Pastoral Care Companion*, 134. The phrase "ashes to ashes" has been questioned, and rightly so. It appeared as a late emendation to the Christian rite of burial in *The Book of Common Prayer*, 1549. Unfortunately, "ashes to ashes" is a phrase that is loaded with tacit inference that cremation is a proper means for disposal of the remains of a deceased Christian. The phrase should be deleted from this reading of the committal. For a discussion of the appearance of "ashes to ashes" in committal readings used by Lutheran churches in America, also in liturgies of other denominations, see Alvin

> May God the Father, who created this body; may God the + Son, who by His blood redeemed this body; may God the Holy Spirit, who by Holy Baptism sanctified this body to be His temple, keep these remains to the day of the resurrection of all flesh. Amen.[387]

At the pastor's discretion, the reading of the committal may be altered, abbreviated, or replaced in various circumstances. This is a sampling of readings:

Placing of Cremated Remains in a Burial Plot or Crypt

We commit his/her body to the elements in the hope of restoration to eternal life on the day of resurrection by our Lord Jesus Christ.[388]

Committal Reading When the Remains Are Not Present

(*This reading serves when there is no immediate interment. It may be spoken at the close of a funeral or memorial service. These instances include occasions when the remains are stored during a severe winter until interment in spring, when the body has been donated to science, or when the body is kept by means of cryogenics. The reading is suitable at a mausoleum where the remains have already been encrypted and the committal is part of a service conducted in the chapel of such a facility.*)

Forasmuch as it has pleased almighty God, in His wise providence, to take out of this world the soul of our departed brother/sister, (name), we therefore commit his/her mortal remains to God in the hope of the resurrection to eternal life, through our Lord Jesus Christ, who will change our lowly bodies so that they will be like His glorious body, by the power that enables Him to subdue all things to Himself.

May God the Father, who has created this body;

May God the Son, who by His blood has redeemed this body together with the soul;

May God the Holy Spirit, who by Baptism has sanctified this body to be His temple, keep these remains unto the day of the resurrection of all flesh. Amen.

J. Schmidt, *Dust to Dust or Ashes to Ashes: A Biblical and Christian Examination of Cremation* (Salisbury, MA: Regina Orthodox Press, 2005), 67–70.

387 The predecessor of *Lutheran Service Book: Pastoral Care Companion*, the agenda titled *The Pastor's Companion*, added words composing this phrase, "redeemed this body *together with the soul*" (italics ours).

388 This reading is adapted from Armin W. Schuetze and Irwin J. Habeck, *The Shepherd Under Christ* (Milwaukee: Northwestern Publishing House, 1974), 293.

Committal of the Remains of a Person Who Had Been a Professed Unbeliever

In this rare circumstance, omit the Christian committal and substitute the following:

Our times are in the Lord's hands. The Lord gives life and He takes life. Blessed be the name of the Lord! We commit these mortal remains to their place of final rest.

When the remains of a person who had been a professed unbeliever were cremated and placed in a crypt, say the following:

Our times are in the Lord's hands. The Lord gives life and He takes life. Blessed be the name of the Lord! Let us pray.

This brief, dignified committal is for persons who refused to be identified as Christians. For them, the Christian committal is inappropriate.

Recipients of the Christian Funeral, Memorial Service, Committal

Christ-Confessing Christians

Principle: The Christian pastor conducts funeral services and memorial services for persons who lived in Christ and died as Christ-confessing Christians.

The Christian pastor's funeral ministry is for Christians, but this practice has been modified extensively. Some pastors oblige any and every request for a funeral, memorial service, or committal. They accommodate requests from the community at large or from morticians who seek a clergyman to serve their clients. Other pastors limit their funeral ministry for members of their Christian congregations. Normally, they do not conduct funerals for persons they do not know. Some pastors, however, make exceptions and conduct funerals for nonmembers in some circumstances. The question is, How open should the Lutheran pastor's funeral practice be?

Pastors pursuing open funeral practice are quite vocal. They assert that the funeral ministry is to those surviving a loss by death and that the faith or confession of the deceased has only marginal significance. Many of these pastors attest that they never refuse a request to officiate at a funeral. Replying to the charge that they are *burying Sams*, they maintain that preaching the Gospel to any and every audience takes priority over criteria for accepting or rejecting funeral requests.

A more moderate practice is to serve the needs of people outside the congregation when it is clear that a deceased stranger was a Christ-confessing

Christian.[389] A mortician calls and reports that a family is seeking a clergyman for a funeral. The body was flown from a distant city. The pastor responds, "My funeral ministry is for Christians. It has to be this way. Is there anyone in the near circle of survivors who may attest that the deceased was baptized and a Christ-confessing Christian?" Although the attestation may be weak, the pastor may concede a point or two and serve this request. Also within the moderate category is a pastor's consent to officiate at a funeral for a person who was baptized but inactive in the Church for many years and distant from the Church's Gospel ministry.

Boundaries for Funeral Practice

The principle cited above regularizes the Lutheran pastor's funeral practice. It implies boundaries that are established by the Christian committal originating in the Early Church. That committal action commends the dead to God in the name of the Holy Trinity, and the remains await the day of the resurrection of the dead at Christ's coming on the Last Day (John 5:25–29). Furthermore, in this Christian rite and committal, the deceased is embraced by all that is Christian: the prayers of the Church, the reading of the Scriptures, the remembrance of Holy Baptism, the Church's confession of faith and profession of Christian teaching in the words of the Apostles' Creed, the Lord's Prayer, and finally the words of the committal followed by the Aaronic Benediction. Should the deceased have a place within this celebration of the death and resurrection of Jesus Christ through whom the Church boasts hope of the resurrection of the body and the life everlasting (John 12:23–26; 1 Cor 15:42–49, 51–57; 1 Thess 4:13–17)? It is clear, a person who professed rank unbelief or indifference to the Gospel in life has no place in the Christian committal at death.

Implications of the Boundaries

The Christian committal described here with regard to the deceased is the criterion for determining arrangements for a funeral or memorial service. The latter is most poignant. The focus is the memory of a person, and does that memory recall a confessing Christian? Further, the Rite of Committal references the deceased as *brother/sister*, meaning a fellow member of the Body of Christ who believes in Christ for life and eternal salvation. Is this true with respect to the deceased? Is the memory of the individual inclusive of that profession of saving faith in Jesus Christ? Broadly speaking, the referent is Holy

389 It is not and has not been the policy or practice of The Lutheran Church—Missouri Synod to limit conduct of funeral or memorial services only for members of congregations of the Synod. Lutheran pastors oblige requests to serve a diversity of families when it is attested that the deceased was a believer who confessed faith in Jesus Christ.

Baptism, which is the Spirit's attestation of the gift of Christian faith. Was the public confession of the deceased an integral confession of his or her Baptism?

The pastor's plea cited above, "My funeral ministry is for Christians, and it has to be this way," appears stern and delimiting. This is not the case. Consider again the boundaries cited above. They are quite inclusive, beginning with baptized members of the congregation. Further, the boundaries warrant funeral ministry and the committal for a broad range of persons who in some manner are audience to the Gospel of Christ. This audience would include persons on their deathbed to whom the pastor ministered, families who attend worship services occasionally as visitors, children or youth attending Sunday School or Bible classes, unchurched individuals who are receptive to the pastor's ministry of the Word of the Gospel of Christ, persons taking instruction in teachings of the Christian faith, and the unchurched person who gives a listening ear to the Gospel witness given by his/her devout Christian spouse (1 Cor 7:12–14, 16). These people are within the larger orbit of the Christian community. They may receive Christian funeral ministry.

The pastor will serve for a Christian who dies while under church discipline and also a Christian who fell into criminal and felonious behavior. In these instances, not all the t's will be crossed or the i's dotted in terms of Confession, repentance, and Absolution. Still, barring a person's outright rejection of the faith, the pastor will serve with Christian committal and funeral or memorial services. Similarly, the pastor serves when a Christian committed suicide. Leaving judgment over the action of suicide to God, the Church's funeral ministry serves because although suicide is not an action of faith, it may not indicate unfaith either, that is, wholesale rejection of the Gospel.

Refusal to Conduct the Committal and/or Public Funeral or Memorial Services

The instances are rare when a pastor refuses to conduct a funeral, but it is necessary when it is clear that the deceased was openly a professing non-Christian. To embrace him with the Christian committal or the Christian funeral or memorial service would not be consonant with his determination to not be named a Christian. To imply in any manner that he had faith given by the Holy Spirit would offend him and blaspheme the Spirit.

Although a public funeral or memorial service is inappropriate, still the pastor serves the surviving family of a deceased non-Christian with a ministry that is generous but also sincere and integral. He meets with the mourners. He listens. He may plan a private service for the immediate family at the church or mortuary followed by words of committal at the grave site or columbarium.

Most likely, the family is best served by a brief private service of interment only. The pastor informs the family that the committal will differ from words in the Christian rite. In a private setting, the pastor may bring a message based on the Gospel of John, the risen Lord's appearance to grieving Mary Magdalene (John 20:14–16).

> This is where we are today. Death lays a heavy burden on our hearts. Who can change this? Who may wipe away tears and dispel sorrow and sadness? We look to Jesus, who does such marvelous, yes, miraculous healing of the wounded heart. He is the risen Lord. From the grave He came, victor over death, and over all the sorrow death causes. That first Easter morning, He spoke tenderly, "Mary!" The risen Lord will not fail us. He calls us by name. So lift up your hearts and believe in Jesus. He is the resurrection and the life. He changes all for the better, and He is for you and with you, today and always!

Funeral Ministry—The Deceased Was a Member of a Non-Christian Lodge or Cult

Christian funeral ministry is complicated when the deceased was a member of the Christian congregation and held membership in a lodge or fraternity whose tenets, rituals, practices, or ceremonies are in conflict with the Church's faith articulated in the ecumenical creeds. That a Christian would participate in fellowships where the Christian confession is not honored or tolerated is an issue for pastoral care and counsel, but care and instruction do not come easily (Matt 10:32–36, 40).[390] Meanwhile, when a Christian caught up in this duplicity of confession dies, how shall the pastor handle his or her funeral or memorial service?

This is not a time to publicly excoriate the lodge and its teaching. Neither is it a time to soft-pedal, but focus on the Gospel in hope that the deceased saw and believed in Jesus Christ, his Savior. If the deceased lodge member attended worship services and communed, he was in reach of the Gospel and the Spirit working in the heart of one hearing the Gospel. The Church grants this much, but its public funeral ministry should never be scheduled back-to-back with ceremonies conducted by the lodge. A minimum of twenty-four hours should separate the Church's worship and the lodge's non-Christian funeral and burial ceremonies.

390 To instruct Christians caught in duplicity of confession with lodges and other fraternal groups inimical to Christianity, see chapter 19 of this work.

Funeral Ministry to a Family When a Loved One Committed Suicide

Ministry to the Surviving Family

Funeral ministry is pastoral care to the mourners, especially when a Christian loved one commits suicide. In the wake of this tragedy, survivors deal with two conflicting emotions. One is *anger*, that is, why did our loved one deal with us so harshly by depriving us of his or her life? Simultaneously, the surviving family is drawn to the person they miss with another emotion, undeniable *love*. What depths of hurt and pain! A third emotion stalks survivors: *guilt*. Questions linger. "What did we not see? Were we not listening? What have we neglected? What could we have done to prevent this tragedy?"

A caring pastor comes alongside the broken family. When the circle of their grief opens, he enters gently. He listens. He represses his urgent need to *say something*. Leave it alone for now. Let the grieving persons sort out their thoughts and feelings. Permit them to verbalize at will, unhindered by the pastor's need to be directive, to pull them out of the mire of confusion, doubt, despair, hopelessness, depression. This is not an occasion for clumsy, worn-out clichés that lack substance. There will be a time for the pastor to speak. That opportunity arises when survivors are ready to express and even confess the core reality of their faith that points upward to Christ the risen Lord. Let the right time for the Gospel come as it will. When the family wants the pastor to speak, he is ready with the Gospel.[391]

The Public Service for a Christian Who Committed Suicide

Our discussion proceeds to the funeral or memorial service conducted for the Christian who took his or her life. Former pastoral practice did not proceed in this direction. In fact, it did not proceed at all. Suicide was interpreted akin to the unforgivable sin against the Holy Spirit, although mostly it is nothing of the kind (cf. Matt 12:31–32; Heb 6:1–6). Sinning against the Holy Spirit is unconditional apostasy. Is this the case with suicide? Pastors and theologians once concluded that suicide forfeited any opportunity to repent for this sin against the commandment "You shall not murder" (Exod 20:13). Without repentance, the consequences are disaster—forfeiting forgiveness, condemnation, and damnation. Pastors in former generations reasoned in this manner, and they refused to conduct a Christian funeral for a suicide victim. This was the accepted practice.[392]

391 Instructive is the account of a Lutheran pastor who worked through the trauma when his wife killed herself. See Peter Preus, *And She Was a Christian: Why Do Believers Commit Suicide?* (Milwaukee: Northwestern Publishing House, 2011).

392 The Agenda used by pastors of The Lutheran Church—Missouri Synod for several generations was

Today, pastoral practice differs significantly. Suicide is certainly serious, because it shortchanges opportunity for repentance, and nonrepentance has terrifying consequences. No argument here. We concede the possibility that by premeditated defiance and action, a Christian may indulge in unbelief and precipitously take away life. This is a serious transgression against God. But who can arrive at such an assessment and judgment in the face of the mystery surrounding suicide? A larger question surfaces here. Does every Christian who commits suicide do so in denial of faith in Jesus Christ? A related question also surfaces. Is mental anguish or mental disorder or mental breakdown leading to suicide always an instance of ultimate unfaith? Answers to these questions transcend our limited capacity to discern. Leave the judgment to God and go forward, conducting the funeral or the memorial service in a manner free from overtones of judgment. Again, this does not question the seriousness of suicide. No impression should be given—especially to the young—that suicide is an option in place of coping with life and its difficulties. Let the Church not trivialize suicide, lest in copycat fashion the young imitate a friend who took his or her life.

Services for a Christian who died by suicide are according to the customary order. No special format is needed. We move with the tribute and the worship similar to services conducted for other Christians. A carefully prepared sermon may include five accents:

1. Acknowledgment of the reality of death that occurred by suicide
2. Questions that are as painful as they are unavoidable
3. The judgment is God's alone
4. The Gospel proclaims God's love in Christ
5. Commendation of the deceased Christian to God

The message of the sermon may develop in a manner similar to this model:

> God gives life, and God takes life (Job 1). This is not what happened. We do not know what strong feelings or what thoughts pressed our loved one. God knows, and we leave all to Him. We shall not judge. God calls everyone to account. But this we know, God is love (1 John 4)! His love embraced our loved one, and God's love will not let him/her go. In God's love, there is forgiveness of sins, yes every sin. The cross of Christ stands to exclaim this truth for eternity that the blood of Jesus shed at the cross

The Pastor's Companion, that contained no service, only a prayer that may be spoken at interment of the remains of a Christian who committed suicide.

cleanses us from all sin (John 1:29; 1 John 1:7b, 9). Our Lord who came to seek and to save reaches into our tragedies. He rescues as He redeems. Therefore, in hope we commend our loved one to God's mercy in Christ Jesus, and we await our Lord's presence and care for us in these and all the days ahead. Amen.

Care for the Dead

An Action Serving the Living

There is added comfort for the living when they know all is well for the loved one who died. The overture *requiescat in pace*, rest in peace, is familiar in the Christian community. This closure in peace is tacit ministry to the living. Resting in the Lord, our loved ones rest in that peace of God surpassing all human comprehension, keeping hearts and minds in Christ Jesus (Phil 4:7). The mortal remains in quiet repose await that last trumpet and the unmistakable call of the Lord, "Come out" (cf. John 11:43; 5:28–29). This is peace for us who survive, peace knowing that nothing can snatch the loved one out of the hands of the Good Shepherd and the heavenly Father (John 10:28–29). Everything that God does in His hidden care touches those who mourn and ministers to them (Josh 1:9; Matt 28:20b).

Care for the Remains—Burial, Cremation, or Others

Burial—The Christian Way

A corollary to peaceful closure is Christian burial. This assertion appears at first to merely project sentiment. After all, disposing of the remains by other means is increasingly commonplace. There is cryogenic preservation, depositing the remains with laboratories in medical schools, and burial at sea. Increasing numbers of Christians choose cremation instead of burial. The number of clergy and professors in the Lutheran Church choosing cremation is on the rise. While many affirm that the Scriptures do not forbid the practice of cremation, can it be said that the Scriptures make no judgment about cremation when the practice was resoundingly dismissed among God's people?[393]

393 On resistance to the practice of cremation in ancient Israel, Alvin J. Schmidt comments, "Throughout the Old Testament there is a marked theological *Sitz-im-leben* that shows cremation is not how God wants his people to dispose of their dead. Even pagan writers were conscious of this ancient Old Testament prescription. For instance, the first-century Roman writer Tacitus wrote that the Hebrews 'bury rather than burn dead bodies'" (*The Histories* 5:5). Alvin J. Schmidt, *Dust to Dust or Ashes to Ashes?*, 31. Elsewhere, Schmidt states, "For there is not a single biblical case where God commanded cremating any individual as an act of honor or blessing." Ibid., 90–91.

The long-standing preference in the Judeo-Christian tradition is burial in the earth or in tombs hewn from the stone of the hills. Burial is in view when the traditional Christian committal says, "earth to earth, dust to dust" (cf. Gen 3:19). The Bible reports numerous accounts of burial. "Abraham buried Sarah, his wife" (Gen 23:19). "Then he [Jacob] commanded them and said to them, 'I am to be gathered to my people; bury me with my fathers in the cave that is in the field of Ephron the Hittite'" (Gen 49:29). This was done as Jacob requested. "So Joseph went up to bury his father" (Gen 50:7). The Lord God administered burial for His servant, Moses (Deut 34:5–6). Later is the account of Solomon's burial, "And Solomon slept with his fathers and was buried in the city of David his father" (2 Chr 9:31). The body of our Lord was buried. He had commented about the woman who anointed Him with precious and costly ointment, "In pouring this ointment on My body, she has done it to prepare Me for burial" (Matt 26:12; cf. Matt 27:58–60). In the apostolic church, observe that the women prepared the remains of Dorcas for burial[394] (Acts 9:36–37; cf. John 19:39–42; 20:5–6; Mark 16:1; Luke 7:12; John 11:38, 44).

Burial vs. Cremation

While not prescriptive, the scenes referenced above demonstrate that among God's people, burial was the preferred disposal of the remains. This ancient practice connotes respect and honor for the body. Does cremation accord the remains of deceased Christians such dignity? Burial conveys a sense of the body intact awaiting the day of resurrection, even though decay occurs in the interim. By contrast, surrendering the body to flames and residual components to pulverization unwittingly conveys a sense of fatal and lasting extinction. This violence King David would not inflict on the bones of Saul and Jonathan (2 Sam 21:13–14).

Admittedly, these are mere sensitivities, and cremation, *caeteris paribus*, is an adiaphoron. This is the fixed opinion of clergy and church bodies who assert that the Scriptures do not forbid the practice of cremation.[395] The motives, however, for choosing cremation are suspect. For instance, it has been a long-standing suspicion in the Church that elective cremation expressed defiance of the notion of the resurrection and restoration of the body.[396] Yet some

394 For a description of burial customs in the Early Church through the second century and beyond, see Edwin Knox Mitchell, "Death and the Disposal of the Dead (Early Christian)," in *Encyclopedia of Religion and Ethics*, ed. James Hastings, vol. 4 (Edinburgh: T & T Clark, 1956), 456–458.

395 Alvin J. Schmidt cites the position taken by numerous churches that the Scriptures do not forbid cremation or are neutral regarding the practice. See *Ashes to Ashes, or Dust to Dust?*, 87ff.

396 This suspicion was confirmed in the nineteenth century. The *Dictionary of Moral Theology*, subject cremation, cites a movement launched in Italy about 1870 by Masonic and other anti-Catholic societies. The Masons had hoped to use cremation to destroy Christian belief in the resurrection of the body. In 1872, crematories or incinerators were constructed in Padua; later, they were constructed in other countries

Christians may choose cremation in order to ostensibly confess their faith in the resurrection of the body, that the resurrection shall indeed override this radical end of the body by means of fiery extinction.[397] These considerations aside, the Church's principle argument for interment versus cremation is consistency with the ancient tradition whereby God's people chose to bury the remains of fellow believers. They followed this ancient practice in the confession that God had created this body, redeemed this body, and keeps this body until the day of resurrection to eternal life through our Lord Jesus Christ.

Furthermore, arguments favoring cremation have little standing in the light of the Old Testament. The Pentateuch legislated burning of bodies as a disgraceful event and a punishment imposed for reason of heinous sins committed in ancient Israel (Lev 20:14; 21:9). Though Judah was no example of virtue, he ordered the burning of Tamar's body as testimony to her sin of whoredom (Gen 38:24). Fierce judgment befell the king of Moab who burned the king of Edom's bones to lime (Amos 2:1–3). Therefore, the question presses, shall the Church accompany the bodies of Christians to the fire that was a means of judgment and punishment exercised by God's people (cf. Josh 7:10–15, 25)? There are exceptional circumstances that warrant cremation—plague, epidemics such as cholera or Ebola, or even a shortage of burial grounds. Such exceptions, however, do not commend the practice of cremation under normal circumstances. Cremation is advertised as an inexpensive alternative to burial, but economic advantage does not make cremation a dignified way to dispose of the body. Incinerating the remains is what it is, a violent action!

The term *Christian cremation* has entered the Church's vocabulary. Is this designation valid? Where does cremation fit in a theology that signals treating the bodies of deceased Christians with dignity, respect, and honor. Consider four factors:

1. *Creation*—Of the body, the Scriptures say, "The Lord God formed man of dust from the ground and breathed into his nostrils the breath of life; and man became a living being" (Gen 2:7 RSV). Was not the body inherent in man as a "being" created in the image of

---

of Europe and in the United States. Civil laws, which until then had recognized only interment, were amended to include cremation as a legally accepted practice. Now it has become a choice even among Christians.

397 Why do numerous clergy and professors in The Lutheran Church—Missouri Synod choose cremation? Could it be the reverse of defiance of the resurrection of the body, that is, an overt confessional assertion that the body so destroyed is no challenge to the Lord who promises resurrection even of the body that is cremated? Could it be that reduction of the body to dust by fire and flame complies with God's speaking to Adam in the curse "for you are dust, and to dust you shall return" (Gen 3:19b)? These reasons, however, are questionable in light of the fact that cremation was unacceptable in the biblical record as shown above. Is cremation ever a corollary to confession of faith?

God? "So God created man in His own image, in the image of God He created him; male and female He created them" (Gen 1:27).

2. *Redemption*—The person, body and soul, were redeemed by our Lord's atoning work on the cross. This assertion finds support in the passage "Do you not know that your body is a temple of the Holy Spirit within you, whom you have from God? You are not your own, for you were bought with a price. So glorify God in your body" (1 Cor 6:19–20). "Do you not know that your bodies are members of Christ?" (1 Cor 6:15a; cf. Rom 12:1).
3. *Resurrection*—The future resurrection of the body is the powerful reality governing the treatment of the bodies of Christians. Jesus said, "Do not marvel at this, for an hour is coming when all who are in the tombs will hear His voice and come out" (John 5:28–29). "For this is the will of My Father, that everyone who looks on the Son and believes in Him should have eternal life, and I will raise him up on the Last Day" (John 6:40; cf. John 6:44b, 54b). "For the Lord Himself will descend from heaven with a cry of command, with the voice of an archangel, and with the sound of the trumpet of God. And the dead in Christ will rise first" (1 Thess 4:16).
4. *Translation (Glorification)*—This body resurrected by the Lord is a candidate for inexpressible glory (cf. Rom 8:18, 23b). "In a moment, in the twinkling of an eye, at the last trumpet. For the trumpet will sound, and the dead will be raised imperishable, and we shall be changed" (1 Cor 15:52; cf. Phil 3:21; Eph 1:20–21).

Respect and care for the body are actions driven by this theology. This is so in life. Why should it not be so in death? Consider that health care is not for comfort and longevity alone, but for the reason that God has placed us in our bodies. Thus, careless risks to bodily safety are discouraged, as are deleterious habits such as smoking, overeating, and the like. Mutilation of the body may be viewed as desecration of what is sacred. Disfigurement, piercings, tattoos, and other unseemly alterations are impositions detracting from the body that God has created. In death, is not cremation—consuming the body in flame—the ultimate abuse of the body?[398]

398 The attempts by mortuaries to provide tasteful descriptions of the cremation process cannot hide the violence incurred upon the remains when fire destroys all body parts except bones, which are then pulverized and mixed with the ashes, then gathered from the cremation chamber and conserved in an urn or vessel, the remaining contents generally weighing between four to eight pounds. For a graphic description, see *Cremation: Facts and Options Guide* (St. Charles, MO: Baue Funeral Homes, Crematory, Cemetery).

Principle: The body of the Christian—created, redeemed, slated for resurrection and glorification—bespeaks the work of God throughout. As such, the body of a Christian who has died deserves disposal in a manner that is respectful, dignified, and honorable.

Post-Funeral Matters

The Motor Procession

Surrounding the Church's ministry to the living and proper care for the deceased—funeral and/or memorial service, committal, interment—are incidental matters that involve the pastor. One is the custom in some communities when the motor procession from the church or mortuary takes a circuitous route to the interment, passing key places such as the home of the deceased, his or her workplace, a favorite restaurant, or schools attended. There is nothing questionable about this custom from a theological viewpoint.

The Funeral or Memorial Dinner

After a funeral or memorial service, the family or the congregation may host a dinner at the church for all who attended the service, or they may arrange for a luncheon at a local restaurant. The obvious rubric is "Pastor, be there!" Nothing more important is happening at this hour. Most likely, the hosts look to the pastor to bring the invocation or lead in the table prayer. These post-service occasions are an opportunity to be with the people. The pastor should be there and not eat and run, or overstay.

Partners with Morticians

Serving bereaved families is the pastor's ministry, and he has a partner, the mortician who also serves the family. When invited, the pastor rides with morticians to and from the cemetery. Funeral directors and morticians befriend the clergy. Pastors should regard them as friends and partners. The pastor, however, shall be guarded in conversation. It has happened that a pastor confided in a mortician who was driving only to learn that his confidence was betrayed when the same mortician drove the next clergyperson. Wise pastors are discreet when expressing opinions or feelings on any subject. The longer the ride, the more guarded is the conversation.

Securing the Grave Site

At the grave site, should the pastor remain with funeral directors until cemetery personnel have closed and sealed the vault? In some states, this is a legal requirement for the funeral director. If the pastor is transported by this person, he may have to remain until all is finalized. If time is a consideration, he may either return with another driver or with a party who attended the committal and interment. Some pastors always drive their own vehicle on these occasions.[399]

The Choice of Funeral Homes

The choice of services—one funeral business establishment or another—is sometimes referred to the pastor for his recommendation. How shall he advise? The pastor must work with numerous mortuaries in the community. Showing preference to one over another could be awkward. Perhaps the pastor may counsel in this manner: "We have several reputable funeral homes in our community. Families of our congregation patronize this funeral home, also this one, and some others." The pastor mentions the funeral homes by name without additional reflection. The family takes the initiative and selects a funeral home.

Memorials vs. Floral Displays

Bereaved families may designate memorials in memory of their loved one to support specific charities or institutions. Some family and friends prefer to give floral tributes. Assertive parties in the congregation may consider floral tributes frivolous and wasteful. They press families to designate memorials to the Church or to missions. How fierce is the debate in some congregations over these designations!

Why not permit the family to decide? If they are accepting of floral gifts and they do not designate alternative memorials, so be it. The church's mission has other venues of support. Furthermore, when accepting memorial gifts, a congregation wisely specifies particular aspects of its mission and ministry in need of financial assistance. Also, the congregation should adopt a fixed policy for dispersing undesignated memorials.

---

399 Remaining at the grave site until all mourners have left is salutary, but staying there is not required. In the earlier discussion of the committal, it was stated that the pastor's continued presence may be interpreted as a sign of the eternal presence of Christ with the departed person. This action, however, is distinguished from remaining at the grave site for security reasons, that is, to prevent tampering or even stealing from the casket prior to sealing of the vault and lowering it into the ground. Security concerns are the responsibility of the morticians and cemetery personnel.

CHAPTER SEVENTEEN

Church Discipline—Admonition, Repentance, Forgiveness

Introduction

Members of the Body of Christ should openly and lovingly minister to one another with friendly counsel toward sincere repentance, and with grace they should declare forgiveness through Christ. This ministry is church discipline.

The Disciplined Church Ministers to Fallen Christians in the Fellowship

Righteousness Expected among the Righteous

The Lord likened His disciples to a city shining atop a hill (Matt 5:14–15). At times, however, the light shines dimly. Petty competing for greatness, loveless condescension, even denial of the Master were sins of the twelve disciples. The light flickered in the Early Church with infighting over distribution to the widows (Acts 6:1) and charity spoiled by selfishness and deceit (Acts 5:1–2). St. Paul wrestled with his dark side (Rom 7:8a, 11a, 25b). Today the Church still reckons with sin in the camp.

Principle: Because sin surfaces within the camp, the people in whom Christ is formed (Gal 4:19) shall minister to one another proper correctives indicated by the words, "Brothers, if anyone is caught in any transgression, you who are spiritual should restore him in a spirit of gentleness" (Gal 6:1).

Unrighteousness Found among the Righteous

The Church uses its own set of tools to deal with its own nature, a fellowship of those who are *simul justus et peccator*, at once both saint and sinner. A conversation goes like this: "I don't know why I am telling you this. I guess I had to get it out in the open. I had to tell someone." The Christian listening to this confession draws the fallen one to the cross to hear Jesus' prayer, "Father, forgive them" (Luke 23:34; cf. John 6:37b).

Unseemly speech, unkind words, and harsh and unloving actions may unsettle a congregation. Fellow Christians respond. "Joe, could you express your strong feelings as our Lord would want to hear you speak?" "Mary, do you really mean what you said?" "George, shall we probe for a speck in the neighbor's eye and ignore the beam in our own?" "Bill, we all have our moments. God is witness to them, and His love and mercy for Jesus' sake is everlasting. How does this good word change things?" Thus, the Gospel that God is eager to forgive equips Christians in proactive care for their fellows when they have fallen (cf. 1 John 1:8–9; Exod 34:7a; Num 14:18a; 1 Kgs 8:34, 36, 39; cf. Ezek 34:15–16). Baptized into Christ, the fellowship of Christians serves and restores the fallen ones (cf. Rom 6:22; 8:5b; Eph 2:13–22; Phil 1:6, 27).

A Pastor's Care for Fallen Christians in the Congregation

A Pastor's Attention to the Congregation's Sanctification

Church discipline does not always go smoothly. Some Christians are content to wash their hands of sin within the camp and say, "Let the pastor deal with it," so he does attend to sanctification or the lack of it. His watching and caring for Christian lives is clearly *dominical.* His example will assist the larger congregation to fulfill their ministry to one another in the way of proper church discipline.

Principle: As bishop and shepherd, the pastor is a spiritual watchman who oversees the doctrine and life of the congregation. This truism of pastoral practice compels close attention to the lives of the baptized. Only when they are careful to live in newness of life out of their Baptism can they care for their fellows in the way of true church discipline.

Our Lord modeled attention to Christian life when He called for discipleship and referenced the sanctified life (Mark 8:35–37). He pressed disciples to hear the Word of God and do it (Luke 8:21; Mark 3:35; Matt 12:50; Matt 7:21, 24–27). He was not, however, merely a programmer of good works or a legislator. The Gospel of the Kingdom breaking forth in His ministry with grace and newness of life prefaces His speaking on many Christian life topics: keeping sexual life within boundaries of the Sixth Commandment, disciplining the tongue, making peace with enemies, prayer, fasting, dealing with worry, stamping out judgment in favor of Christian love, and the like (Matt 4:23; 5:1ff.).

Similarly, St. Paul oversaw the sanctified lives of Christians. He addressed them—justified by grace and heirs according to the hope of eternal life—and then he exhorted, "Those who have believed in God may be careful to devote themselves to good works" (Titus 3:7–8). Again, Paul exalted the life transformed by the Gospel in terms of genuine love and abhorrence of evil; he does this with remarkable specificity (Rom 12:1–2, 9, 14–21; cf. 13:8–10; Eph 5:1–2). He contrasts the mind that is set on the Spirit with the mind that is set on the flesh, and he encouraged the former as the way for the Christian life (Rom 8:3–7; cf. Gal 5:16–24; Eph 2:10). He boldly pressed Christians to "be imitators of God" (Eph 5:1), and he counseled, "Let everyone who names the name of the Lord depart from iniquity" (2 Tim 2:19). Throughout the Pauline corpus, these exhortations show how the apostle monitored the sanctified lives of Christians in congregations that he served as apostle, preacher, and teacher.

The Pastor Models Care for the Congregation

Today, a faithful pastor monitors what is going on in the lives of the people, but he does so as a caring shepherd, not a severe judge. His genuine interest in the people earns their respect. They welcome his concern. He inquires, listens, and affirms. He is prepared to give gentle correction when needed. He cites the Scriptures when they apply to Christian lives, but he is not brusque or *in your face* with the people. Instead, his appeal is from the Gospel. Certainly, the pastor is proactive in this sensitive care for the individual Christian. He is proactive in caring because warped belief and false teaching abound everywhere. The people are vulnerable. Christians live in a world that denounces moral absolutes, so the pastor calls them back to solid mooring in the words of the Lord because those who keep and do His words have God's blessing (Matt 7:24–25; cf. Deut 6:1–9).

The Church Exercises Discipline of Impenitent Christians

The Church and Public Sin

The Church's care takes a serious turn when flagrant sin and impenitence occur in the Christian community. The apostle Paul confronted the Christians at Corinth when they did not admonish the man in their fellowship who pursued an affair with his father's wife (1 Cor 5:1–2). He called attention to mortal sins (such as those cited in 1 Cor 6:9–10) that forfeit the kingdom of God and separate one from the community of faith (1 Cor 5:11; SA III III 44–45; Ap IV 64). These sins call for intense church discipline.[400]

400 Observe this situation. A husband and father returns from work for the evening meal with his wife

Sins That Call for Intense Church Discipline

In the world, God judges the wicked, but He requires the Church to address public sin among its own[401] (1 Cor 5:3–5, 12–13; cf. 1 Tim 1:18–20; Titus 3:10–11). Public sins are defined thusly:

1. Manifest sins of the flesh, that is, immoral behavior (1 Cor 6:9; Gal 5:19–21; 1 Tim 1:10; 1 Cor 5:11)
2. Persistent adherence to false doctrine—public teaching and influence that is contrary to the Word of God

These sins include openly entertaining false teaching that causes confusion and division (Rom 16:17; 1 Tim 4:1–2; 6:3; 2 Tim 2:18b; Titus 1:9), altering the meaning of the Scriptures (Deut 4:2; 12:32; Rev 22:18–19), and distracting from the truth (2 Tim 2:16–18; 3:1–8; Titus 1:14; 3:9–11). On these counts, the Church invokes two actions of intense church discipline:

1. Admonishment (Lev 19:17; Matt 18:15–17; Luke 17:3; 2 Thess 3:14)
2. Restoration (Luke 17:4; Jas 5:19–20; Gal 6:1; 2 Cor 2:5–11; 2 Thess 3:15)

Principle: When a fellow Christian is overtaken by flagrant sin—sins of the flesh or advocacy of teaching that is contrary to the Scriptures—the Church is proactive in its care by administering admonishment and, upon repentance, giving Absolution leading to restoration.

Christian congregations neglect church discipline to their disadvantage. Erring persons are emboldened. They rationalize, "everyone is doing it," yet the Bible warns that sins of the flesh and setting one's mind on the flesh is death (Rom 8:6a). Moreover, teaching false doctrine is as egregious as are sins of the flesh. Theologians may err, and the laity may court unorthodox beliefs and advocate false teaching in the congregation. Church discipline must begin[402]

and two daughters. Subsequently, he leaves the house for another residence two blocks away for an overnight stay with his mistress. He returns "home" at 6:00 a.m. to shower and go off to work. His adultery is known in the community. His behavior indicates crass impenitence. The pastor intervenes and admonishes this man. The congregation stands by to assist with church discipline if there is no repentance and return to moral living.

401 The apostle Paul's severe action of pressing the Church at Corinth to deliver one guilty of flagrant sin to Satan indicates how proactive the Church should be when open sin flares up. The saying "To deliver this man to Satan for the destruction of the flesh, so that his spirit may be saved in the day of the Lord" (1 Cor 5:5) is either a reference to putting out and away an errant Christian, the action of excommunication, or it refers to imposition of an unknown infliction of evil in the body. The purpose, however, is "so that his spirit may be saved in the day of the Lord" (1 Cor 5:5b). How certainly and seriously the Church should address open and public sin *within the camp* is most clear from the apostle's pastoral care in this instance at Corinth.

402 Discerning theologians know better than to teach falsely. This egregious error calls for swift action and a prompt conclusion of the matter. Theologians know full well the judgment upon any who misrepre-

(Titus 3:9; 1 Tim 6:3–5; Rom 16:17–18; 2 Tim 4:14–15). The Church cannot ignore heretical teaching.[403] Furthermore, foregoing needed church discipline forfeits use of the Office of the Keys (cf. John 20:23; Matt 18:18), and it places church leaders in jeopardy (cf. 1 Tim 5:22; Ezek 3:18). The Lord censured the Church at Thyatira for failing to admonish public sin (Rev 2:19–23).

Procedure in Church Discipline

Preliminary Consideration

The pastor oversees church discipline, beginning with measured response to complaints. A sincere but misguided Christian woman inquired, "Pastor, did you know that James was seen exiting a local bar one night last week? He had a lady on each arm, and he is a married man!" Such a complaint may be hearsay. The pastor replies, "Did you approach our friend and fellow Christian? Oh, you did not observe the incident? You were not there?" In this instance, the pastor does not get involved, though he may check on James. Other situations call for the pastor to intervene. For example, children may observe inappropriate behavior by a teacher. They cannot approach the teacher. A church employee observes unchristian behavior by a staff member. The employee cannot be involved because he or she could be fired. In these instances, the pastor takes the initiative and makes appropriate inquiries.

Principle: Church discipline follows procedure, but concern for the spiritual life of a fallen Christian transcends procedural details. Rather than showing hostility and judgment against an errant Christian, the Church both loves and cares for him or her as God our Father loves His children in Christ Jesus (Rom 12:10; Eph 5:2; 1 Cor 13; 1 John 4:7–8, 11; cf. 2 Thess 3:15).

Steps of Church Discipline—Matthew 18:15–17

The Church proceeds with discipline, either spontaneously or by a proce-

sent God and His Word and falsify that which is true (Prov 30:5–6; Jer 23:25–32; Gal 1:8–9). Neither shall theologians add to or diminish the Word of God (Deut 4:2; 12:32; Rev 22:18–19—cited above). Then, a Christian layman is absorbed with a menagerie of false teaching garnered from listening to a kaleidoscope of religious broadcasts. On Sundays, he presses fellow Christians at church to accept spurious teachings that he has absorbed. It appears that Satan has a grip on the man. Active dissemination of false teaching and open proselytizing both call for church discipline.

403 The word *heresy* derives from the Greek term *hairesis*, which has as its root the word meaning "choice" or "assertive self-will." The term implies choosing one's own personal will over the truth. It is a term that was applied to early interpretations of Christianity that differed markedly from apostolic testimony. It was a poignant term in the light of stressful conditions that required unflinching loyalty to the apostolic teaching under the pain of violent persecution. See Thomas C. Oden, "Can We Talk about Heresy?" *The Christian Century* 113, no. 12 (April 12, 1995): 391. Dr. Martin Luther viewed heresy as stubborn error in an article of faith in opposition to Scripture. For additional references to Luther's understanding, see the subject "heresy" in *Lutheran Cyclopedia*, rev. ed., ed. Erwin L. Lueker (St. Louis: Concordia Publishing House, 1975), 375.

dure specified by our Lord in the Gospels. When the flagrant sin arouses public outrage, the Church cuts to the quick and openly admonishes (cf. 1 Tim 5:20; 1 Cor 5:1–2). Otherwise, the Church proceeds with discipline according to our Lord's instruction in Matthew 18:15–17 (cf. Luke 17:3–4).[404] Jesus' words apply directly when one Christian sins against a fellow Christian. Indirectly, His words assist the Church to admonish an errant Christian and minister to that person in the event that he or she elects to remain in a state of stubborn impenitence. The Absolution cannot be administered. Finally, the Lord instructs the Church to excommunicate a persistent impenitent sinner, declaring the person to be outside the community of faith. By persistent sinning, one gives notice that he or she is an unbeliever. The steps of discipline are the following:

"If your brother sins against you, go and tell him his fault, between you and him alone" (Matt 18:15a).

A Christian privately counsels with one who has sinned against him, but the reference may be more inclusive than one Christian against another (cf. Gal 6:1; Jas 5:19–20; 2 Thess 3:14–15). The sin may be public, and one or another Christian—the pastor or lay Christian—may admonish the person, keeping the matter private. "If he listens to you, you have gained your brother" (v. 15b). When he acknowledges the sin and expresses repentance before God and apologizes, seeking forgiveness, speak the Absolution and rejoice. The matter is closed.

"But if he does not listen, take one or two others along with you, that every charge may be established by the evidence of two or three witnesses" (Matt 18:16).

If the matter is not closed, if the sinning Christian persists, denying guilt or making light of it, the Lord instructs that the first Christian who admonished take *one* or *two* witnesses and counsel the errant Christian again. These fellow Christians may not have been eyewitnesses, but now they establish the truth of "every word," the nature of the sin and the good counsel that the first Christian brought to the errant one. Luther comments about the one who sinned, "If he will not accept your counsel, then you must bear with him in patience and take with you one or two witnesses who can verify your contentions or bear witness that you have admonished and instructed and told him."[405] The added presence

404 From close study of these verses and in light of their context and the structure of Matthew 18, Dr. Jeffrey Gibbs and Dr. Jeffrey Kloha show that the principal subject of the Lord's words on discipline is the Christian who has sinned against another Christian and is in danger because of that sin. The implication is that the sin fractures *koinonia* in Christ, the bond wherein Christians have identity with one another. Restoration of the fallen one to this *koinonia* and, for that matter, repair of the fellowship harmed by a member who has sinned is a priority. See Jeffrey A. Gibbs and Jeffrey J. Kloha, "'Following' Matthew 18: Interpreting Matthew 18:15–20 in Its Context," *Concordia Journal* 29, no. 1 (January 2003): 6–25.

405 Luther's comments are cited by Edgar J. Otto, "Church Discipline," *Abiding Word*, vol. 2 (St. Louis:

of *one* or *two* witnesses presses the gravity of the matter and is occasion to plead, "Friend, this course that you are pursuing is not God-pleasing and if you continue in this way, you endanger your own soul."

"If he refuses to listen to them, tell it to the church. And if he refuses to listen even to the church, let him be to you as a Gentile and a tax collector" (Matt 18:17).

Before taking this step of admonishment, steps one and two may be repeated. With the third step, those who admonish intensify love and care for an errant Christian. In the face of continuing resistance and refusal to repent, Jesus instructs, "Tell it to the church." Tell it to the assembled congregation or the congregation's governing assembly, council, board of elders, or a special commission. This is the venue where the errant Christian can secure a hearing. The Church is eager to listen and then serve with good counsel. Coming together in this manner, the Church receives the errant Christian as a brother or sister in Christ (2 Thess 3:15). Although it convenes to address sin and impenitence, it does so in a spirit of Christian love that is patient and forbearing (1 Cor 13).

The Christian who is invited to this gathering may not appear. Then, the congregation may extend repeated invitations to meet with the church over a period of weeks or months. The admonished person may turn bitter and hostile and cynical. "You goody-goody people think that you are going to come down on me. What I do and how I live is between me and God. All of this is none of your business." Then, speaking for the Church, the pastor may respond:

> Friend, if the matter of your actions and the way that you live your life is between you and God, then please let those whom God has gifted with the right and the privilege to declare forgiveness of sins do just that for you (John 20:23; Luke 17:3; Gal 6:1; cf. 2 Tim 2:19). Come clean with the Lord and His Church, and He will declare to you forgiveness of the sin for which you are sincerely repentant. This is not just about *sin*. This is about *forgiveness* of sin, a blessing for you. Please listen and hear the Church's desire to speak Absolution in the name of Jesus so that you may be at peace and the Church may be assured that she has cared for you.

The Hearing by the Church

The Church convenes. If the errant Christian appears, listens, and responds

---

Concordia Publishing House, 1947), 540. The precise *locus* for the citation from Luther is *Dr. Martin Luther's Sämmtliche Schriften* 7, ed. Johann Georg Walch (St. Louis: Concordia Publishing House, 1891), 921. Dr. Otto's treatment of church discipline is exacting and comprehensive, an indispensable resource.

with appreciation for the Church's care, confesses responsibility for the sin, and seeks forgiveness, a victory is won. The assembly collectively declares the freeing words of the Absolution. However, if the party does not appear and refuses to meet with the Church, the assembly firms up three factors that relate to care for this errant Christian:

1. Establish the sin, that is, that the person admonished has sinned.
2. Establish the care, that is, demonstrate how fellow Christians in Christian love have admonished and called the person to repent.
3. Celebrate repentance, or establish continued impenitence, that is, there is no evidence of contrition or softening of the heart, and the person appears to continue in the sin that is of great concern.

The impenitent person might appear at the Church's hearing to defend against the admonishment or get the Church off his or her back, so to speak. He or she is entitled to bring support, that is, character references or witnesses who support the person's denial that he or she is guilty of public sin.[406] Still, healthy discussion and exchange should lead to resolution of the matter.

The errant Christian, however, may ostensibly demonstrate impenitence. The Church cautions that such a spirit spurns the grace and mercy of God and places a fallen Christian in danger of God's judgment (cf. 1 Cor 6:9a; Isa 57:20–21; et al.). Further, the Church wants to declare forgiveness and say to a penitent person, "Be free as Christ has set you free, and go and sin no more!" Then the Church may welcome the errant one back into the fellowship of the Church with celebration (cf. Eph 4:4–6).

Administering Excommunication (*The Major Ban*)

Initial Understanding

Principle: Not out of spite, nor a spirit of hostility, but acting in Christian love and sadness, the Church follows the Lord's teaching and puts away from the Christian fellowship one who persists in impenitence and continues to sin.

Finally, if a fellow Christian remains belligerent and pursues deliberate sinning and impenitence,

406 Rules of evidence in these proceedings were engaged to determine both the sin and the impenitence. The late Rev. Arnim Polster, who was by profession both an attorney and a pastor, distinguished between the use of evidence in civil courts and adjudication in church assemblies. We may question such a proceeding. When discipline moves to the hearing by the church (Matt 18:17), the admonished party is held accountable for the sin and his or her impenitence, factors that are already known and established by two or three witnesses (Matt 18:16). Is there a need for proceedings in which the "guilty" one is addressed as a defendant? Doubtless, our Lord did not have a church court in mind when He counseled, "Tell it to the church" (Matt 18:17a). See Arnim Polster, "Rules of Evidence in Church Disciplinary Procedure" (unpublished essay, n.d.). Also see a lengthy discussion of church court proceedings cited from A. L. Graebner by John H. C. Fritz, *Pastoral Theology*, 245–256.

then Christian discipline comes to this: "And if he refuses to listen even to the church, let him be to you as a Gentile and a tax collector" (Matt 18:17). Yes, "a Gentile," one who is no longer a member of the Body of Christ. Yes, "a tax collector," an inveterate sinner who shows no interest in the forgiveness of sins. Then comes to pass Jesus' words, "Whatever you bind on earth shall be bound in heaven" (Matt 18:18b). Note that the impenitent one does not exclude himself. The Church acts on the word of our Lord, and this action is exclusion or inclusion.

The Action of Excommunication

God forbid that church discipline should come to excommunication, but it happens. The Church renders its judgment and excommunicates the impenitent sinner. Again, this action is upheld by the Lord of the Church (Matt 18:18; cf. 1 Cor 5:2b; Titus 3:10–11; 1 Pet 3:12b). When the Church's governing assembly convenes for excommunication, the pastor reviews the situation: the egregious sin, the care that the sinning person has received, and his or her refusal to repent and be accepted by the congregation as a fellow Christian.

The Church executes excommunication with a resolution to this effect, supported by unanimous decision of the assembly. If any person in the assembly dissents, they should either show just cause for their dissent or be admonished for obstructing the Church's action. When the Church excommunicates, the pastor announces it to the larger congregation. He speaks in the Lord's name and in His stead (John 20:23). The congregation—the Church in action—has formally *bound* the sin of the impenitent person (Matt 18:18). This is the procedure:

1. The pastor informs the congregation of the meeting to consider the action of excommunication. He asks for prayers on behalf of the impenitent person.
2. The pastor informs the errant person and invites him or her to appear at this meeting.
3. Whether or not the person appears at the meeting, the pastor monitors the procedure of excommunication by unanimous decision.
4. The pastor informs the person that he or she has been the subject of this action by the congregation.
5. In the following public worship service(s), the pastor informs the larger congregation of the excommunication with accompanying prayer for the impenitent person.

Attitude of the Church toward a Person Who Has Been Excommunicated

The words of our Lord stand! He says of the impenitent sinner, "Let him be to you as a Gentile and a tax collector" (Matt 18:17b). This command raises the question "What is the relationship of the Church to the one who has been excommunicated?" Our Lord's words have been interpreted to support shunning the person. In some tight-knit Lutheran communities, congregational practice literally stigmatized excommunicated persons. As a result, they found it difficult to function in the community, to do things such as securing employment, enrolling children in schools, and even shopping for necessities. We question ostracizing excommunicated persons based on the apostle Paul's mandate to Christians at Corinth, "Purge the evil person from among you" (1 Cor 5:13b; cf. 5:2b).

There is no doubt that the apostle raised the guard at Corinth against the influence that an immoral man might have in the congregation. He put the guard down, however, when the man showed repentance (2 Cor 2:5–11). Until then, Paul's censure stood firm, but it was not outright rejection or repudiation of the excommunicated man. Instead, censure was necessary to shield the congregation from the influence of blatant sin, for example, when Hymenaeus and Philetus upset the faith of some at Ephesus (2 Tim 2:18b). Likewise, consider that he counseled Titus to have nothing to do with the factious person after admonishing him once or twice (Titus 3:10).

Censure of the impenitent person to protect fellow Christians from negative influence does not preclude showing civility and kindness toward this person. There is no place in the Christian community for hatred and hostility toward one who has been excommunicated (Rom 12:17–18; 1 John 4:20; cf. 3:16–18). To the contrary, Christian love means that the excommunicated person is welcome at public worship services. The Church shall never deny any person the privilege of hearing the Gospel. Partaking of the Lord's Supper, however, is a different matter. While under the *major ban*, the excommunicated person is also under the *minor ban*. A person who is impenitent of public sin may not partake of the Lord's body and blood for the remission of sin, but hearing and listening to the Word of the Lord is the means for the Holy Spirit to work in heart and life with great promise (cf. Isa 55:11; Rom 10:8, 13, 17). Frankly, it would be unconscionable for the Church to do less than welcome the sinner who is in need of both the judgment of the Law and the comfort of the Gospel. How could excluding him or her stand in the light of our Lord's parables, the lost sheep and the lost coin (Luke 15:3–10)?

Restoration of an Excommunicated Person Who Repents

Doubtless, the action of Christian love essentially helped restore the fallen but repentant man at Corinth (2 Cor 2:7–8). The devil would have the congregation continue to pummel the repentant one and not let him forget shame over his sin. Some in the congregation may always hold his sin against him. This is cruel and ungodly treatment. Excommunication got his attention and brought him to sorrow for how he was living. This is a Lutheran view. Now, love that forgives surely welcomes and affirms the repentant soul, and Christ blesses such ministry (2 Cor 2:10). Forgiving love is a ministry that saves the man from the pits of despair (2 Cor 2:7).

The fallen man at Corinth repented, and he was forgiven. What joy even among the angels in heaven when an impenitent sinner returns to receive forgiveness (Luke 15:7, 10)! The day that the pastor reports a person's repentance, the Church receives the report and by formal resolution and unanimous vote lifts the *major ban* (excommunication) from the person. The pastor announces this action to the larger congregation at the next worship hour with a prayer of thanksgiving.

Principle: Excommunication does not relieve the Church from Christian love—showing openness to hear repentance and receive the repentant sinner. Therefore, the Church stays in contact with the excommunicated person, as far as this is possible, in order to open the door for return in humble repentance, seeking our Lord's forgiveness administered by the congregation and executed by the pastor.

With the major ban lifted, must the restored Christian make a public apology to the congregation? Former practice was definite. "Public apology must be made before that congregation to which the offense was given."[407] Another view is that the person's repentance tacitly included any apology expected by the Church. Further, the Absolution administered the Gospel of forgiveness of sin (John 20:23; Matt 18:18b). The inherent offense of the public sin is removed. The forgiven person, however, may volunteer to make a public apology that gives glory to God and is edifying to all.

Miscellaneous Subjects Related to Church Discipline

Honoring the Absolution Spoken by the Pastor

These paragraphs have set forth the procedure of administering church discipline. Additional subjects call for comment. The first is administering the

407 John H. C. Fritz, *Pastoral Theology*, 239.

Absolution to a person during the process of church discipline. If, at any time during the Church's ministry of discipline (Matt 18:15–18), an errant person approaches the pastor in sincere repentance and receives Absolution from the pastor, the matter is closed. The pastor reports to the church elders and the congregation that Confession has been heard and Absolution administered. All give thanks and rejoice with exceeding great joy (Jas 5:19–20; Luke 15:7; Gal 6:1)!

Respecting the Disciplinary Action of Sister Congregations

A second subject is respecting the disciplinary actions of sister congregations. When a person who is under admonishment or has been excommunicated seeks membership at a neighboring congregation, the matter must first be resolved at his or her home congregation. In the instance of excommunication, only the congregation that administered this final action can lift the major ban, and then only when the errant Christian has repented.

These matters can be sensitive. An excommunicated person who seeks membership at a neighboring congregation may appeal the action of his or her home congregation that administered the major ban.[408] Perhaps the pastor of that neighboring congregation willingly assumes pastoral care of the excommunicated person. If he or she repents and is absolved of the sin, the former home congregation may then lift the major ban so that the person may join the new congregation.

Direct Engagement of Step Three in the Procedure of Church Discipline

A third subject is the necessity to deal promptly with any Christian who refuses to repent for committing egregious sins (cf. 1 Cor 5:1–2). In instances of flagrant sin, the Church moves swiftly and holds a hearing. If this hearing is rebuffed by the errant Christian, the Church executes the apostolic counsel, "As for those who persist in sin, rebuke them in the presence of all, so that the rest may stand in fear" (1 Tim 5:20). St. Paul did not hesitate. With dispatch he publicly admonished Peter because his suspected Judaizing was openly damaging to the Gospel. "I said to Cephas [Peter] before them all" (Gal 2:14). Of course, a pastor will counsel one-to-one with the errant person even though the Church holds its hearing. If the reaction of the one who sinned is defensive, callous, or belligerent, the Church must administer the major ban.

408 A person who was excommunicated may appeal to another congregation or to the local circuit or consistory of congregations, or even to the larger district or diocese. Adjudication at any level will examine disciplinary actions to determine if they were rightly executed and that proper care was given to an errant Christian according to the Word of God.

Admonition of Weak Christians Who Absent Themselves from Word and Sacrament

A fourth subject in this field of miscellanea can be stated as a question: "Should church discipline apply to weak Christians who do not attend worship services or partake of the Sacrament?" Worshiping with fellow Christians on the Lord's Day is not an option.[409] The mandate prevails, "Not neglecting to meet together, as is the habit of some, but encouraging one another, and all the more as you see the Day drawing near" (Heb 10:25). Some professing Christians neglect hearing the Word of God (which is life from God, Deut 8:3; Matt 4:4; cf. John 6:33, 58, 63b) and sin against the Third Commandment, "Remember the Sabbath day, to keep it holy" (Exod 20:8). How shall the Church minister to these weak Christians? Are they candidates for intense church discipline? In large parishes, is it possible to move through the three steps (Matt 18:15–17) with hundreds of members who do not attend worship services?

Many congregations address worship delinquency in nontheological ways. They designate numbers of nonworshipers as inactive church members. At length, these members who do not worship or commune are regarded as evangelism prospects, or they are simply removed from the membership rolls. They are viewed as former members who excluded themselves by persistent absence from the worshiping congregation.

Principle: Ministry to Christians who persistently neglect public worship will place them under the Word of God as the means whereby the Spirit increases faith and aids the weak to recover faithful worship practice.

Consider an acceptable alternative to arbitrary dealing with delinquent Christians. Assumed is a ministry of visitation to delinquents by the pastor and church elders. Then, we recommend forming a special class that places weak Christians under the Spirit's teaching (Rom 10:17; John 8:31–32; 16:12–15; Eph 6:17b). Observe that congregations host instruction classes for new members. Why not offer similar care for absent members? If they are separating from Him who is the Vine because they eschew His Word, call them to be under that Word. Form a mini class of three to six ninety-minute sessions. Conduct the class in a nonthreatening setting. Provide for socializing—pleasant and comfortable surroundings with palatable refreshments—and make the experience

409 In early New Testament times, the community of faith assembled in the local synagogue for teaching and prayer, a custom followed by the Church as far back as Pentecost (Acts 2:46; 19:8–10; Heb 10:24–25; cf. Luke 4:16ff.). Also, they found places where they could come together for the teaching of the apostles, which was the teaching of the Lord (Acts 2:42; John 8:31–32; 14:25–26; 16:12–15; 17:6b–8; cf. Matt 28:20; Luke 24:44–49). The Lord's Table was central, for He had said of His Holy Supper, "Do this in remembrance of Me" (1 Cor 11:24b–25).

pleasant. Often, lapsed church members have hurt feelings. They were offended by someone. This member renewal class provides a fresh experience with fellow Christians, an opportunity to reconnect. The curriculum may be the following:

MEMBER RENEWAL CLASS

A CHRISTIAN IS . . .

I. I Became a Christian

- Human condition (the fall, second use of the Law)
- Call of the Holy Spirit through the Gospel (Holy Baptism)
- Focus—seeing Jesus Christ, His person and work (my Redeemer, my Lord)

II. I Am a Christian

- Ongoing power and use of Holy Baptism
- Sanctified Christian life
- Member of the Body of Christ (the Church)

III. I Belong as a Christian

- Where the Word of the Lord is preached and taught
- With the Lord at His Table (the Lord's Supper)
- With this Congregation of fellow Christians
- These are my gifts (gifts, abilities, talents—inventory)
- This is what I can do and contribute (stewardship)

IV. I Live Daily as a Christian

- Intake (personal Bible reading, prayer, public worship)
- Output (living for God and my fellows—Christian ethics)
- Sharing Christ with others (witness, the missionary task)

This outline is flexible. Amend it; alter it. Fill it with Scriptures and key passages from the Lutheran Confessions. The point is, gather the weak where there is strength. Place them under the Word and the power of the Holy Spirit. Offer this mini-class, a member renewal effort, on different days, at different times, in different select locations such as church/school premises, local library facilities, and the like. A family may host the class in their home.

Will this fresh initiative of a member renewal class bring results? We count on the Holy Spirit. Some persons will recover the blessing of belonging at public worship. Others may refuse this special care that the Church is giving. Their action, refusing this care and continuing to reject public worship and the Lord's Supper, is self-exclusion. Formal ministry to them has come to a close. The congregation removes them from the member roster and notifies them of this action. The Church wishes them God's blessing and bids them farewell.[410]

410 In this litigious society, the Church carefully frames the notion of membership in the congregation and also carefully articulates just cause for dismissal, precisely stating that release from membership is devoid of any claim to the congregation's treasury, property, or other assets. Legal counsel is advisable when the congregation draws up these rubrics or revises them in its constitution and bylaws. These initiatives are regrettable, to be sure, but they are necessary.

CHAPTER EIGHTEEN

Men and Women in the Church

Introduction

Since the mid-twentieth century, the subject of ordaining women to the pastoral office has overshadowed a larger discussion of how men and women serve the Lord in His Church. This chapter engages that discussion, but not before addressing women's ordination. For two reasons, ordaining women is both sensitive and controversial. The first reason is the inescapable stigma borne by some church bodies because they reject the practice of ordaining women to the pastoral office. A second reason is the increasing pressure on these churches to reverse their current practice and imitate the practice of the Evangelical Lutheran Church in America and numerous Protestant churches that ordain women to the pastoral office.

Deferring the larger subject of men and women in the Church until later, this initial discussion of women's ordination opens in nautical terms—taking a reading of the situation, getting our bearings, and setting a course for appropriate practice. The first two moves are general. The third move, setting the course for practice, engages specific Scriptures that must decide the issue of accepting or declining the practice of ordaining women.

Women and Men and the Office of the Holy Ministry—Reading and Bearing

Reading the Situation

Female enrollment in seminaries of mainline denominations across the nation exceeds the number of male enrollees. More women than men are preparing to be pastors. While celebrating the thirty-fifth anniversary of women's ordination in 2005, the Evangelical Lutheran Church in America saw women passing men in ordination numbers.[411] The trend continues unabated in Protestantism, and reports from Roman Catholic sources disclose frequent overtures favoring ordination of women to the priesthood.

The press for ordaining women is indicative of a continuing struggle against sexist ways that limit women's ministry in the Church. Dominant male leadership of local congregations is a factor. In the view of many women, male leadership has little interest in viable roles for women that offer fulfillment in service to the Gospel. An added frustration is the inconsistency in public teaching and practice regarding the roles that women may or may not occupy in the local church. Many women, therefore, view the practice of ordaining women as a symbol. They believe that ordination promotes a liberating ethos that will lead to resolving ambiguity over the place of women in the local ministry.

Getting Our Bearings

Where does the Church go from here? It is a matter of getting our bearings, that is, in nautical terms, assessing vital factors essential to setting a course and moving forward. Confessional churches secure their bearings from the Word of God. This means redoubling efforts to assure right interpretation of Scriptures that apply to women and ministry. The subject of women's ordination has been addressed in hundreds of papers and studies during the latter half of the twentieth century. This vast amount of literature is daunting. Finally, we must take a position integral with the Scriptures and the Lutheran Confessions. In this way, we find our bearings and point forward to practice that honors women in service of their Lord.[412]

---

411 "Women Pass Men in Ordination Numbers," *The Lutheran* (May 2005), cited in *Christian News* (May 23, 2005): 14.

412 Works for and against this subject abound. Advocating women's ordination are Cynthia Jo Dentinger, *Report: Women in the Church* (Rochester, NY: Cynthia Jo Dentinger, 1973); Marie Meyer et al., *Different Voices/Shared Vision: Male and Female in the Trinitarian Community* (Delhi, NY: American Lutheran Publicity Bureau, 1992); "The Ordination of Women," a National Council of Churches document condensed by Raymond Tiemeyer (Minneapolis: Augsburg Press, 1970). Here are a few more titles of works taking a position against women's ordination: *Women Pastors? The Ordination of Women in Biblical Lutheran Perspective*, ed. Matthew C. Harrison and John T. Pless, 3rd ed. (St. Louis: Concordia Publishing House, 2012); Fritz Zerbst, *The Office of Women in the Church*, trans. Albert G. Merkens (St. Louis: Concordia Publishing House, 1955); Peter Brunner, *The Ministry and the Ministry of Women* (St. Louis: Concordia Publishing House, 1971); *Women in the Church: Scriptural Principles and Ecclesial Practice; A Report of the Commission on Theology and Church Relations* (St. Louis: The Lutheran Church—Missouri Synod, 1985); Laurence L. White, "The Role of Women in the Lutheran Church—Missouri Synod" (unpublished essay, Houston, TX: Our Savior Lutheran Church, July 1991); *The Service of Women in Congregational and Synodical Offices: A Report of the Commission on Theology and Church Relations* (St. Louis: The Lutheran Church—Missouri Synod, November 1994). For six essays presenting arguments for retaining the ordination of men only and arguments for introducing the ordination of women, see *Lutheran Theological Journal* 39, 1 (May 2005). These essays by theologians of the Lutheran Church of Australia's Commission of Theology and Inter-Church Relations are preceded by earlier discussions accessed at www.alc.edu.au.

Two Scriptures That Speak to the Subject—Women and the Pastoral Office

Prologue to Discussion of 1 Corinthians 14:33b–38 and 1 Timothy 2:11–15

The question of whether women may be ordained to the Office of the Ministry is addressed by two Scriptures, 1 Corinthians 14:33b–38 and 1 Timothy 2:11–15. Seeking the answer elsewhere proves confusing and futile. For instance, the proposition that women can qualify for and do the tasks of the office and function as well as men is pragmatic in nature. Many voices speak about the notion of gender equality in support of ordaining women. It is true that the effect of functions of the office—preaching and the Sacraments—is by the Word only, regardless of the person occupying the office. Nevertheless, does neutrality with respect to the person potentially using the Word and representing Christ imply gender neutral occupants of the pastoral office? Equally unsubstantial is the argument that only men should be ordained because all the apostles were men. Also, the argument that the passages from 1 Corinthians and 1 Timothy cited above (the apostle Paul's directives that the women be silent) may be mutable, thus opening the door to women's ordination, is specious.[413]

This brief representation of several arguments for women's ordination calls for pause to focus attention on 1 Corinthians 14:33b–38 and 1 Timothy 2:11–15. These passages depict Christians at public worship where preaching, teaching, and logically, the Sacraments, too, are visible actions of the Office of the Ministry. In the assembly for public worship, the women present are to remain hearers. They are not to be preachers (cf. 1 Cor 14:34, 35; 1 Tim 2:11, 12). This directive is clear. It is *apostolic* and therefore *dominical*, of the Lord (1 Cor 14:37b; cf. John 14:24, 26; 17:8, 14a). Also, Paul states that it is a directive con-

413 Pastor Rolph Mayer of the Lutheran Church of Australia infers that Pauline directives that women be silent may be among those "traditions" not set down as necessary acts of worship but a means of preserving order in the Church for the sake of peace. He asks whether these directives may have been among those things that the apostles reportedly ordained but which they did not set down as though they could not be changed (Ap XXVIII 15, 16). We have no way of knowing what these things were because Melanchthon does not mention what the apostles tentatively ordained. Furthermore, the sentence that begins "for they did not contradict their own writings . . ." must be a reference also to the apostle's writing about the silence of women in the church's worship assembly as well as many other subjects—for example, the present reference to his intent to free the Church from the notion that human rites are required acts of worship (Ap XXVIII 16b; cf. 1 Cor 14:36, 37b). Therefore, in the view of the confessors, Paul's directives that women be silent were not subject to change because such alterations would contradict the apostle's writing. Further, if the Pauline directives were indeed viewed as things that could be changed, the Lutheran confessors would have considered this factor binding. In that event, it is likely that we should have seen the practice of women's ordination advocated by the Lutherans of the sixteenth century. See Rolph Mayer, "The Confessions, the Public Ministry, and the Ordination of Women," *Lutheran Theological Journal* 31, no. 2 (August 1997): 82–88.

sistent with the intention of the Law under the old covenant (1 Cor 14:34b). Does the authoritative Word engaged in the Church's public worship address the matter of occupants of the Office of the Ministry (cf. 1 Cor 14:26)? It seems so. Ordering the conduct of public worship, the apostle Paul demonstrates how the Word governs the Church's practice (1 Cor 14:36). This includes the practice of the Office of the Ministry. In reference to the office and its functions, the apostle teaches that the women remain hearers. Men who are properly trained and qualified, then called, exercise this public office.

First Corinthians 14:33b–38

These general comments lead to passages that are key to this subject, beginning with 1 Corinthians 14:33b–38 (and set within the larger context, 1 Cor 14:26–40). Dr. John Kleinig states that the *pericope*, verses 34–37, is a coherent piece of Pauline rhetoric presented in the form of regulations for the operation of the Church as a liturgical community.[414] The structure of the passage in its context and pattern of rhetoric establishes the unity of verses 33b–38 as a coherent argument. Dr. Kleinig presents the structured argument as follows:

a. As in all the churches of the saints,
the women *must remain silent* in the churches,
  for it is not permitted for them to speak,
  but they must be subordinate, as the law says.

b. If they wish to learn something,
let them question their husbands at home,
  for it is shameful for a woman to speak in church—
  did the word of God really originate from you,
  or has it reached you alone?

c. If any considers that he is a prophet or a spiritual person,
let him acknowledge that what I write is a command of the Lord.

d. If, on the other hand, anybody disregards it,
he is disregarded (by God).

Setting forth the argument as it is structured by the text, Dr. Kleinig adds these expository remarks:

> In keeping with the pattern established in vv. 26–33b, the flow

414 John Kleinig, "Scripture and the Exclusion of Women from the Pastorate," *Lutheran Theological Journal* 39, no. 2 (Part I, August 1995): 77. In Part I of his essay, Dr. Kleinig prefaces exposition of 1 Corinthians 14:33b–38 with hermeneutical presuppositions for the Lutheran interpreter. He adds theological presuppositions about the Ministry of Word and Sacrament drawn from the Scriptures. In Part II, December 1995, he expounds 1 Timothy 2:11–15.

> of the argument is determined by two categorical third person imperatives for silence and subordination in v. 34 followed by two conditional imperatives about the questioning of husbands and the acknowledgment of Christ's authority in vv. 35–36. This culminates in the conditional threat about the rejection of dissenters in v. 37. Moreover, as Paul develops his argument, he gives six reasons for his instructions, in subordinate clauses: ecumenical practice (33b), the prohibition of women speaking in church (34a), the content of the law (34b), the shamefulness of women speaking in church (35), the origin of the apostolic teaching (36a), and its reception (36b).[415]

From this reading of the text, 1 Corinthians 14:33b–38, both the assertion that women are to remain silent in the worshiping assembly with regard to preaching and teaching the Word, and the authority for this directive support the validity of the practice of not ordaining women to the calling of pastor/leader in the Office of the Ministry. Five facets of this subject are the following:

1. The setting—the public worship of the assembled congregation of Christians—is determined within the context where the apostle Paul states that he is talking about the whole Church assembling, and he comments on decorum and behavior in this setting (1 Cor 14:23).
2. The "speaking" in this setting referenced by the apostle is *lalein*, a term with many uses in the New Testament, but used here as a synonym for authoritative teaching, likely formal preaching and teaching[416] (cf. 1 Tim 2:12; Matt 9:18; 28:18; John 18:19; Acts 4:1; 18:25; 1 Cor 2:6–7; 2 Cor 2:17; Heb 13:7). Observe that in the liturgical assembly there was a plethora of other "speaking"—speaking in tongues, interpretation of "tongue" speaking, prophesying and weighing what was said when prophets spoke, liturgical prayer, open discussions—and women participating in all of this "speaking" (1 Cor 11:5; 14:28, 29; 1 Tim 2:1–10; cf. 1 Thess 5:19–22). The apostle Paul's intent is to keep order (1 Cor 14:40) and make sense out of this mixture of speaking so that all is done for edification (1 Cor 14:26b, 33).

415 Ibid., 78.
416 Ibid., 79.

3. The Christian woman's place with regard to public preaching and teaching is to remain silent, to listen and be subordinate presumably to the leader's preaching and teaching (1 Cor 14:34). For that matter, silence is the posture for prophets and those speaking in tongues as well as for women when it comes to speaking God's Word, which has come as an apostolic word via emissaries from Jerusalem[417] (1 Cor 14:28, 30, 34; 1 Cor 14:36; cf. Acts 1:8).

4. That women in the public worshiping assembly shall remain silent is asserted further by the directive that a woman should consult with her husband at home when reflecting on the meaning and implications of the Word preached or given as instruction (1 Cor 14:35). For her to be forward in the public setting and assume the "speaking" role—also breaking out of the "subordinate" posture—would be shameful (1 Cor 14:35b).

5. These directives are given by special authority—not the apostle Paul's misogynous or sexist psyche—but the definitive Word of the Lord (1 Cor 14:37b–38). Any who contradict this dominical authority of the apostolic directive clearly show hubris, as if the word directing governance in the Church originated not with Christ and His Word but with individuals and their subjective assertions (1 Cor 14:36).

The ordaining of women to the Office of the Holy Ministry places them in a position of speaking and leading by the instrument of the Word in the public assembly of the congregation—vocally preaching and teaching—and displaces them from subordinate in this setting to assume a function with authority that the apostle Paul rejects. He has more to say on this point in 1 Timothy 2:11–15.

First Timothy 2:11–15

The other passage in this discussion of women's ordination is 1 Timothy 2:11–15. The immediate context addresses the demeanor of women in the church assembly at worship. "Likewise also that women should adorn themselves in respectable apparel, with modesty and self-control, not with braided hair and gold or pearls or costly attire, but with what is proper for women who profess godliness—with good works" (1 Tim 2:9–10). Not only does the woman's apparel reflect her high calling as the Lord's disciple, but she also pursues good works, not least the calling for which she is specially equipped, the vocation of motherhood (1 Tim 2:10, 15).

417 Ibid., 80.

The apostle Paul's directives go beyond women's apparel and demeanor. They also focus on the place of women in public worship, the liturgical fellowship (1 Tim 2:11–12). Paul's teaching on this subject references Adam's priority as the leader in the first marriage, family, and then the larger human family. Dr. Kleinig anchors Adam's headship Christologically. "The role of Adam as the liturgical head of the human family," he states, "was fulfilled by Christ (see Col. 1:15–23); it is now exercised by him through the male teachers of the church."[418] The headship of Adam was established from the beginning of the human race. God created Adam first. Adam's headship stands out in the structure of 1 Timothy 2:8–15 set forth by Dr. Kleinig:

1. I therefore (as teacher of the gentiles) require that in every place (of worship) men should pray, lifting consecrated hands without anger and quarreling, and women too (should pray), decorating themselves with modesty and chastity by means of respectable deportment, not by means of gold-braided hair or pearls or expensive dress, but through good works, as is suitable for women who profess reverence for God.

2. Let a woman learn in quietness with entire subordination.

   On the other hand, I do not permit a woman to teach or to have authority over a man, but she must remain in quietness; for Adam was formed first, then Eve; and Adam was not deceived, but the woman, being deceived, came into transgression. Nevertheless a woman will be saved even as she bears children (Greek: through child bearing), provided that she remains with *chastity* in faith and love and sanctification.[419]

What does the apostle Paul require with respect to women in the worship assembly? Clearly, he requires that women should not teach or have authority over a man (1 Tim 2:12). The man in this instance is the leader, the pastor. The teaching is the apostolic witness to the Lord (Acts 1:8; 2:42); the Gospel (2 Tim 1:10–11), inclusive of all that the Lord taught; what the Spirit would bring to the apostles' memory (John 14:25–26); and teaching or doctrine, the Word of God (1 Thess 2:13). Further, the teaching is inclusive of Paul's apostolic instructions (1 Tim 1:3; 4:6; 2 Tim 4:2b), in this instance, counsel about conduct in the household of God (1 Tim 3:15).

418 John W. Kleinig, "Scripture and the Exclusion of Women from the Pastorate (II)," *Lutheran Theological Journal*, 39, no. 3 (December 1995): 126.

419 Ibid., 123.

The Christian woman defers to those who are called or appointed to lead the worship—including public teaching and prayer and other liturgical actions, such as the Sacrament (cf. 1 Tim 2:8; Acts 2:42). The apostle's instruction is clear. Even though she is a disciple of Jesus, the woman is not the *teacher*. She attends as a disciple to learn, quietly and unobtrusively (1 Tim 2:11–12). She refrains from outbursts and, instead of asserting authority over the men, defers to the leader, the *episcopus*, the bishop or pastor in this liturgical assembly.

Paul's instruction about the role of women in public worship is not from his opinion, but on the authority of his call from God to order how the household of God should conduct itself as the Church of the living God (1 Tim 3:14–15). For this leadership, the apostle was appointed by God as preacher and apostle to be "a teacher of the Gentiles in faith and truth" (1 Tim 2:7; also Acts 26:16–18; 2 Tim 4:17; Eph 3:8). Dr. Kleinig observes that the strength of St. Paul's apostolic authority extends everywhere the Church is gathered, transcending particular local circumstances in Ephesus.[420] Both the authority and the teaching about conduct apply universally to congregations of Christians gathered for public worship in any time and place.

Moreover, besides ordering conduct in the worship assembly, Paul focuses on the conduct of public teachers. Dr. Kleinig explains the apostle's instruction about both the role and vocation of teachers:

> As "bishops" they supervise the worship and life of the congregation (1 Tim 3:2). As "elders" they arrange the worship of the congregation and manage its operation (1 Tim 5:17). As "servants" of the risen Lord they represent him in their teaching and work with him (2 Tim 2:24). Their basic qualification is that they are teachable and skilled in teaching (1 Tim 3:2; 2 Tim 2:24). Such teachers teach God's word in the congregation (1 Tim 5:17) and use the healing doctrine of Christ to encourage the faithful and to refute those who contradict it (Tit. 1:9).[421]

Dr. Kleinig summarizes, "So then, for Paul a teacher is one who has been authorised to teach the apostolic doctrine and engage in the apostolic ministry of the word."[422] He concludes, "Thus, while Paul teaches the full involvement of all women in the public worship of the church as intercessors, as disciples of their risen Lord, and as holy people together with the angels, he forbids them to be teachers in the church."[423] If any do not recognize this teaching as

420 Ibid., 124.
421 Ibid., 125
422 Ibid.
423 Ibid., 127.

a command of the Lord, they are not to be recognized (1 Cor 14:37b–38). The Church shall honor the Lord's command and call or appoint only trained and qualified men to the Office of the Holy Ministry.

Women and Men in the Congregation

Mutuality

The previous discussion of women's ordination in light of apostolic directives for public worship is part of the overarching subject of women and men in the life of the Church. Mutuality orders the life of the two sexes in the Christian congregation; that is, women and men live and serve together, showing mutual Christian love, respect, and honor.[424] Although women and men baptized into Christ are the priesthood of believers (Gal 3:26–28; 1 Pet 2:9–10), this identity, also mutuality, does not obviate their roles in God's order of creation. This fact differs profoundly from the constructs of gender equality or gender homogeneity advanced by secularists.

Interdependence

Sexism and feminism have polarized the sexes in Western culture. Observe that the Church offers a different model. Against the background of the divine order of creation, the apostle Paul affirms that in the Lord woman is not independent of man, nor is man independent of woman (1 Cor 11:11). He continues, "For as woman was made from man, so man is now born of woman" (1 Cor 11:12). Further, the relationship between men and women observed in the Church arises from the matrix of Christian marriage, where a woman is never without a man. She accepts the headship of her husband (1 Cor 11:3b–9; Eph 5:23, 25). In marriage, she is submissive as to the Lord (Eph 5:22–24). Also, in Christian marriage a man is never without a woman (Gen 2:18, 23–24; 24:4; Judg 14:1–3; Prov 18:22). The husband rejoices in the blessing of his wife's help, support, partnership, and loyalty (Gen 2:18; 8:18; 23:2). In turn, he secures her protection and he spends himself in loving care for her (Gen 2:23; 3:8, 20; 1 Pet

424 Mutuality is framed in Ephesians 5:21 as "mutual submission" or "submitting to one another" or "submitting yourselves one to another," but mutual submission does not override the roles of women and men in God's order of creation that are honored in the fellowship of the Church. God's place for women and men ennobles mutual submission, though submitting to one another within His order is more complex than appears at first. John Nordling argues against an interpretation of Ephesians 5:21 that either obviates the differences of roles according to divine ordering in creation or presses for a strict egalitarian relationship of the sexes in the fellowship. Nordling's exegesis leads him to observe that Ephesians 5:21 functions as a kind of "general heading" for the specific callings of Christians that follow in the household code of Ephesians 5:22–6:9; namely, wives with regard to husbands (5:22–33), children with regard to parents (6:1–4), and slaves with regard to masters (6:5–9). See John G. Nordling, "Does Ephesians 5:21 Support Mutual Submission?" *Logia* 24, no. 4 (Reformation 2015): 20.

3:7; Col 3:19; 1 Tim 5:8; cf. Matt 1:20, 24; 2:13, 19–23; Luke 2:4–5, 39–40). Marriage, family, and home compose a microcosm of life together in the Church. This configuration illustrates the point.

	Order	Role	Duty
Marriage			
Husband	Head of wife	Leader, protector, provider	Love, care, protect
Wife	Looks to husband as head	Complement, helper	Love, honor, assist
Home			
Husband	Headship	Provider, overseer, leader	Provide, protect, lead
Wife	Looks to husband	Partner overseeing, leading	Love, care, serve
Parents	Over children	Providers, teachers, leaders	Love, teach, train
Children	Submit to parents	Learners, helpers	Love, honor, obey/serve
Church			
Men	Headship	Leaders, teachers, administrators	Oversee public doctrine, teach, lead/follow
Women	Look to headship of men	Parents, teachers, counselors	Support, serve, follow, lead (outside the pastoral office)

Application to Woman's Place in the Congregation

Within this organic configuration, there is room for gender-neutral ministry. The apostle Paul recognizes the gifts and functions of the members of the Body, the Church—giftedness for serving, teaching, exhortation, contributing material goods, leadership, ministry of mercy and care (Rom 12:4–8). Women and men are both so gifted. Barring ordination to the pastoral office and exercise of functions closely related to the office, women may serve in most every aspect of the congregation's ministry including leadership roles as chairpersons of boards and committees, voting in the governing assembly, ushering in the worship assembly, and so forth. This was the opinion rendered by a majority of members of the Commission on Theology and Church Relations of The Lutheran Church—Missouri Synod in 1994.[425]

The Diaconate

Mutuality of women and men in the Church would be served by the nomenclature of deacons and deaconesses, with the congregation's ministry configured accordingly.[426] The term and the office of elder in today's congregations would be expendable. In its place, deacons would assist with duties assigned to the pastor, feeding the congregation with the Word of God and overseeing spiritual welfare. The service of deacons also embraces caring ministries and administration (Acts 6:2–3). Deaconesses would also serve in important roles: prayer and devotion with the sick and distressed, aid to needy persons and families, counseling troubled persons, teaching children and women, and assisting the laity to carry out various ministries such as music, evangelism and mission, youth ministry, social welfare, and other ministry *iure humano*, by human arrangement[427] (cf. Titus 2:3–5). Recovery of the diaconate offers possibilities for mutuality in the ministry of women and men in the Church.

Principle: As baptized Christians, women and men are free in the Gospel to serve the Lord and His people within boundaries established by the order of creation and according to apostolic exhortations addressing the proper exercise of authority in the Church.

425 See the Commission's document *The Service of Women in Congregational and Synodical Offices* (November 1994), 11. The Commission, however, was divided. A minority expressed their concern that this opinion would benefit from further investigation and study, principally the doctrine of the order of creation (1 Cor 11:3, 8–12, 16) and the concept of αυθεντέιν articulated in 1 Timothy 2:12–14 in order to see how these two factors instruct about women's service within the Christian congregation. The minority response was published as a document titled "Dissenting Opinion on Women in Congregational Offices," in *Reporter*, December 1994. The Executive Committee of the CTCR published their response to the "dissent" document in the Workbook for the 1995 Convention of The Lutheran Church—Missouri Synod, 314–316.

426 The CTCR of The Lutheran Church—Missouri Synod offered this suggestion in its report *The Service of Women in Congregational and Synodical Offices*. See the discussion of "Case One: The Office of Elder," 13.

427 The possibilities of the diaconate in Lutheran pastoral and ecclesiastical practice are evident in the pivotal work that documents this ministry from the early centuries to the present. See Jeannine E. Olson, *Deacons and Deaconesses through the Centuries* (St. Louis: Concordia Publishing House, 2005).

CHAPTER NINETEEN

Christians and Lodges, Fraternal Orders, Sects, Cults

Introduction

Theological pluralism—tolerance of many religions—is an outlook that usually is intolerant of the particularity professed by Christianity. This is an issue for Christians attracted to various non-Christian fellowships. The belief and confession that Jesus Christ, the Son of God, is the one in whom alone is salvation (Acts 4:12) is incompatible with the spirit of pluralism that dictates if there be religion, then all *religions* have a place at the table. This is not the first age of popular pluralism. Williston Walker opens his monumental work, *A History of the Christian Church*, with this observation:

> Christianity entered no empty world. Its advent found men's minds filled with conceptions of the universe, of religion, of sin, and of rewards and punishments, with which it had to reckon and to which it had to adjust itself. Christianity could not build on virgin soil.[428]

Walker's observation about the advent of Christianity resonates today. Current conceptions of reality—man and God and life and hope and salvation and destiny—vary greatly from Christian teaching. Those variations appear in the teachings and practices of lodges, fraternities, sects, and cults. Certainly, the distinctions are also acute with regard to secular humanism.

We live in an age of pluralism. This factor challenges pastors who are watchmen for Christians. There are prophets of one kind or another who are eager to accommodate a Christian who is curious about something *other* than the faith confessed in the Church's creeds. Christians are a mouse-click away from religious options that offer divergent notions about God and the world

428 Williston Walker, *A History of the Christian Church*, 3rd ed. (New York: Charles Scribner's Sons, 1970), 3.

and life. They conflict with the one Gospel of the Savior, who declared, "I am the way, the truth, and the life" (John 14:6). How shall the pastor minister to baptized Christians who are curious about other belief systems or may be interested in joining an alternative religious organization or fraternity, one of the sects, or even a cult?

Distinctive Religions and Quasi Religious Groups

The Variety of Religious Persuasions

Principle: If the pastor is to minister effectively to Christians who are drawn to non-Christian fellowships, he will attempt to comprehend the appeal of such groups and understand their teachings and practices.

Access to numerous religious affiliates may distract Christians. Various fraternities, principally lodges—Freemasonry, the animal lodges (Elks, Moose, etc.), the International Order of Odd Fellows—supplement creedal religion professed by the Christian churches. Candidates need not leave their churches to affiliate with the lodge. Many Protestants are quite comfortable with dual church and lodge membership. Even the clergy in some of these churches hold dual membership. The sects, however—Jehovah's Witnesses, the Mormons, Christian Science, for example—present a clear distinction between the Christian Church and sectarian beliefs. Similarly, the cults totally absorb persons and insist on severance of ties with one's religion.

The Variety of Attractions

Attraction to alternative religions requires serious attention by confessing Lutherans. Why would Lutheran Christians look elsewhere? Why would they either supplement fellowship in the Body of Christ or seek a substitute for this fellowship? Perhaps it is because they are caught in dysfunction of the *Body*. This occurs in various ways. Within the congregation, insensitivity to earnest questions posed by a Christian, doctrinaire or heavy-handed delivery of the Gospel, a judgmental attitude, either rigidity or perceived lack of seriousness about the requirements of faith, laxity with doctrine, mean-spirited treatment, or social ostracism are some of the reasons that drive Christians to look in other directions.[429]

429 For ten years, a pastor ministered to a severely disabled, homebound person, bringing the Lord's Supper to her and her elderly father once a month. Their home was a cabin nestled in the hills of a remote area. They were poor. One afternoon, the pastor visited. As he set out the Communionware on the kitchen table, he was stopped cold. "No, no, I don't want that," was the outburst. "I don't understand. Why this sudden concern?" the pastor replied. He retreated and said, "Perhaps another time." "No, No!" The pastor learned in these moments that this handicapped aging lady had been visited by members of the Jehovah's Witness

Essential personal or social needs that go unmet in the Christian community are fertile ground for attraction to alternative religions of one kind or another. For instance, when a thoughtful Christian harbors unresolved spiritual unrest—even doubts—the sects offer alternative belief systems. They frame attractive teaching that proposes to correct what is amiss in the corpus of Christian doctrine and confession. They may suggest, "You can still follow Jesus, but your belief must change. Let us supply details about the Lord that you never heard in your former church." The cults are more extreme. They propose to convince the confused Christian that the Bible is not important. In fact, it should be abandoned so that one may welcome new revelations and insights that are waiting in the cult experience.

Preparing for Counsel and Instruction

Securing Opportunity to Bring Pastoral Counsel

Upon hearing that a member of the congregation contemplates involvement in the lodge, one of the sects, or even a cult, a pastor immediately prays for this Christian. He prays that the person may be drawn back to the Scriptures. The pastor asks the Holy Spirit to lead this Christian to remain in his or her faith in Jesus Christ. Thus, a mistake of eternal proportions may be averted. The pastor also prays for patience, wisdom, and skill to effectively minister to the distracted Christian.

The challenge to care for a Christian who is toying with membership in a non-Christian group or fraternity can be disquieting. The pastor reflects, "I don't need this new problem." In addition to all that he is dealing with in a busy pastorate, patient and lengthy counsel with a distracted Christian is not easy. He is tempted to procrastinate and avoid the matter. Or, in the interest of solving it quickly, he may be impatient and descend on the weak Christian like a traffic patrolman apprehending an errant motorist. Caution! A Christian astray who senses impatience or condescension or judgmental scolding may be swiftly driven to the lodge, sect, or cult.

Timing of Pastoral Counsel of the Christian Astray

Our Lord's parables of the shepherd seeking the lost sheep and the humble woman seeking the lost coin apply to the restless pastor who faces an absorbing pastoral care challenge (Luke 15:3–10). When caring for Christians drawn to

sect. They had befriended her and persuaded her to reject the Lord's Supper, and for that matter, her pastor too. What was happening? While the pastor's visits over the years had resulted in a close bond—shepherd and sheep—the other members of the flock were conspicuously absent. Others in the congregation had neglected this poor family in their humble home locked back in the hills. They had failed this lady and her father. But the Jehovah's Witnesses had filled the vacuum.

non-Christian organizations, the timing must be right, that is, when the person is ready to explore his or her attraction to alternative religions. Hesitation to engage in this conversation may call for a gentle reminder that our Lord voices a strong "Beware!" He cautioned that false christs abound (Matt 24:24; Mark 13:22). The apostle John counseled, Test the teaching of other belief systems. His advice was, "Beloved, do not believe every spirit, but test the spirits to see whether they are from God, for many false prophets have gone out into the world" (1 John 4:1). St. Paul noted that some will depart from the faith by giving themselves to other doctrines. These could be doctrines of demons (1 Tim 4:1). Perhaps it is time for a frank discussion about these issues.

Approaches in Pastoral Counsel of the Straying Christian

In addition to proper timing, patient attention to factors that led a Christian to an alternative religion is essential. A pastor may cut to the quick and focus on the doctrinal differences between Christianity and the other religion. He may directly scrutinize the teachings advanced by this religion, but he may be moving too swiftly. Why is this Christian attracted to the lodge? What needs are not being met in the Church that he or she perceives are fulfilled in the lodge? We alluded to these factors above. They cannot be ignored and it is best to explore them early in the discussion. Handling the need factor is essential for the person to be receptive to discussing the confessional issues.

The approach to discussing doctrinal and confessional issues is through introspection. The pastor may frame key questions. "Why am I a Christian? How did I become a Christian? What do I believe? What does Jesus Christ mean to me? How has our Lord redeemed me to be His own? Have my current answers to these and similar questions changed? Why? How binding is God and His Word on my thinking, my goals, my life?" Reviewing and reconsidering a Christian's identity and confession, sets the stage for honest comparison between the teachings of the Christian faith and the non-Christian alternative religion—a lodge, sect, or cult.

The Content of Counsel with Distracted Christians

Paradigm for Counsel

Principle: Having attended to a Christian's felt needs that presumably are met by an alternative religion, the pastor moves to concrete comparisons that demonstrate how the teaching of Christianity can have no part with non-Christian teachings and practices of the lodge, sect, or cult that attracts this person.

A Christian who is attracted to non-Christian groups may not realize how devotion to deities other than the triune God is heretical confession and practice. Satan is a master at deception. Therefore, the pastor asks, "Now, can we be honest, not only about your feelings at this point but also about the teachings of the fellowship that attracts you and how those teachings compare with Bible teaching? What does the Bible say; what does (the lodge, sect, or cult) teach?"[430] Here is a list of doctrines and subjects for comparison:

Holy Scripture, the Bible	Prayer
The Triune God	Initiation Rites
Jesus Christ	Oaths
Salvation	Sacraments
Works/Righteousness	Spiritual Leadership
Justification before God	Community/Fellowship
Death and Beyond/Eschatology	Witness vs. Compromise
Worship/Ritual	Syncretism

When these doctrines and subjects are the focus, the discussion moves toward solid ground and becomes more than a friendly chat. The pastor assists the Christian to review the salient teachings of Holy Scripture. Using the Bible and reading it aloud is important.[431] The aim is to consider the non-Christian teachings from a position of strength when a Christian has reaffirmed the right doctrine according to the Scriptures. Certainly, the Holy Spirit will impart a clear understanding and assist in the reaffirmation of faith and confession of the true doctrine (John 14:25; cf. Matt 10:32–33, 37–39; Rom 10:9; 1 John 4:1–3).

Examples of Dialogue

It goes without saying that the pastor prepares well before counseling the distracted Christian. First, he is informed about the teachings and practices of the lodge, sect, or cult that troubles the Christian he is counseling.[432] Second, he is conversant about the Scriptures that apply to the issues. In dialogue, the pastor may pose the right doctrine and the opposing teaching in terms of *thesis* and *antithesis*. Here are a few examples:

The Doctrine of God

The *thesis* may be expressed in this manner: "On the basis of the teachings

430 For comparisons, see *Masonry in the Light of the Bible* (St. Louis: Concordia Publishing House, 1969).

431 Need we state the wisdom of the pastor and counselee having in their hands Bibles of the same identical version and edition?

432 A primary source of information from the Commission on Theology and Church Relations of The Lutheran Church—Missouri Synod is the document titled *Membership in Certain Fraternal Organizations: A Pastoral Approach* (February 2009). This document and other helps are found at www.lcms.org?2150.

of the Scriptures, we believe, teach, and confess that God is revealed to us by His Word, the triune God—Father, Son, and Holy Spirit—three divine persons in one divine essence or being." This concise revelation and the First Commandment permit no other notions of God. The teaching in conflict, the *antithesis*, may be expressed, "Freemasonry worships the Grand Architect of the universe, a vague notion of deity." This distinction raises a question, "How can a Christian look to God and worship Him in both the Church and the lodge?"

Worship Practices

Regarding worship practices, the *thesis* may be expressed this way. Christians at worship gather in the name of the triune God. They expect that God's Word will be proclaimed and taught in truth and purity as He intended it to be. Our response of honor, adoration, and sacrificial offerings shall be directed only to the true God. Contrast the *antithesis*, the arrangement of ceremonies of the lodge where the deity goes by different names and the rituals engage persons with varying notions of deity. In some lodges, even atheists are welcome to participate on their own terms. Frequently, the spoken rite or ceremony departs from monotheism and also from articulation of God in terms of His revelation to us as the one triune God who is worshiped only through Jesus Christ (2 Cor 4:6). For the Christian who bears the name of the true God from Baptism, participation in ceremonies of the lodge poses inescapable questions: "Which altar is right? Which altar is right for me?"

The seriousness of these two questions cannot be overemphasized. At times in ancient Israel, the people forsook Yahweh. They worshiped other gods, or they attempted to straddle the issue by professing loyalty to Yahweh while devoting themselves to false deities. In both instances, reprisal by God's wrath was formidable (cf. Exod 32:1–10; 1 Kgs 18:20–40; Amos 5:25–27; et al.). Intriguing as secret ceremonies and worship practiced by lodges and others are, Joshua's mandate and stern warning still apply (Josh 24:14, 20). Now what is Joshua saying to the Christian who ventures into the arena of any lodge, sect, or cult?

Death and Beyond—Eschatology

Fraternal organizations often direct their members to the hereafter. The "grand lodge above," "the eternal happy home" are examples of euphemisms for the bliss that supposedly awaits members in good standing after death. Funeral and burial rites give expression to such aspirations. Freemasonry speaks of the summons from the "Grand Warden of heaven" and points to the celestial "lodge above" where the "Supreme Architect of the universe" presides. In the funeral ritual of the Elks lodge, members look to the "light beyond the valley of the shadow of death." Similarly, the ritual of the Moose lodge points to blessed immortality or eternal rest beyond the grave.

Furthermore, many lodges and fraternal organizations focus on their brotherhood in the hereafter. Brothers and sisters pursued the pure and the good during their lifetime on earth. Now they look forward to a more blessed fraternity. In these projections and the collective imagery of the hereafter, there is no reference to Jesus Christ. The *antithesis*, therefore, opens with the frank observation that Christians consider any notion of the hereafter without Christ repugnant. It is He who redeemed us—the robes of the saints washed in His blood. In heaven, the saints worship the Lamb of God, who is on the throne (Rev 5:8–14). Who is central in that vision of the saints before God (Rev 7:13–17)? It is the Lamb. Jesus Christ alone is the agent for eternal life with God (John 3:16; 6:40; 10:27–30; Rom 6:22b–23; Titus 3:4–7). How lacking is any funeral service or burial rite that deliberately dismisses Jesus Christ!

Salvation

Salvation, that is, getting on with God in peace and confidence, is a subject related to the hereafter. The *thesis* embraced by many fraternal organizations, sects, and cults is that salvation is man's own doing. He must accomplish it, if and when he has a mind to do so. The notion of *deity* is left to individual members to frame as they will, and the program of reaching acceptance with that deity is also one's own making. For example, in Freemasonry, each member works out his own conception of God and achieves salvation by his own initiative.[433] In the history and teachings and sayings of the respected masters, Masonry does not teach salvation by faith. The vicarious atonement for sins by Jesus Christ has no credence. There is no plan for redemption from sin. Instead, a platform of good works is the focus and emphasis. In the Masonic funeral service, there is an allusion to a certain *pass* into the "grand lodge above," which is cited as the *pass* of a pure and blameless life.[434]

The Christian *antithesis* to Masonry's design for salvation and any similar scheme in other fraternities is threefold. First, the Scriptures dismiss the notion that *pure and blameless* may be ascribed to any who fashion their own notion of salvation. "All have sinned and fall short of the glory of God" (Rom 3:23). Honesty about the human condition compels the sad conclusion that all "are under the power of sin" (Rom 3:9 RSV; cf. vv. 10–18 RSV) and are helpless to remedy this sinful condition by any means contrived by sinful man. The Scriptures consign the sinful race to death (Rom 5:12; 6:23).

433 Ward, *Freemasonry: Its Aims and Ideals*, cited in *Masonry in the Light of the Bible* (St. Louis: Concordia Publishing House, 1969), 17.
434 *Masonry in the Light of the Bible*, 19.

Second, salvation can only be by God's design and creation that He graciously accomplished when He sent His Son, Jesus, to save His people from their sins (Matt 1:21). Jesus Christ, the God-man, gave Himself into death on the cross "as a ransom for many" (Mark 10:45). He gave His life on the cross to atone for our sins and by His stripes we are healed (Rom 3:23–25; Isa 53:5). Thus, the apostle exclaimed that salvation is in none other than Jesus Christ, for there is no other saving name (Acts 4:12). In Him, we have freedom, that is, the forgiveness of sins, and we are reconciled to God in peace (1 Pet 2:24; 2 Cor 5:19; Rom 5:1). Our sins are no longer charged to us but to Christ so that we are justified before God for time and eternity by faith in Jesus Christ (Rom 5:1; 3:25; cf. Gal 3:8, 11, 22).

Third, this salvation is by the Gospel, not by man's design or effort as numerous organizations and fellowships assert. They would program their followers back to God on the platform of good works. In His grace, God has made such futile efforts unnecessary, and we are saved by His grace alone (2 Cor 5:18a; Eph 2:8–9). How can a Christian who is saved by Jesus Christ participate in rituals or ceremonies that press faulty human works and remove Jesus from the notion of salvation?

Good Works

The good works accomplished by the lodge and other fellowships and organizations are admirable. Observe, however, that charity programs advanced by the lodge such as the Shriners' medical care for children, though commendable, are tainted with the works-righteousness motif that is apart from faith in Jesus Christ. A Christian wants to do good works, but can a Christian participate in the works of the lodge and avoid the faulty work-salvation ethic? Perhaps a Christian may discover other organizations or groups that permit doing good works as evidence of faith in Jesus (Eph 2:10; Titus 3:4–8; cf. Jas 1:22; 2:14–18).

Confession

Jesus Christ is the Savior who frees us from sin and death. Grafted in Him, we can do good works (John 15:5–6). The Masonic Order and similar lodges or fraternities, however, silence the Christian's confession of Jesus Christ.[435] Their opening exercises, prayers, rituals, and ceremonies are dismissive of Jesus Christ—a breach of confession for any Christian. It is uncontestable that Chris-

---

435 Masonry discourages discussion of Jesus among its members and in its meetings. So resistant are some Masons to Jesus Christ that when reading the Bible in Masonic meetings the leaders either select passages that do not name Jesus or they elect to excise His name from the Scripture text as they read. In the Royal Arch Degree, 2 Thessalonians 3:6–16 is read. In both verses 6 and 12 the reference to Christ is omitted. See Mackey, *Masonic Ritualist*, 348–349, cited by *Masonry in the Light of the Bible*, 14.

tians believe, teach, and confess what the Scriptures say, that Jesus is the Son of God, that He is one with the Father, that to acknowledge the Father is possible only when we confess Jesus, and that abiding in the doctrine of Jesus Christ we have both the Father and the Son (Matt 10:32–33; John 5:23; 14:9; 1 John 2:23; 2 John 9; 2 Cor 4:6).

This confession of Jesus Christ by the Holy Spirit (1 Cor 12:3) shares no likeness with Masonry or any organization that dismisses our Lord and presses man's delusion of self-ascribed purity. In this regard, the funeral rite of Masonry is telling. Denying the biblical teaching that salvation and heaven are ours only by faith in Jesus Christ, Masonry engages the symbol of the lambskin to make the impression that: "In all ages the lamb has been deemed an emblem of innocence; he, therefore, who wears the Lambskin as a badge of Masonry is continually reminded of that *purity of life and conduct which is necessary to obtain admittance into the Celestial Lodge above*, where the Supreme Architect of the Universe presides."[436] Christians cannot abide with this confession of the lodge.

Conclusion

These exhibits of teaching and practice compared to the Christian confession assist the pastor in his dialogue with Christians who are attracted to lodges, fraternities, organizations, sects, or cults. In similar fashion, a pastor may frame discussion of other pertinent subjects for comparison. At length, a Christian will consider how participation in alternative non-Christian groups may affect confession of Jesus Christ and witness to Him and His saving work. Will the Christian retain faith as confessed in the Church's creeds, Apostles', Nicene, Athanasian? Can he or she be faithful to this confession in settings where the Christian *credo* is frankly *anathema*? Scrutiny of fraternal organizations will raise issues framed by this summary statement:

> When any organization makes religious promises contrary to Holy Scriptures . . . requires calling upon God as a witness to an unnecessary oath or one pertaining to unrevealed matters . . . promises eternal life apart from Jesus Christ as a reward for virtue . . . regards the Bible as one moral code among many . . . pronounces that all religious beliefs are equally valid before God . . . practices quasi-sacramental rites with religious meanings . . . or requires prayer, but at the same time by rule and for a purpose forbids the use of Jesus' name in prayer—then the Christian must

436 Cited in "Membership in Certain Fraternal Organizations: A Pastoral Approach," 5; emphasis added.

> avoid membership in the organization because it is involved in sub-Christian religion.[437]

Following Jesus Christ and His Word may lead to the conclusion that certain lodges, fraternal orders, sects, or cults are false teachers of whom the apostle Peter spoke, "who will secretly bring in destructive heresies, even denying the Master who bought them, bringing upon themselves swift destruction" (2 Pet 2:1). Instead of engaging with such teachings and practices, let us take up our cross and walk with Jesus!

437 Cited from "Christians and Their Affiliations," in "Membership in Certain Fraternal Organizations: A Pastoral Approach," 8–9.

CHAPTER TWENTY

Church and Ministry in the Public Domain

Introduction

Across America, Christian churches mark the presence of the Gospel of Christ. Though some of the venerable houses of worship have gone the way of secular makeover—museums, restaurants, retail outlets, and such—the Church's presence and its mission still remain in the public arena. Our Lord positioned His disciples, saying, "I have sent them into the world" (John 17:18).

God's Divine Presence and Rule

God Rules in Two Realms

The two subjects in this discussion are how the Church conducts its mission to society and how pastors conduct themselves in public. The springboard for the discussion is the Lutheran theology of church and state, which is known as the two-kingdom theology. God created both realms, and He rules both realms. Centuries prior to the Constantine paradigm—the Church *legalis*, lawful or legal—and subsequent institutionalizing of the church, the apostle Paul placed Christians subject to the state, the higher power ordained by God (Rom 13:1–2). Through temporal kings, rulers, and parliaments, God rules, for He wills that state authorities govern and promote civil order so that all may live a peaceable life in this fallen age (Rom 13:1–7; 1 Pet 2:13–17; Mark 12:13–17; 1 Tim 2:1–2; AC XVI 1; XXVIII 11).

The other realm where God rules is the Church—the kingdom of God that came and is here in the Word made flesh, the incarnate Christ (John 1:14; Mark 1:14–15). God rules this realm by grace through Christ. The means for His rule is through the Church's primary mission of preaching the Gospel (Matt 28:18–20; Acts 1:8; cf. Eph 3:7–10). Through the Gospel, the Holy Spirit calls hearts to believe in Christ and keeps them in this faith (Acts 2:4f., 4:4, 29–31; 1 Cor 12:3; cf. AC XXVIII 5–8). The Church is God's doing, and His kingdom remains to the close of the age and beyond (Isa 9:7; Luke 1:33).

The Two Realms Distinguished

The Lutheran Confessions declare a clear distinction between the two realms, citing the kingdom of the *right* (the authority to preach the Gospel and administer the Sacraments) and the kingdom of the *left* (the authority and power of the state to maintain civil order). The Confessions honor both realms with their respective authority under God's rule as the highest gifts on earth (AC XXVIII 4, 18). However, the two realms shall remain separate from one another, and they shall not be confused or mingled (AC XXVIII 12–18). This distinction is made by God. Jesus Christ replied to Pontius Pilate, "But my kingdom is not from the world" (John 18:36b).

This distinction implies several points. God calls the Church to preach the Gospel that brings eternal gifts. The Church, therefore, does not interfere with the temporal authority of government[438] (AC XXVIII 10; cf. 13). Melanchthon wrote that the Gospel does not legislate for the state or undermine the state, for Christians are subject to governments (Ap XVI 3, 5–6; AC XVI 5–7; cf. Mark 12:17). Government, however, has a clear mandate to not interfere with preaching the Gospel. Government has its domain. It was instituted by God not to protect the soul but the body. The Augsburg Confession is clear. It states, "Secular power does not protect the soul but, using the sword and physical penalties, it protects the body and goods against external violence"[439] (AC XXVIII 11).

The Distinction of Realms Expedited

The United States Constitution acknowledges the distinction between the spiritual and the temporal realms. The First Amendment of the Constitution reads:

> Congress shall make no law respecting an establishment of religion, or prohibiting the free exercise thereof; or abridging the freedom of speech, or of the press; or the right of the people

438 Melanchthon confines the Church's focus within the spiritual realm. See his discussion of the marks of the Church (Ap VII and VIII 5–10a).

439 For representative essays on this subject, the distinction between the spiritual and temporal realms, see *God and Caesar Revisited*, ed. John R. Stephenson (Lutheran Academy Conference Papers, No. 1, Spring 1995). Also *Render unto Caesar . . . and unto God: A Lutheran View of Church and State; A Report of the Commission on Theology and Church Relations* (St. Louis: The Lutheran Church—Missouri Synod, September 1995). Also see LCMS President Matthew Harrison's letter to pastors, "President Harrison Provides a Lutheran View of Church and State," March 3, 2016.

> peaceably to assemble, and to petition the government for a redress of grievances.[440]

These well-crafted statements articulate separation between church and state, but they defy any notion of absolute separation. A caveat is unmistakable. Observe that the amendment does not forbid interaction between church and state where reasonable exchange is acceptable for the common good.[441] Furthermore, Lutheran theology informs understanding of the boundaries for the Church's wider participation in the public domain. Four essential principles emerge.

1. In the name of the Gospel, the Church does not interfere with the governing structure and administration of the state. It has no calling to make laws in the civil realm. Instead, the Gospel commands us to obey the present laws (AC XXVIII 13; Ap XVI 3, 5).
2. The Church may interact with governmental authorities when public policy matters involve choice or decision to uphold or ignore clear moral duty essential for peace and the welfare of the public (cf. Acts 5:29; Jer 44:22–23).
3. The Church has no mandate under Christ to convert government into a "Christian state," nor should the Church undertake any initiative to accomplish the same. It is sufficient to encourage Christians to be good citizens (cf. Rom 13:5–7).
4. Christians in the kingdom of the *right* are at liberty to occupy roles within government—the kingdom of the *left* (AC XVI 1–3; Ap XVI 1).

---

440 "Constitution of the United States"; signed on September 17, 1787, at Independence Hall in Philadelphia.

441 For further clarification of church and state with regard to the First Amendment, see Bill Hecht, *Two Wars We Must Not Lose* (Fort Wayne, IN: Concordia Theological Seminary Press, 2012). Most pertinent are passages in the Introduction, 21–22, 29–47, and chapter 6, "The Cultural War Being Waged by the Radical Secularists," 393ff. Historical background to the church-state doctrine is addressed by Philip Hamburger, *Separation of Church and State* (Cambridge, MA: Harvard University Press, 2004), and *Church and State under God*, ed. Albert G. Huegli (St. Louis: Concordia Publishing House, 1964). Engaging the debate about church-state relations, see Richard John Neuhaus, *The Naked Public Square: Religion and Democracy in America*, 2nd ed. (Grand Rapids: Wm. B. Eerdmans, 1984). For a thorough treatment of the Lutheran distinction between the two kingdoms, with application to twenty-first-century American society, see Robert Benne, *The Paradoxical Vision: A Public Theology for the Twenty-First Century* (Minneapolis: Fortress Press, 1995).

Boundaries for Church and Ministry in the Public Domain

Retaining the Church's Primary Identity

These principles infer that the Church should retain a visible and public identity as the Body of Christ and chief exponent of Christ and His Word. Visibility of the Church is as real and concrete as the marks of the Church, the preaching of the Gospel and the public administration of the Sacraments[442] (Ap VII and VIII 5). The Church should not relinquish or diminish this essential identity and visibility by resorting to activism. Many causes knock on the doors of the Church, and opportunities abound to respond, to wear *hats* other than the identity given by Christ. This is not to say that every cause from the public domain is suspect. Certainly, appeals for mercy and compassion are compelling. In the name of Jesus, the Church always responds to human need (Matt 25:40; Gal 6:9–10; cf. Mal 3:5b; Amos 2:6–7a; 8:4).

However, there are questionable causes. For instance, the temptation is real for the Church to reform American society and government. The Church's identity and mission are at stake. In the late twentieth century, there were two high profile ministries in America: the Rev. Dr. Jerry Falwell's movement known as the "moral majority" and the Rev. D. James Kennedy's proactive effort to turn America to Christ. The core ministry of both preachers was proclaiming the Gospel of Christ, but their ministries also called for reforms in legislation and execution of laws. In the heat of pursuing those initiatives, the retention of the proper distinction between church and state could be questioned. Pressing Christian principles as foundational and essential for government, it appeared that the distinction asserted here was, at times, either blurred or dismissed.

Again, the primary identity of the Church is at stake with respect to elections. The morality of candidates and moral implications of public policy issues are concerns for Christians, so pastors and church leaders may give counsel when the people vote. Their counsel must abide within boundaries that govern the acceptable influence of the Church under the laws of the state.[443] One stipulation is clear: pastors in the United States may not instruct their congregations to vote for a specific candidate.

442 Dr. Kurt Marquart emphasizes that the Church is about more than sharing "inward" spirituality. It possesses signs of an outward institution as surely as the temporal realm has its external marks. He explains, "Yes, the church is mainly an inward fellowship, but she is also an outward one, precisely because the inward faith is given only through the outward gospel and sacraments." Kurt E. Marquart, "The Two Realms ("Kingdoms") in the Lutheran Confessions," *God and Caesar Revisited*, ed. John R. Stephenson (Luther Academy Conference Papers, No. 1, Spring 1995), 41.

443 Requirements set by the Federal Election Campaign Act and the Internal Revenue Code clarify the parameters of public address and counsel that pastors and churches may advance under the law.

Appropriate Action vs. Activism

In addition to boundaries set by the state, the confessional principles of the Lutheran Church prevent inappropriate interference with government (AC XVI 5; XXVIII 10, 13). Issues arise, however, in the public sector that call for a definitive Christian response. The Church must speak. For example, under the Patient Protection and Affordable Health Care Act (2009), the United States federal government required that certain churches and church agencies pay health-care benefits inclusive of contraceptives and abortifacients for their employees. The Rev. Dr. Matthew Harrison, president of The Lutheran Church—Missouri Synod, took swift action to confront this issue. He appeared before the House Oversight and Government Reform Committee at the nation's capital in Washington, DC, on February 16, 2012. President Harrison and other church leaders objected to the measure that presses Christian conscience to be subservient to governmental authority.[444] The public witness given by Harrison and others gained national attention. The principle below abides.

Principle: Not of the world, stated Christ, but nevertheless in the world, the Christian Church gives open testimony to the Gospel and God's order for right conduct according to natural law articulated in divine statutes and ordinances for human life.

The Church weighs her words carefully in the public domain. She speaks as the Body of Christ. It is proper that the Church leave the gloves in the locker room. She is not hostile. Actions that are meant to intimidate and control the public mind are atypical for the Church, and internally there is a risk of division among church members over public issues. Although zealots and extremists may find their way into Christian congregations, they shall not be emboldened. Conversations that turn negative and caustic against the president or other officials have no place in the Church (Exod 22:28; Eccl 10:20; cf. 2 Pet 2:10; Jude 8). In public or behind closed doors, political activism is out of character for the Christian Church, but so is blatant quietism—the silence of Christians in the face of issues that they should and must address. Martin Luther's essay attached to correspondence with Nicholas von Amsdorf, titled "To the Christian Nobility of the German Nation Concerning Reform of the Christian Estate," is a model for walking the fine line between activism and quietism.[445]

444 Clearly, stipulations by the Affordable Health Care Act stood to press consciences of persons in the Church and related agencies who recognized that providing contraceptives and abortifacients is contrary to their beliefs.

445 See Martin Luther, "To the Christian Nobility of the German Nation Concerning the Reform of the Christian Estate, 1520," trans. W. A. Lambert, rev. James Atkinson (LW 44:123). See Richard H. Warneck, "The Pastor as Religious and Civic Leader: Breaking with Quietism," in *Witness & Worship in Pluralistic America*, ed. John F. Johnson and associate editors, Charles P. Arand, Joel P. Okamoto, Paul Raabe (St. Louis: Concordia Seminary, 2003), 28ff.

The Pastor's Conduct in the Public Domain

Identity as a Christian Pastor

Church and ministry in the public domain is the matrix for the pastor's conduct in society. In every circumstance, the pastor is a minister of the Gospel of Jesus Christ (Rom 1:1; 1 Cor 4:1; 1 Tim 3:7). Prioritizing in this manner does not obscure the fact that the pastor is also a citizen of the state, though his calling to the pastoral ministry may limit his options to speak and influence the public. When he participates in public gatherings—forums where the public addresses mayors and aldermen, or when the pastor's counsel is sought as testimony before public officials—does the pastor wear two hats, one as Christian pastor and the other as a citizen?

The understanding that the pastor wears one hat is preferred. His singular identity and *vocation* is that of a servant of Jesus Christ, yet he may function and speak as a citizen, being mindful that he is viewed as a churchman. As a citizen, he represents his own informed views, or he speaks on behalf of his congregation when mandated to do so. In either instance, he may advise officials to correct public policy, or he may recommend change and improvement. He does so in order to be helpful. The pastor is not a complainer. He speaks what is edifying and for the common good, fully aware that he is a servant of the Gospel of Christ. This truth steadies the pastor in the public domain as this comment suggests: "And when a pastor concludes that it would be possible for him to participate in a civic event, he should keep in mind that his very presence there—and the public witness given by his participation—introduces at least to some extent a 'religious dimension' to the event."[446]

Civic leaders know the difference between counsel from an informed churchman and the tirades of a zealot. A wise pastor also knows the difference. He practices in accord with this distinction. When stepping into the public arena, the pastor is conscious of his integral obligation to the Holy Scriptures and the Lutheran Confessions, and his well-informed words are helpful and edifying. Civic leaders are indebted to him.

Visibility

Beyond formal civic events, there are occasions when the pastor makes informal appearances. He is a public figure. When a crisis occurs—flood, fire, quake, or epidemic—the pastor is there. Compassion thrusts him in the midst of hurting people. Reaching far beyond church borders is the apostle's counsel,

---

446 *Guidelines for Participation in Civic Events: A Report of the Commission on Theology and Church Relations* (St. Louis: The Lutheran Church—Missouri Synod, 2004), 6n5.

"Rejoice with those who rejoice, weep with those who weep" (Rom 12:15). At scenes where the public is hurting, the pastor is there to assist. At other times, the pastor joins those who cheer and are happy. What does this mean? Picture a few scenes. The pastor is in the stands rooting for the local high school team playing the football or basketball game. Not every Friday evening, but frequently he is there. At town celebrations and fairs when the community gathers, the pastor is there. Or, midmorning now and then, he is away from his desk, strolling down Main Street. He has coffee with the local guys at the town café. Pleasant surprises await the pastor who is wise enough to be visible in the community.

Acquaintances

It is healthy for pastors to have relationships with key persons in the community—the mayor, the chief of police, the local superintendent of schools, or the high school principal. When the pastor takes the initiative to contact community leaders, they will welcome him for a few minutes of conversation. Consider others—the bank president, the hospital administrator, the funeral director, a family physician, the pharmacist. Consider a brief visit with the editor and/or publisher of the local newspaper or the manager of the radio or TV station. Much good comes from these contacts. The pastor is a professional person; he is a neighbor and a team member. He befriends key persons in the community.

The Open Public Square

Etiquette is important when the pastor engages in public discourse. Sooner or later, he will be in the thick of community life where his speech and conduct are visible. In his speaking, he is both wise as a serpent and innocent as a dove. So spoke our Lord (Matt 10:16). Forceful but gentle, the pastor's words are graced with kindness and love for all persons. He is charitable. He recognizes others for their sincerity and for the good they seek to accomplish. What about people who are not up to goodness? The pastor keeps his distance from them. He avoids conflict in public. The pastor has courage of his convictions and he champions moral rectitude, even in a hostile environment. He is also civil and courteous when he addresses opposing viewpoints. He speaks to issues, not persons. He doesn't *take on* opponents. He doesn't go on the attack. He never shoots from the hip. He doesn't demean. The pastor is not condescending but builds up others. He is a Christian gentleman.

Causes

The pastor knows that he cannot lend the weight of his office to any and every social cause. He is guarded, lest the ministry be blamed (2 Cor 6:3). The stances that he takes in public must be consistent with the majority viewpoint of his congregation. This is the rubric most of the time. In any public forum, the pastor is well informed. He refrains from speaking if he lacks sufficient data.

Prudence in speech and conduct covers a multitude of situations. Before or after meetings and events, in those informal conversations, the pastor is careful that his words help rather than hurt. He is especially careful when addressing the media or when he sends correspondence to newspapers and publications. He cannot be too careful when he utilizes email, Twitter, and Facebook. A wise pastor refrains from participation in any venue where he does not know who reads his words or how they may be misunderstood, misrepresented, or misused. Our Lord's words "Let what you say be simply 'Yes' or 'No'" may suggest that frequently, less is more (Matt 5:37). Also to the point, with regard to electronic correspondence, silence is golden.[447]

Protest Movements

At their own risk, the clergy participate in public protests.[448] The causes for public protest may be salutary, yet frequently these random assemblies get out of control. Most of the participants may be peaceful, but others appear to intentionally engage in hostile action. This is a red flag. Is it advisable for a Christian pastor to join people who protest in ways that are abusive or injurious to others? Perhaps the pastor may *protest* by communicating concerns to community leaders in a manner that is both rational and respectful. The pastor's exemplary conduct—leading by example—is a powerful communicator (1 Tim 3:2ff.; 2 Tim 2:24–26).

Involvement in Politics

The pastor remains politically neutral in public. He does not divulge how he votes in elections, and he is reluctant to appear on panels when the program is about political aims or ends. He should remember that he ministers to per-

447 In the chapel of Concordia Seminary, St. Louis, the dean authorized the use of streamers in the processional on a feast day, a liturgical gesture of praise to the Lord. The use of these streamers set off upwards of 130 blog-type messages on one church-related website. Most were negative comments. Many were uncharitable. Some were downright ugly. And these were from an audience of clergy. *Kyrie eleison!*

448 In the aftermath of a grand jury decision regarding a police shooting in Ferguson, Missouri, hundreds of people, most of them anonymous, marched and protested. This was in late November 2014. Some participants were notably revving up the intensity of protest. Clergypersons were among them. Some Lutheran clergy were observed approaching protesters to understand their concerns. The aim was to lower the level of intensity. Is there any social phenomenon more explosive and unpredictable than public protests organized to oppose perceived injustices?

sons and families who represent a variety of political persuasions. Therefore, the pastor does not join the campaign of any candidate for public office.

Does the pastor stand for election to public office? American politics records a few instances when the clergy held public office.[449] In the state of Missouri during the late twentieth century, the Rev. Dr. John Danforth, an ordained Anglican priest, served three terms in the United States Senate. Nothing stands in the way of such an arrangement (Ap XVI 1; cf. AC XVI 2), but serious issues surface when a parish pastor considers candidacy for public office. The issues raise this question: can a Christian pastor fulfill his calling to the Office of the Ministry with faithfulness to the Lord and His people when he devotes himself to the demands of public service? An unqualified affirmative answer is difficult. It bears repeating that holding public office under the auspices of a particular political party may hinder the pastor's ministry to persons of opposite political persuasions. Because of potential philosophical differences, the dual role of pastor and politician is discouraged. If a pastor perceives that his true calling is service in the temporal realm, he should resign from the pastoral ministry and freely pursue vocations in the public arena.

Affiliations

A Christian pastor may be invited to join civic groups—Rotary International, Kiwanis, Lions Club to name a few. A pastor may join fellowships that have no objectionable theology or worship practices or ceremonies. How does the pastor make good decisions about membership in civic groups? First, he consults with his congregation. Their counsel is invaluable. Only with support of the congregation does a pastor become a member or leader in service organizations. He should be cautious before accepting appointments to boards of businesses or corporations or schools. Second, the pastor assesses the demands of his ministry. Will participation in a civic group overtax time and energy? If he cannot be an active member, he should hesitate. Civic groups do not need members in name only. Third, the pastor's current or prospective involvement in church district or synod is a factor. Finally, the pastor determines whether membership in an organization will enhance the positive influence he brings if membership could subtly muzzle his witness to the Gospel of Jesus Christ.

Principle: When a pastor is invited to join and be active in civic groups or organizations, he accepts invitations only when service to the Gospel and God's people remain a priority, that is, when the public ministry to which he is called receives the firstfruits of his time and energy and life.

449 Ordained Lutheran pastors, Peter and Frederick Muhlenberg, sons of the Rev. Heinrich Melchior Muhlenberg, were both members of Congress.

Conclusion

The Church's teaching and confession regarding the relationship of church and state is foundational for the pastor's ministry in the public domain. By abiding within boundaries that are established by confessional norms, the pastor attends to Christian ethics that inform and guide his conduct in public. Always and everywhere, he is a Christian pastor!

CHAPTER TWENTY-ONE

The Practice of Christian Stewardship

Introduction

A congregation faced a shortage of income. Therefore, concerned lay leaders requested that the pastor preach a stewardship sermon. He was not sure of his ground. He could not preach *money* to encourage offerings, he thought, because his calling was to preach the Gospel. Are giving and the Gospel mutually exclusive? Not if we consider stewardship in the way of biblical theology.

The Lutheran Church—Missouri Synod operates with this definition: "Christian stewardship is the free and joyous activity of the child of God and God's family, the church, in managing all of life and life's resources for God's purposes."[450] Within that larger story—managing all of life and life's resources—is the specific managing of money and material assets in support of Gospel ministries. *Dominical* and *apostolic* authority sustains the stewardship of treasures (Mark 12:13–17, 41–44; 14:3–9; 1 Cor 16:1–2; 2 Cor 8:6–11; 9:3–7).

Givers in the World of God the Giver

From the Order of Creation—Stewardship

Principle: On good authority—*dominical* and *apostolic*—the Christian pastor attends to the congregation's practice of sacrificial giving as proper Christian living to the glory of God and for supporting the mission of preaching the Gospel.

The biblical teaching about stewardship derives from both the order of creation and the order of redemption. Speaking to the Greek intellectuals on Mars Hill, St. Paul referenced human existence to the true God, "who made the world and everything in it, being Lord of heaven and earth" (Acts

450 Department of Stewardship Ministry of The Lutheran Church—Missouri Synod, "Biblical Stewardship Principles," in *Congregational Stewardship Workbook, 2000,* cited on the inside cover of the publication.

17:24). God is both creator and provider, "since He himself gives to all mankind life and breath and everything" (Acts 17:25). Man's relationship to *materia*—material things and stuff—as steward or manager is anchored in the truth for "in Him we live and move and have our being" (Acts 17:28). From all that the Creator provided, the people brought tangible offerings to God when King David announced the building of the temple (1 Chr 29:9–19). Clearly, God gives, and man praises Him with tangible offerings.

From the Order of Redemption—Stewardship

In the order of redemption, baptized Christians manage *materia* in a manner that serves the Gospel. Transformed by the Spirit, they are no longer slaves to self-serving passion (Rom 6:12). Christ's love controls and impels them to express their love in tangible ways (2 Cor 8:8–15, 24). From the giving heart that confesses joyfully, "I am baptized into Christ Jesus!" they yield sacrificial offerings (2 Cor 8:7; 9:7). This discipline is ancient as the old covenant when parcels of land were viewed by God's people as His provision within His created order. And they yielded to God the firstfruits from that land (Lev 25:23, 28; Deut 11:31–32; 26:1–4; cf. Exod 19:5–6).

A Pastor's Stewardship Initiative

The Apostolic Example

St. Paul was not hesitant to teach stewardship of treasures and call for offerings to meet a dual need:

1. He pressed congregations like the Church at Corinth to take a collection that he would direct to alleviate destitute Christians in the east (1 Cor 16:1–4; 2 Cor 9:12). They were to join the effort already begun by fellow Christians in Achaia and Macedonia (2 Cor 9:1–5; 8:1–7, 20–21).
2. The second need was closer to home. Paul appealed for support of himself and others who preached the Gospel (1 Cor 9:14; cf. Gal 6:6).

Courage to Teach and to Ask

Pastors can learn from the apostle to teach stewardship and ask for offerings from their congregations. Indeed, this ministry will meet resistance. A seasoned lay Christian counseled his new pastor, "One word you shall not speak from this pulpit is the word *money*." Such misguided counsel may intimidate a pastor, but not St. Paul. If ever he avoided the subject of stewardship, it was because he did not want to be misunderstood as eager to fill his own coffers (1 Cor 9:3ff.). No, he was not a celebrity, and he would not boast his apostleship. If he had to boast, however, he would rather glory in his right, if any, to bring the Gospel freely to the Corinthians (1 Cor 9:1, 15b, 18; cf. 2 Cor 11:5–6). He lived only to preach the Gospel for the salvation of many (1 Cor 9:13–23).

Although devoted to preaching the Gospel, Paul did not back away from asking the Corinthians to support this ministry for the sake of all (cf. 1 Cor 9:19–23). Certainly, he and his partners refrained from burdening the Corinthians (2 Cor 11:9b). Later he declared, "And I will not be a burden, for I seek not what is yours but you" (2 Cor 12:14). That said, preaching the Gospel for free did not relieve the Corinthians of their duty to support those who brought the Gospel to them. "If we have sown spiritual things among you," he asserted, "is it too much if we reap material things from you?" (1 Cor 9:11–12; cf. 2 Cor 12:15b) Yes, if plowmen deserve wages and servants in the tabernacle and the temple received provisions from the tangible offerings brought by the people, certainly the Corinthians should bring offerings and provide for those who preach the Gospel (1 Cor 9:9–14; cf. 1 Tim 5:17–18; Gal 6:6).[451]

Leading a Ministry of Stewardship

Teaching Christian stewardship and asking congregations to bring their offerings is not for faint hearts and weak resolves. A large congregation faced grim reality. Their treasury could not meet the payroll of church and school. This was an emergency. The pastor and lay leaders decided to ask the membership to contribute the next month in this manner: each giving unit was asked to bring a tithe or tenth of their income on the first and third Sundays, and a double tithe on the second and fourth Sundays. The shocked membership responded and saved the congregation from financial meltdown.

Principle: Honoring the Lord's exhortation to be witnesses to Him in Judea, Samaria, and to the end of the earth (Acts 1:8), the Church intentionally gathers gifts to support preaching of the Gospel everywhere in every generation.

The pastor must lead the congregation in stewardship of treasures. As long as congregations are configured institutionally, there will be financial issues.

451 Broken relationships between the laity and their pastors adversely affect the giving of many persons in our congregations. They dislike either the pastor or members of the church staff, thus they resist giving to the congregation's treasury from which these called or appointed persons are salaried. A corrective to this small thinking is the blessing our Lord promised to those who transcend personal issues and generously support pastors and teachers and other workers in the Church's ministry. He said to His disciples, "For truly, I say to you, whoever gives you a cup of water to drink because you bear the name of Christ, will by no means lose his reward" (Mark 9:41 RSV).

The congregation pays salaries, maintains buildings and properties, and fosters new initiatives in mission and ministry. The congregation also joins fellow Christians in a synod to educate future pastors, teachers, missionaries, and other professional workers. Producing literature for the Church—catechisms, hymnals, liturgical helps, and devotional pieces—is a formidable collective challenge. There is no escape from financial support of Christian ministry in this age.

Principles of Christian Giving

Regular and Proportionate Giving—1 Corinthians 16:1–2

When Paul made an appeal for faithful stewardship, he taught Christians how to assemble their gifts and bring them to the Lord. His instruction answers two questions: "When should I give?" and "How much should I give?" In his words, the apostle taught, "On the first day of every week, each of you is to put something aside and store it up, as he may prosper, so that there will be no collecting when I come" (1 Cor 16:2). Every first day of the week, Christians give as God has loved them in Christ Jesus and then proportionately as God has blessed them—"according to what a person has, not according to what he does not have" (2 Cor 8:12). This is clear guidance. Pastors can teach Christians both *regular* and *proportionate* giving.

Arriving at a Proportionate Gift

Principle: Christian giving is a discipline characterized by good timing—giving that is *regular* and consistent and then generous, that is, *proportionate* in relation to the abundance of God's blessings represented in levels of wealth and material prosperity.

Christians give in relation to the abundance of God's blessings—good health, opportunity, privileged education, adjusted and happy home life. One may surmise that the medium can be time and talent, but here the apostle Paul designates money or funds transportable to Jerusalem and translated into economic assistance to destitute fellow Christians (1 Cor 16:1; 2 Cor 8:1–7). Some interpreters equate a proportionate gift with a tithe or tenth. This equation can be misleading. The wealthy may easily render a tenth that is hardly proportionate. A family gripped in poverty may render less than a tenth, and their gift is extra proportionate. The tithe or tenth is useful when calculating proportion, but the particulars of the ancient ordinances regulating tithing are not binding on Christians in the New Testament era (Col 2:16–17; cf. Mark 7:19b).

Motivations for Stewardship of Treasures

Primary Motivation—the Gospel

Calculating gifts and offerings is a matter of priorities. What things are important to the Christian? "For if we are beside ourselves, it is for God. . . . For the love of Christ controls us, because we have concluded this: that one has died for all . . . and He died for all, that those who live might no longer live for themselves but for Him who for their sake died and was raised" (2 Cor 5:13–15; cf. Gal 2:20). What shall I give? The prior question is, how shall I *live*? "For me to live is Christ" (Phil 1:21a). Thus, for me to *give* is Christ who loved me and gave Himself for me. All that I am and all that I might be is for God and His purposes. With the grace of God on my heart, giving is never by compulsion, but free and cheerful (2 Cor 8:5; 9:7).

Secondary Motivations—Circumstantial Factors

In addition to the primary motivation, the Gospel, other factors may foster generosity. The *example* of the generous churches in Macedonia who gave in the face of their own economic adversity was powerful motivation. The apostle hoped that the Macedonians would inspire the Corinthians to excel in the grace of giving just as they excelled in everything—in faith, in speech, in knowledge, in love (2 Cor 8:7, 24).

A second motivation is the pressing *need* for monetary assistance. We have noted that the congregation at Corinth had resources to meet the need of destitute fellow Christians by contributing money as the apostle directed them (1 Cor 16:1). Centuries earlier, the need was great and the time was right when the prophet Haggai directed the people to rebuild the house of the Lord (Hag 1:1–8). Compelling need calls for faithful stewardship.

A third motivation is *opportunity* to prove our love for God by bringing tangible gifts or offerings. Are Christians alive in Christ, or are they comatose? Lest we forget, they are as living stones in God's spiritual house (1 Pet 2:5). While offering spiritual sacrifices that are acceptable to God, why not bring tangible sacrifices as well? In this matter of giving, earnest Christians seek to "understand what the will of the Lord is" (Eph 5:17b). With that understanding, they go for it. They prove their love is genuine by generous giving.

A fourth motivation is the *blessing* that God promises to those who are stewards of their bounty for His purposes. God blesses such giving (Mal 3:10–12). No, a Christian does not *work* God for special favors. There is no *give to get* formula (cf. Deut 14:28–29; cf. Mal 3:6–9). The Christian simply shares, trusting the promises of God. The apostle encourages waiting for God's blessing. He argues, "Whoever sows sparingly will also reap sparingly, and whoever sows bountifully will also reap bountifully" (2 Cor 9:6). Paul assured the Christians at Philippi, "And my God will supply every need of yours according to His riches in glory in Christ Jesus" (Phil 4:19). Not least of His blessings is a spirit of thanksgiving that results from generous giving (2 Cor 9:11–13).

A fifth motivation may be that Christian giving is an occasion to *glorify* God. When the apostle referred to the test put to Christians at Corinth to provide for the saints who suffered in the east, he commented: "Under the test of this service, you will glorify God by your obedience in acknowledging the gospel of Christ, and by the generosity of your contribution for them and for all others" (2 Cor 9:13 RSV).

Education and Training in the Practice of Stewardship of Treasures

Readiness

There are numerous motivations, but readiness for giving depends upon the level of spiritual maturity that varies from Christian to Christian. A pastor assesses readiness before he launches into public appeals that the people give. The readiness of the Christians at Corinth was certainly a factor when Paul sent for their gifts intended to meet the needs in the east (2 Cor 8:11; 9:2, 5, cf. 9:12). Pastoral leadership in stewardship ministry does not leap beyond the people who are growing in the grace of giving. The principle below applies.

Approach

Again, educating and training a congregation in the grace of giving is a challenge to pastoral leadership. Misinformation and misunderstanding surround the subject of stewardship. Therefore, a pastor assesses the congregation for its readiness first to learn this discipline of Christian giving. The task to teach and train may require intentional and formal initiatives.

Principle: As beneficiaries of a gracious and giving God, Christians grow into the grace of giving and to that end they are open to heed training in the stewardship life according to the Scriptures.

Types of Stewardship Education and Training

Education and Training Distinguished from Programs

The methods to grow faithful stewards by education and training differ from programs designed for specific stewardship efforts such as Loyalty Sunday, pledge programs, and Every Member Visitation. These programs include some amount of education, but conditions in a congregation may require immersing the membership in the theology of stewardship, that is, the clear teaching of the Scriptures regarding this discipline. Only then will the people grow spiritually and mature in a way that prepares them to receive specific direction in the stewardship of treasures. The present discussion may assist in getting started with stewardship education and training.[452]

The Practice of Pledging

Thorough preparation is required when a congregation introduces a program of pledging weekly offerings. There is value in both individual pledging and the larger collective commitment of the pledging congregation. The pledge is conditional on God's continuous blessing that enables a family to commit offerings every week. Any instrument that solicits pledges or gathers them should convey this truth clearly. The pledge is driven by the truth that the Holy Spirit works in Christians the will to do what is pleasing to the Lord (Phil 2:13; 4:13). Undergirding the pledge are the promises of God, for they are "yes" in Christ (2 Cor 1:20; cf. John 3:16; 2 Pet 3:13; Mal 3:10–12). Frame the thesis for pledging in this manner: "Can we be less than venturous in our promises to God when He is faithful in His commitment to us?"

---

452 Other resources are: Carl W. Berner Sr., *The Power of Pure Stewardship* (St. Louis: Concordia Publishing House, 1970); August W. Brustat, *Partnership with God* (Ernst Kaufmann, 1947); J. E. Herman, *The Chief Steward* (St. Louis: Department of Stewardship, Missionary Education and Promotion, The Lutheran Church—Missouri Synod, 1951); T. A. Kantonen, *A Theology for Christian Stewardship* (Philadelphia: Muhlenberg Press, 1956); *Congregational Stewardship Workbook* 2000 (St. Louis: Department of Stewardship Ministry, The Lutheran Church—Missouri Synod, 2000); Guido A. Merkens, *Living Lutheran Leadership* (Austin, TX: G. E. Saegert, 1968); R. C. Rein, *Adventures in Christian Stewardship* (St. Louis: Concordia Publishing House, 1955); Armin W. Schuetze and Irwin J. Habeck, *The Shepherd Under Christ* (Milwaukee: Northwestern Publishing House, 1974): 241–262; Carl W. Berner Sr., "Stewardship in General," in *The Pastor at Work* (St. Louis: Concordia Publishing House, 1960), 299–316; Erwin Kurth and Herman Zehnder, "The Stewardship of Money," in *The Pastor at Work* (St. Louis: Concordia Publishing House, 1960), 317–338; John F. Brug, "The Principles of Financial Stewardship in Paul's Letter to the Philippians," *Wisconsin Lutheran Quarterly* 86, no. 3 (Summer 1989): 215–224; David P. Kuske, "Principles of Stewardship in First Corinthians 16:1, 2 and Second Corinthians 8:1–9," *Wisconsin Lutheran Quarterly* 84, no. 4 (Fall 1987): 248–269; David J. Vallesky, "Stewardship of Possessions in the Gospels," *Wisconsin Lutheran Quarterly* 84, no. 3 (Summer 1987): 168–185; Armin J. Panning, "Be Cheerful Givers—2 Cor. 9:8–15," *Wisconsin Lutheran Quarterly* 86, no. 2 (Spring 1989): 131–142; Ronald D. Roth, "Characteristics of Joyful Giving: A Stewardship Study of 1 Chronicles 19:1–20," *Wisconsin Lutheran Quarterly* 84, no. 3 (Summer 1987): 168–185.

Pledging may be sealed or open. The annual sealed pledge is private. It remains sealed and is returned to the giver next church year. The sealed pledge serves to counsel a Christian with respect to his or her pattern of giving. The open pledge is entrusted to lay leaders who view all pledges in order to calculate resources available to the congregation as it budgets for its total ministry. The financial plan must be in line with total offerings anticipated. On Pledge Sunday or Loyalty Sunday, the order of service includes a ceremony when congregation members come forward and place their pledges in a special receptacle prepared for this event. The pastor frames the ceremony as an action of prayer and devotion, and the people participate prayerfully. Not every attendee at the Sunday worship service will present a pledge. In some stewardship programs, those who did not pledge in the worship service will receive a visit between Sunday afternoon and Tuesday evening of the following week. The visitors will encourage faithful stewardship of treasures to support Gospel ministry.[453]

Lutheran congregations have launched a variety of stewardship programs, including the traditional Every Member Visitation (EMV), direct mail appeals, series of weekly letters coordinated with sermons and stewardship emphases on Sundays, and banquets orchestrated to foster pledging. For several decades in the late twentieth century, congregations engaged professional fund-raisers to organize and execute stewardship programs. The merits of any or all such programs must be weighed by the pastor and congregation leaders.

If stewardship in the Christian congregation becomes materialistic in nature and spirit, great harm results. Lost are the benefits of cheerful giving that leads both giver and recipients of charity in joyful thanksgiving directed to God (2 Cor 9:11–12). The antidote is connecting giving to the Christian's worship. True, contributing electronically online may be efficient for both giver and the congregation's administration, but there is no substitute for the ancient discipline whereby God's people brought and presented their gifts in hand before the Lord (Deut 12:10–11; 26:1–4, 10).

453 Dr. Guido Merkens, founding pastor of Concordia Lutheran Church of San Antonio, Texas, developed and perfected a Loyalty Sunday stewardship effort. The outline of this program is available in Dr. Merkens' unpublished notes titled "Living Lutheran Leadership."

Epilogue

Though heretofore unspoken, the tacit purpose of this work about pastoral ministry is to invite young Christian men to aspire to the pastoral office and to encourage pastors who currently practice the profession. There is no higher calling than an appointment to represent Jesus Christ and to speak God's Word in His name to His people. This means that we shall search far and long to discover the privilege of vocation equal to that of serving Christ in His public ministry.

Our Lord's pastoral ministry is what it is. The Gospels seldom record promises to the Lord's first apostles that they would have comfort and security, satisfaction and fulfillment, exuberance and hilarity within the Office of the Ministry. He did assure that as the heavenly Father cares for the birds of the air and flowers of the field, God would take care of them, and the Holy Spirit would abide with them. He talked about the supreme joy of finding one sinner who repents, turns to God, and receives the forgiveness of sins. Jesus was eloquent about welcoming back the wayward son and the excitement of finding faith where it appears and is confessed. Are there any takers of these things which are promised by Jesus today?

Pastors may look for tangibles. There are few such things in the pastoral ministry. If you are looking for wealth or celebrity status or a giddy feeling of grabbing the American dream, you probably will be disappointed in your calling as a Christian pastor. If you seek an easy path, then go down another road. Faithfulness in the pastoral ministry costs a man dearly. Long before Dietrich Bonhoeffer eloquently expounded on the way of the disciple in an evil world, pastors in the Early Church followed in the steps of the prophets and apostles before them and sacrificed comforts, material affluence, family, and their lives in order to work long day after long day in faithful service to Him who gave all for us. Who follows in His train?

This former pastor would not trade it for all the kingdoms of the world. There is nothing on earth to surpass knocking heads [dialoguing] with prophets and apostles *ala* the Bible text and stepping forth at length and at last before the people with the Word that God wants to speak to them on Sunday morning. What compares to the ministry of the Holy Spirit when a word from the Scriptures brings God and His love to a soul who is eager to know that just one party in the universe truly cares about him or her? Who is not encouraged to see newly baptized Christians finding themselves at home with a congregation who warmly welcomed them and genuinely includes them? There are sufficient victories witnessed by a pastor that he is assured every day that Christ is Lord. Satan has had his day, and he is history.

The privilege to be in the pastoral ministry, the opportunity to declare God and His Word, the assurance that a pastor's faithfulness is not forgotten by Jesus are all reasons enough to get excited about becoming or being a pastor. To that end, may this work not only help but also point Christ's men to Him, and by His Spirit, fill their hearts with quiet joy.

FINIS

Appendices

Appendix 1

Fifteen Steps from Scripture Text to a Central Thought

by Martin H. Scharlemann

1. Know the text!

Establish the text by scrutinizing the critical apparatus.

2. Know all the words in the text.

List all the words verse by verse. Omit obvious particles. Listing words as they appear in the text, analyze verbs and nouns. Identify pronouns. Determine the meaning of all words. Note the prepositions.

3. Know all grammatical forms.

Pay close attention to the parts of speech. Observe moods and tenses of verbs: number, gender, case of nouns. Relate modifiers (adjectives) to nouns, (adverbs) to verbs. Note conjunctions and particles.

4. Relate words and sentences to one another.

This step addresses syntax, the sentence structure or arrangement of words and phrases related to one another. Therefore, relate subject/verb/object. Note punctuation, series of words, the strength of adjectives and adverbs, the use of prepositions and the thrust of prepositional phrases, the color of meaning signified by tenses and moods of the verbs. In summary, how is the holy writer employing language to convey the Word given by the Holy Spirit?

5. Render a rough translation.

On the basis of your textual and grammatical studies, render the passage into clear English. ***Translate***, do not paraphrase. Do not be concerned, for now, if your translation is somewhat wooden. Accuracy is the priority at this point.

6. Determine the thought progression in the text.

Discover main emphases in the text, ascertain the progression of thought, the movement and thrust manifest in the text, the development of an idea, the manner in which subordinate thoughts relate to the larger concepts. How does the meaning of the text unfold? How do major ideas surface? How are the major ideas related to one another? Is there a natural progression of thought discernible in the text?

7. Relate the passage to its context. See the text within its setting.

General Context—The entire Epistle, Gospel, or book; the message of the book—how does this text relate to the larger picture, the general situation? How does the larger setting impact on this text and assist understanding the text?

Immediate Context—The passages immediately before and immediately following the text—how does this text fit with this material? What significance does the nearer context have for interpretation of this text?

8. Relate the passage to the unifying theme of Scripture.

How does this text speak the Gospel? How does it express the central theme of God's grace to sinners through Christ and salvation by faith in Jesus Christ? What aspects of this central theme does the text express or represent? Does the text link up with other clear Gospel passages in the Scriptures?

9. Do *word studies* of the main concepts.

Identify the key words in the text. Discover their usage elsewhere in the Scripture. How do your findings relate to the use of these words in this preaching text? Decide on usage of the words *here*! Then marshal support from similar usage elsewhere in Scripture. Use the concordance. Be alert, then, to parallel or support passages.

10. List parallel passages.

Discover and list passages that parallel the text, either in vocabulary, doctrine, concept, thought, or idea. **Note:** Begin with parallels cited in the margin of the text, those suggested by the editors. From your knowledge of the Bible, garner other parallels. Also review again your word studies from step 9.

11. Study the doctrines related to the text.

Consult the Lutheran Confessions, dogmatics, essays such as *The Abiding Word,* vols. 1–3, and other works in doctrinal and biblical theology. Study in depth the doctrines expressed or taught in the preaching text.

12. Compare your translation with other translations.

Look to the precise rendering of words and phrases in the text. How do others translate the original? Compare five or more translations with your own.

13. Render a final translation.

Note: This final translation is for your own study. In the pulpit, read the text in a standard English translation.

14. Ruminate on the text, its teachings and implications.

What do you hear God saying in this text? What is He saying to people? Can you support your answers to these questions with solid text material? Then note the insights as they apply to the hearer's need. How shall the hearer receive this text and its meaning in light of his present experience? Are there applications and illustrations in the text itself? Focus attention on major ideas as the text directs these ideas, thoughts, concepts, and teachings to the hearer. Consult commentaries for two reasons:

1. Compare your exegesis and interpretation with other authorities.
2. Note how others interpret and apply this text.

15. Write out a trial central thought or theme.

While textual study and reflection are fresh in your mind, attempt to articulate a central thought or theme—or even a proposition that reflects the major message of the text as help for the hearer. **Note:** This theme or central thought will govern development of the structure and body of the sermon. Note once again that this statement of theme or central thought brings together the text and the hearer and also addresses the text to the needs of the hearer!

Note: Be patient to try and try again! The first expression of theme or central idea may be adequate. Then again, it may be only a precursor to a better and improved statement. And the latter may not surface until the tenth or twelfth attempt. It is a "trial and error" process; and the process requires patience and persistence. But the yield is bountiful!

Appendix 2

Thirteen Reminders for the Exemplary Pastor

1. He is a man—"a man's man."

- Someone has divided the world into men, women, and ministers. The pastor carries himself in a manner and with bearing as one who is conscious that he is a leader of people and that he is responsible for the spiritual lives of others. He is aware that so much depends upon what he says, how he says it, and how he conducts himself, how his life communicates to others. He is a shepherd, not a sheep.
- The pastor is a man who compels respect from the world (1 Tim 3:7), not only because he is a man but also because of the kind of man he is.

2. He is a man in Christ—*en Christo.*

- He is driven by the realization of his personal sinfulness and sinning, complemented by a deep appreciation for God's grace that reached down to save the sinner from his sin, guilt, and deserved punishment and worked in him faith, calling him to that saving faith by the Gospel. He is a man, therefore, who rejoices in his heart over the treasure of the Gospel, the forgiveness of sins through Jesus Christ.
- As a man in Christ, he is always surprised and amazed that God would place him in the ministry. "Unto me, who am less than the least of all saints, is this grace given, that I should preach among the Gentiles the unsearchable riches of Christ" (Eph 3:8 KJV). He is a man who says, "but I obtained mercy" (1 Tim 1:13 KJV). "And the grace of our Lord was exceeding abundant with faith and love which is in Christ Jesus" (1 Tim 1:14 KJV; cf. 1 Cor 15:10).
- He has a strong faith in Christ, Christian faith, faith that appropriates the blessings of his Baptism into Christ, his old Adam daily dying and with Christ he rises again in the confidence that the dominion of sin over him and over his people is broken by Christ. His old Adam does not live robust and healthy in midday because the old one has died in the morning by remembering Baptism.
- The "man in Christ" has a vision of the ministry and what it can do to lead others who need grace to realize their need, to accept forgive-

ness and salvation, and to go on to abundant enjoyment of all that the Savior has to offer. These factors have solidified in the heart of the man who is a candidate for the office of the pastoral ministry.

- "The pastor ought to be a humble believer in his Savior, Jesus, and his desire to serve as pastor ought to be a fruit of that faith. (cf. Jn. 21:15–17; 2 Cor. 5:14)" (Schuetze and Habeck, *The Shepherd Under Christ* [Milwaukee: Northwestern Publishing House, 1974], 2).

3. He is a Christ-man who lives the Christlike life.

- God has called us to holiness. The pastor lives and works as a man affected in heart and life "by the mercies of God" (Rom 12:1–2), and he is consciously aware of the fact that his mind is "renewed," that he dare not any longer be conformed to the world, but that above all others, he will "prove what is that good, and acceptable, and perfect, will of God" (Rom 12:2b KJV).
- A man of God called to holiness of living (cf. 1 Thess 4:7b), the pastor does not let sin grow in his life. He curbs temptation and sin. Though he, too, will admit with the apostle that he has by no means attained perfection ("Not that I have already obtained this or am already perfect" [Phil 3:12]), he dare not settle for the lowest level of sanctification. For to him the apostle's instruction is given: "Set the believers an example" (1 Tim 4:12; 1 Pet 5:3b; Phil 3:17).
- He lives consistently on all fronts as the same sanctified man in Christ.
    - Within, he lives in control of himself. He is temperate, curbing the lusts and appetites and passions of the flesh. He behaves "with all purity" (1 Tim 5:2 KJV) and he observes what St. Paul said to Timothy, "flee youthful passions" (2 Tim 2:22). Sin lurks at the door, but the pastor does not open the door to sin and temptation. He runs from pornography and the like. At home when he disengages the "pastoral" role and image, he lives consistently as a man in Christ. He can be depressed emotionally—down time—but he is ever up spiritually.
    - Without, the pastor is in the public eye either in the midst of his people or under the scrutiny of the community at large. He is alert. He is careful that lapses do not in any way hinder the effectiveness of how his ministry is viewed and received.

- The pastor does not lead two lives. The man within, the private man, the man away from his parish, is the same man in the public eye where he is known as a Christian pastor or, for that matter, where he is unknown. Always and everywhere he is at all times in his heart and in his comportment a pastor, the representative of the Lord Jesus Christ, the Lord's man. He is never his own man. He is always a man in Christ, serving Christ.

4. He devotes himself entirely to his calling.

- The pastor is a man intrigued by the ministry. He is absorbed by it. He is not a man for whom the ministry and ministerial tasks are an unwelcome distraction, always making it obvious that he is a pastor, compelled by the necessity to hold a job.
- The pastor is a man with one calling. "No man can serve two masters" (Matt 6:24 KJV). St. Paul was a tentmaker and pursued his craft in order to support himself, yet he was entirely devoted to his life as an apostle of Jesus Christ (1 Cor 9:19–23). He is ever challenged by the "noble task" that is the pastoral ministry (1 Tim 3:1).
- Singularly devoted to his calling as a Christian pastor, he does not engage in distracting pursuits or avocations. For example, he does not take on jobs that accrue extra income, such as selling insurance or investments, soliciting sales for cemetery lots, or clerking at local retailers. Nor does he pursue other interests (e.g., hobbies, sports, fishing, hunting, camping) as if he considers these pursuits to be his real interest and essential calling, which can absorb amounts of energy and time and diminish concentration and focus on his pastoral duties (1 Tim 3:1).

5. He is not mercenary.

- The Christian pastor has no roving eye for money. He is not covetous, not given to absorption in pursuit of money or things [filthy lucre] (1 Tim 6:10–11; cf. Acts 8:20). He does not complain about his salary. He has accepted less in order to serve the Lord more. He will never be a rich man, nor does he seek to be a rich man.
- He refrains from dealing with retailers sporting a subtle sense of self-pity to get breaks on prices. He is not overly solicitous of favors. He does not shame others into taking up the cause and donating to him in order to provide support.
- He is an example to the flock in his own proportionate stewardship of treasures for the sake of the Gospel and preaching the Word of

God. In this stewardship the pastor is saying to the laity of the congregation, "I seek not what is yours but you" (2 Cor 12:14). By his exemplary stewardship he assures them, "I will most gladly be spent for your souls."

- The pastor graciously receives honorariums, gifts, favors—gestures of love and honor and respect from the people. He does not refuse these in a spirit of pietistic deprecation. Nor does he send subtle hints and messages that he seeks such tributes. At all times, he and his family acknowledge gifts presented to them. A written note expressing sincere gratitude—sent by surface mail—is still a proper courtesy.

6. He is truthful.

- He truly loves his congregation and sincerely devotes himself to them (John 15:12).
- His *word* is good as his bond, so good, he needs no bond.
- There is no doubt in anyone's mind, "What will he say next?"
- He demonstrates straight talk, no "bull!"
- His speech is consistent, with no double meanings.
    - He does not make empty promises.
    - He keeps his word and stands by his word.
- He does not send anonymous letters.

7. He is honest.

- He pays his bills—(some pastors move from parish to parish with unpaid bills and debts).
- He pays back what he borrows (Ps 37:21).
- He is careful to return borrowed equipment in good condition.

8. He is humble.

- A pastor is meek (2 Tim 2:25; Matt 11:29), but also strong.
- He is not a man who must be the "center" of every event, as if when he enters the room, all bow; he is not a "celebrity."
- He does not seek the limelight.
- Like St. Paul, he is a "fool" for Christ but never "foolish."
- He is a servant of God and man, while maintaining the dignity of the office.
- But he is not a codependent doormat.

9. He is genuine, sincere.

- Others see Christ in him!
- He exhibits no false piety, the euphemism for pride and arrogance.
- He puts on no phony airs.

10. He is circumspect, dignified, and cheerful.

- He lives as an "example" to the flock (1 Pet 5:3)
- He gives no offense so that the ministry shall not be blamed (2 Cor 6:3).
    - He is a man who always remembers who he is.
    - In public, he remembers, he is ***always*** a Christian pastor—thus, he curbs outbursts such as road rage.
- He is neither a clown nor the funniest man in town.
- He is not given to coarse jokes or jesting or, for that matter, tawdry gestures—His conversation is "Yes, yes!" and "No, no!" (Matt 5:37 KJV), but he can still laugh and exhibits a healthy sense of humor.
- He is not a *cold stiff*—not formal to the point of making others uncomfortable.
- His reading is circumspect, as is his use of the Internet.
- He is prudent in what his eyes see: "The eye is the lamp of the body. So, if your eye is sound, your whole body will be full of light" (Matt 6:22 RSV).
- His pursuit of entertainment is prudent, upscale, and decent.
    - He has no use for pornography; if tempted, he emphatically declines, ceases, quits—compulsive attraction to pornography requires consultation with a therapist.
    - He does not play poker or frequent the casinos, does not gamble.
    - He does not patronize unsavory establishments, bars, and some pubs.
    - He is not after "faster horses, younger women, older whiskey!"
    - He knows when to leave a party and return home.
- He is a man in the world, and with his people in the world, but he is not of the world.
- His thoughts and fantasies are formed and framed by Philippians 4:8 (RSV): "Finally, brethren, whatever is true, whatever is honorable, whatever is just, whatever is pure, whatever is lovely, whatever is gra-

cious, if there is any excellence, if there is anything worthy of praise, think about these things."

11. He has an even temperament.

- His temperament is even and predictable, with no unexpected explosions.
- He is not moody or sullen.
- He is not disgruntled or angry.
- He is not jocular, unable to settle down to reality, unable to get serious; not a comedian.
- He handles depression, seeking professional help, when necessary.

12. He is fair and impartial.

- He is all things to all men (cf. Rom 14).
- He shows kindness to all!
- He does not run with the "jet set," the rich and the powerful; he is not the prize or pet of any group or clique.
- He does not cultivate the "pastor's pets."
- He is available to all the people.
- At public events, he seeks out the disabled, the "wallflower," the socially disenfranchised persons—he cares about the lonely, the withdrawn.
- He seeks out the "lost sheep."
- He shows compassion for the sinners.
- He shows empathy and compassion for the forlorn, the lonely, and those hurting.

13. He is a Christian gentleman.

- He has good manners and cultivates social graces, consulting experts on etiquette, such as Emily Post.
    - He is prompt (on time) and meets agreed commitments.
    - He is courteous and considerate.
    - He practices acceptable table etiquette—he does not gesture by waving the fork.
    - He acknowledges favors and gifts with formal but friendly notes sent by surface mail, enlisting his wife to assist in writing proper thank-you notes.
- He dresses for the job—clothes make the man!
    - He upgrades his dress code in and about the parish from customary garb worn to seminary classes.

    - His dress is in good taste, neither flamboyant nor dull.
    - He wears clothing that is clean and well kept.
    - His trousers and coats regularly see the back side of a hot iron!
    - His shoes are shined—again, and again, and again!
    - He has changes of clothing, as he is able to afford them.
    - He wears clergy garb, but not day and night. He does not sleep in them.
- He practices good grooming.
    - Hair and hirsute growth—he adopts hair and beard styles not only to his liking and preference but, more important, also to how his people will best receive him as their pastor. In these matters, he makes no *statement*. The only statement he ever makes is the Gospel of Jesus Christ!
    - Nails—always clean and well manicured [He distributes the Lord's Supper!]
    - Bathing—he showers daily and wears appropriate deodorant, but avoids shaving lotions or cologne that may annoy the sensitivities of others.
- His body is healthy and strong.
    - He exercises regularly.
    - He gives attention to nutrition and diet without fanatical preoccupation.
    - He curtails the vices of smoking, overconsumption of alcohol, and assiduously avoids the use of illicit drugs.
    - Conscious of St. Paul's reminder (1 Cor 6:19), he thinks hard before enlisting tattoos, piercings, or other body mutilation. As stated above, he makes the Gospel his only statement. Much body altering or mutilation may be perceived as a bold statement of self, which has no place in the ministry.

Appendix 3

Priorities for New Testament Congregations

Preface: "This is My commandment, that you love one another as I have loved you" (John 15:12). Except love permeate active ministry represented by the following priorities, efforts will founder. Mutual love—pastor and people—was the emphasis in a sermon preached on Call Day, April 26, 2016, at Concordia Seminary, St. Louis, Missouri, by the Rev. Dr. Dean Nadasdy.

Worship

In the earliest gatherings, Christians came together for public worship. The first Christians at Jerusalem continued to observe the hours for prayer and worship in the temple (Acts 2:46). The Church, assembled for public preaching and teaching of the Word and for the Sacrament, was representative of the early Christian fellowship (1 Cor 11:20; 14:23). Long before the fifth-century axiom, *lex orandi, lex credenda*, Christians confessed the faith as they assembled for worship and prayer on the first day of the week (1 Cor 16:2).

Witness

A second priority is the urgency not only to come together but also to disperse into the community and world and tell the "Good News." Jesus commenced His ministry preaching the Gospel of the kingdom of God (Mark 1:14–15). Simultaneous with the outpouring of the Spirit at Pentecost, the apostles came forth, preaching the Gospel, urging the crowds in Jerusalem to repent and be baptized in the name of Jesus Christ for the forgiveness of sins (Acts 2:38). The spontaneous and urgent proclamation of Jesus Christ for salvation by faith in His saving name (Acts 4:12) remains a priority of first importance for every Christian congregation. Neither inhibitions nor intimidation or persecution shall hinder the Church's witness to Christ and His saving name because God is in this ministry (2 Cor 5:18; cf. Acts 9:31).

Teaching

A third priority for the New Testament congregation is nurture of the new Christian by equipping him or her for service to God and man (Eph 4:12–13;

6:6; Mark 9:33–35; 10:38–45). The first disciples of Jesus followed the Master with a sense of commitment strengthened in company with Him and by means of His constant teaching and nurture (Mark 1:20; 10:23–31; Luke 24:13–35; John 21:15–19). Nurture was our Lord's priority (Matt 28:19), and the early congregations gave themselves to teaching (Acts 20:28). The Lord's apostles taught, and the first Christians devoted themselves to the teaching of the apostles (Acts 2:42; cf. Acts 11:26; 15:41; 18:26–28; 20:20). Maturing in the knowledge of Christ and in all things profitable for faith and life was a primary objective in the teaching ministry of the Early Church. It was understood that following conversion, spiritual growth was of utmost importance. To that end, teaching was a vital ministry.

Fellowship

Koinonia, the fellowship of Christians, a fourth priority, was not so much a topic for discussion in the Early Church as it was a way of life. As stated above, the first Christians were together in the temple, later for teaching, prayer, the Sacrament, and at mealtime (Acts 2:42, 46–47; 4:31; 13:1–3). Togetherness in Christ as members of His Body is expressed as one calling unto one hope, one Lord, one faith, one Baptism, one God and Father (Eph 4:3–6). This fellowship transcends every apparent difference (Rom 12:3–8; 1 Cor 12:12ff.).

By no means was this fellowship of early Christians a utopian community. Early on, deception, strife, and unloving actions plagued the Church. The lying speech of Ananias and Sapphira (Acts 5), the struggle over the care of widows (Acts 6:1ff.), the exchange of strong feelings over the mission to the Gentiles (Acts 15) are the marks of an imperfect fellowship. Still, constrained by the love of Christ, this fellowship was sensitive to need. These Christians brought their assets to fulfill dire need (Acts 2:44–45), and they conducted ministries of mercy, love, and care. The Church gave tangible help and support where needed in the congregation and in the larger community.

Service

Love and service to God and man are another priority for every new person in Jesus Christ and for the congregation (2 Cor 5:15; Gal 5:13; Rom 12:13). Christians are the priesthood of believers (1 Pet 2:9; Rev 1:5–6), but priesthood before God is not a matter of status. It is priestly service like unto Him who "came not to be served but to serve, and to give His life as a ransom for many" (Mark 10:45). The first-century church pursued numerous avenues of service. Caring for the spiritual life of its own was the primary service (cf. 1 Cor 12:25;

Mark 9:50; Gal 6:1ff.; Heb 10:24; Jas. 5:19–20; Acts 4:23–31; 12:12). Also, attending to the emotional and physical needs of the faithful together with showing hospitality to strangers were distinctive congregational services (cf. Acts 2:44–45; 6:1; 1 Tim 5:1–14; Heb 13:1–3, 16; Gal 6:9–10).

Growth (Mission)

Sensitive to church growth strategies, some Lutherans object to the notion that growth in numbers of Christians is a priority for the Christian congregation. Our Lord, however, envisioned the Church, the company of believers, as large as the human race itself (2 Cor 5:15, 21; John 3:16; Matt 28:19–20). The testimony to Christ in all the world (Acts 1:8), the post-Pentecost activity of the apostles in the Early Church, the expanding mission to the Gentiles arose from a compelling assumption that the Lord had redeemed *all* (cf. John 10:16). In the light of the Lord's universal redemption, a Christian congregation presses to reach all persons of the present generation with the Gospel. Not only Gospel proclamation to all but accession of new Christians is a priority of first importance (cf. Acts 2:38–41, 47; 6:7; 9:31).

Richard H. Warneck, PhD

April 16, 2016

Appendix 4

Examples of Sermon Development

Three examples of sermon development are the following:

Rhetorical/Deductive

Arriving at the meaning of a Scripture text through careful exegesis, the preacher formulates that meaning in a central theme or thought or idea usually framed in a single sentence. From this central theme, the major parts of the sermon unfold, each part related to the theme and to the other parts, always proclaiming the text or portions thereof.

Example: Text—Romans 3:19–26

Central Thought: Sinners are justified not through their deeds but because of God's grace for the sake of redemption in Jesus Christ through faith.

Introduction
I. Sinners are not justified because of their deeds.
II. Sinners are justified because of God's grace for the sake of the redemption in Jesus Christ.
III. Sinners are justified through faith.
Conclusion

—Richard R. Caemmerer

Inductive

Beginning with careful study of the Scripture text, the truth conveyed by the text is reserved for discovery at the close of the sermon. In one such inductive format, the sermon moves from the hearer's concerns, to conflict or question, to resolution, to delayed summary and conclusion. The "goal" or "effect" of the sermon is not captive within a central idea but shows up as the Word impacts the experience of the hearer. According to Eugene L. Lowry, evocation in this direction is more significant than a central governing idea. The sermon is shaped as *movement* marked by the following:

Conflict→ Complication→Sudden Shift→Unfolding (resolution)

The *moving* toward *resolution* may engage forms such as argument, story, or image. Where the Gospel, the Good News, makes its appearance in this movement, Lowry discusses at length. See Eugene L. Lowry, *The Sermon: Dancing the Edge of Mystery* (Nashville: Abingdon Press, 1997), 54–55, 81; the larger discussion, 62–89.

Expository

Expository preaching is not bookish setting forth of the text—vocabulary, grammar, syntax—but exposition of the Bible and its meaning, with the needs of the hearer in view. Expository preaching, with respect to the text, has depth, weight, and the power of truth. It also has relevance, life, and animation. It looks backward to the Bible where God has spoken, and it looks forward to the needs of a given audience (Bernard Ramm). The attitude is one of faithful representation of the text in some depth. Meticulous attention to the text—close exegesis, taking the text apart, setting out the details—lends objectivity to preaching, highlighting more of the Word and less of the preacher's opinions or even sanctified insights. While unfolding particulars of the text with attention to its language, the expository sermon is governed by an overarching subject that surfaces from close study of a chapter or book of the Bible. The exposition may cluster around numerous subtopics of the overarching subject.

Example: "Glorifying God"

Text: Acts 6:3–8:2

Introduction
Proposition: Stephen's life illustrates three ways by which we can glorify God.
I. He Glorified God in His Character: Acts 6:3, 5, 8
II. He Glorified God in His Testimony: Acts 6:8–9, 10; 6:11–7:56
III. He Glorified God in His Death: Acts 7:57–8:2
Conclusion

—Ferris D. Whitesell

Whatever the format of the sermon, three essentials are critical:

1. Unity: The sermon must be a unit with a single aim or purpose in the faith and life of the hearer. When the sermon is completed, the hearer is prepared to easily remember one major thought.

2. Organization: The parts of the sermon relate to one another logically, and their arrangement develops, governed by a unifying theme, aim, and purpose.
3. Progress: Like a river flowing constantly toward its end, the open sea, the sermon unfolds in a process of movement steadily to its close.

Appendix 5

Caring for the Sick—Response to Anxiety

The crisis of illness gives rise to anxiety that takes numerous forms. The pastor may minister to anxiety with skillful use of the Scriptures—meaning, interpretation, and application. Consider five exhibits of anxiety and a sixth exhibit, convalescence.

Fear

Fear in the face of illness is not necessarily a sign of weak faith or lack of faith. It is a common reaction to insecurity brought on by sickness. When a patient can speak freely about his fears, the opportunity for supportive ministry of Word and prayer is at hand.

Scripture: Josh 1:1–9; Ps 27:1–5, 14; 34:1–10; 46; 91:1–6, 9–12, 14–16; Isa 41:10; Matt 8:23–27; Rom 8:31–32, 35–39; 1 Pet 5:7.

Guilt

The question "Why does God send this affliction?" may be a symptom that the patient has already answered the question in terms of his lack of standing with God because of his sinful ways. He narrowly interprets illness as punishment.

When the pastor helps a patient clarify guilt feelings, he is ready with the Absolution when guilt is real under the judgment of God's Law. He speaks the cross of Christ, His atonement for our sins, and God's complete forgiveness of *all* our sins. He assures the patient that in Christ we may feel better about ourselves and about God.

Scripture: Ps 32; 51; 130; Matt 9:1–9; Luke 19:1–10; John 8:3–11; Rom 3:10–12, 22–25; 5:1–10; 6:6–12; 2 Cor 5:17–21; Gal 2:16, 20–21; 3:26–29; 5:1; Phil 3:8–11; 1 John 1:8–9; 2:1–2.

Rejection

Feelings of rejection may be founded or unfounded. Unable to clarify such feelings, a patient may reason, "I don't need anyone. Besides, no one cares if I live or die." A patient may accuse God of rejecting him.

The pastor will not question these strong feelings. Instead, he assures the patient that he or she is God's child by Baptism. On the patient is a price paid by the precious blood of Christ (1 Cor 6:20). That price was paid out of God's great love, and sickness, disability, or even death cannot come between the patient and the love of God in Christ Jesus (Rom 8:37–39). In Christ, God's love, acceptance, and care abide true always (1 Pet 5:7).

Scripture: Ps 13; 16; 18:1–6; 23; 29; 61; 62; 71; Matt 28:20; Luke 15; 18:31–43; John 6:37; Rom 8:32–39; Heb 13:5, 8, 14; 1 John 3:1–2.

Loneliness

Feelings of rejection frequently intermingle with a sense of loneliness. The days are long and the nights longer when a patient struggles alone with the burden of illness. It is an individual and personal burden. Lonely persons easily exaggerate their strong feelings. They are vulnerable to self-pity.

The pastor is careful not to overempathize with the lonely in ways that will feed their strong feelings. He meets persons in their loneliness with warmth and companionship of a friend who does not forget. He is there for them, and he draws them into the larger picture of their life as a child of God, who loves them and cares for them.

Scripture: Gen 37:28, 36; 37:36; 39:1–4, 20–23; Josh 1:1–9; 6:27; Ps 1; 23; 34:15–18; 72:12–14; Prov 30:5; Isa 40:1–11; 55; Matt 6:24–34; Luke 15:1–7; John 18:3–11; Acts 7:54–60; 12:5–9; 16:22–25; Rom 8:35–39.

Despair

A patient is pushed to the brink, so to speak. Despair may be precipitated by permanent disability accompanied by prolonged discomfort and pain. Medical professionals cannot provide a positive prognosis. The situation is grim.

These patients defy any attempts to rationalize that their condition is less dire than it truly is. They may ask, "Why doesn't God take me?" Perhaps the best pastoral care is to help them to have hope in God and call them to readiness, that is, repentance of sins and trust in Jesus Christ for forgiveness and the assurance of eternal life. Point them to things eternal.

Scripture: Ps 16:1–2, 7–8; 31:15; 85:1–9; Isa 41:10; Luke 13:10–13; 23:46; John 3:14–18; Acts 7:54–60; Rom 8:18; 12:12; 2 Cor 12:7–10; Phil 4:4–7, 19–20; 2 Tim 4:6–8; Heb 9:27–28;12:1–7; Jas 5:10–15; 1 Pet 1:3–7; 4:12–13; 2 Pet 1:4–8; Rev 1:4–6; 7:13–17.

Convalescence

For these patients, the crisis is in the past. The prognosis is good. Recovering, they are relieved of anxiety. Healing and the prospect of good health is occasion to "rejoice with those who rejoice" (Rom 12:15).

The pastor encourages these patients to give thanks to God, to wait upon Him for blessings of healing and strength, and to consecrate body, mind, and soul to serve God in the strength He grants for such dedication and service.

Scripture: Ps 63:7; 77:11–15; 84; 103:1–5, 8–14, 20–22; 105:1–6; 106:47–48; 113; Isa 38:15–17, 19–20; Matt 9:27–31; Mark 1:29–31; Luke 17:11–19; 18:41–43; John 9:24–38.

Appendix 6

Holy Ground—Returning to the Lord's Altar

This exhibit is for initial counseling when troubled marriages are on the precipice of divorce.

His Story

- Our marriage—of His making (not our making only)
- Two became one
- For happiness (but we are unhappy in marriage)
- What did God give that we are missing in our marriage?
- To her, He gave a husband
- To him, He gave a wife
- To both, He gave the gift to love and be loved
- Love given and received in sexual life
- Love that supports, helps, builds up
- Love, giving, sacrificing, serving
- To both, He gave a home, children, family
- To both, He gave and gives essentials—provisions for life and living
- To both, He gave lasting marriage, two committed persons
- To both, He gave Himself (the cross)
- To both, He pledged His blessing

Summary

- Oneness, unity
- Love—*agape*, sexual love
- Commitment
- Endurance, survival, longevity
- Emotional support
- Companionship, friendship
- Home, family
- God and God's blessing
- Word, Sacrament
- Prayer

Our Story

- Distance, fragmentation vs. oneness, unity
- Growing apart vs. coming together
- Conflict vs. friendship, companionship
- Toleration vs. love
- Sex vs. intimacy, warmth, tender love
- Absence of God, Word, Sacrament, prayer
- Three persons vs. two-who-are-one (the other "significant other")
- Unhappiness vs. happiness and mutual welfare

Our Future (God and Us)

- From here, where do we go, where do we turn?
- Separation?
- Divorce?
- Regroup, grow, and live?
- God's stake in our (His) marriage
- His love
- His will
- His promises
- His blessing
- Alternative courses of action
- Continue here, with our pastor
- Seek professional counseling
- Work positively, constructively as a couple
- Combination of the above

Priority No. 1

- Our marriage is divine; it is God's life for us
- Save the marriage!

Appendix 7

Premarital Counseling Sessions

Premarital Counseling—Three Interviews

I. First Interview

A. General information shared both ways, couple to pastor, then pastor/church (policy) shared with the couple.

B. Getting to know the couple and their aspirations for marriage. If used, provide a questionnaire or other inventory instrument that shall be the basis of discussion in the second interview.

C. Discuss marriage in creation and empowered by redemption—theology of a life together created and then redeemed, the prospects of happy marriage after the fall. Make the discussion practical.

II. Second Interview

A. The pastor begins by addressing issues within the couple's relationship, issues surfacing from the questionnaire or inventory—strengths, weaknesses that require attention.

B. The pastor may present an overview of Christian marriage—family and home, undergirded by the Scriptures and energized by the Gospel for life together in Christ. Perhaps he will speak about the three loves: *eros*, *philia*, and *agape*.

C. Then, narrow the focus.

1. Husband and wife, servants together, headship and submission, the catalyst of love (Eph 5:21ff.; cf. Col 3:17–19). He may focus attention on the role of husband and wife in the light of Ephesians 5 and Colossians 3. He will accent commitment in marriage: love as devotion, serving each other, living and dying for each other.
2. Dimensions of commitment, fidelity—physical, emotional, spiritual.
3. Maintaining the tension between "intimacy" and individual "privacy."

4. The quiet power of mutual acceptance.
    a. Cease analyzing!
    b. Cease changing, "reforming!"
    c. Pleasing vs. agitation, irritation
    d. The power of acceptance
5. The seasoning of civility.
    a. Common courtesies
    b. Keeping the signposts visible (transparency)
    c. Thinking
    d. Feelings
    e. Readiness to discuss, debate, conflict
6. Building high the walls.
    a. Against intrusion of the unlovely, the tawdry, the impure (Phil 4:8–9)
    b. Setting a shared agenda re: social contacts
    c. Guarded discussion about ourselves and our marriage beyond these walls
    d. In situations and places, it is the "two" of us, never one without the spouse
    e. When we need to say it, then say it: "I'm married!"
    f. Fending away temptation and the "tempter"
7. Marital/family consciousness of the Lord God.
    a. "God" talk
        i. Deepening the spiritual life in marriage (1 Pet 3:7)
        ii. Family altar, a couple's devotional life—a discipline that is learned
        iii. Referencing questions, issues, to the Scriptures
        iv. Interpreting life and existence—family, society, church, culture according to the Scriptures—what says our Lord?
        v. Approaching major decisions—Scripture and prayer
    b. The Church
        i. Public worship and the Lord's Supper

ii. Seeking instruction from the Scriptures—Bible classes

iii. Opportunities for Christian service

iv. A missionary family sharing the Gospel with others

III. Third Interview

A. What has the couple discussed in light of the first and second interviews?

B. Unity in love and marriage expressed in sexual intimacy (neither over attention, nor neglect of the subject).

1. Ennoble more than inform.
2. The "one flesh" union, physical and especially beyond the physical.

C. Home responsibilities—house, finances, budgeting, living within means, saving, day-to-day domestic tasks, and such.

D. Children.

1. Biblical mandate, "Be fruitful and multiply" (Gen 1:28; cf. Gen 16:1a; 17:15–19).
2. Pros and cons of family planning.
3. Keeping a positive attitude toward having children.
4. Interpreting infertility if children are not in the picture.

E. Keeping the marriage relationship alive.

F. The Rite of Marriage—the final interview may include walking through the Rite of Marriage; or, this may be deferred later, close to the wedding day. Words and responses should be familiar. Some pastors build their premarital counseling ministry around the rite.

Premarital Counseling—One Interview

I. Christian Marriage

II. "God Talk" and Church

III. Intimate Life

IV. Home—Privileges and Responsibilities

V. Children

VI. Keeping the Marriage Alive

VII. Rite of Marriage

Appendix 8

Grief and the Sense of Loss[454]

Grief is a normal human reaction to any important loss: moving from a neighborhood or a school, losing a job, a brother or sister leaving for college or getting married, a pet dying, parents divorcing, or a parent, friend, or relative dying. As you journey through life, you encounter many turning points or crises that may cause you to grieve. The ancient people of God grieved over losses. Israel mourned Jacob, Moses, and Samuel (cf. Gen 50:10; Deut 34:8; 1 Sam 28:3). Jesus mourned the loss of His friend Lazarus (John 11:35).

Noteworthy is the time assigned to mourning in the Old Testament. This is to acknowledge what is affirmed today. When we experience a major loss, the need to grieve this loss appropriately is an acute need. Turning from the grief that you feel, repressing grief, attempting to bury it within yourself, it becomes what is called "unresolved grief" and can have a destructive effect on one's life.

There are five recognized stages of grief:

Denial • Anger • Bargaining • Depression • Acceptance

1. **Denial** is a period of rejecting or not believing what is taking place. It is often characterized by a sense of numbness of all emotions or shock. You could find yourself saying, "This can't be happening to me."

2. **Anger** is a deep-seated rage over what is happening. The anger is displaced in all directions and projected at random. The anger may be directed at your parents for letting you down, to doctors or hospitals, friends, teachers, yourself, family, or God. It is essential to experience and express your anger, yet you must be careful to do this in appropriate ways. You might find yourself asking the question "Why me?"

3. **Bargaining** is an attempt to exchange something you are willing to do or give up for something you want to keep. You "deal" with someone who is in control when you are not. It is an attempt to postpone or fix up the inevitable. It is also a time when you experience unrealistic guilt. You might find yourself saying, "If only . . ." or "What if . . . ?"

454 This exhibit, adapted from an anonymous source, is based on the configuration of grief adjustment set forth in Elisabeth Kubler-Ross, *On Death and Dying* (New York: Macmillan, 1969).

4. **Depression** is when you can't cope, your life is out of control, and you feel overwhelmed. It happens when the reality of your situation sets in. It may be a time of highs and lows, and you need to work at keeping a balance. This is also a time when you could turn to drugs, alcohol, and even become suicidal. You might find yourself saying, "What's the use?"

5. **Acceptance** is learning to live with the changes in your life. It is a time when you no longer dwell on the past and begin to look forward to your tomorrows.

According to many psychologists, it is important to pass through each of the five stages of grief so that you may go on with your life. This will be a time of pain, anger, sadness, bitterness, and tears. Going through the initial four stages toward acceptance is a jagged journey. It isn't timed or smooth, orderly or predictable. You don't necessarily go through the stages in order. It is possible to go back and forth, in and out of these stages, but, in time, you will arrive at acceptance and stay there. Along the way, you may seek strength that God gives in the words and promises of the Gospel. The comfort of God and His Word will see you through the rough times.

If you avoid the grieving process by denying or avoiding the emotions, they will eat away at you from the inside. This unresolved grief may become destructive of your emotional health.

One of the best ways to work through your grief is to share your story, what exactly happened—events, circumstances, and feelings—with someone you care about and who cares enough to devote to you a listening ear and tender heart. This person could be your pastor.

Index